DATE DUE

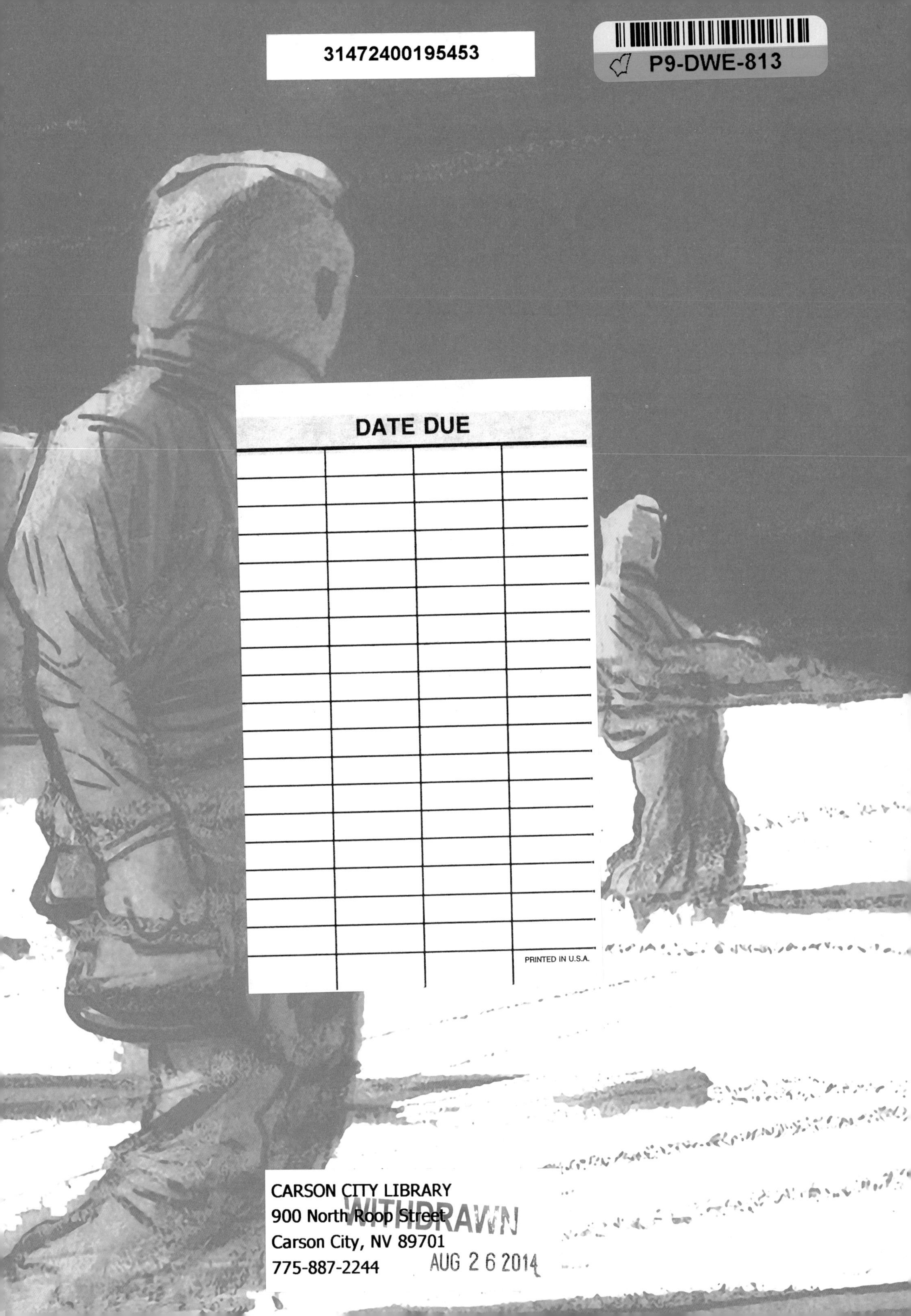

PRINTED IN U.S.A.

SNOW PIERCER

2 : THE EXPLORERS

LEGRAND • ROCHETTE

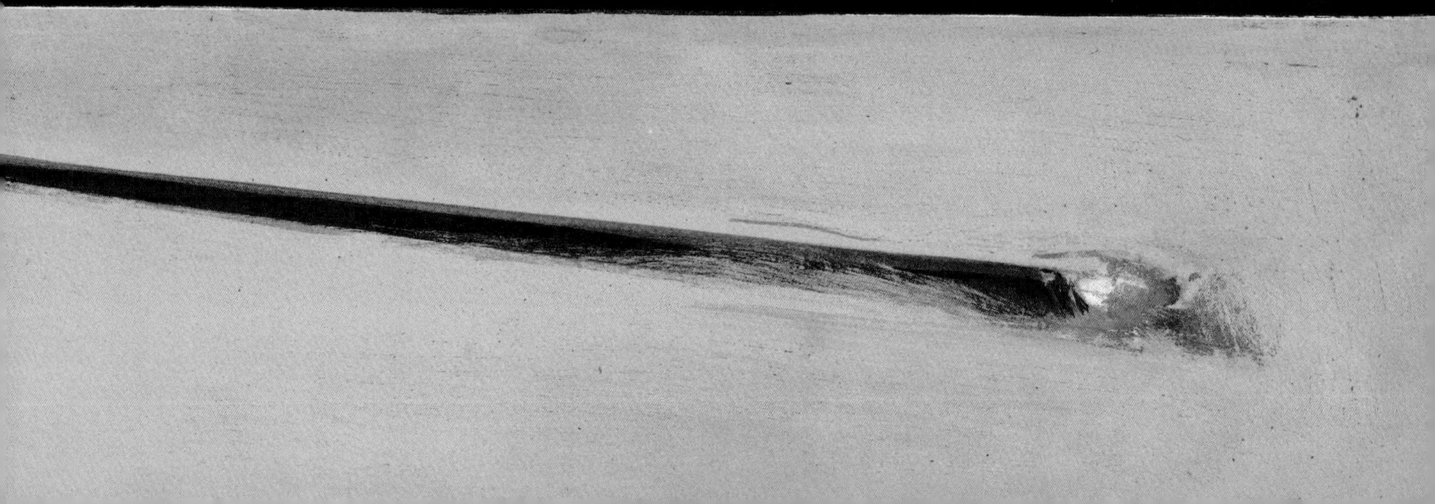

SNOWPIERCER

2 : THE EXPLORERS

WRITTEN BY

BENJAMIN LEGRAND

ART BY

JEAN-MARC ROCHETTE

TRANSLATED BY

VIRGINIE SELAVY

LETTERING BY

GABRIELA HOUSTON

What did you think of this book?
We love to hear from our readers.
Please email us at: **readercomments@titanemail.com,**
or write to us at the address opposite.

To receive news, competitions, and exclusive offers online,
please sign up for the Titan Comics newsletter on our website:
www.titan-comics.com

Follow us on Twitter **@ComicsTitan**

Visit us at **facebook.com/comicstitan**

TITAN COMICS

EDITOR
GABRIELA HOUSTON
COLLECTION DESIGNER
SARA GREASLEY

Senior Editor
Steve White
Titan Comics Editorial
Andrew James, Jon Chapple
Production Supervisors
Kelly Fenlon, Jackie Flook
Interim Production Assistant
Peter James
Art Director
Oz Browne
Studio Manager
Selina Juneja
Circulation Manager
Steve Tothill
Marketing Manager
Ricky Claydon
Senior Marketing and Press Executive
Owen Johnson
Marketing Assistant
Tara Felton
Publishing Manager
Darryl Tothill
Publishing Director
Chris Teather
Operations Director
Leigh Baulch
Executive Director
Vivian Cheung
Publisher
Nick Landau

SNOWPIERCER VOLUME 2: THE EXPLORERS

ISBN: 9781782761365

Published by Titan Comics
A division of Titan Publishing Group Ltd.
144 Southwark St.
London
SE1 0UP

A CIP catalogue record for this title is available
from the British Library.

First edition: March 2014

Originally published in 1984 by
Casterman, France as *Transperceneige; L'arpenteur (1999)*
and as *Transperceneige: La traverse (2000)*

10 9 8 7 6 5 4 3 2

Printed in China.
Titan Comics. TC0235

SNOWPIERCER

2 : THE EXPLORERS

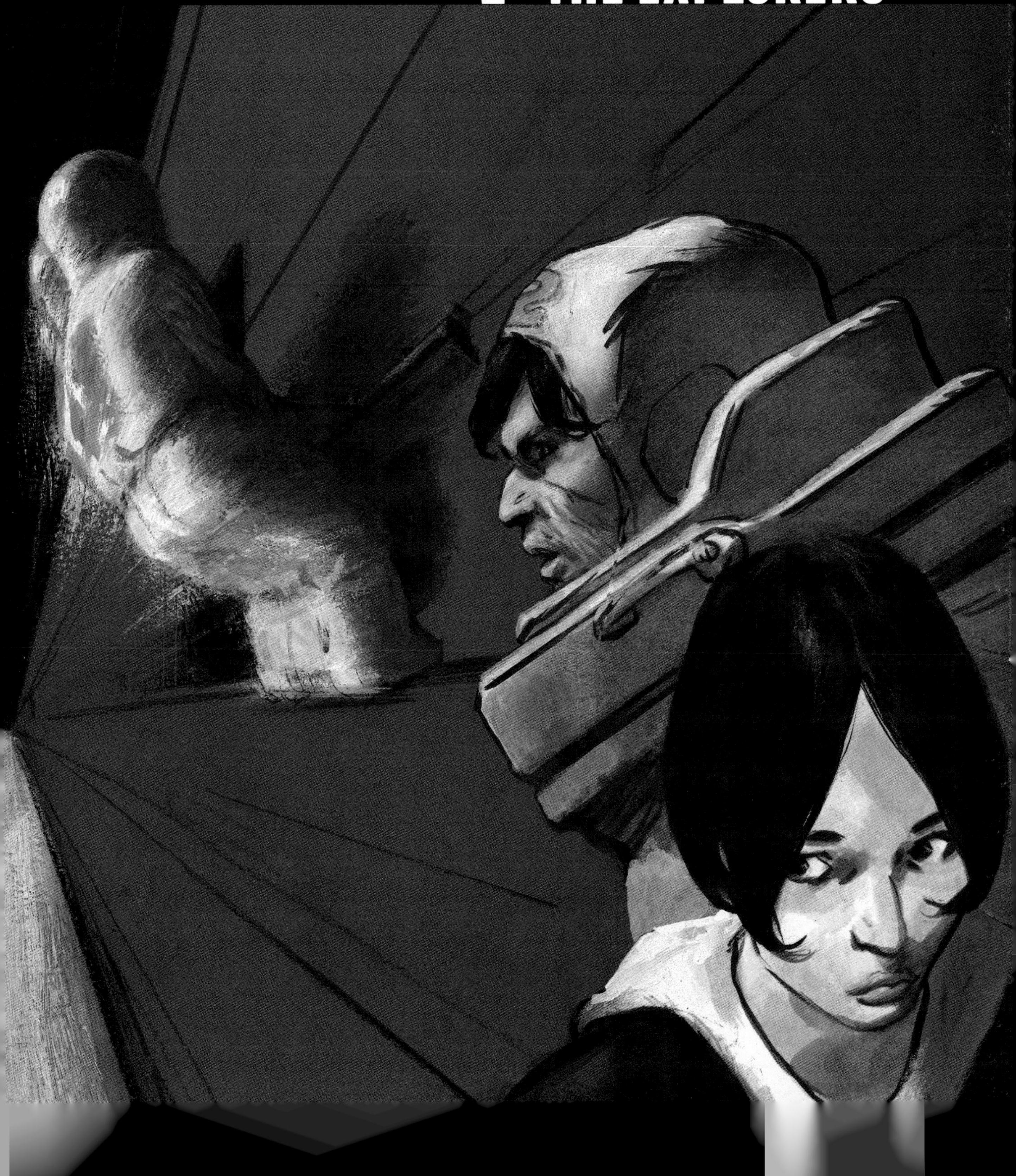

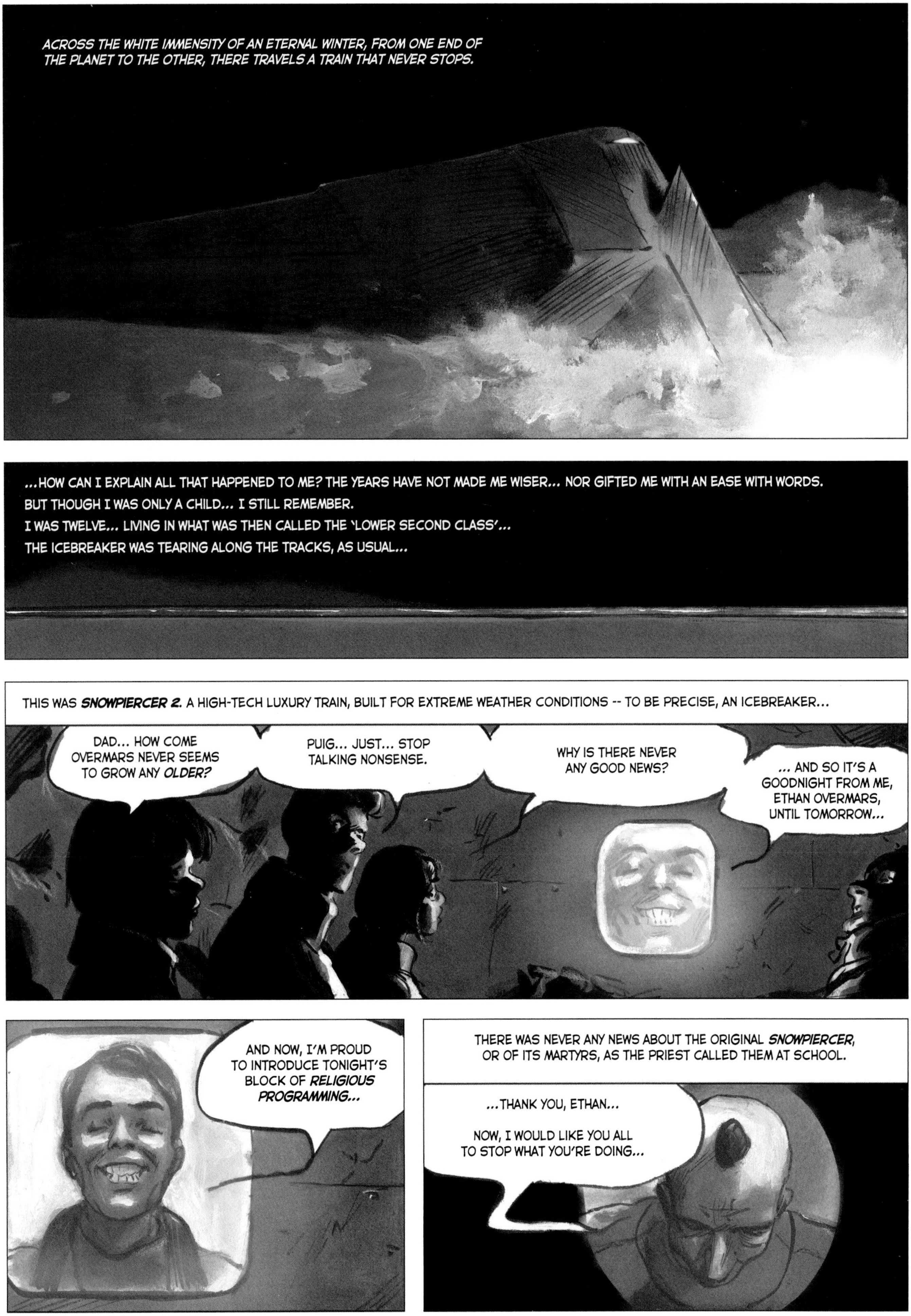
ACROSS THE WHITE IMMENSITY OF AN ETERNAL WINTER, FROM ONE END OF THE PLANET TO THE OTHER, THERE TRAVELS A TRAIN THAT NEVER STOPS.
...HOW CAN I EXPLAIN ALL THAT HAPPENED TO ME? THE YEARS HAVE NOT MADE ME WISER... NOR GIFTED ME WITH AN EASE WITH WORDS.
BUT THOUGH I WAS ONLY A CHILD... I STILL REMEMBER.
I WAS TWELVE... LIVING IN WHAT WAS THEN CALLED THE 'LOWER SECOND CLASS'...
THE ICEBREAKER WAS TEARING ALONG THE TRACKS, AS USUAL...
THIS WAS *SNOWPIERCER 2*. A HIGH-TECH LUXURY TRAIN, BUILT FOR EXTREME WEATHER CONDITIONS -- TO BE PRECISE, AN ICEBREAKER...
DAD... HOW COME OVERMARS NEVER SEEMS TO GROW ANY *OLDER?*
PUIG... JUST... STOP TALKING NONSENSE.
WHY IS THERE NEVER ANY GOOD NEWS?
... AND SO IT'S A GOODNIGHT FROM ME, ETHAN OVERMARS, UNTIL TOMORROW...
AND NOW, I'M PROUD TO INTRODUCE TONIGHT'S BLOCK OF ***RELIGIOUS PROGRAMMING...***
THERE WAS NEVER ANY NEWS ABOUT THE ORIGINAL *SNOWPIERCER*, OR OF ITS MARTYRS, AS THE PRIEST CALLED THEM AT SCHOOL.
...THANK YOU, ETHAN...
NOW, I WOULD LIKE YOU ALL TO STOP WHAT YOU'RE DOING...

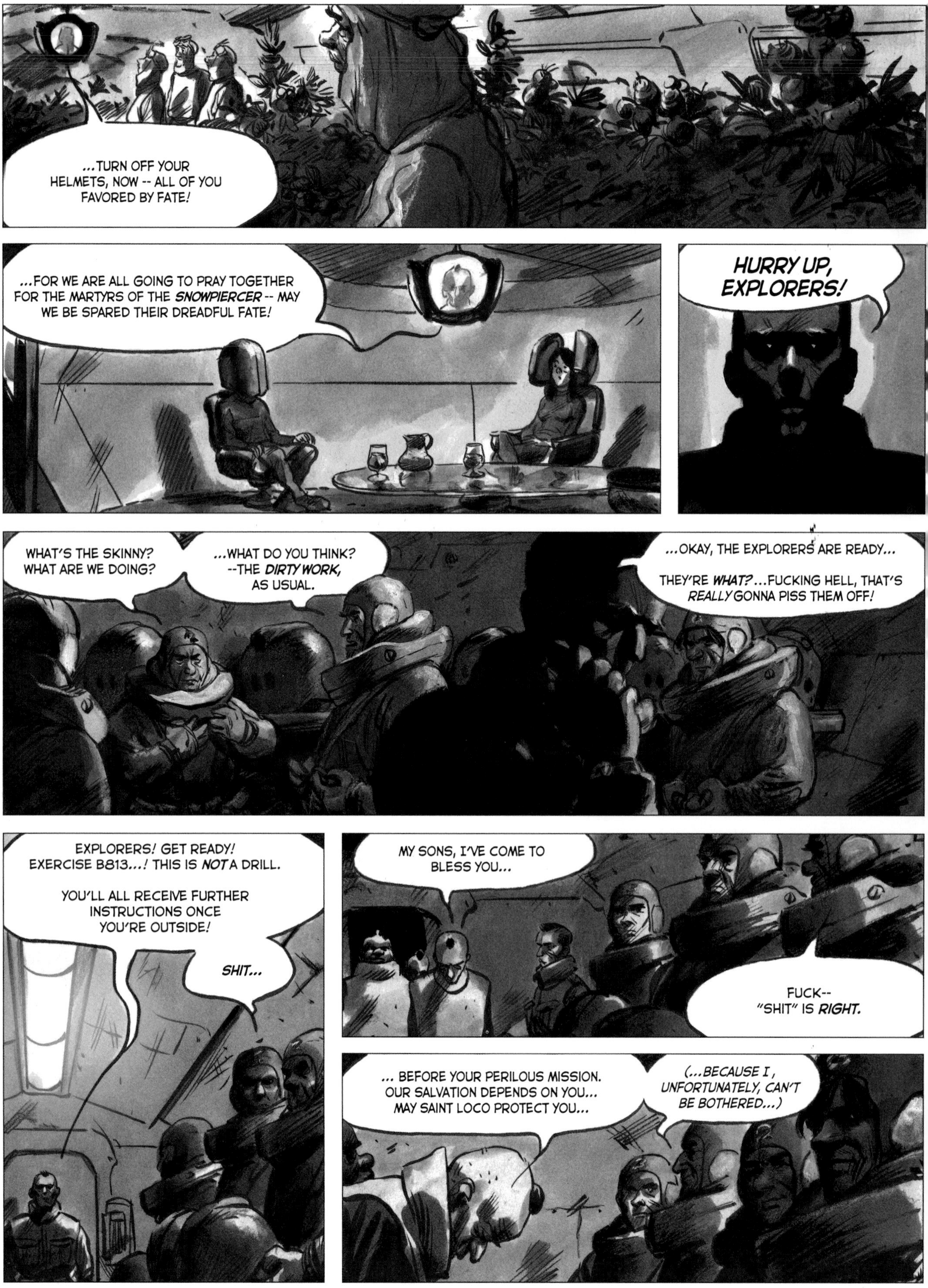
...TURN OFF YOUR HELMETS, NOW -- ALL OF YOU FAVORED BY FATE!
...FOR WE ARE ALL GOING TO PRAY TOGETHER FOR THE MARTYRS OF THE *SNOWPIERCER* -- MAY WE BE SPARED THEIR DREADFUL FATE!
HURRY UP, EXPLORERS!
WHAT'S THE SKINNY? WHAT ARE WE DOING?
...WHAT DO YOU THINK? --THE *DIRTY WORK*, AS USUAL.
...OKAY, THE EXPLORERS ARE READY...
THEY'RE *WHAT?*...FUCKING HELL, THAT'S *REALLY* GONNA PISS THEM OFF!
EXPLORERS! GET READY! EXERCISE B813...! THIS IS *NOT* A DRILL.
YOU'LL ALL RECEIVE FURTHER INSTRUCTIONS ONCE YOU'RE OUTSIDE!
SHIT...
MY SONS, I'VE COME TO BLESS YOU...
FUCK-- "SHIT" IS *RIGHT.*
... BEFORE YOUR PERILOUS MISSION. OUR SALVATION DEPENDS ON YOU... MAY SAINT LOCO PROTECT YOU...
(...BECAUSE I, UNFORTUNATELY, CAN'T BE BOTHERED...)

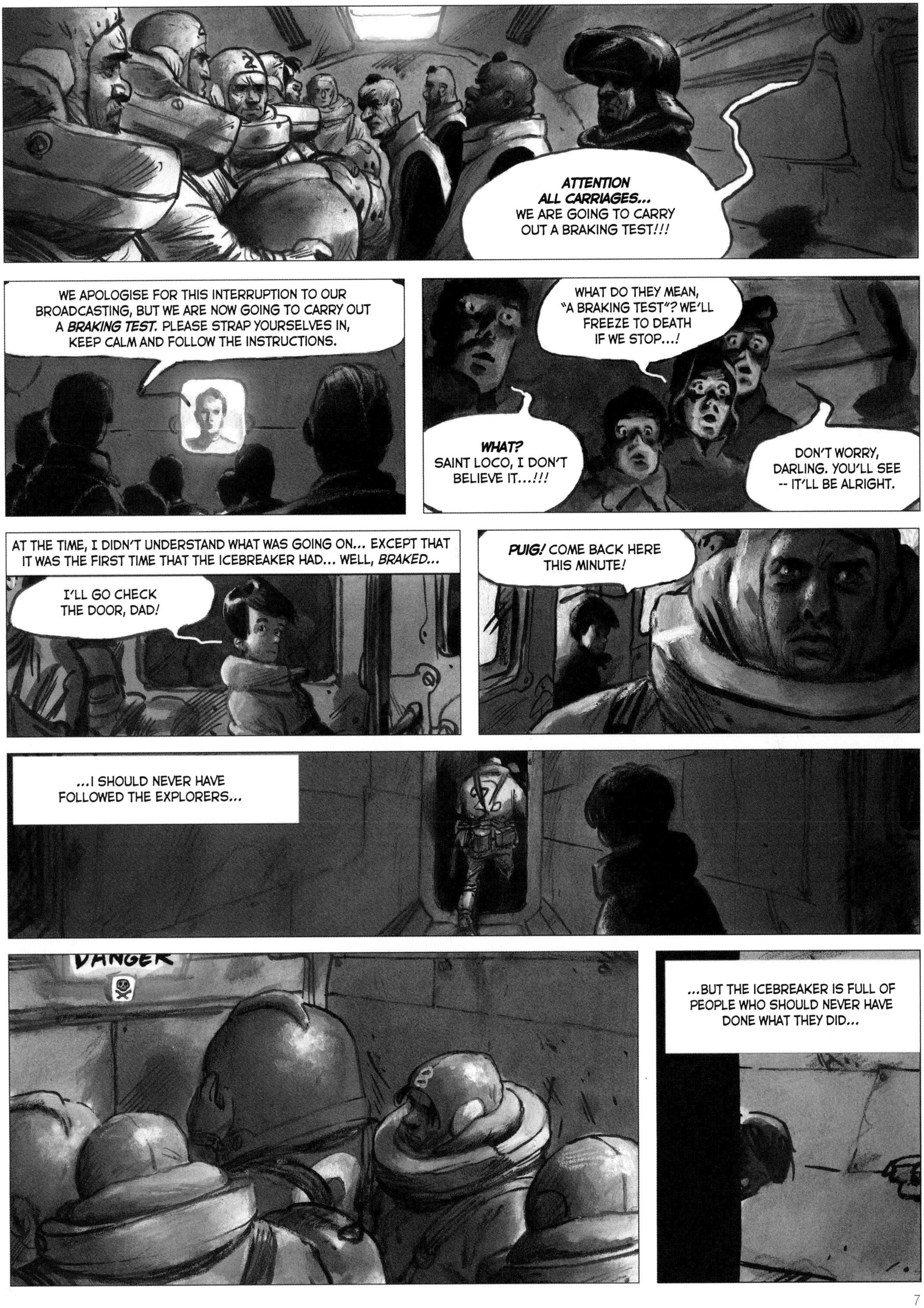

ATTENTION ALL CARRIAGES... WE ARE GOING TO CARRY OUT A BRAKING TEST!!!
WE APOLOGISE FOR THIS INTERRUPTION TO OUR BROADCASTING, BUT WE ARE NOW GOING TO CARRY OUT A BRAKING TEST. PLEASE STRAP YOURSELVES IN, KEEP CALM AND FOLLOW THE INSTRUCTIONS.
WHAT DO THEY MEAN, "A BRAKING TEST"? WE'LL FREEZE TO DEATH IF WE STOP...!
WHAT? SAINT LOCO, I DON'T BELIEVE IT...!!!
DON'T WORRY, DARLING. YOU'LL SEE -- IT'LL BE ALRIGHT.
AT THE TIME, I DIDN'T UNDERSTAND WHAT WAS GOING ON... EXCEPT THAT IT WAS THE FIRST TIME THAT THE ICEBREAKER HAD... WELL, BRAKED...
I'LL GO CHECK THE DOOR, DAD!
PUIG! COME BACK HERE THIS MINUTE!
...I SHOULD NEVER HAVE FOLLOWED THE EXPLORERS...
DANGER
...BUT THE ICEBREAKER IS FULL OF PEOPLE WHO SHOULD NEVER HAVE DONE WHAT THEY DID...

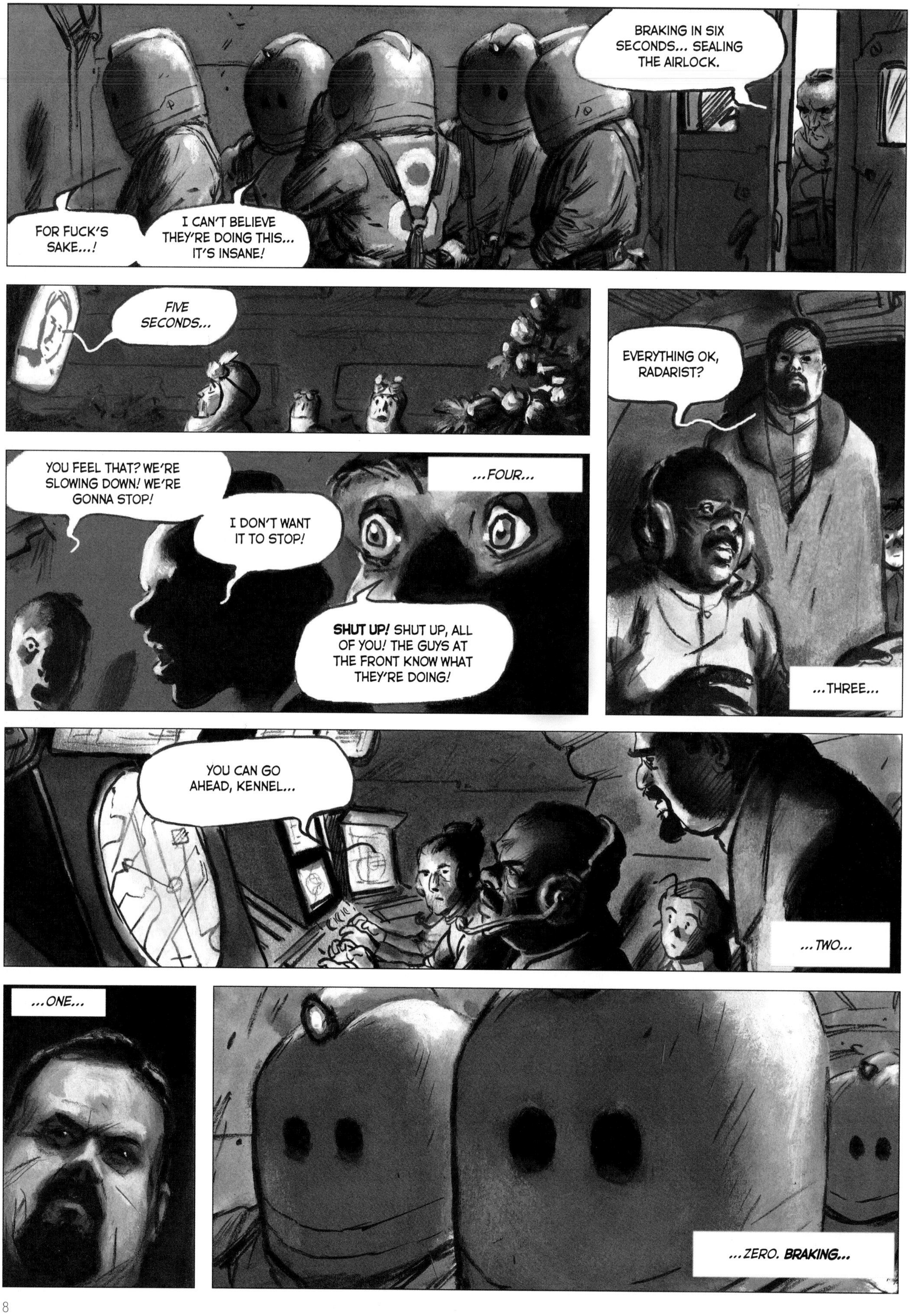
BRAKING IN SIX SECONDS... SEALING THE AIRLOCK.
FOR FUCK'S SAKE...!
I CAN'T BELIEVE THEY'RE DOING THIS... IT'S INSANE!
FIVE SECONDS...
EVERYTHING OK, RADARIST?
YOU FEEL THAT? WE'RE SLOWING DOWN! WE'RE GONNA STOP!
I DON'T WANT IT TO STOP!
...FOUR...
SHUT UP! SHUT UP, ALL OF YOU! THE GUYS AT THE FRONT KNOW WHAT THEY'RE DOING!
...THREE...
YOU CAN GO AHEAD, KENNEL...
...TWO...
...ONE...
...ZERO. BRAKING...

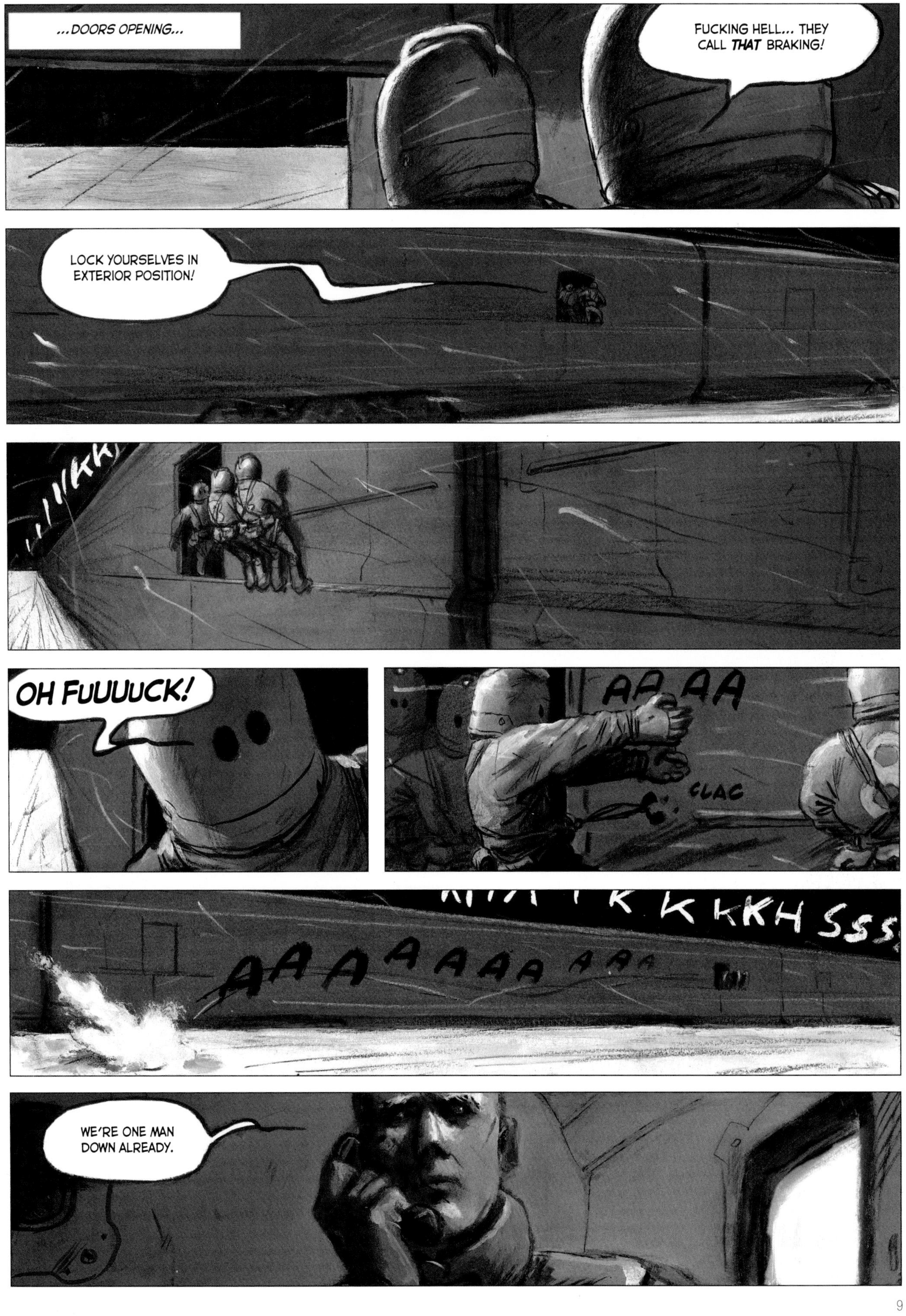
...DOORS OPENING...
FUCKING HELL... THEY CALL **THAT** BRAKING!
LOCK YOURSELVES IN EXTERIOR POSITION!
OH FUUUUCK!
AA AA
CLAC
WE'RE ONE MAN DOWN ALREADY.

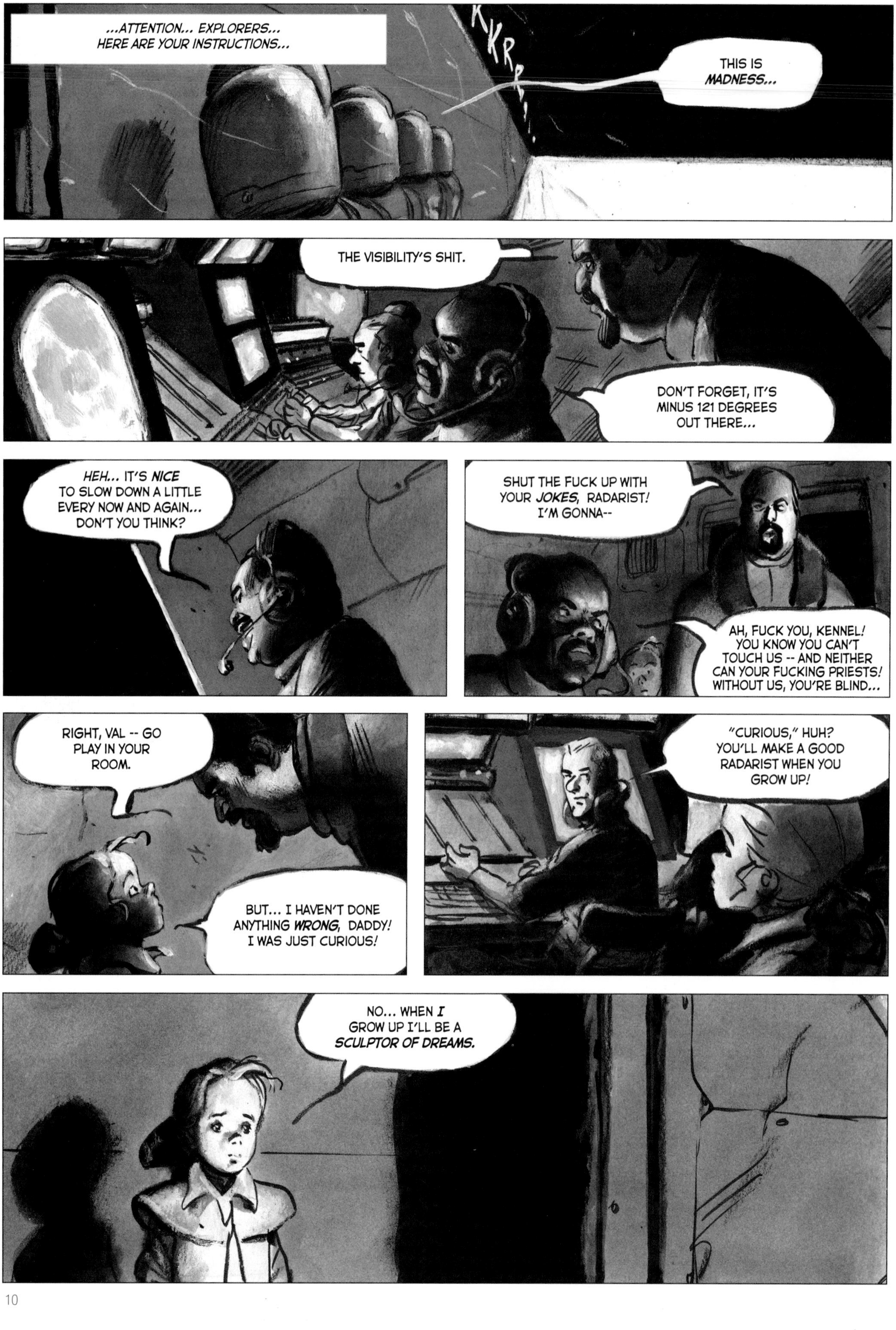
...ATTENTION... EXPLORERS... HERE ARE YOUR INSTRUCTIONS...
THIS IS MADNESS...
THE VISIBILITY'S SHIT.
DON'T FORGET, IT'S MINUS 121 DEGREES OUT THERE...
HEH... IT'S NICE TO SLOW DOWN A LITTLE EVERY NOW AND AGAIN... DON'T YOU THINK?
SHUT THE FUCK UP WITH YOUR JOKES, RADARIST! I'M GONNA--
AH, FUCK YOU, KENNEL! YOU KNOW YOU CAN'T TOUCH US -- AND NEITHER CAN YOUR FUCKING PRIESTS! WITHOUT US, YOU'RE BLIND...
RIGHT, VAL -- GO PLAY IN YOUR ROOM.
BUT... I HAVEN'T DONE ANYTHING WRONG, DADDY! I WAS JUST CURIOUS!
"CURIOUS," HUH? YOU'LL MAKE A GOOD RADARIST WHEN YOU GROW UP!
NO... WHEN I GROW UP I'LL BE A SCULPTOR OF DREAMS.

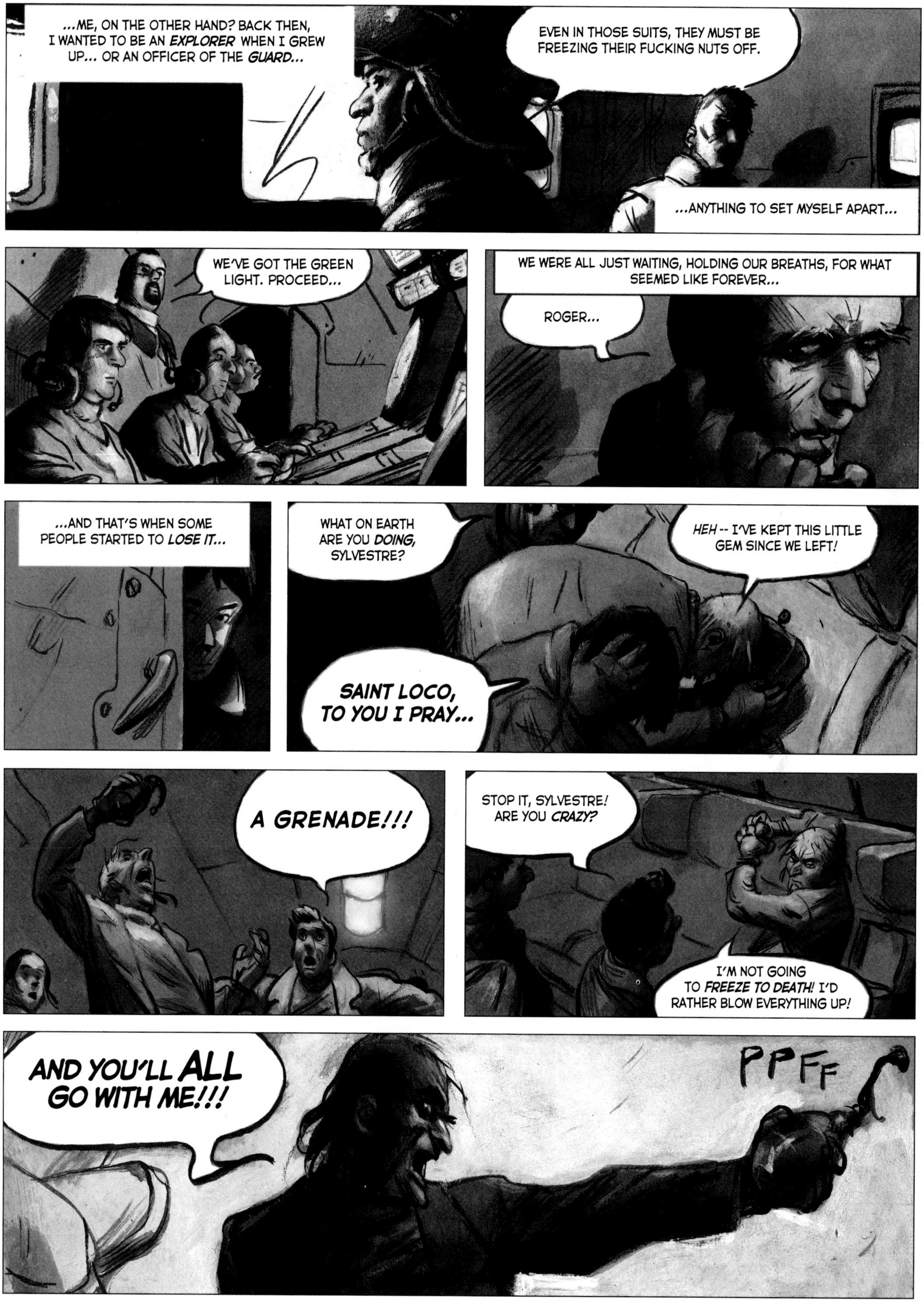
...ME, ON THE OTHER HAND? BACK THEN, I WANTED TO BE AN EXPLORER WHEN I GREW UP... OR AN OFFICER OF THE GUARD...
EVEN IN THOSE SUITS, THEY MUST BE FREEZING THEIR FUCKING NUTS OFF.
...ANYTHING TO SET MYSELF APART...
WE'VE GOT THE GREEN LIGHT. PROCEED...
WE WERE ALL JUST WAITING, HOLDING OUR BREATHS, FOR WHAT SEEMED LIKE FOREVER...
ROGER...
...AND THAT'S WHEN SOME PEOPLE STARTED TO LOSE IT...
WHAT ON EARTH ARE YOU DOING, SYLVESTRE?
HEH -- I'VE KEPT THIS LITTLE GEM SINCE WE LEFT!
SAINT LOCO, TO YOU I PRAY...
A GRENADE!!!
STOP IT, SYLVESTRE! ARE YOU CRAZY?
I'M NOT GOING TO FREEZE TO DEATH! I'D RATHER BLOW EVERYTHING UP!
AND YOU'LL ALL GO WITH ME!!!
PPFF

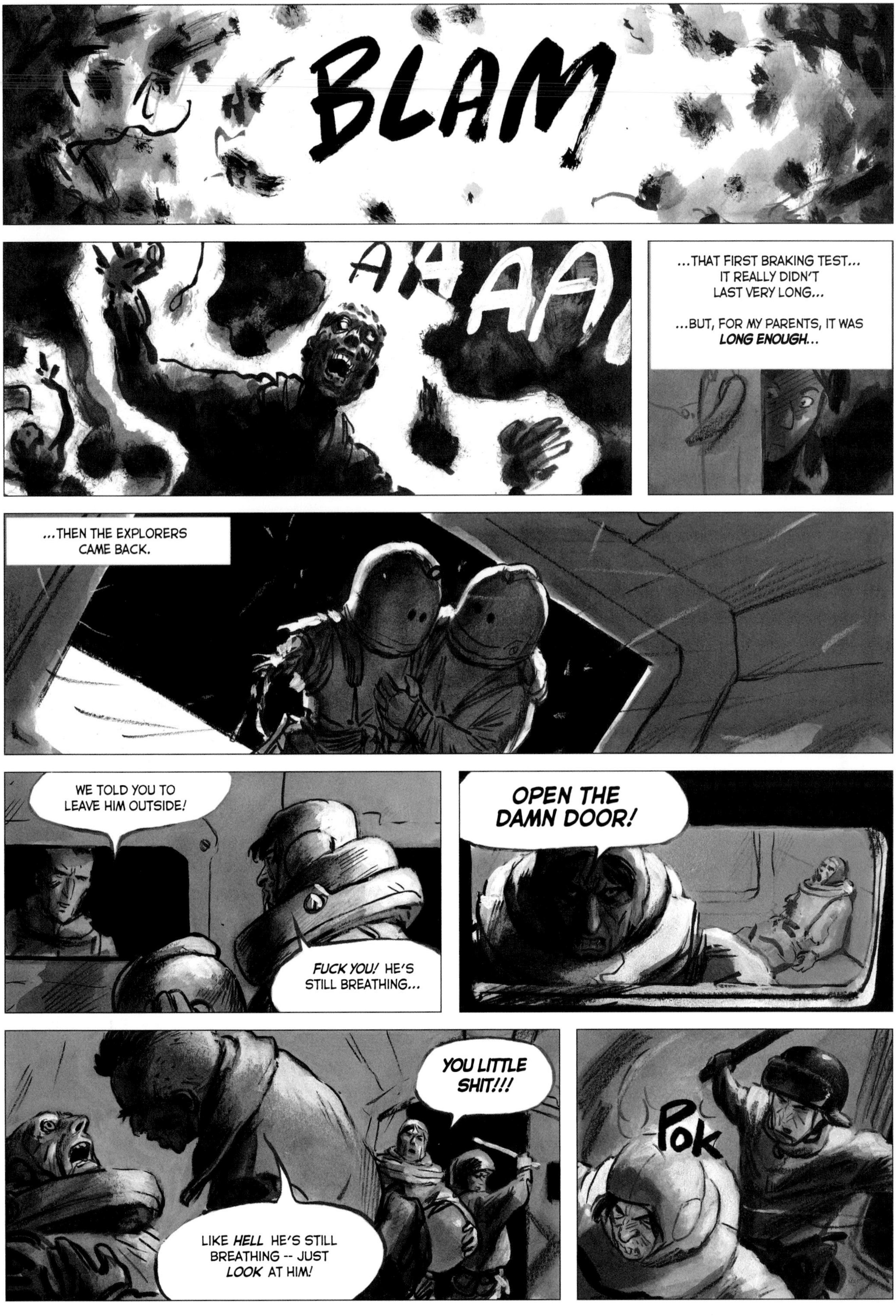
BLAM
AAAAA
...THAT FIRST BRAKING TEST... IT REALLY DIDN'T LAST VERY LONG...
...BUT, FOR MY PARENTS, IT WAS LONG ENOUGH...
...THEN THE EXPLORERS CAME BACK.
WE TOLD YOU TO LEAVE HIM OUTSIDE!
FUCK YOU! HE'S STILL BREATHING...
OPEN THE DAMN DOOR!
YOU LITTLE SHIT!!!
LIKE HELL HE'S STILL BREATHING -- JUST LOOK AT HIM!
POK

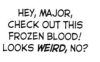

YES, GENERAL. HE'S ON HIS WAY. *YES,* SIR.

SON -- YOU'RE IN SOME *SERIOUSLY* DEEP SHIT NOW! REVEREND DICKSEN *ALREADY* HAD HIS EYE ON YOU...

HEY, MAJOR, CHECK OUT THIS FROZEN BLOOD! LOOKS *WEIRD,* NO?

ONCE IT WAS ALL QUIET AGAIN, I SNUCK BACK OUT OF MY HIDING PLACE... I NOTICED THAT THE EXPLORER HAD DROPPED SOMETHING.

AN EARRING! IT WAS SO COLD THAT IT STUCK TO MY FINGER.

...SO MY PARENTS WERE KILLED BY SOME LUNATIC WITH A HAND-GRENADE AS WE BRAKED.

BUT THAT WAS JUST THE *START* OF THE MADNESS.

THIS WAS FIFTEEN YEARS AGO... FIFTEEN YEARS, TRAPPED ABOARD THE ICEBREAKER.

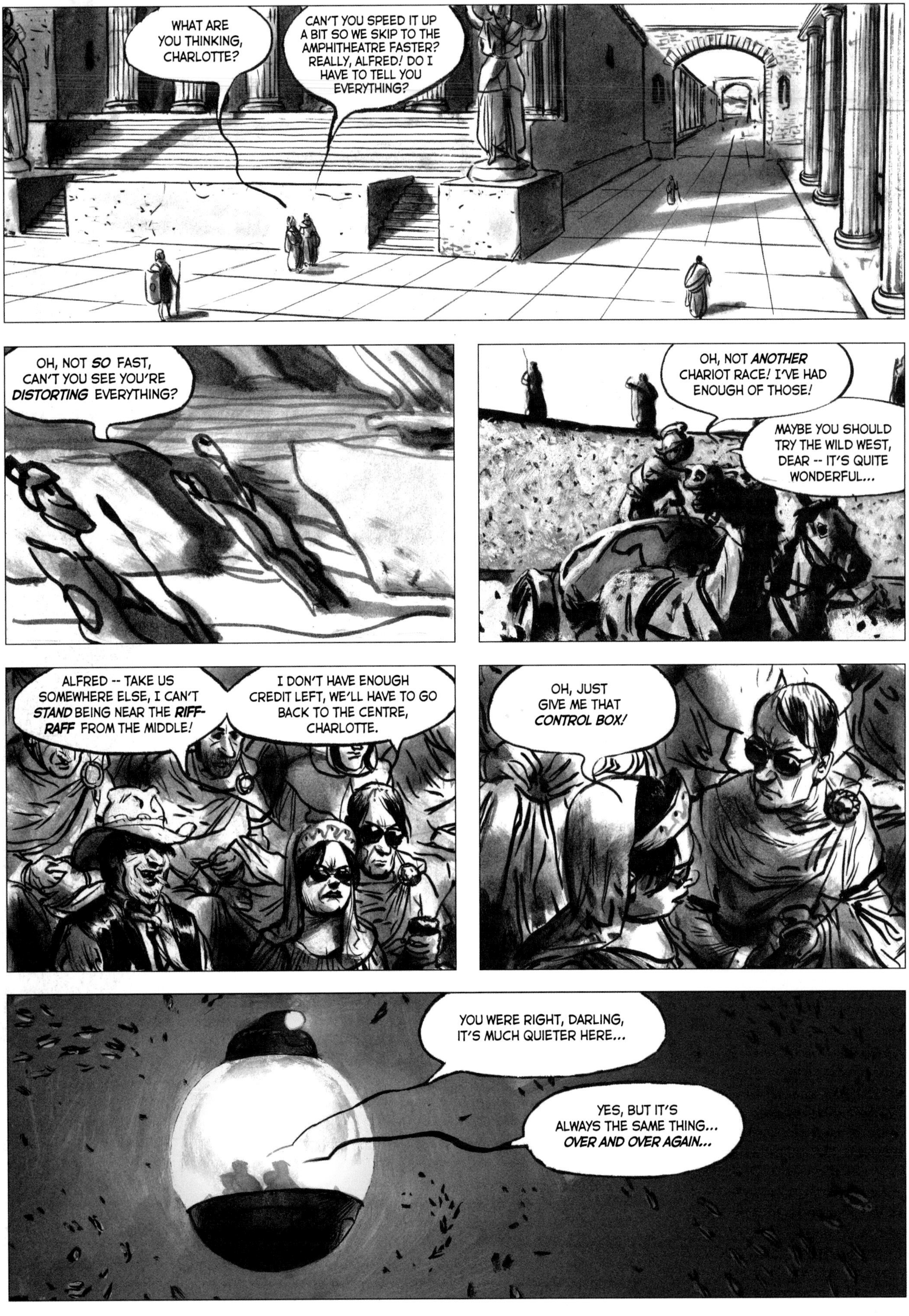
WHAT ARE YOU THINKING, CHARLOTTE?
CAN'T YOU SPEED IT UP A BIT SO WE SKIP TO THE AMPHITHEATRE FASTER? REALLY, ALFRED! DO I HAVE TO TELL YOU EVERYTHING?
OH, NOT *SO* FAST, CAN'T YOU SEE YOU'RE *DISTORTING* EVERYTHING?
OH, NOT *ANOTHER* CHARIOT RACE! I'VE HAD ENOUGH OF THOSE!
MAYBE YOU SHOULD TRY THE WILD WEST, DEAR -- IT'S QUITE WONDERFUL...
ALFRED -- TAKE US SOMEWHERE ELSE, I CAN'T *STAND* BEING NEAR THE *RIFF-RAFF* FROM THE MIDDLE!
I DON'T HAVE ENOUGH CREDIT LEFT, WE'LL HAVE TO GO BACK TO THE CENTRE, CHARLOTTE.
OH, JUST GIVE ME THAT *CONTROL BOX!*
YOU WERE RIGHT, DARLING, IT'S MUCH QUIETER HERE...
YES, BUT IT'S ALWAYS THE SAME THING... *OVER AND OVER AGAIN...*

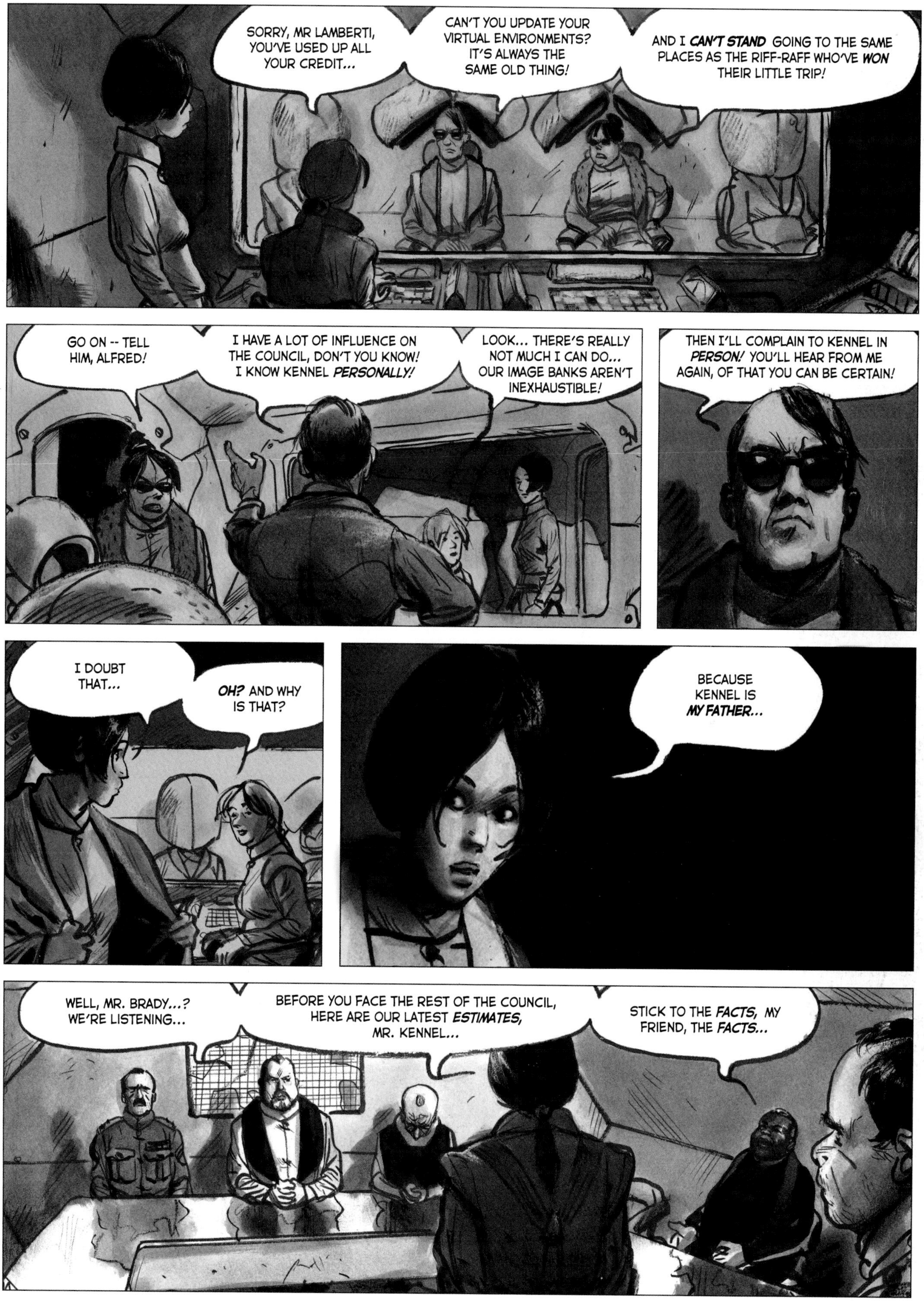

SORRY, MR LAMBERTI, YOU'VE USED UP ALL YOUR CREDIT...
CAN'T YOU UPDATE YOUR VIRTUAL ENVIRONMENTS? IT'S ALWAYS THE SAME OLD THING!
AND I **CAN'T STAND** GOING TO THE SAME PLACES AS THE RIFF-RAFF WHO'VE **WON** THEIR LITTLE TRIP!
GO ON -- TELL HIM, ALFRED!
I HAVE A LOT OF INFLUENCE ON THE COUNCIL, DON'T YOU KNOW! I KNOW KENNEL *PERSONALLY!*
LOOK... THERE'S REALLY NOT MUCH I CAN DO... OUR IMAGE BANKS AREN'T INEXHAUSTIBLE!
THEN I'LL COMPLAIN TO KENNEL IN *PERSON!* YOU'LL HEAR FROM ME AGAIN, OF THAT YOU CAN BE CERTAIN!
I DOUBT THAT...
OH? AND WHY IS THAT?
BECAUSE KENNEL IS ***MY FATHER...***
WELL, MR. BRADY...? WE'RE LISTENING...
BEFORE YOU FACE THE REST OF THE COUNCIL, HERE ARE OUR LATEST *ESTIMATES,* MR. KENNEL...
STICK TO THE *FACTS,* MY FRIEND, THE *FACTS...*

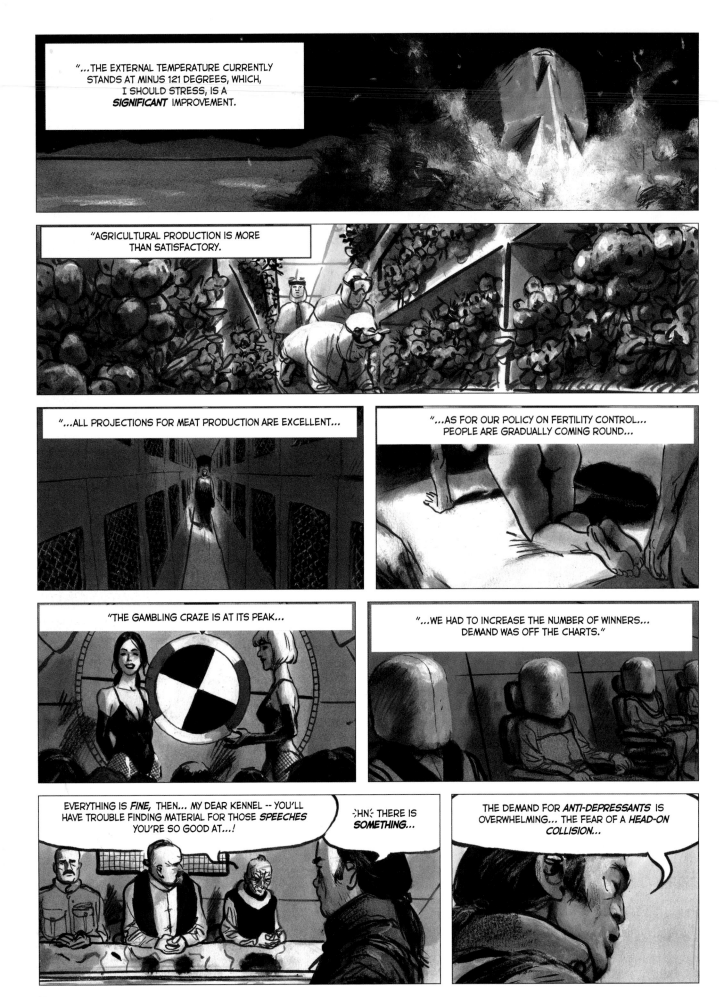

"...THE EXTERNAL TEMPERATURE CURRENTLY STANDS AT MINUS 121 DEGREES, WHICH, I SHOULD STRESS, IS A **SIGNIFICANT** IMPROVEMENT.

"AGRICULTURAL PRODUCTION IS MORE THAN SATISFACTORY.

"...ALL PROJECTIONS FOR MEAT PRODUCTION ARE EXCELLENT...

"...AS FOR OUR POLICY ON FERTILITY CONTROL... PEOPLE ARE GRADUALLY COMING ROUND...

"THE GAMBLING CRAZE IS AT ITS PEAK...

"...WE HAD TO INCREASE THE NUMBER OF WINNERS... DEMAND WAS OFF THE CHARTS."

EVERYTHING IS **FINE,** THEN... MY DEAR KENNEL -- YOU'LL HAVE TROUBLE FINDING MATERIAL FOR THOSE **SPEECHES** YOU'RE SO GOOD AT...!

:HN: THERE IS **SOMETHING...**

THE DEMAND FOR **ANTI-DEPRESSANTS** IS OVERWHELMING... THE FEAR OF A **HEAD-ON COLLISION...**

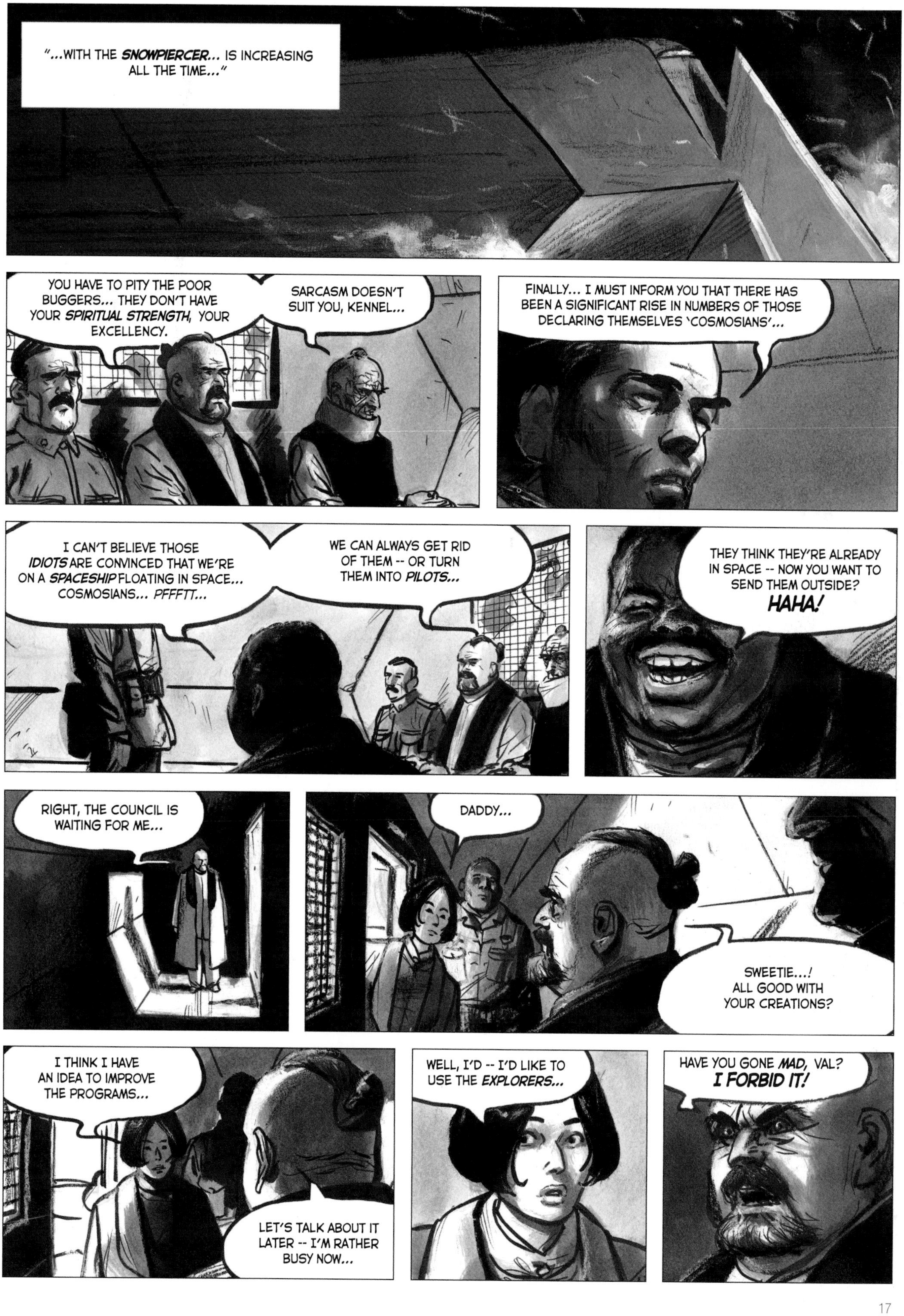
"...WITH THE *SNOWPIERCER*... IS INCREASING ALL THE TIME..."
YOU HAVE TO PITY THE POOR BUGGERS... THEY DON'T HAVE YOUR *SPIRITUAL STRENGTH*, YOUR EXCELLENCY.
SARCASM DOESN'T SUIT YOU, KENNEL...
FINALLY... I MUST INFORM YOU THAT THERE HAS BEEN A SIGNIFICANT RISE IN NUMBERS OF THOSE DECLARING THEMSELVES 'COSMOSIANS'...
I CAN'T BELIEVE THOSE *IDIOTS* ARE CONVINCED THAT WE'RE ON A *SPACESHIP* FLOATING IN SPACE... COSMOSIANS... *PFFFTT*...
WE CAN ALWAYS GET RID OF THEM -- OR TURN THEM INTO *PILOTS*...
THEY THINK THEY'RE ALREADY IN SPACE -- NOW YOU WANT TO SEND THEM OUTSIDE? **HAHA!**
RIGHT, THE COUNCIL IS WAITING FOR ME...
DADDY...
SWEETIE...! ALL GOOD WITH YOUR CREATIONS?
I THINK I HAVE AN IDEA TO IMPROVE THE PROGRAMS...
LET'S TALK ABOUT IT LATER -- I'M RATHER BUSY NOW...
WELL, I'D -- I'D LIKE TO USE THE *EXPLORERS*...
HAVE YOU GONE *MAD*, VAL? **I FORBID IT!**

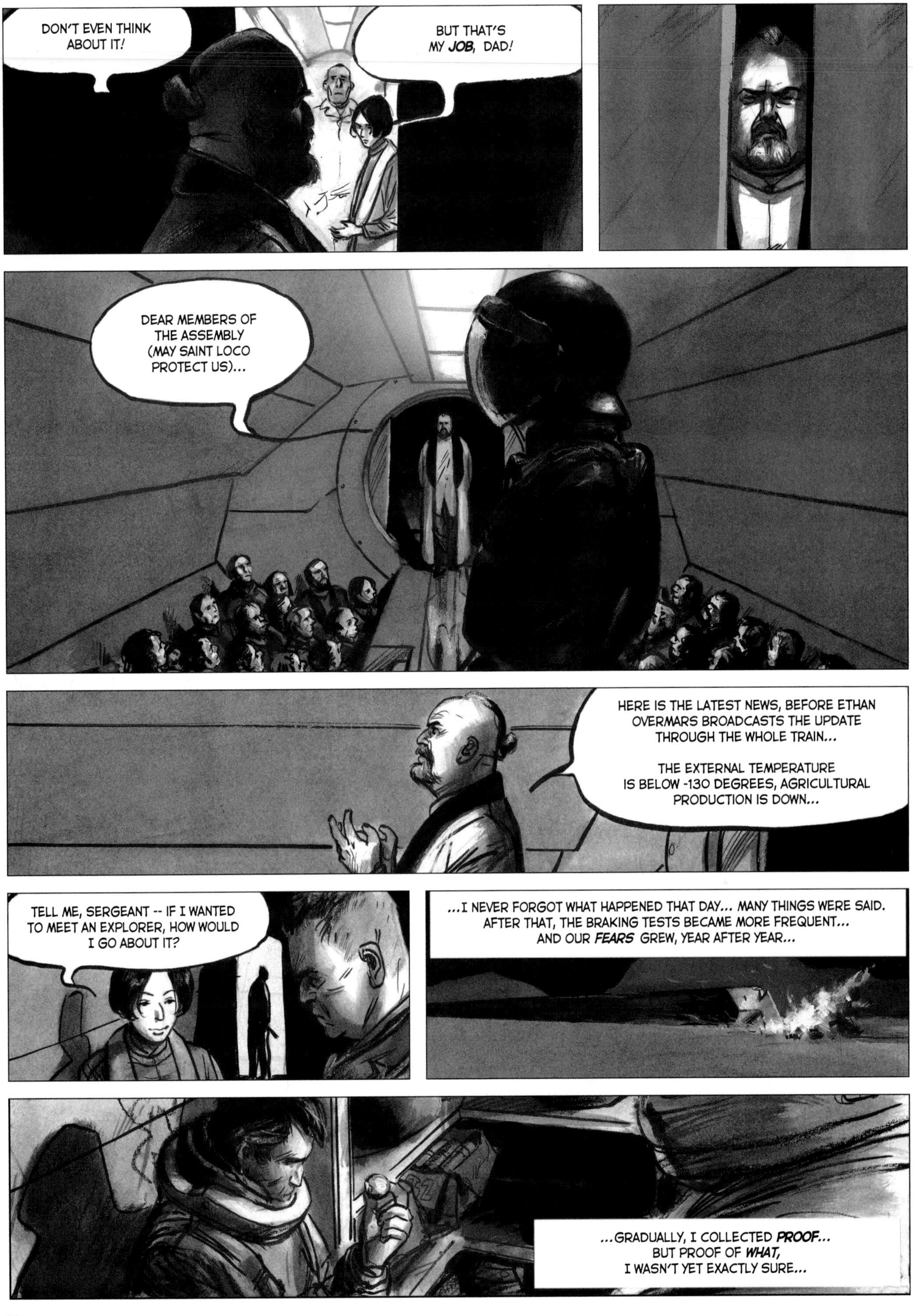

DON'T EVEN THINK ABOUT IT!
BUT THAT'S MY *JOB*, DAD!
DEAR MEMBERS OF THE ASSEMBLY (MAY SAINT LOCO PROTECT US)...
HERE IS THE LATEST NEWS, BEFORE ETHAN OVERMARS BROADCASTS THE UPDATE THROUGH THE WHOLE TRAIN...
THE EXTERNAL TEMPERATURE IS BELOW -130 DEGREES, AGRICULTURAL PRODUCTION IS DOWN...
TELL ME, SERGEANT -- IF I WANTED TO MEET AN EXPLORER, HOW WOULD I GO ABOUT IT?
...I NEVER FORGOT WHAT HAPPENED THAT DAY... MANY THINGS WERE SAID. AFTER THAT, THE BRAKING TESTS BECAME MORE FREQUENT... AND OUR *FEARS* GREW, YEAR AFTER YEAR...
...GRADUALLY, I COLLECTED *PROOF*... BUT PROOF OF *WHAT*, I WASN'T YET EXACTLY SURE...

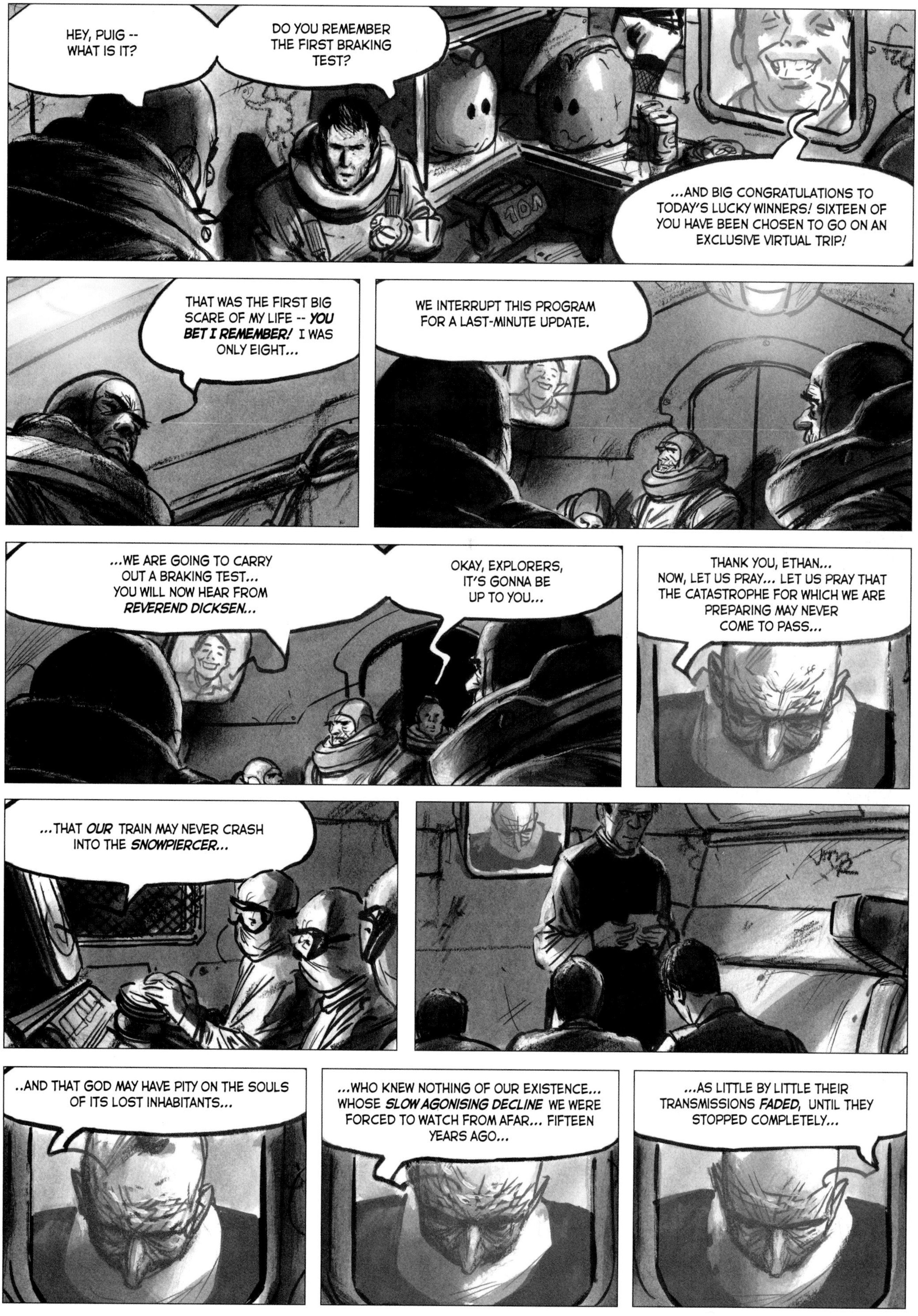
HEY, PUIG -- WHAT IS IT?
DO YOU REMEMBER THE FIRST BRAKING TEST?
...AND BIG CONGRATULATIONS TO TODAY'S LUCKY WINNERS! SIXTEEN OF YOU HAVE BEEN CHOSEN TO GO ON AN EXCLUSIVE VIRTUAL TRIP!
THAT WAS THE FIRST BIG SCARE OF MY LIFE -- *YOU BET I REMEMBER!* I WAS ONLY EIGHT...
WE INTERRUPT THIS PROGRAM FOR A LAST-MINUTE UPDATE.
...WE ARE GOING TO CARRY OUT A BRAKING TEST... YOU WILL NOW HEAR FROM *REVEREND DICKSEN...*
OKAY, EXPLORERS, IT'S GONNA BE UP TO YOU...
THANK YOU, ETHAN... NOW, LET US PRAY... LET US PRAY THAT THE CATASTROPHE FOR WHICH WE ARE PREPARING MAY NEVER COME TO PASS...
...THAT *OUR* TRAIN MAY NEVER CRASH INTO THE *SNOWPIERCER...*
..AND THAT GOD MAY HAVE PITY ON THE SOULS OF ITS LOST INHABITANTS...
...WHO KNEW NOTHING OF OUR EXISTENCE... WHOSE *SLOW AGONISING DECLINE* WE WERE FORCED TO WATCH FROM AFAR... FIFTEEN YEARS AGO...
...AS LITTLE BY LITTLE THEIR TRANSMISSIONS *FADED,* UNTIL THEY STOPPED COMPLETELY...

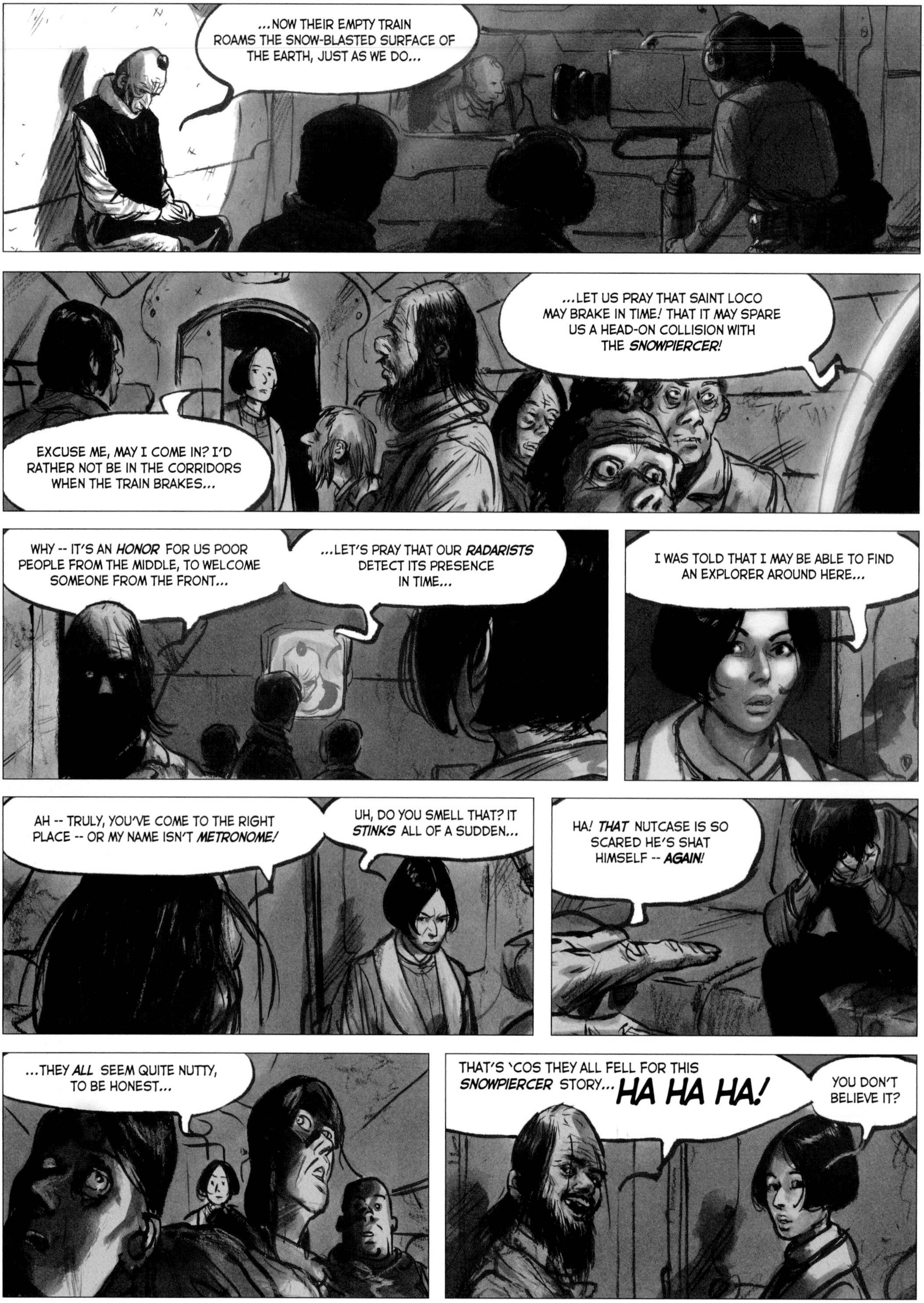
...NOW THEIR EMPTY TRAIN ROAMS THE SNOW-BLASTED SURFACE OF THE EARTH, JUST AS WE DO...
...LET US PRAY THAT SAINT LOCO MAY BRAKE IN TIME! THAT IT MAY SPARE US A HEAD-ON COLLISION WITH THE SNOWPIERCER!
EXCUSE ME, MAY I COME IN? I'D RATHER NOT BE IN THE CORRIDORS WHEN THE TRAIN BRAKES...
WHY -- IT'S AN HONOR FOR US POOR PEOPLE FROM THE MIDDLE, TO WELCOME SOMEONE FROM THE FRONT...
...LET'S PRAY THAT OUR RADARISTS DETECT ITS PRESENCE IN TIME...
I WAS TOLD THAT I MAY BE ABLE TO FIND AN EXPLORER AROUND HERE...
AH -- TRULY, YOU'VE COME TO THE RIGHT PLACE -- OR MY NAME ISN'T METRONOME!
UH, DO YOU SMELL THAT? IT STINKS ALL OF A SUDDEN...
HA! THAT NUTCASE IS SO SCARED HE'S SHAT HIMSELF -- AGAIN!
...THEY ALL SEEM QUITE NUTTY, TO BE HONEST...
THAT'S 'COS THEY ALL FELL FOR THIS SNOWPIERCER STORY... HA HA HA!
YOU DON'T BELIEVE IT?

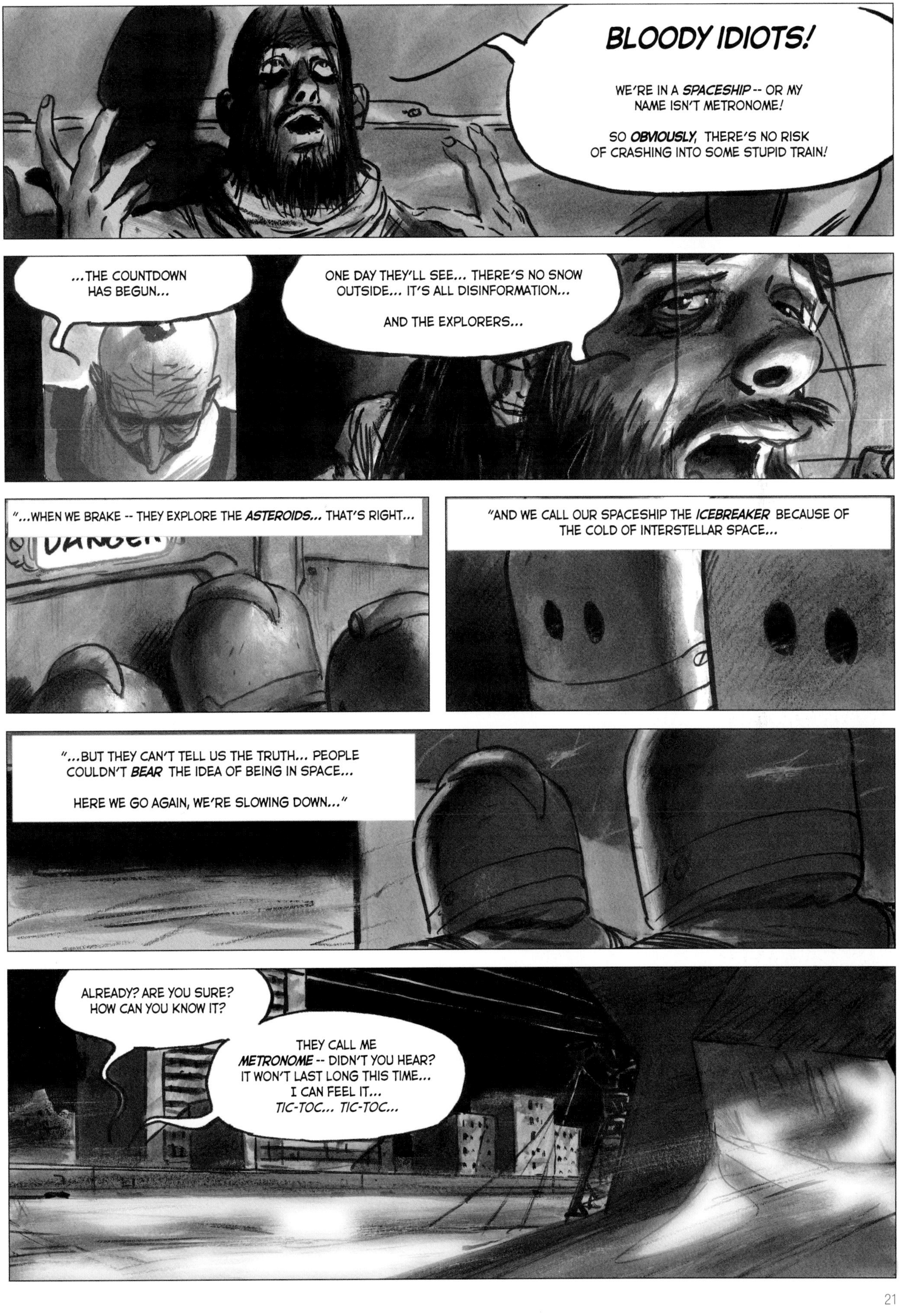
BLOODY IDIOTS!
WE'RE IN A SPACESHIP -- OR MY NAME ISN'T METRONOME!
SO OBVIOUSLY, THERE'S NO RISK OF CRASHING INTO SOME STUPID TRAIN!
...THE COUNTDOWN HAS BEGUN...
ONE DAY THEY'LL SEE... THERE'S NO SNOW OUTSIDE... IT'S ALL DISINFORMATION...
AND THE EXPLORERS...
"...WHEN WE BRAKE -- THEY EXPLORE THE ASTEROIDS... THAT'S RIGHT...
"AND WE CALL OUR SPACESHIP THE ICEBREAKER BECAUSE OF THE COLD OF INTERSTELLAR SPACE...
"...BUT THEY CAN'T TELL US THE TRUTH... PEOPLE COULDN'T BEAR THE IDEA OF BEING IN SPACE...
HERE WE GO AGAIN, WE'RE SLOWING DOWN..."
ALREADY? ARE YOU SURE? HOW CAN YOU KNOW IT?
THEY CALL ME METRONOME -- DIDN'T YOU HEAR? IT WON'T LAST LONG THIS TIME... I CAN FEEL IT... TIC-TOC... TIC-TOC...

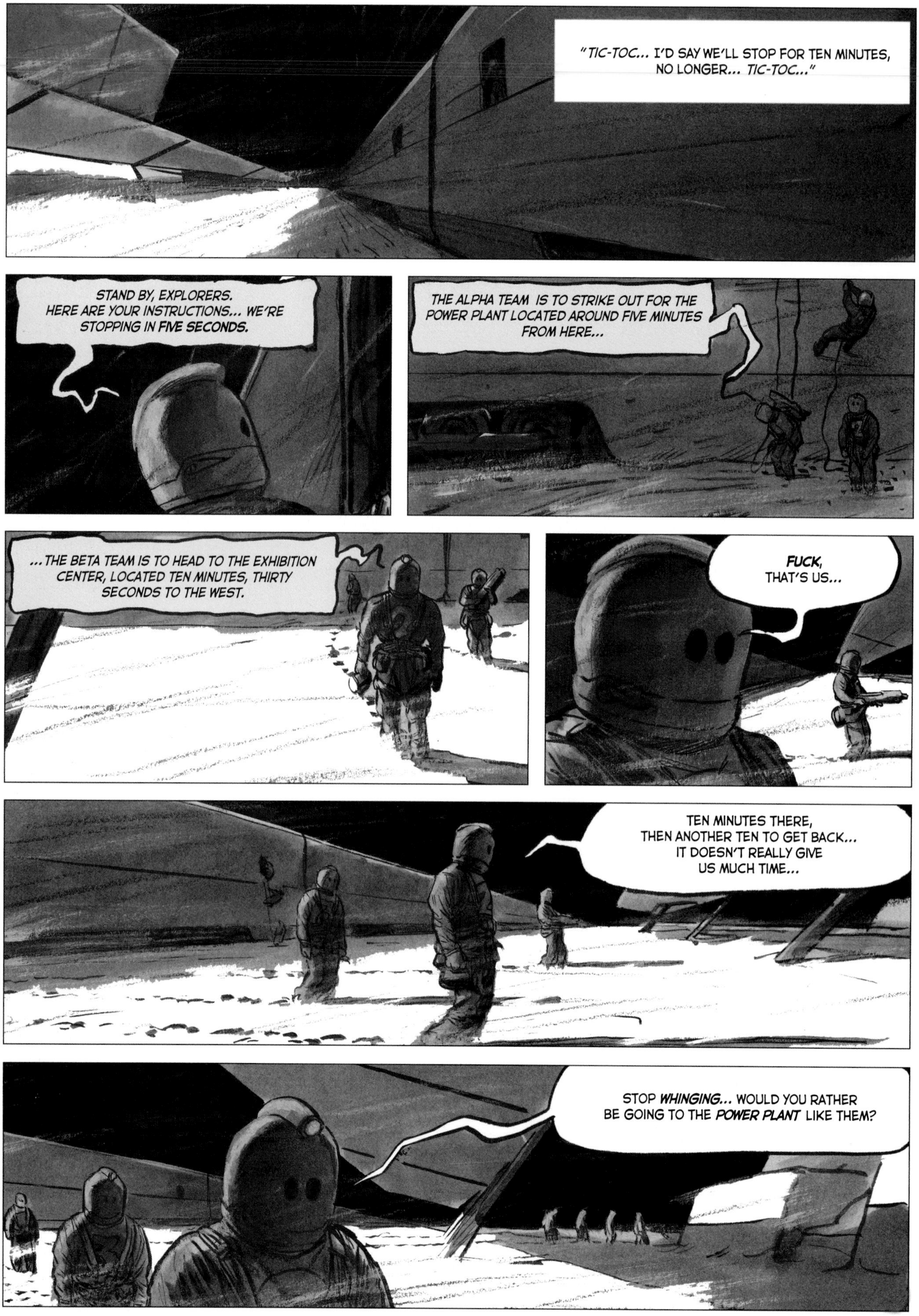
"TIC-TOC... I'D SAY WE'LL STOP FOR TEN MINUTES, NO LONGER... TIC-TOC..."
STAND BY, EXPLORERS. HERE ARE YOUR INSTRUCTIONS... WE'RE STOPPING IN FIVE SECONDS.
THE ALPHA TEAM IS TO STRIKE OUT FOR THE POWER PLANT LOCATED AROUND FIVE MINUTES FROM HERE...
...THE BETA TEAM IS TO HEAD TO THE EXHIBITION CENTER, LOCATED TEN MINUTES, THIRTY SECONDS TO THE WEST.
FUCK, THAT'S US...
TEN MINUTES THERE, THEN ANOTHER TEN TO GET BACK... IT DOESN'T REALLY GIVE US MUCH TIME...
STOP WHINGING... WOULD YOU RATHER BE GOING TO THE POWER PLANT LIKE THEM?

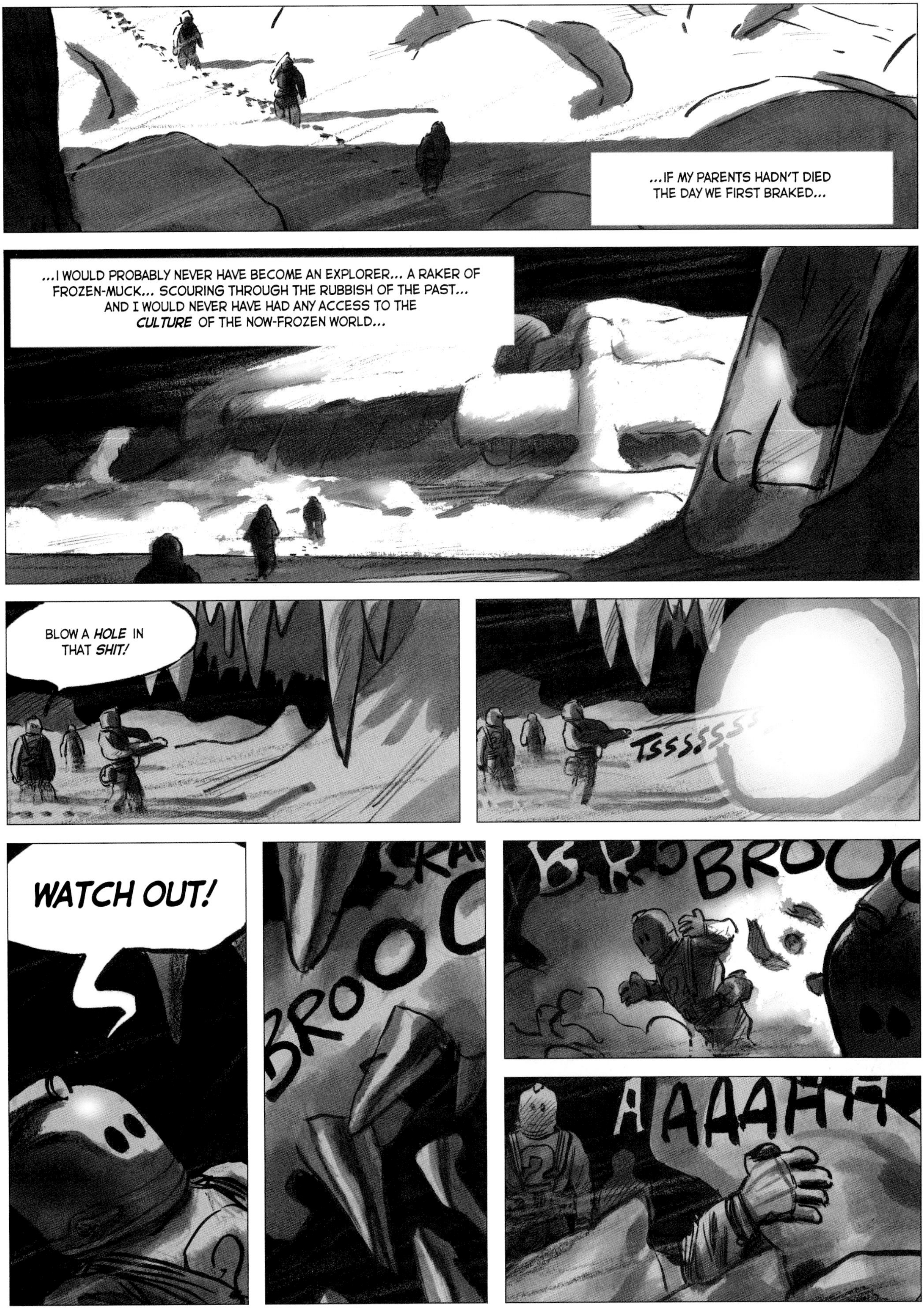
...IF MY PARENTS HADN'T DIED THE DAY WE FIRST BRAKED...
...I WOULD PROBABLY NEVER HAVE BECOME AN EXPLORER... A RAKER OF FROZEN-MUCK... SCOURING THROUGH THE RUBBISH OF THE PAST... AND I WOULD NEVER HAVE HAD ANY ACCESS TO THE *CULTURE* OF THE NOW-FROZEN WORLD...
BLOW A *HOLE* IN THAT *SHIT!*
TSSSSSS
WATCH OUT!
BROO
BROOO
AAAAHH

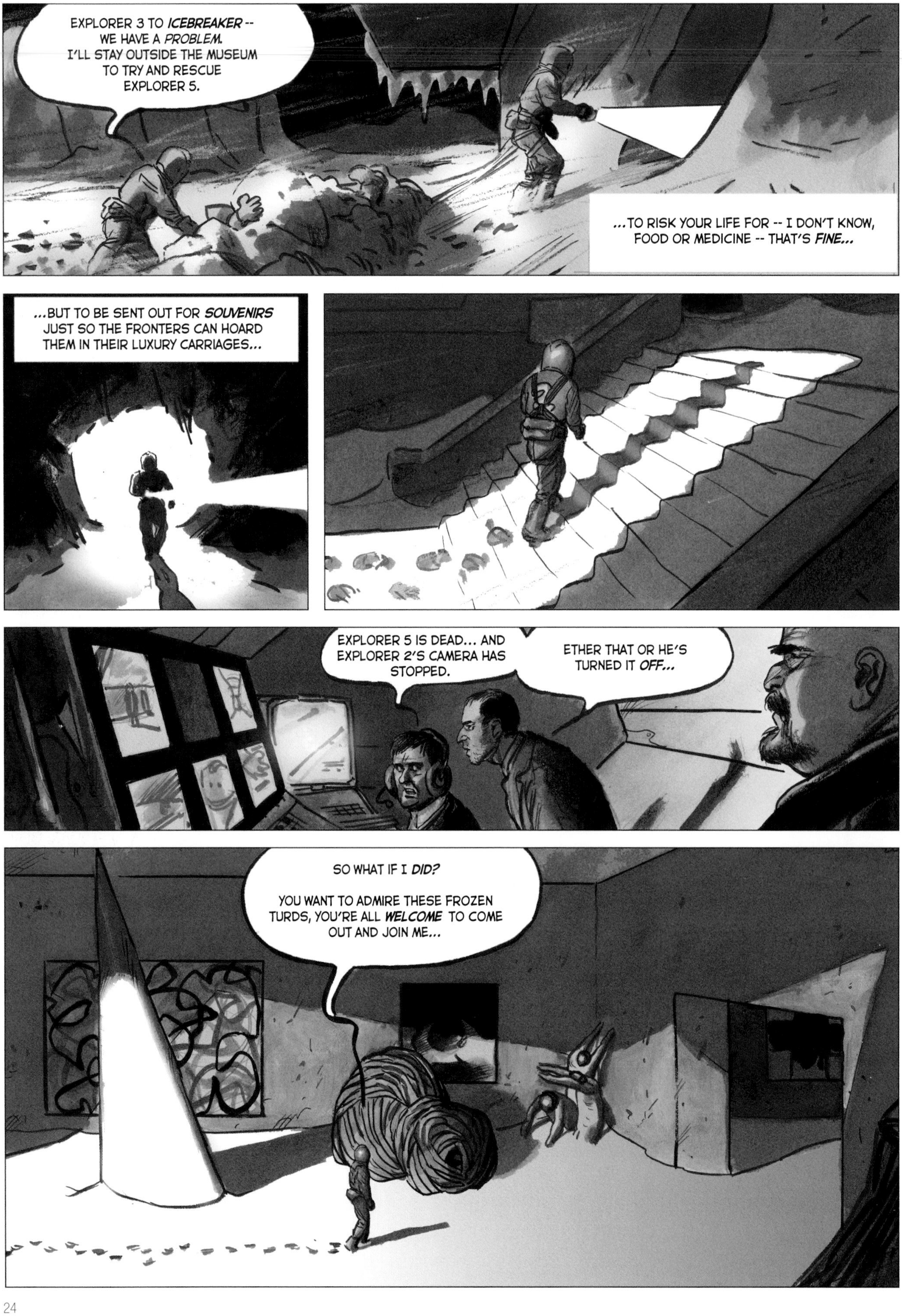
EXPLORER 3 TO *ICEBREAKER* -- WE HAVE A *PROBLEM*. I'LL STAY OUTSIDE THE MUSEUM TO TRY AND RESCUE EXPLORER 5.
...TO RISK YOUR LIFE FOR -- I DON'T KNOW, FOOD OR MEDICINE -- THAT'S *FINE*...
...BUT TO BE SENT OUT FOR *SOUVENIRS* JUST SO THE FRONTERS CAN HOARD THEM IN THEIR LUXURY CARRIAGES...
EXPLORER 5 IS DEAD... AND EXPLORER 2'S CAMERA HAS STOPPED.
ETHER THAT OR HE'S TURNED IT *OFF*...
SO WHAT IF I *DID?*
YOU WANT TO ADMIRE THESE FROZEN TURDS, YOU'RE ALL ***WELCOME*** TO COME OUT AND JOIN ME...

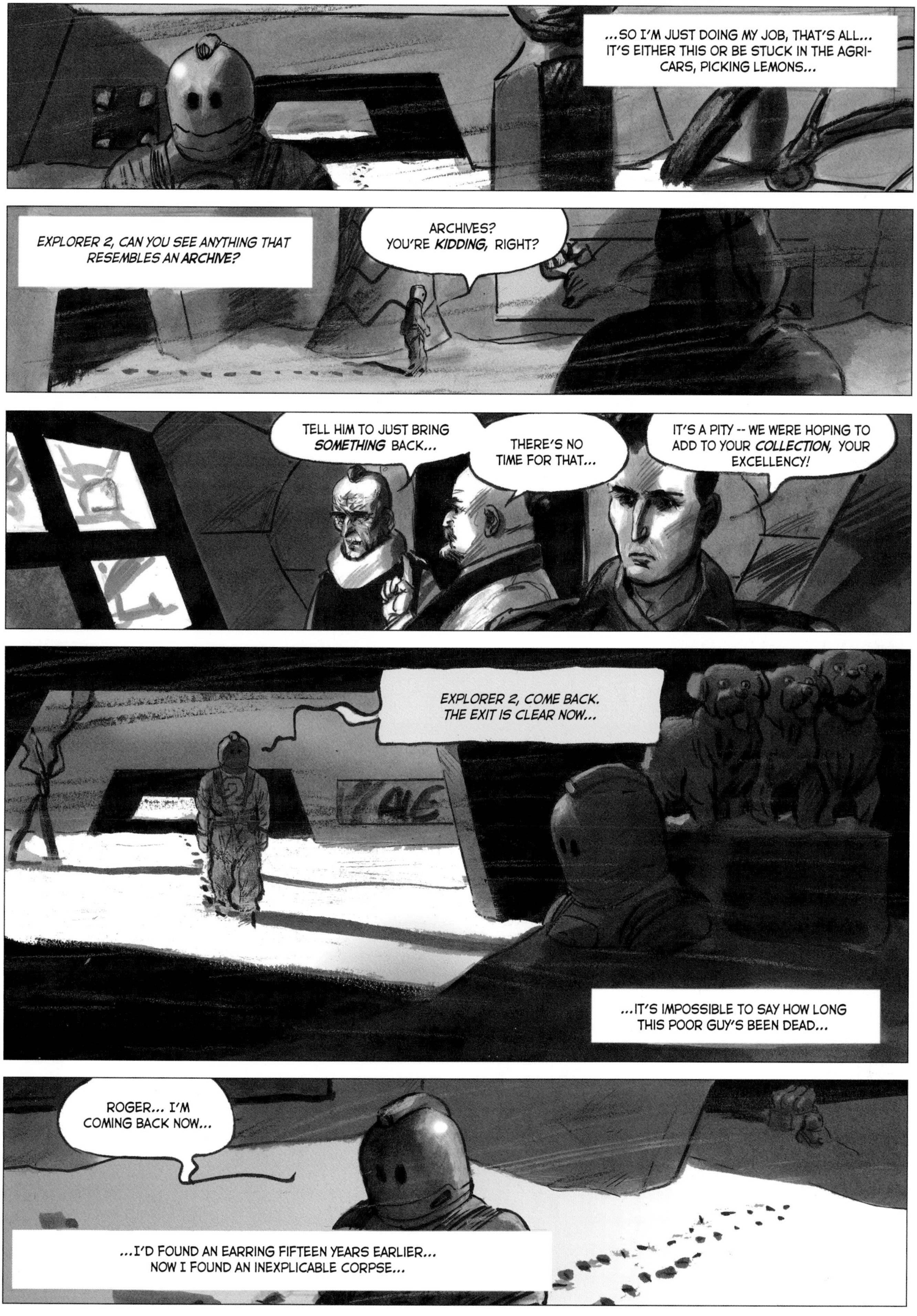
...SO I'M JUST DOING MY JOB, THAT'S ALL... IT'S EITHER THIS OR BE STUCK IN THE AGRI-CARS, PICKING LEMONS...
EXPLORER 2, CAN YOU SEE ANYTHING THAT RESEMBLES AN ARCHIVE?
ARCHIVES? YOU'RE KIDDING, RIGHT?
TELL HIM TO JUST BRING SOMETHING BACK...
THERE'S NO TIME FOR THAT...
IT'S A PITY -- WE WERE HOPING TO ADD TO YOUR COLLECTION, YOUR EXCELLENCY!
EXPLORER 2, COME BACK. THE EXIT IS CLEAR NOW...
...IT'S IMPOSSIBLE TO SAY HOW LONG THIS POOR GUY'S BEEN DEAD...
ROGER... I'M COMING BACK NOW...
...I'D FOUND AN EARRING FIFTEEN YEARS EARLIER... NOW I FOUND AN INEXPLICABLE CORPSE...

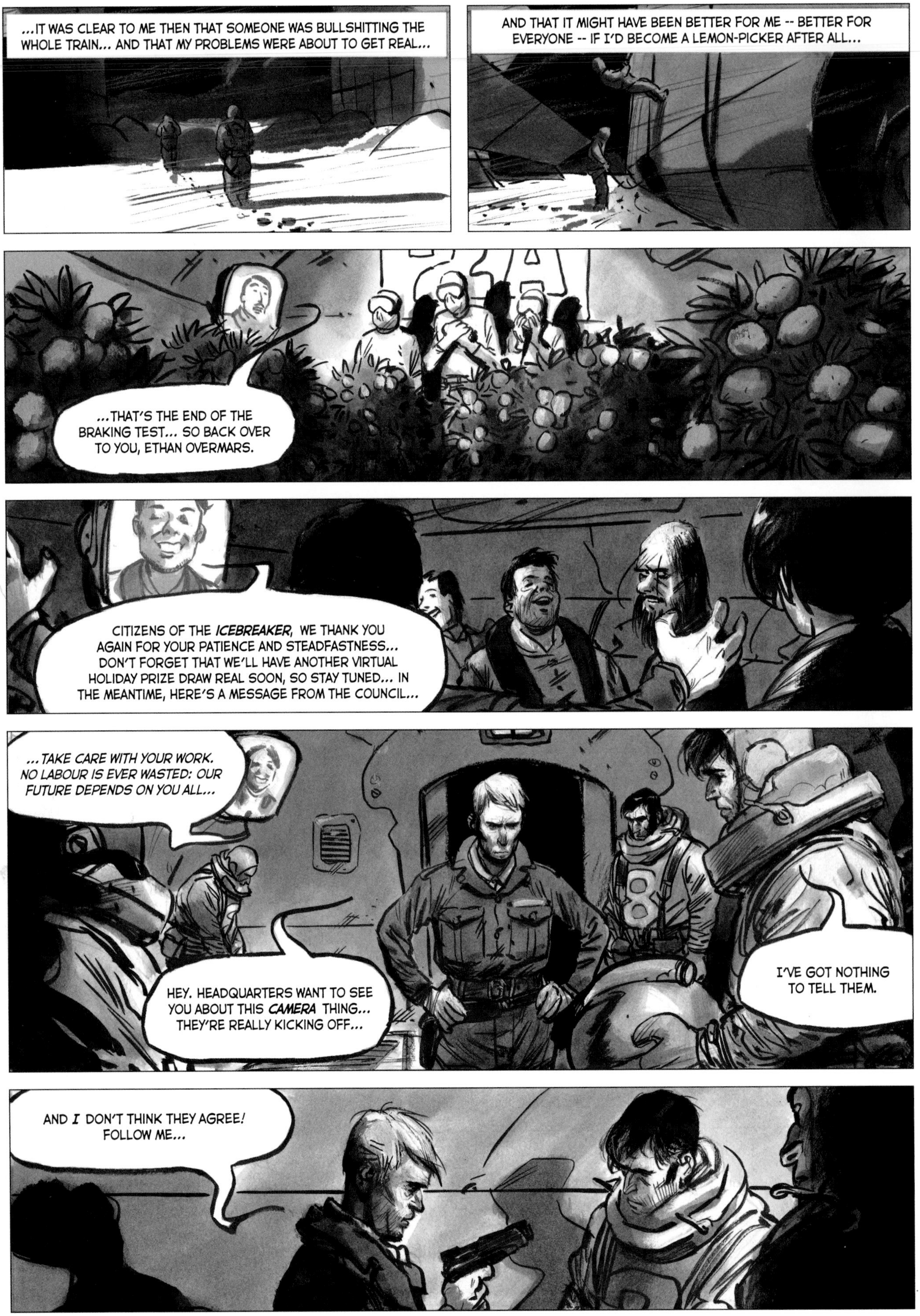
...IT WAS CLEAR TO ME THEN THAT SOMEONE WAS BULLSHITTING THE WHOLE TRAIN... AND THAT MY PROBLEMS WERE ABOUT TO GET REAL...
AND THAT IT MIGHT HAVE BEEN BETTER FOR ME -- BETTER FOR EVERYONE -- IF I'D BECOME A LEMON-PICKER AFTER ALL...
...THAT'S THE END OF THE BRAKING TEST... SO BACK OVER TO YOU, ETHAN OVERMARS.
CITIZENS OF THE ICEBREAKER, WE THANK YOU AGAIN FOR YOUR PATIENCE AND STEADFASTNESS... DON'T FORGET THAT WE'LL HAVE ANOTHER VIRTUAL HOLIDAY PRIZE DRAW REAL SOON, SO STAY TUNED... IN THE MEANTIME, HERE'S A MESSAGE FROM THE COUNCIL...
...TAKE CARE WITH YOUR WORK. NO LABOUR IS EVER WASTED: OUR FUTURE DEPENDS ON YOU ALL...
HEY. HEADQUARTERS WANT TO SEE YOU ABOUT THIS CAMERA THING... THEY'RE REALLY KICKING OFF...
I'VE GOT NOTHING TO TELL THEM.
AND I DON'T THINK THEY AGREE! FOLLOW ME...

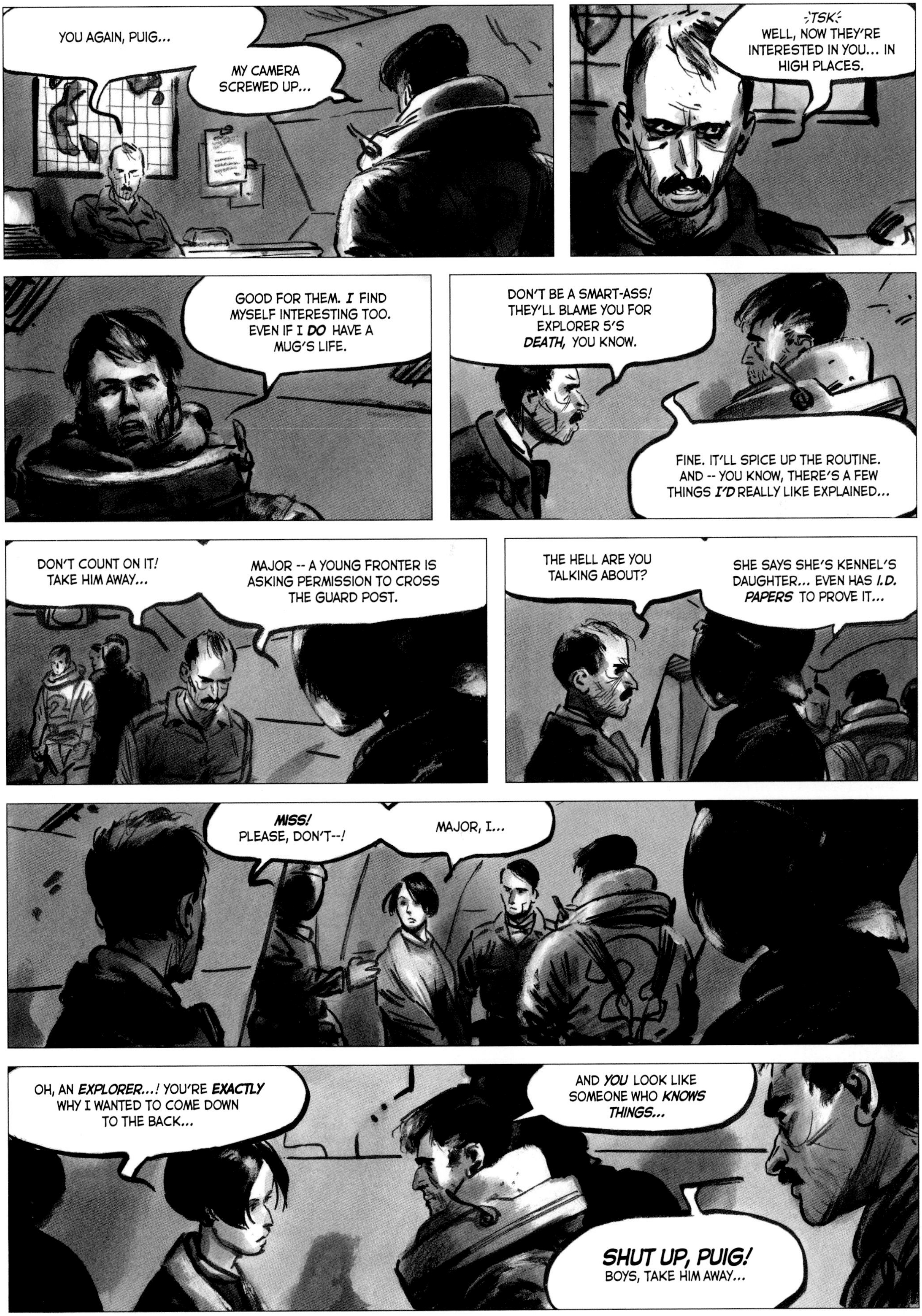
YOU AGAIN, PUIG...
MY CAMERA SCREWED UP...
-TSK- WELL, NOW THEY'RE INTERESTED IN YOU... IN HIGH PLACES.
GOOD FOR THEM. I FIND MYSELF INTERESTING TOO. EVEN IF I DO HAVE A MUG'S LIFE.
DON'T BE A SMART-ASS! THEY'LL BLAME YOU FOR EXPLORER 5'S DEATH, YOU KNOW.
FINE. IT'LL SPICE UP THE ROUTINE. AND -- YOU KNOW, THERE'S A FEW THINGS I'D REALLY LIKE EXPLAINED...
DON'T COUNT ON IT! TAKE HIM AWAY...
MAJOR -- A YOUNG FRONTER IS ASKING PERMISSION TO CROSS THE GUARD POST.
THE HELL ARE YOU TALKING ABOUT?
SHE SAYS SHE'S KENNEL'S DAUGHTER... EVEN HAS I.D. PAPERS TO PROVE IT...
MISS! PLEASE, DON'T--!
MAJOR, I...
OH, AN EXPLORER...! YOU'RE EXACTLY WHY I WANTED TO COME DOWN TO THE BACK...
AND YOU LOOK LIKE SOMEONE WHO KNOWS THINGS...
SHUT UP, PUIG! BOYS, TAKE HIM AWAY...

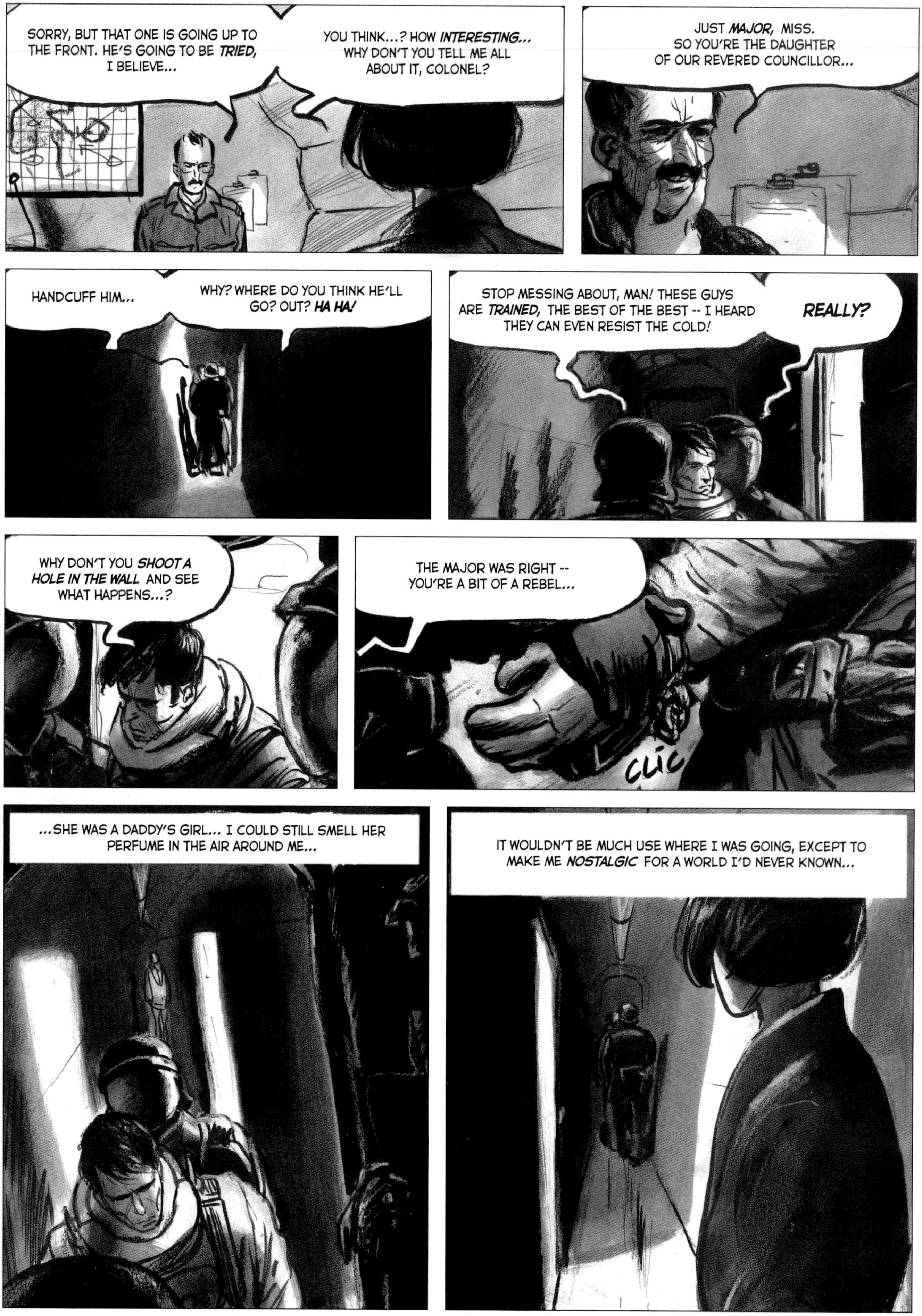
SORRY, BUT THAT ONE IS GOING UP TO THE FRONT. HE'S GOING TO BE *TRIED,* I BELIEVE...
YOU THINK...? HOW *INTERESTING...* WHY DON'T YOU TELL ME ALL ABOUT IT, COLONEL?
JUST *MAJOR,* MISS. SO YOU'RE THE DAUGHTER OF OUR REVERED COUNCILLOR...
HANDCUFF HIM...
WHY? WHERE DO YOU THINK HE'LL GO? OUT? *HA HA!*
STOP MESSING ABOUT, MAN! THESE GUYS ARE *TRAINED,* THE BEST OF THE BEST -- I HEARD THEY CAN EVEN RESIST THE COLD!
REALLY?
WHY DON'T YOU *SHOOT A HOLE IN THE WALL* AND SEE WHAT HAPPENS...?
THE MAJOR WAS RIGHT -- YOU'RE A BIT OF A REBEL...
CLIC
...SHE WAS A DADDY'S GIRL... I COULD STILL SMELL HER PERFUME IN THE AIR AROUND ME...
IT WOULDN'T BE MUCH USE WHERE I WAS GOING, EXCEPT TO MAKE ME *NOSTALGIC* FOR A WORLD I'D NEVER KNOWN...

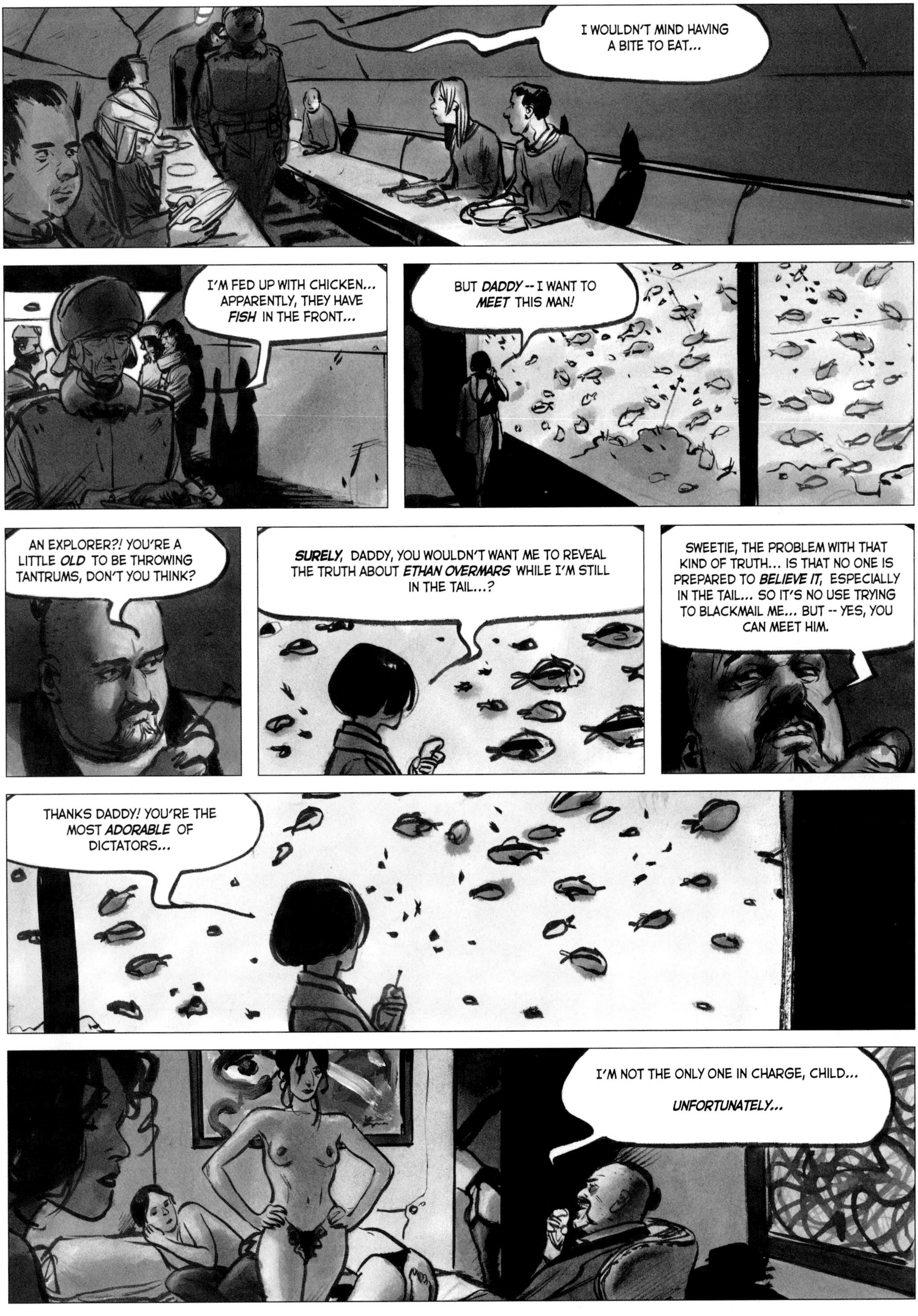
I WOULDN'T MIND HAVING A BITE TO EAT...
I'M FED UP WITH CHICKEN... APPARENTLY, THEY HAVE *FISH* IN THE FRONT...
BUT *DADDY* -- I WANT TO *MEET* THIS MAN!
AN EXPLORER?! YOU'RE A LITTLE *OLD* TO BE THROWING TANTRUMS, DON'T YOU THINK?
SURELY, DADDY, YOU WOULDN'T WANT ME TO REVEAL THE TRUTH ABOUT *ETHAN OVERMARS* WHILE I'M STILL IN THE TAIL...?
SWEETIE, THE PROBLEM WITH THAT KIND OF TRUTH... IS THAT NO ONE IS PREPARED TO *BELIEVE IT*, ESPECIALLY IN THE TAIL... SO IT'S NO USE TRYING TO BLACKMAIL ME... BUT -- YES, YOU CAN MEET HIM.
THANKS DADDY! YOU'RE THE MOST *ADORABLE* OF DICTATORS...
I'M NOT THE ONLY ONE IN CHARGE, CHILD...
UNFORTUNATELY...

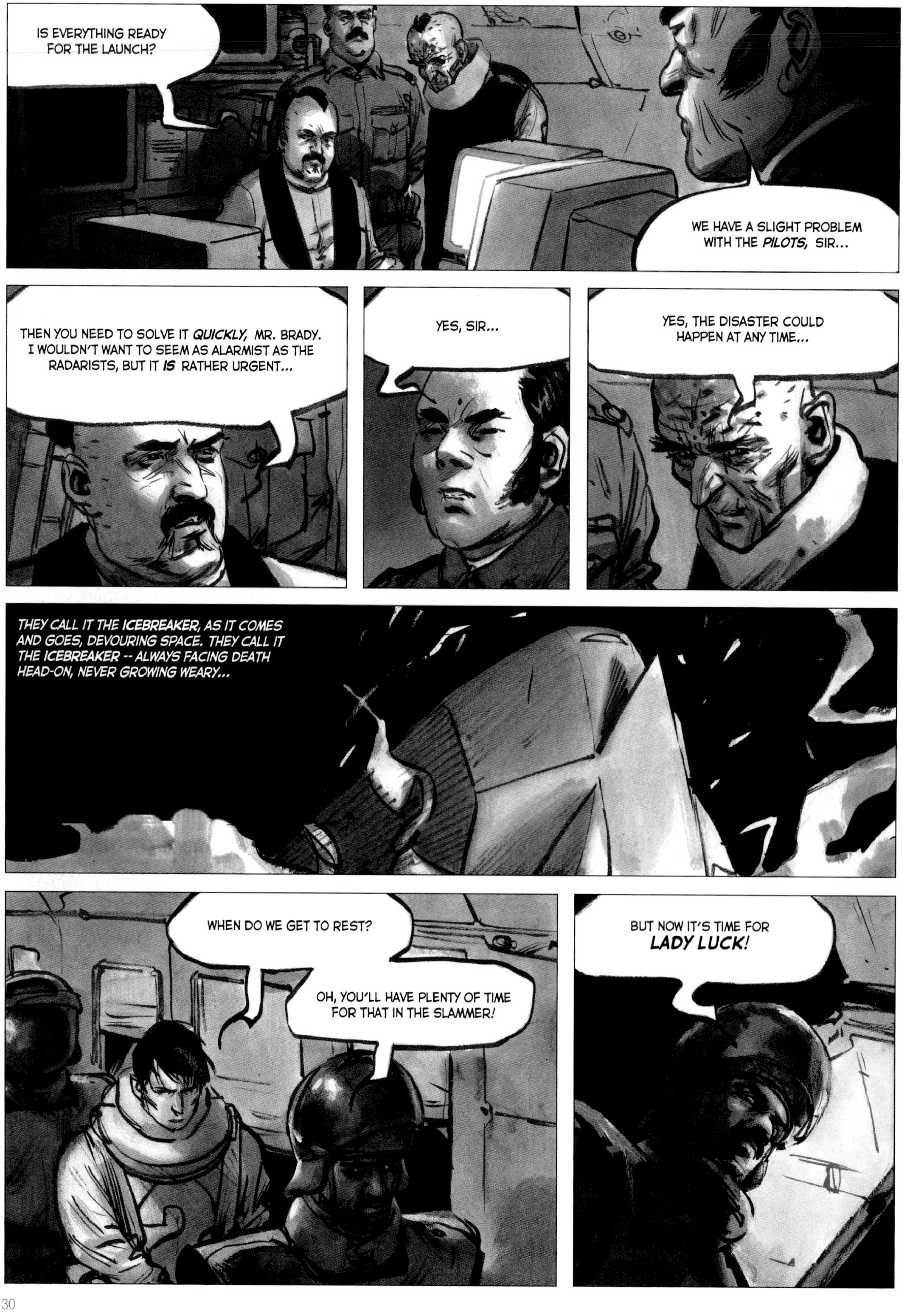
IS EVERYTHING READY FOR THE LAUNCH?
WE HAVE A SLIGHT PROBLEM WITH THE *PILOTS,* SIR...
THEN YOU NEED TO SOLVE IT *QUICKLY,* MR. BRADY. I WOULDN'T WANT TO SEEM AS ALARMIST AS THE RADARISTS, BUT IT *IS* RATHER URGENT...
YES, SIR...
YES, THE DISASTER COULD HAPPEN AT ANY TIME...
*THEY CALL IT THE **ICEBREAKER**, AS IT COMES AND GOES, DEVOURING SPACE. THEY CALL IT THE **ICEBREAKER** -- ALWAYS FACING DEATH HEAD-ON, NEVER GROWING WEARY...*
WHEN DO WE GET TO REST?
OH, YOU'LL HAVE PLENTY OF TIME FOR THAT IN THE SLAMMER!
BUT NOW IT'S TIME FOR ***LADY LUCK!***

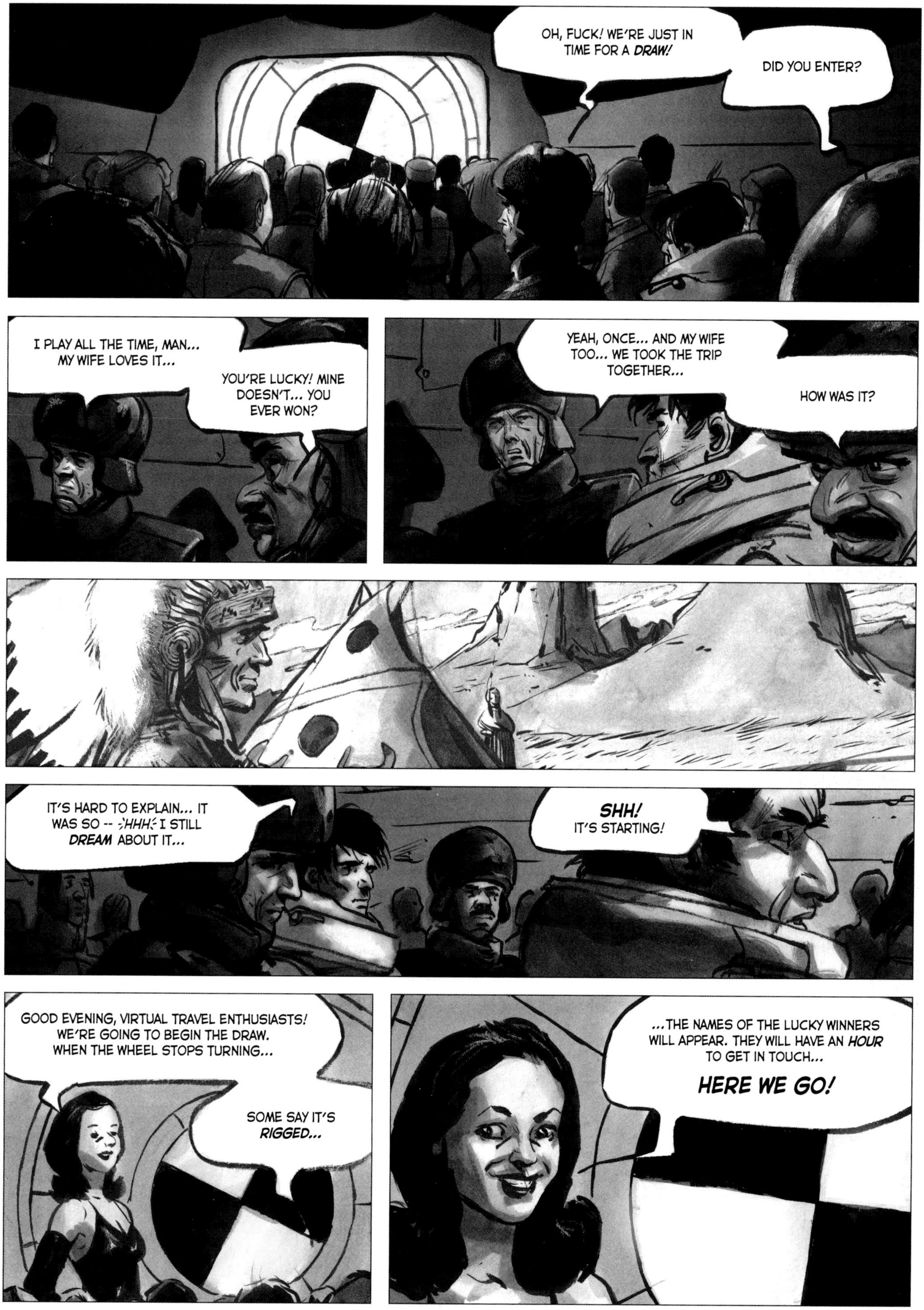
OH, FUCK! WE'RE JUST IN TIME FOR A *DRAW!*
DID YOU ENTER?
I PLAY ALL THE TIME, MAN... MY WIFE LOVES IT...
YOU'RE LUCKY! MINE DOESN'T... YOU EVER WON?
YEAH, ONCE... AND MY WIFE TOO... WE TOOK THE TRIP TOGETHER...
HOW WAS IT?
IT'S HARD TO EXPLAIN... IT WAS SO -- *HHH* I STILL *DREAM* ABOUT IT...
SHH! IT'S STARTING!
GOOD EVENING, VIRTUAL TRAVEL ENTHUSIASTS! WE'RE GOING TO BEGIN THE DRAW. WHEN THE WHEEL STOPS TURNING...
SOME SAY IT'S ***RIGGED...***
...THE NAMES OF THE LUCKY WINNERS WILL APPEAR. THEY WILL HAVE AN *HOUR* TO GET IN TOUCH...
HERE WE GO!

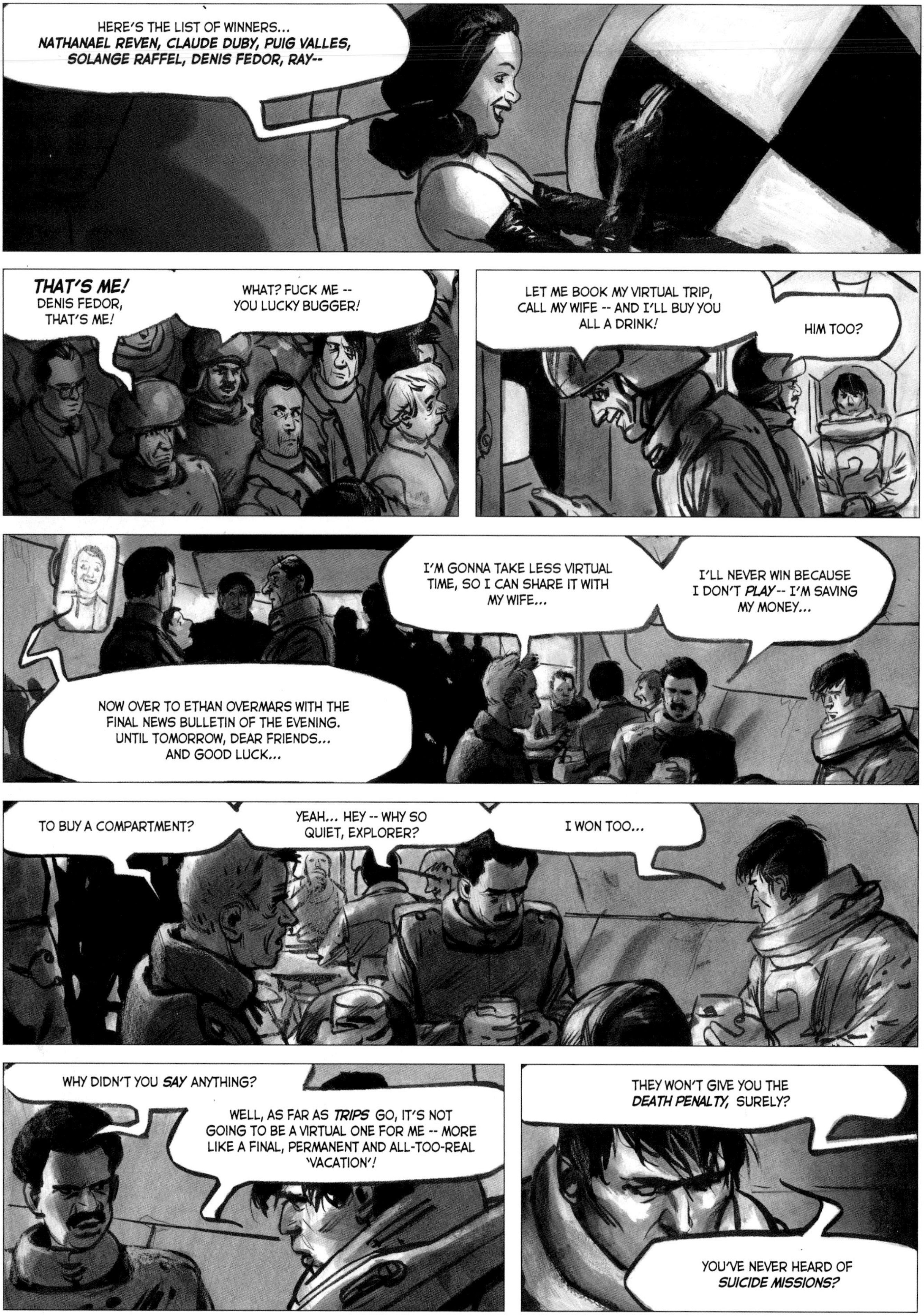
HERE'S THE LIST OF WINNERS... NATHANAEL REVEN, CLAUDE DUBY, PUIG VALLES, SOLANGE RAFFEL, DENIS FEDOR, RAY--
THAT'S ME! DENIS FEDOR, THAT'S ME!
WHAT? FUCK ME -- YOU LUCKY BUGGER!
LET ME BOOK MY VIRTUAL TRIP, CALL MY WIFE -- AND I'LL BUY YOU ALL A DRINK!
HIM TOO?
NOW OVER TO ETHAN OVERMARS WITH THE FINAL NEWS BULLETIN OF THE EVENING. UNTIL TOMORROW, DEAR FRIENDS... AND GOOD LUCK...
I'M GONNA TAKE LESS VIRTUAL TIME, SO I CAN SHARE IT WITH MY WIFE...
I'LL NEVER WIN BECAUSE I DON'T PLAY -- I'M SAVING MY MONEY...
TO BUY A COMPARTMENT?
YEAH... HEY -- WHY SO QUIET, EXPLORER?
I WON TOO...
WHY DIDN'T YOU SAY ANYTHING?
WELL, AS FAR AS TRIPS GO, IT'S NOT GOING TO BE A VIRTUAL ONE FOR ME -- MORE LIKE A FINAL, PERMANENT AND ALL-TOO-REAL 'VACATION'!
THEY WON'T GIVE YOU THE DEATH PENALTY, SURELY?
YOU'VE NEVER HEARD OF SUICIDE MISSIONS?

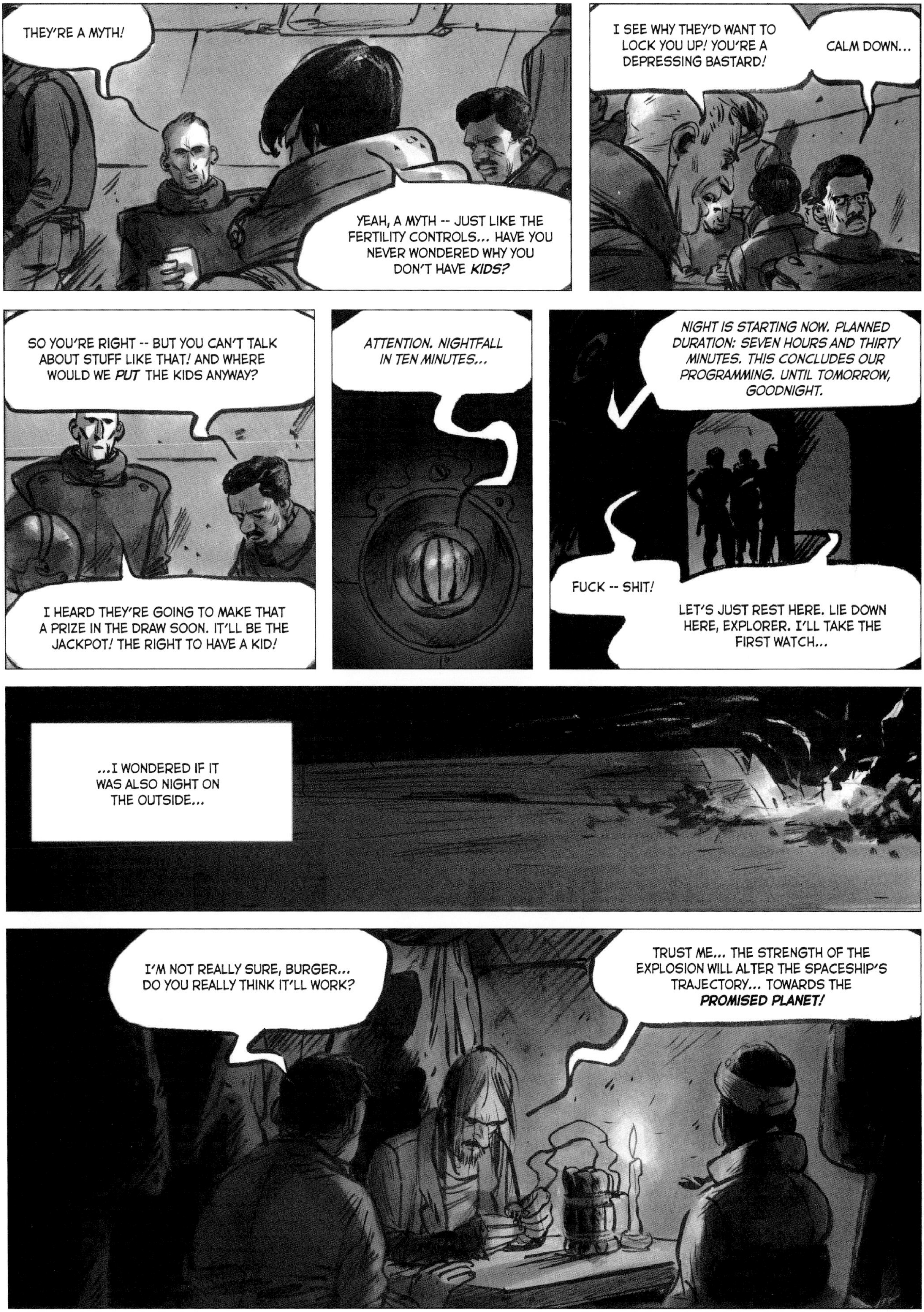
THEY'RE A MYTH!
YEAH, A MYTH -- JUST LIKE THE FERTILITY CONTROLS... HAVE YOU NEVER WONDERED WHY YOU DON'T HAVE *KIDS?*
I SEE WHY THEY'D WANT TO LOCK YOU UP! YOU'RE A DEPRESSING BASTARD!
CALM DOWN...
SO YOU'RE RIGHT -- BUT YOU CAN'T TALK ABOUT STUFF LIKE THAT! AND WHERE WOULD WE *PUT* THE KIDS ANYWAY?
I HEARD THEY'RE GOING TO MAKE THAT A PRIZE IN THE DRAW SOON. IT'LL BE THE JACKPOT! THE RIGHT TO HAVE A KID!
ATTENTION. NIGHTFALL IN TEN MINUTES...
NIGHT IS STARTING NOW. PLANNED DURATION: SEVEN HOURS AND THIRTY MINUTES. THIS CONCLUDES OUR PROGRAMMING. UNTIL TOMORROW, GOODNIGHT.
FUCK -- SHIT!
LET'S JUST REST HERE. LIE DOWN HERE, EXPLORER. I'LL TAKE THE FIRST WATCH...
...I WONDERED IF IT WAS ALSO NIGHT ON THE OUTSIDE...
I'M NOT REALLY SURE, BURGER... DO YOU REALLY THINK IT'LL WORK?
TRUST ME... THE STRENGTH OF THE EXPLOSION WILL ALTER THE SPACESHIP'S TRAJECTORY... TOWARDS THE **PROMISED PLANET!**

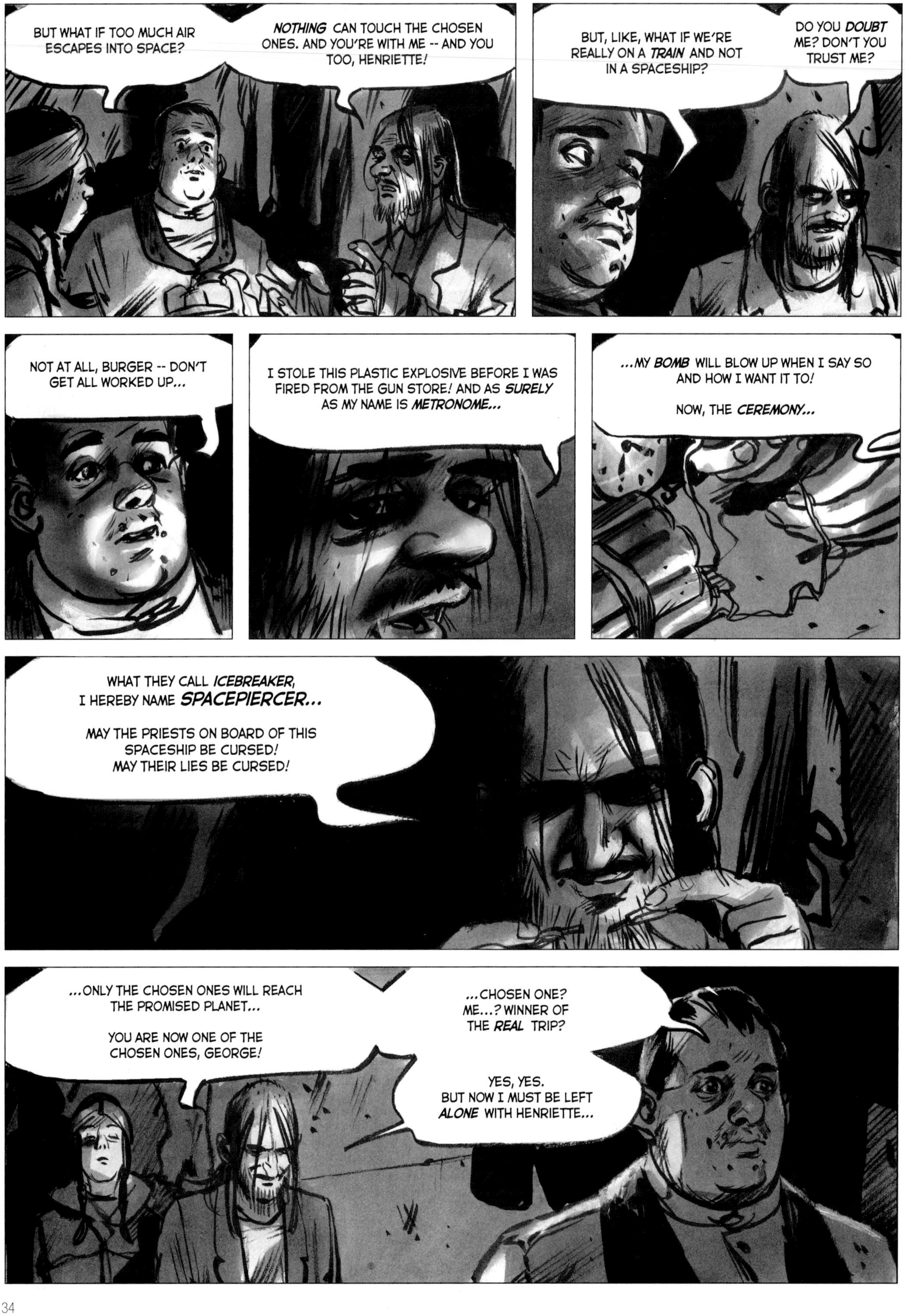
BUT WHAT IF TOO MUCH AIR ESCAPES INTO SPACE?
NOTHING CAN TOUCH THE CHOSEN ONES. AND YOU'RE WITH ME -- AND YOU TOO, HENRIETTE!
BUT, LIKE, WHAT IF WE'RE REALLY ON A TRAIN AND NOT IN A SPACESHIP?
DO YOU DOUBT ME? DON'T YOU TRUST ME?
NOT AT ALL, BURGER -- DON'T GET ALL WORKED UP...
I STOLE THIS PLASTIC EXPLOSIVE BEFORE I WAS FIRED FROM THE GUN STORE! AND AS SURELY AS MY NAME IS METRONOME...
...MY BOMB WILL BLOW UP WHEN I SAY SO AND HOW I WANT IT TO!
NOW, THE CEREMONY...
WHAT THEY CALL ICEBREAKER, I HEREBY NAME SPACEPIERCER...
MAY THE PRIESTS ON BOARD OF THIS SPACESHIP BE CURSED! MAY THEIR LIES BE CURSED!
...ONLY THE CHOSEN ONES WILL REACH THE PROMISED PLANET...
YOU ARE NOW ONE OF THE CHOSEN ONES, GEORGE!
...CHOSEN ONE? ME...? WINNER OF THE REAL TRIP?
YES, YES. BUT NOW I MUST BE LEFT ALONE WITH HENRIETTE...

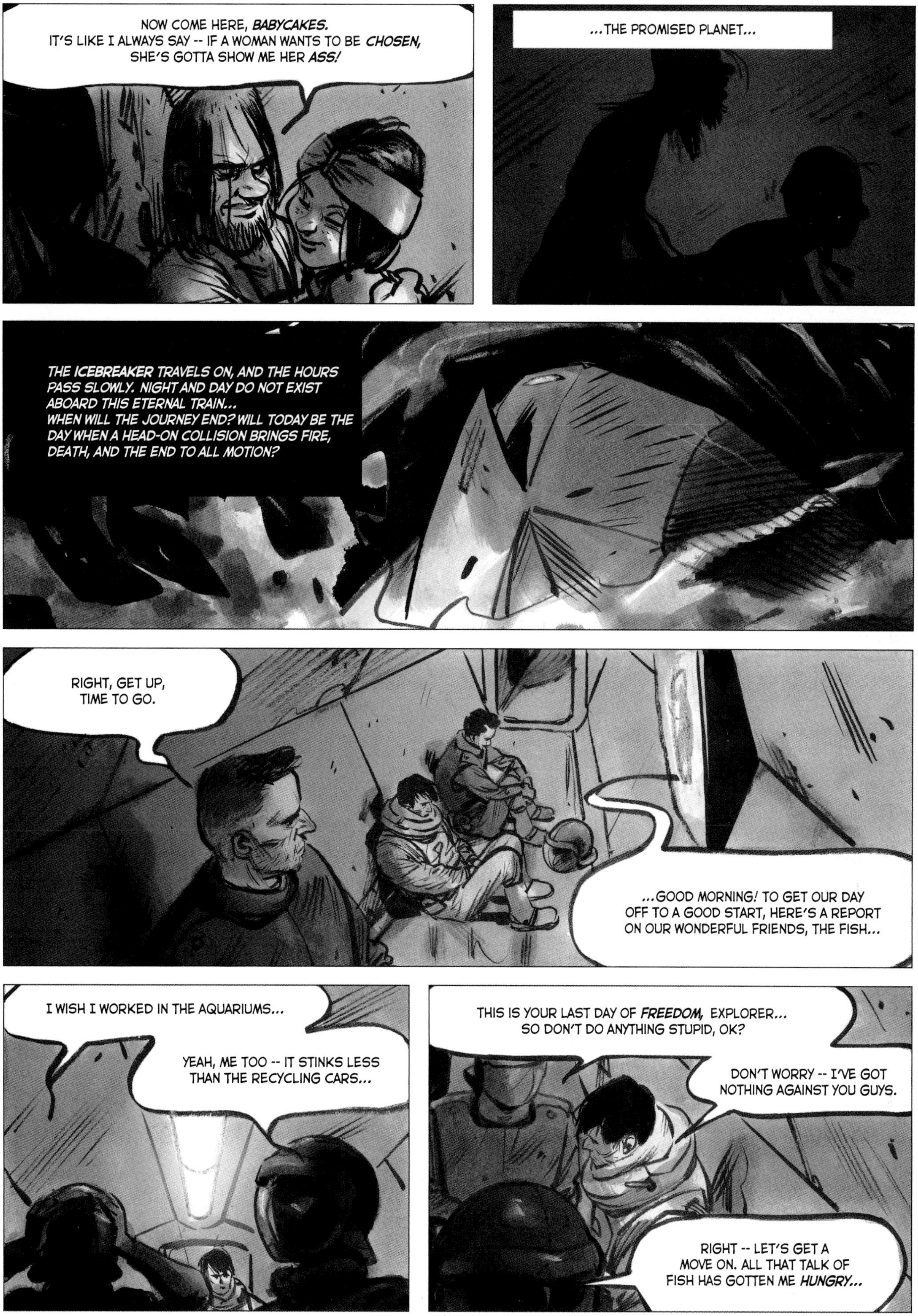
NOW COME HERE, *BABYCAKES.* IT'S LIKE I ALWAYS SAY -- IF A WOMAN WANTS TO BE *CHOSEN,* SHE'S GOTTA SHOW ME HER *ASS!*
...THE PROMISED PLANET...
THE ICEBREAKER TRAVELS ON, AND THE HOURS PASS SLOWLY. NIGHT AND DAY DO NOT EXIST ABOARD THIS ETERNAL TRAIN... WHEN WILL THE JOURNEY END? WILL TODAY BE THE DAY WHEN A HEAD-ON COLLISION BRINGS FIRE, DEATH, AND THE END TO ALL MOTION?
RIGHT, GET UP, TIME TO GO.
...GOOD MORNING! TO GET OUR DAY OFF TO A GOOD START, HERE'S A REPORT ON OUR WONDERFUL FRIENDS, THE FISH...
I WISH I WORKED IN THE AQUARIUMS...
YEAH, ME TOO -- IT STINKS LESS THAN THE RECYCLING CARS...
THIS IS YOUR LAST DAY OF *FREEDOM,* EXPLORER... SO DON'T DO ANYTHING STUPID, OK?
DON'T WORRY -- I'VE GOT NOTHING AGAINST YOU GUYS.
RIGHT -- LET'S GET A MOVE ON. ALL THAT TALK OF FISH HAS GOTTEN ME *HUNGRY...*

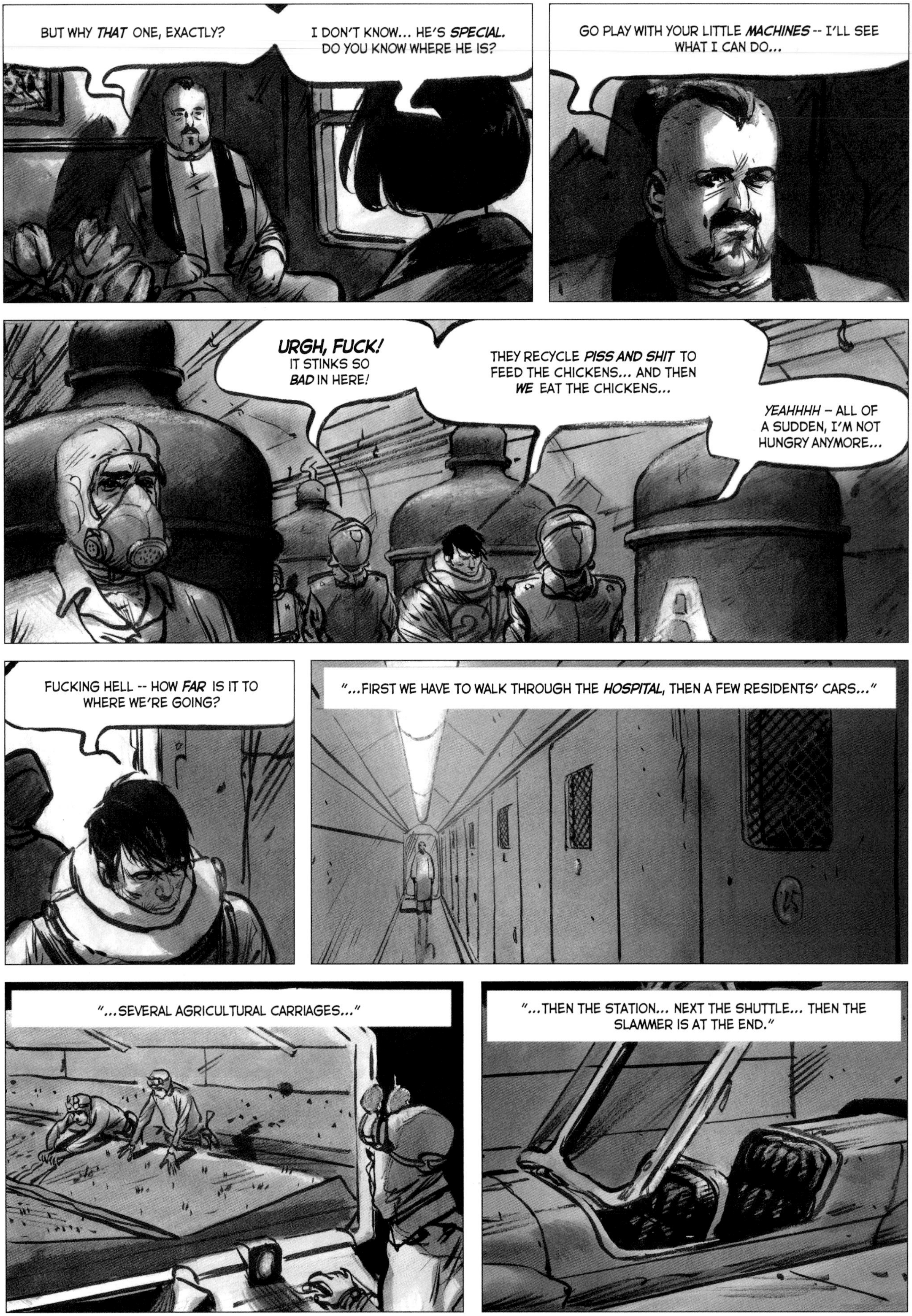
BUT WHY THAT ONE, EXACTLY?
I DON'T KNOW... HE'S SPECIAL. DO YOU KNOW WHERE HE IS?
GO PLAY WITH YOUR LITTLE MACHINES -- I'LL SEE WHAT I CAN DO...
URGH, FUCK! IT STINKS SO BAD IN HERE!
THEY RECYCLE PISS AND SHIT TO FEED THE CHICKENS... AND THEN WE EAT THE CHICKENS...
YEAHHHH – ALL OF A SUDDEN, I'M NOT HUNGRY ANYMORE...
FUCKING HELL -- HOW FAR IS IT TO WHERE WE'RE GOING?
"...FIRST WE HAVE TO WALK THROUGH THE HOSPITAL, THEN A FEW RESIDENTS' CARS..."
"...SEVERAL AGRICULTURAL CARRIAGES..."
"...THEN THE STATION... NEXT THE SHUTTLE... THEN THE SLAMMER IS AT THE END."

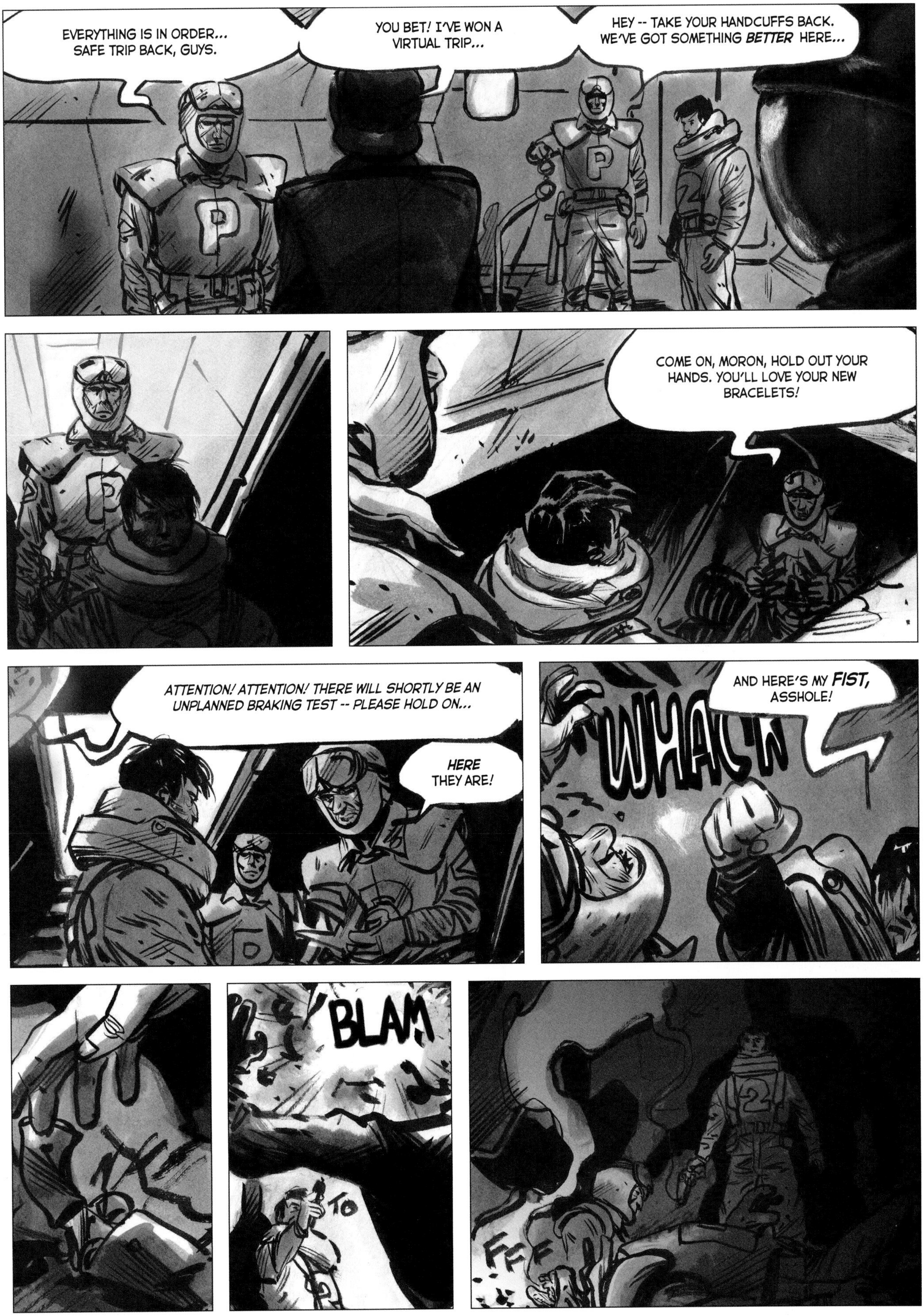
EVERYTHING IS IN ORDER... SAFE TRIP BACK, GUYS.
YOU BET! I'VE WON A VIRTUAL TRIP...
HEY -- TAKE YOUR HANDCUFFS BACK. WE'VE GOT SOMETHING *BETTER* HERE...
COME ON, MORON, HOLD OUT YOUR HANDS. YOU'LL LOVE YOUR NEW BRACELETS!
ATTENTION! ATTENTION! THERE WILL SHORTLY BE AN UNPLANNED BRAKING TEST -- PLEASE HOLD ON...
HERE THEY ARE!
AND HERE'S MY *FIST,* ASSHOLE!
BLAM

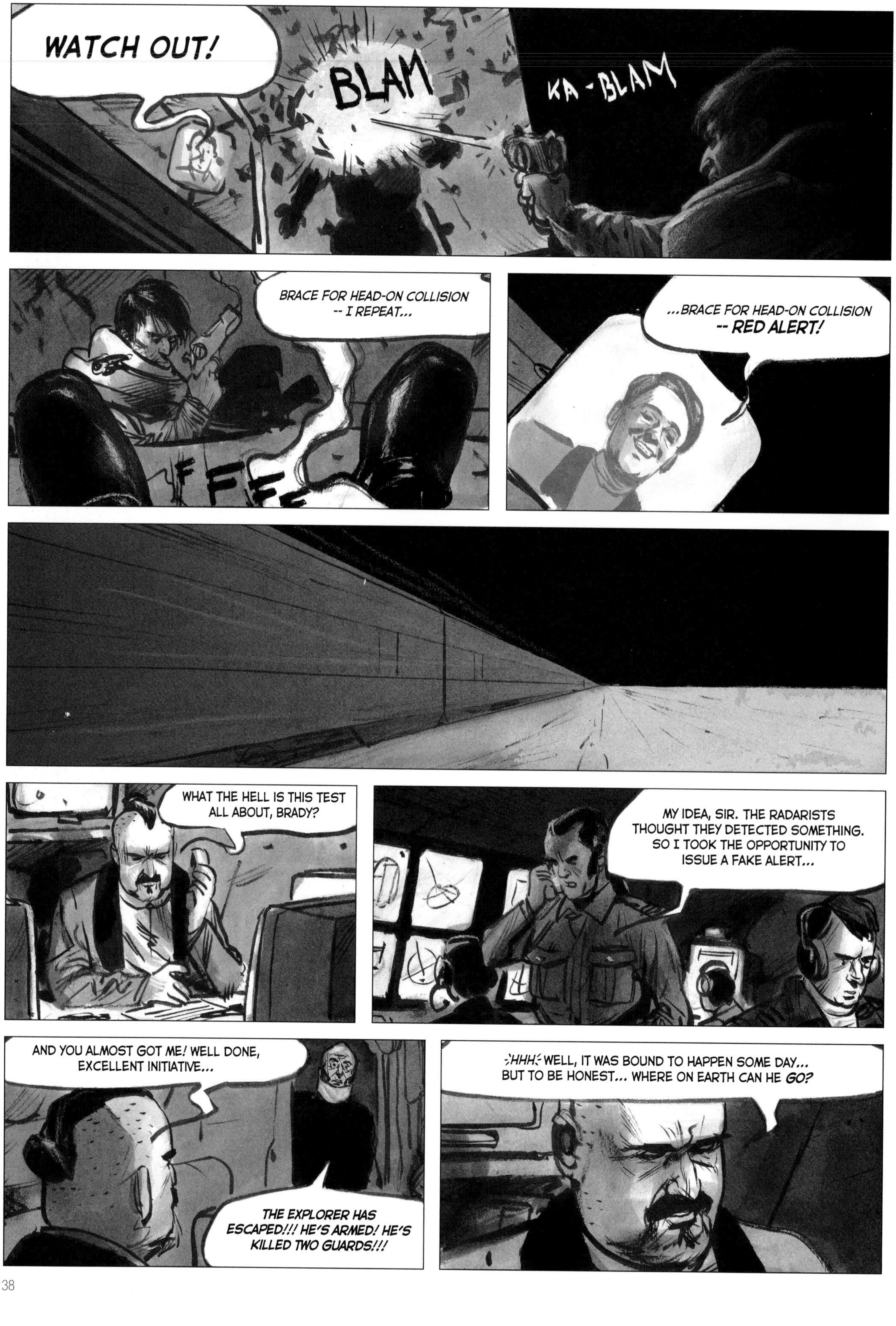
WATCH OUT!
BLAM
KA-BLAM
BRACE FOR HEAD-ON COLLISION -- I REPEAT...
FFF
...BRACE FOR HEAD-ON COLLISION -- RED ALERT!
WHAT THE HELL IS THIS TEST ALL ABOUT, BRADY?
MY IDEA, SIR. THE RADARISTS THOUGHT THEY DETECTED SOMETHING. SO I TOOK THE OPPORTUNITY TO ISSUE A FAKE ALERT...
AND YOU ALMOST GOT ME! WELL DONE, EXCELLENT INITIATIVE...
THE EXPLORER HAS ESCAPED!!! HE'S ARMED! HE'S KILLED TWO GUARDS!!!
HHH WELL, IT WAS BOUND TO HAPPEN SOME DAY... BUT TO BE HONEST... WHERE ON EARTH CAN HE GO?

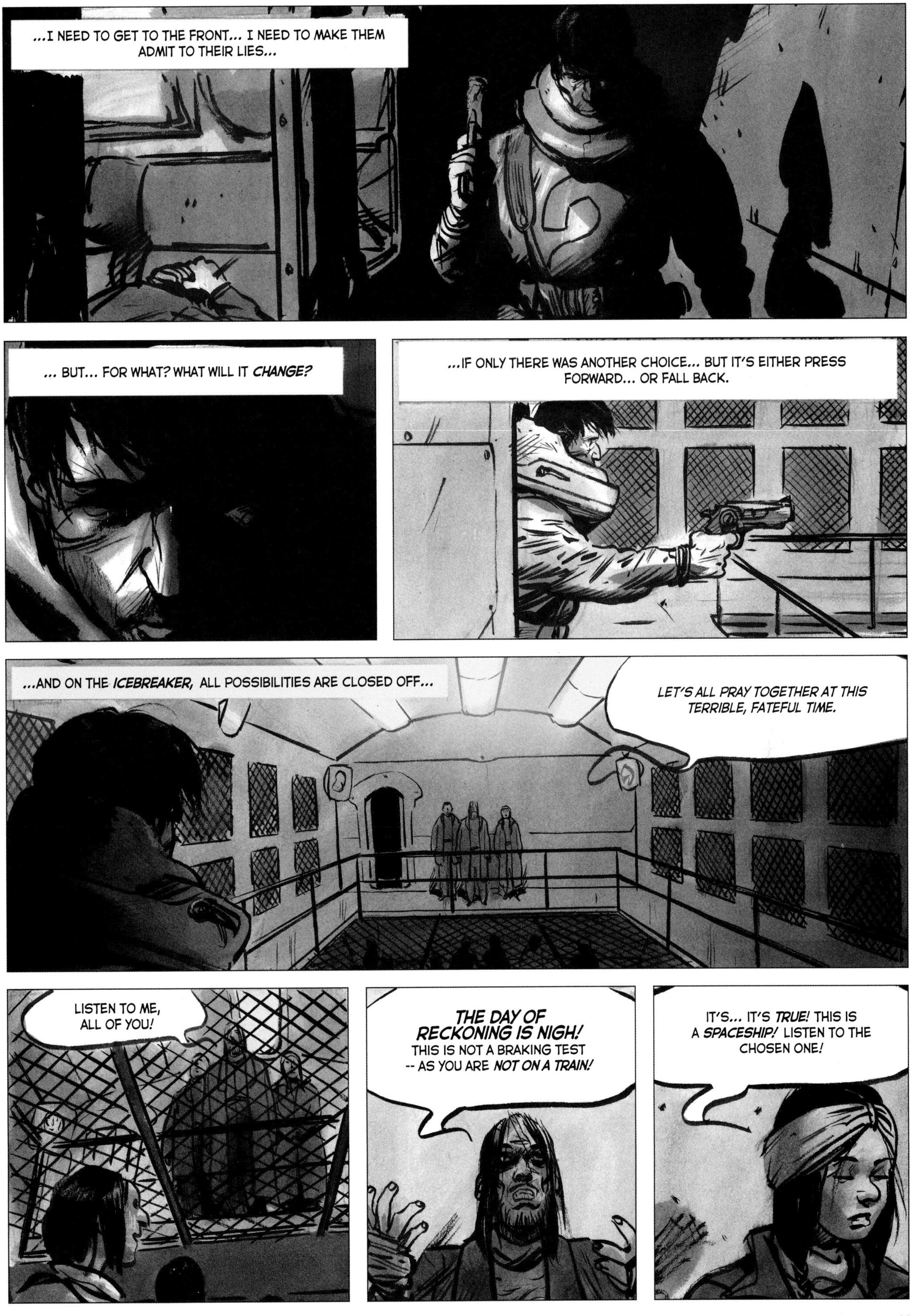
...I NEED TO GET TO THE FRONT... I NEED TO MAKE THEM ADMIT TO THEIR LIES...
... BUT... FOR WHAT? WHAT WILL IT *CHANGE?*
...IF ONLY THERE WAS ANOTHER CHOICE... BUT IT'S EITHER PRESS FORWARD... OR FALL BACK.
...AND ON THE *ICEBREAKER,* ALL POSSIBILITIES ARE CLOSED OFF...
LET'S ALL PRAY TOGETHER AT THIS TERRIBLE, FATEFUL TIME.
LISTEN TO ME, ALL OF YOU!
THE DAY OF RECKONING IS NIGH! THIS IS NOT A BRAKING TEST -- AS YOU ARE ***NOT ON A TRAIN!***
IT'S... IT'S ***TRUE!*** THIS IS A ***SPACESHIP!*** LISTEN TO THE CHOSEN ONE!

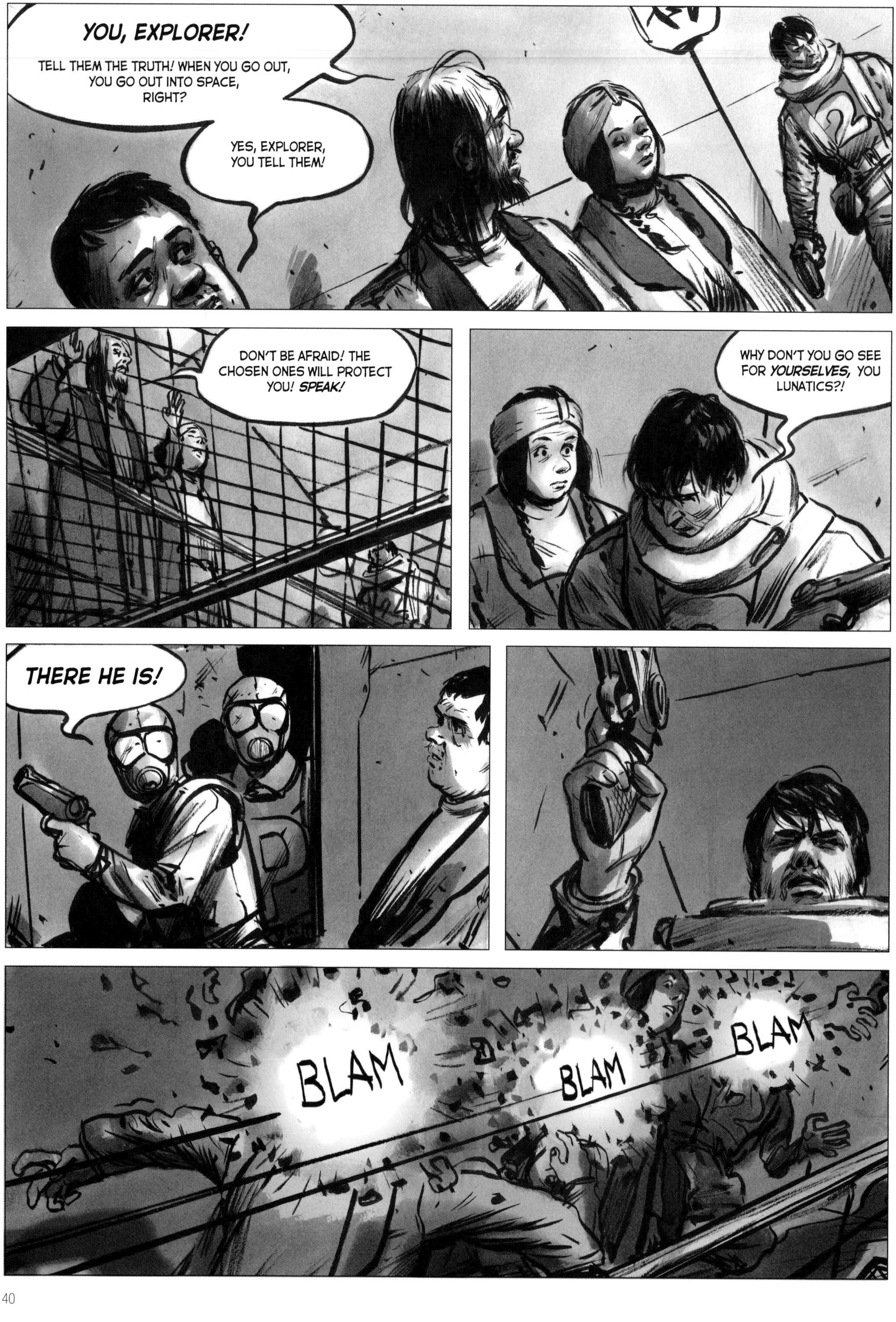
YOU, EXPLORER!
TELL THEM THE TRUTH! WHEN YOU GO OUT, YOU GO OUT INTO SPACE, RIGHT?
YES, EXPLORER, YOU TELL THEM!
DON'T BE AFRAID! THE CHOSEN ONES WILL PROTECT YOU! SPEAK!
WHY DON'T YOU GO SEE FOR YOURSELVES, YOU LUNATICS?!
THERE HE IS!
BLAM
BLAM
BLAM

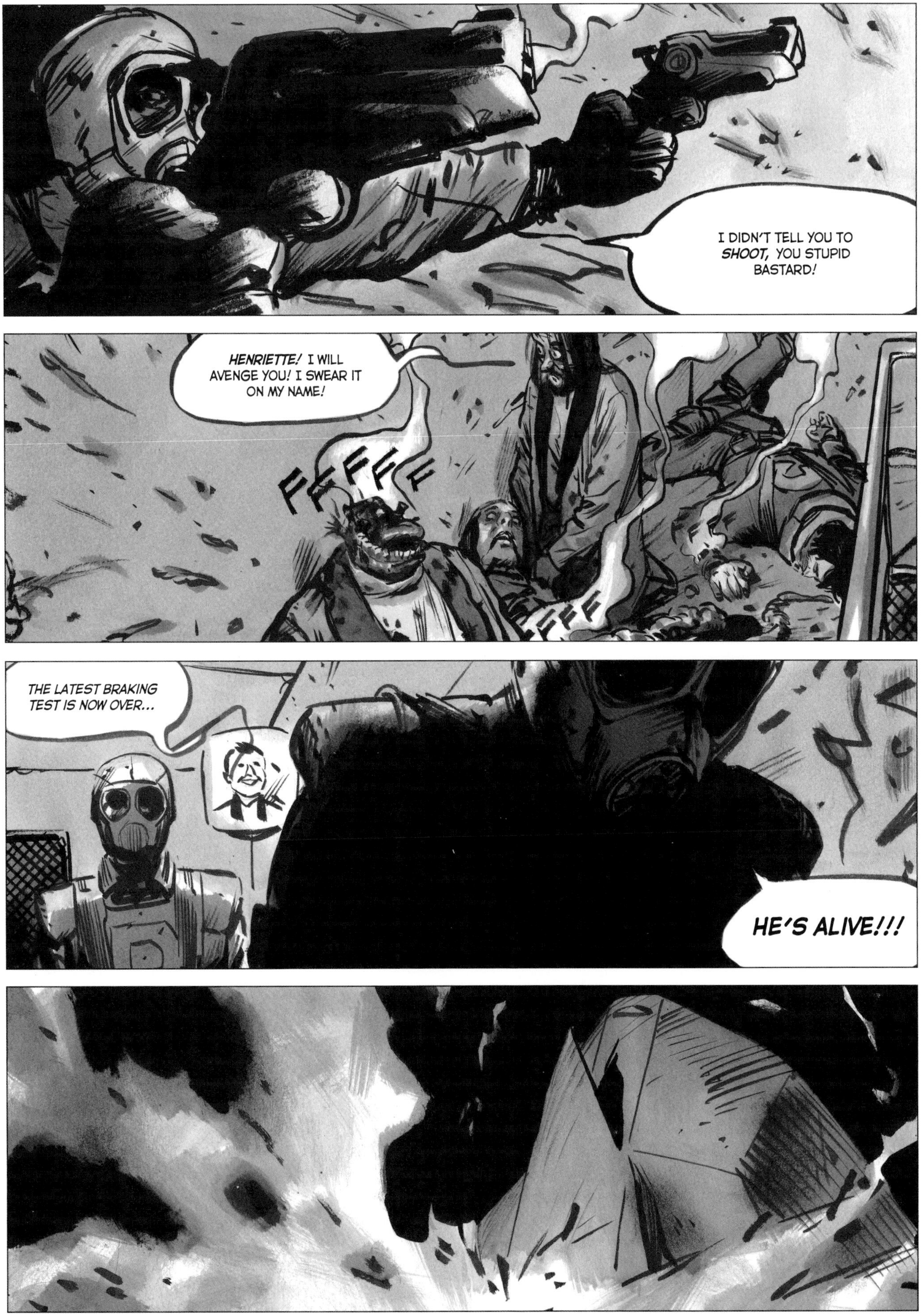
I DIDN'T TELL YOU TO SHOOT, YOU STUPID BASTARD!
HENRIETTE! I WILL AVENGE YOU! I SWEAR IT ON MY NAME!
FFFFF
FFF
THE LATEST BRAKING TEST IS NOW OVER...
HE'S ALIVE!!!

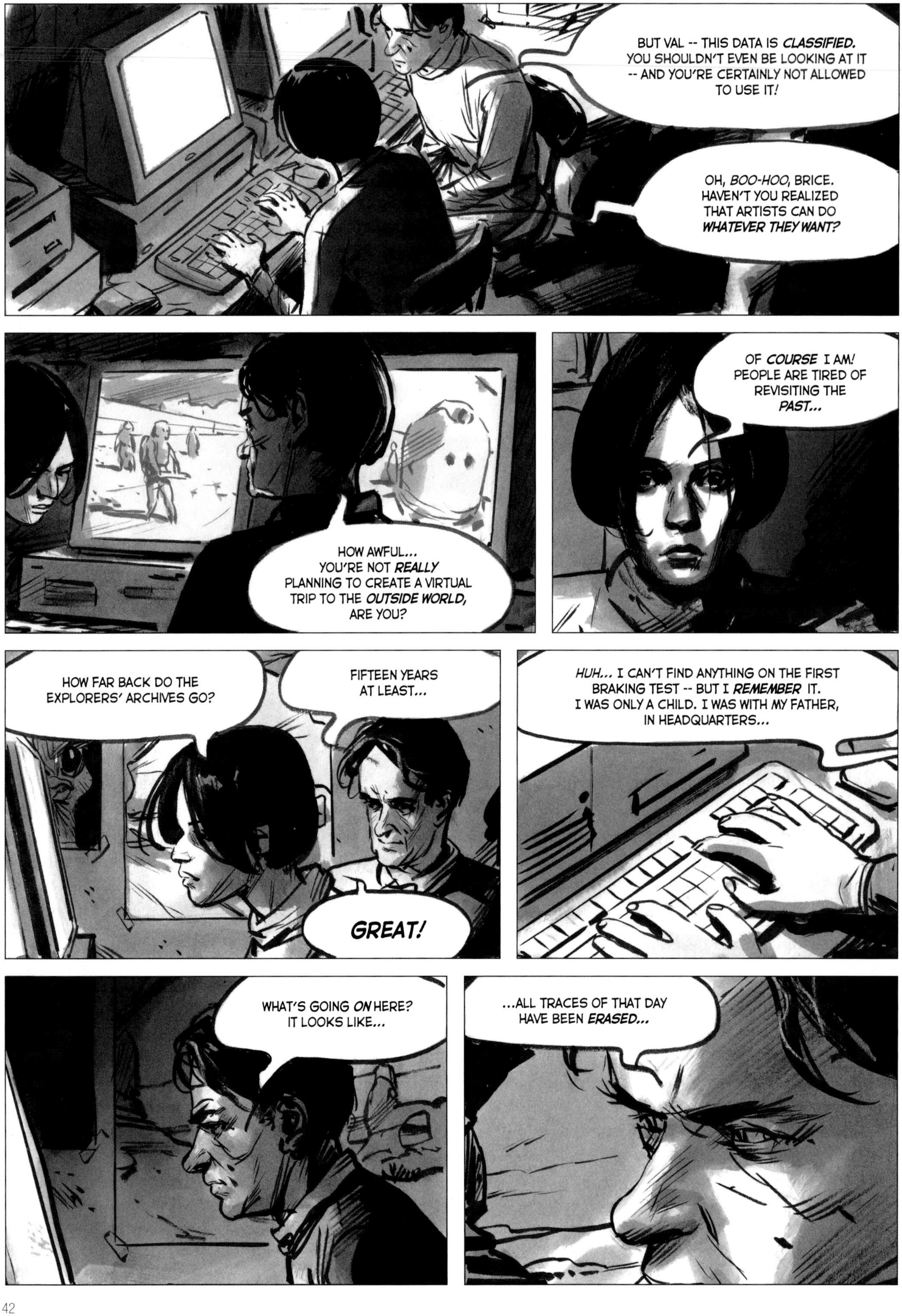

BUT VAL -- THIS DATA IS *CLASSIFIED.* YOU SHOULDN'T EVEN BE LOOKING AT IT -- AND YOU'RE CERTAINLY NOT ALLOWED TO USE IT!
OH, *BOO-HOO*, BRICE. HAVEN'T YOU REALIZED THAT ARTISTS CAN DO *WHATEVER THEY WANT?*
HOW AWFUL... YOU'RE NOT *REALLY* PLANNING TO CREATE A VIRTUAL TRIP TO THE *OUTSIDE WORLD,* ARE YOU?
OF *COURSE* I AM! PEOPLE ARE TIRED OF REVISITING THE *PAST...*
HOW FAR BACK DO THE EXPLORERS' ARCHIVES GO?
FIFTEEN YEARS AT LEAST...
GREAT!
HUH... I CAN'T FIND ANYTHING ON THE FIRST BRAKING TEST -- BUT I *REMEMBER* IT. I WAS ONLY A CHILD. I WAS WITH MY FATHER, IN HEADQUARTERS...
WHAT'S GOING *ON* HERE? IT LOOKS LIKE...
...ALL TRACES OF THAT DAY HAVE BEEN *ERASED...*

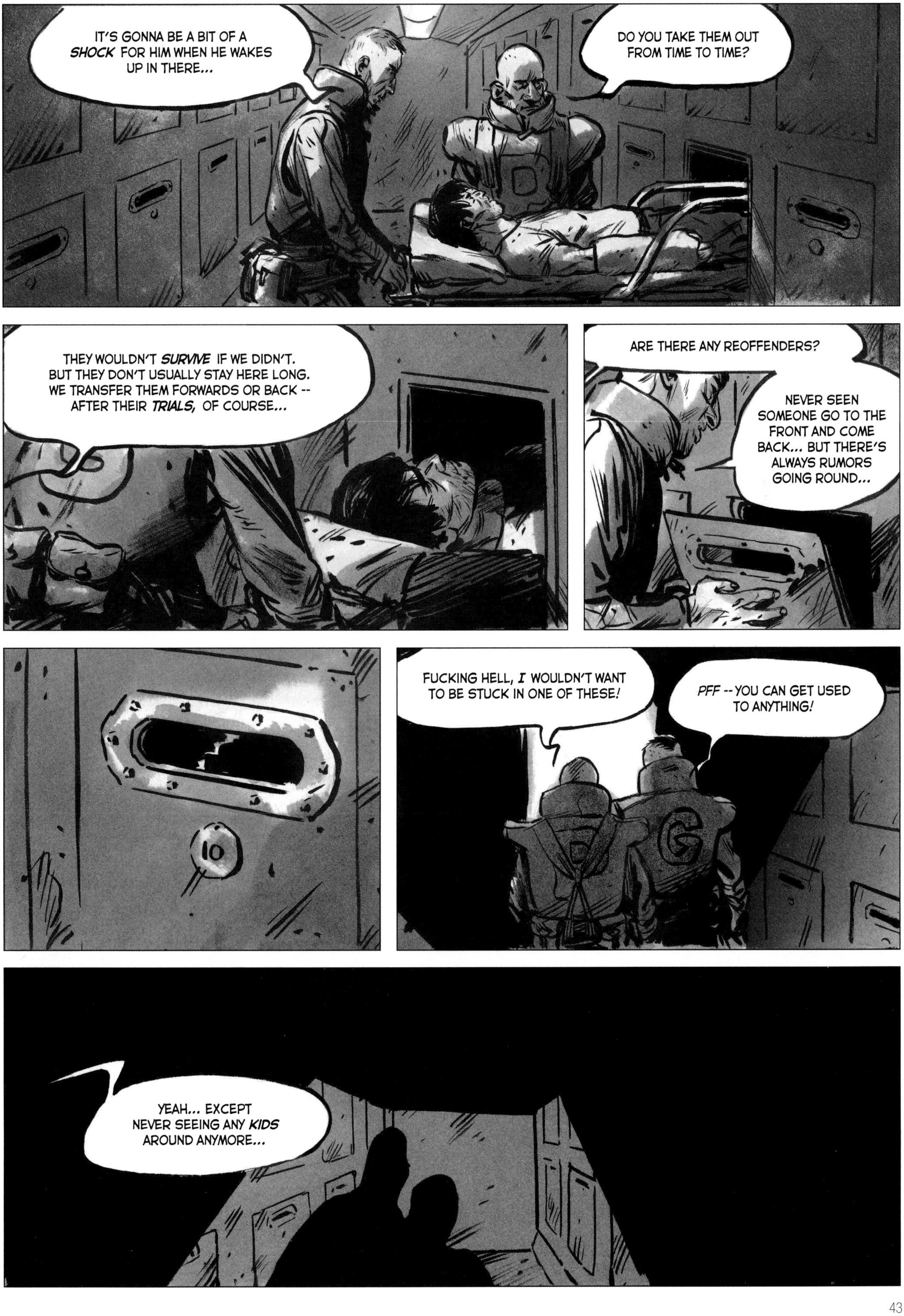
IT'S GONNA BE A BIT OF A SHOCK FOR HIM WHEN HE WAKES UP IN THERE...
DO YOU TAKE THEM OUT FROM TIME TO TIME?
THEY WOULDN'T SURVIVE IF WE DIDN'T. BUT THEY DON'T USUALLY STAY HERE LONG. WE TRANSFER THEM FORWARDS OR BACK -- AFTER THEIR TRIALS, OF COURSE...
ARE THERE ANY REOFFENDERS?
NEVER SEEN SOMEONE GO TO THE FRONT AND COME BACK... BUT THERE'S ALWAYS RUMORS GOING ROUND...
10
FUCKING HELL, I WOULDN'T WANT TO BE STUCK IN ONE OF THESE!
PFF -- YOU CAN GET USED TO ANYTHING!
YEAH... EXCEPT NEVER SEEING ANY KIDS AROUND ANYMORE...

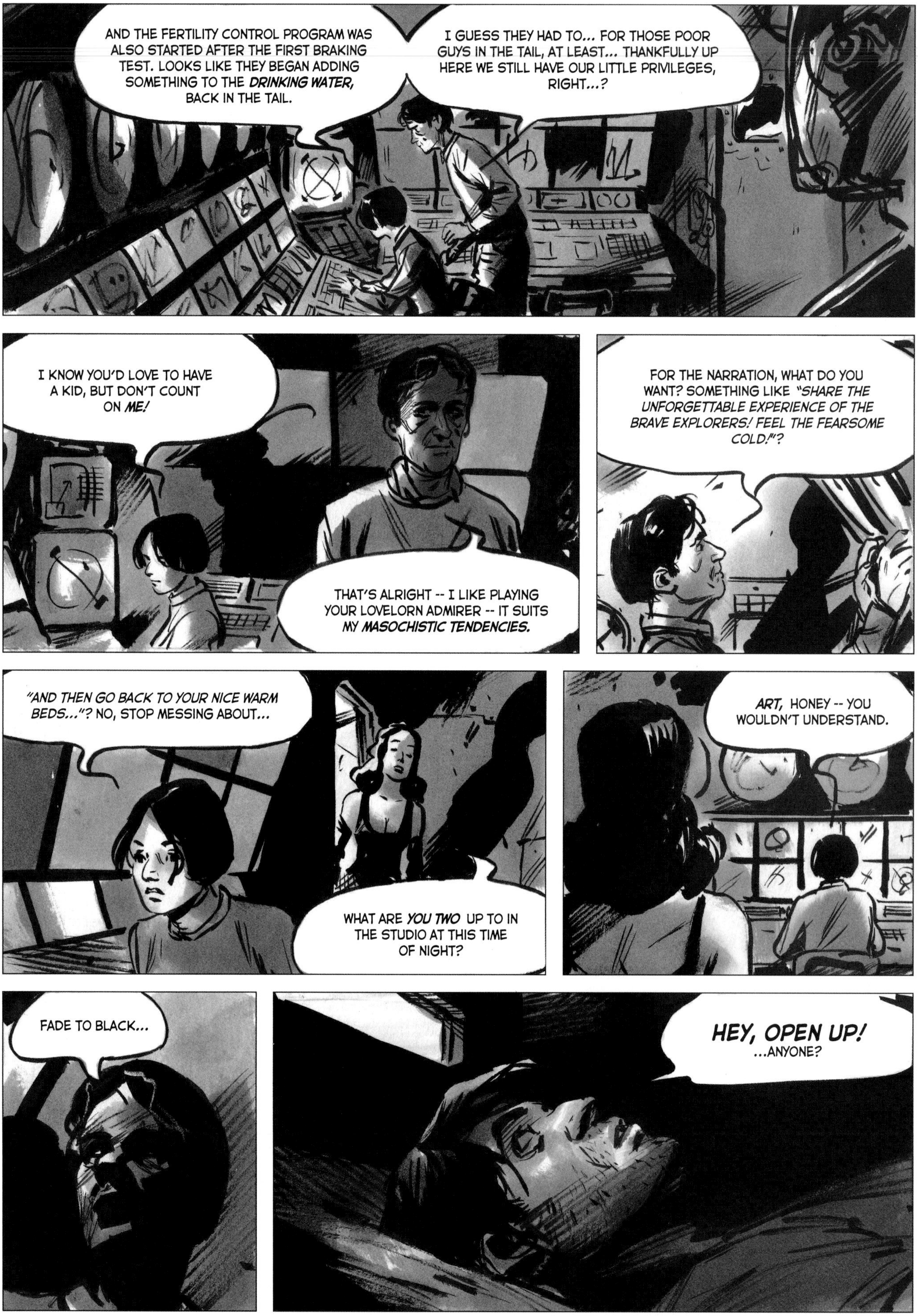
AND THE FERTILITY CONTROL PROGRAM WAS ALSO STARTED AFTER THE FIRST BRAKING TEST. LOOKS LIKE THEY BEGAN ADDING SOMETHING TO THE *DRINKING WATER,* BACK IN THE TAIL.
I GUESS THEY HAD TO... FOR THOSE POOR GUYS IN THE TAIL, AT LEAST... THANKFULLY UP HERE WE STILL HAVE OUR LITTLE PRIVILEGES, RIGHT...?
I KNOW YOU'D LOVE TO HAVE A KID, BUT DON'T COUNT ON *ME!*
THAT'S ALRIGHT -- I LIKE PLAYING YOUR LOVELORN ADMIRER -- IT SUITS MY *MASOCHISTIC TENDENCIES.*
FOR THE NARRATION, WHAT DO YOU WANT? SOMETHING LIKE *"SHARE THE UNFORGETTABLE EXPERIENCE OF THE BRAVE EXPLORERS! FEEL THE FEARSOME COLD!"*?
"AND THEN GO BACK TO YOUR NICE WARM BEDS..."? NO, STOP MESSING ABOUT...
WHAT ARE *YOU TWO* UP TO IN THE STUDIO AT THIS TIME OF NIGHT?
ART, HONEY -- YOU WOULDN'T UNDERSTAND.
FADE TO BLACK...
HEY, OPEN UP!
...ANYONE?

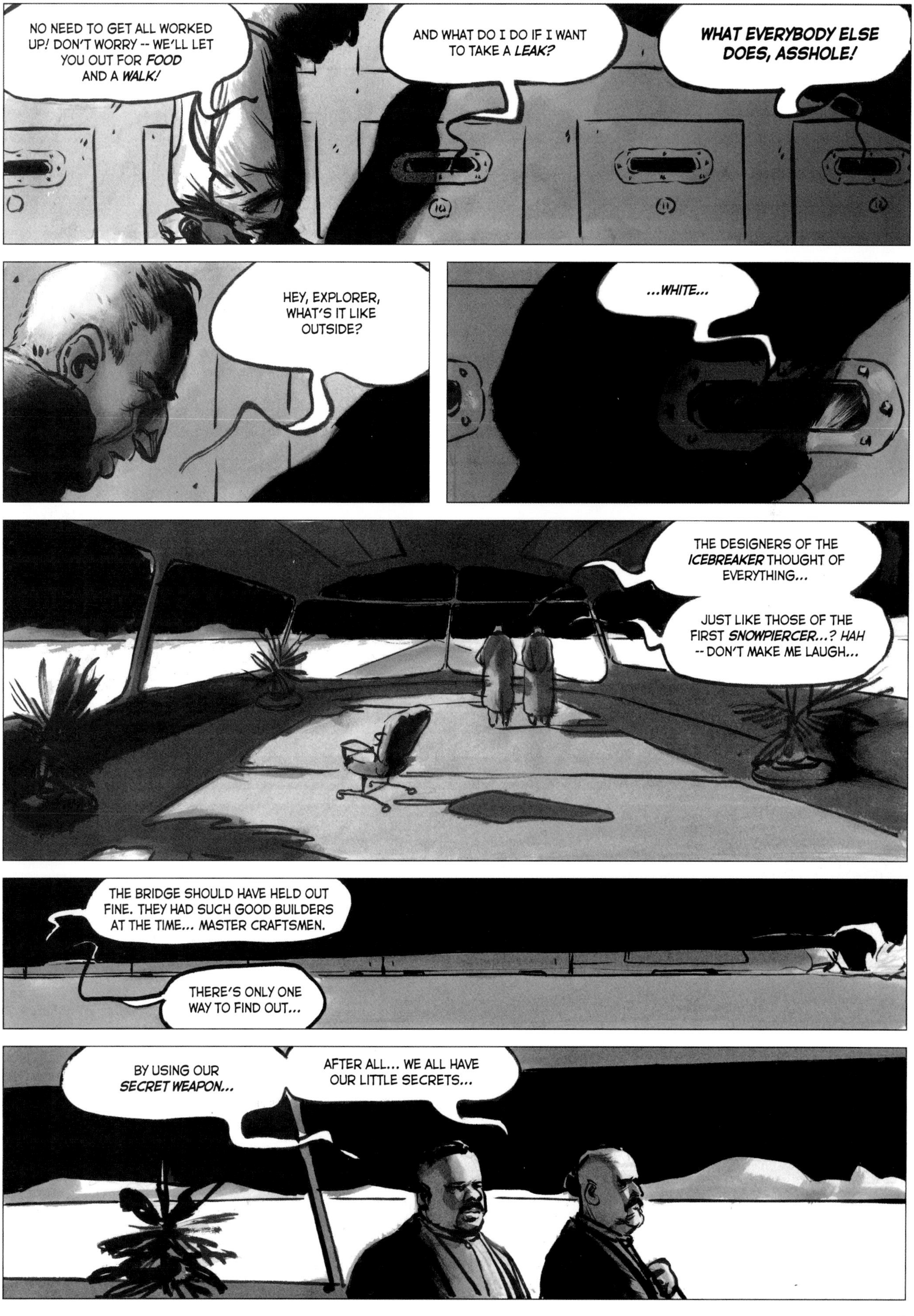
NO NEED TO GET ALL WORKED UP! DON'T WORRY -- WE'LL LET YOU OUT FOR *FOOD* AND A *WALK!*
AND WHAT DO I DO IF I WANT TO TAKE A *LEAK?*
WHAT EVERYBODY ELSE DOES, ASSHOLE!
HEY, EXPLORER, WHAT'S IT LIKE OUTSIDE?
...WHITE...
THE DESIGNERS OF THE *ICEBREAKER* THOUGHT OF EVERYTHING...
JUST LIKE THOSE OF THE FIRST *SNOWPIERCER...? HAH* -- DON'T MAKE ME LAUGH...
THE BRIDGE SHOULD HAVE HELD OUT FINE. THEY HAD SUCH GOOD BUILDERS AT THE TIME... MASTER CRAFTSMEN.
THERE'S ONLY ONE WAY TO FIND OUT...
BY USING OUR *SECRET WEAPON...*
AFTER ALL... WE ALL HAVE OUR LITTLE SECRETS...

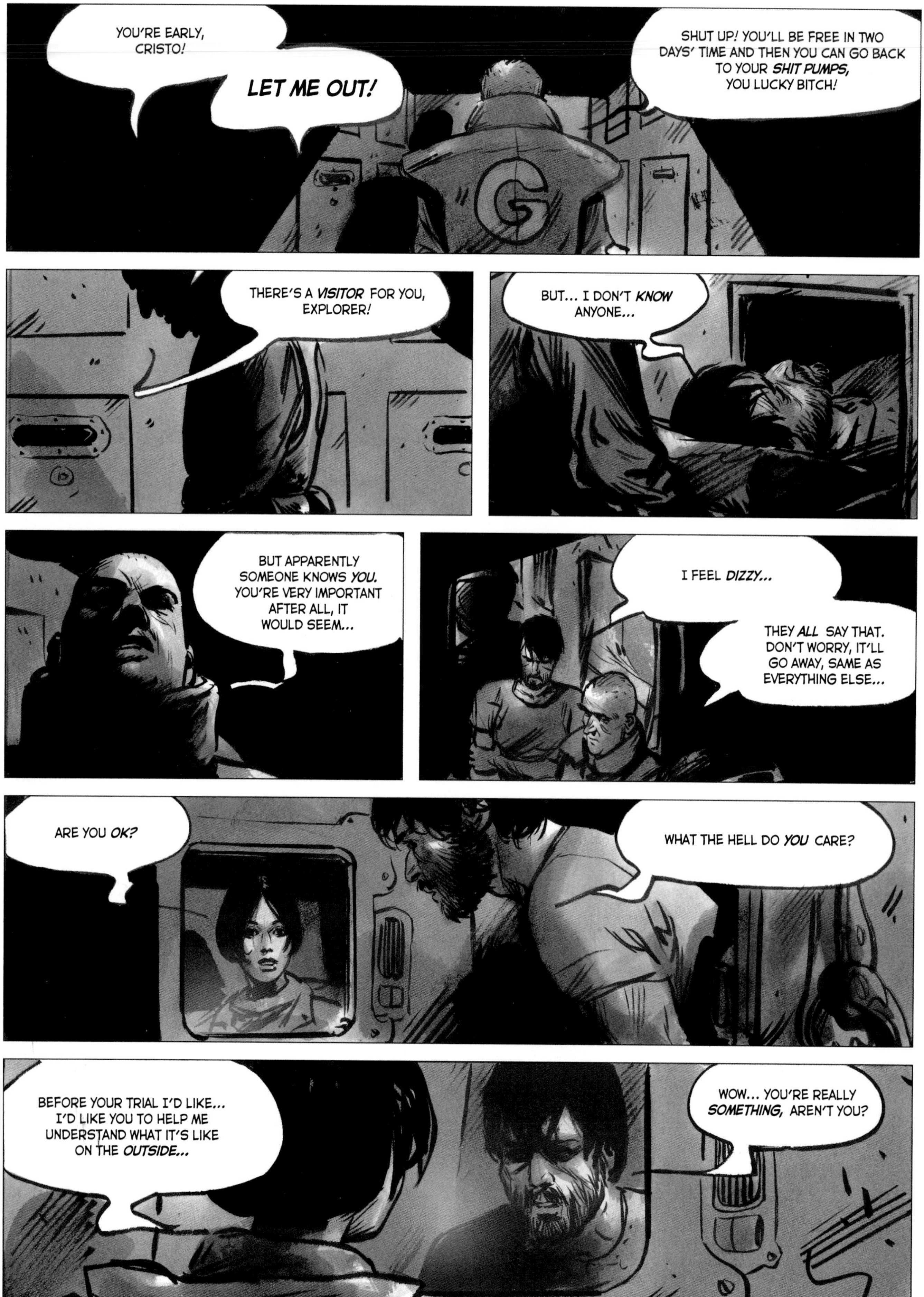
YOU'RE EARLY, CRISTO!
LET ME OUT!
SHUT UP! YOU'LL BE FREE IN TWO DAYS' TIME AND THEN YOU CAN GO BACK TO YOUR SHIT PUMPS, YOU LUCKY BITCH!
THERE'S A VISITOR FOR YOU, EXPLORER!
BUT... I DON'T KNOW ANYONE...
BUT APPARENTLY SOMEONE KNOWS YOU. YOU'RE VERY IMPORTANT AFTER ALL, IT WOULD SEEM...
I FEEL DIZZY...
THEY ALL SAY THAT. DON'T WORRY, IT'LL GO AWAY, SAME AS EVERYTHING ELSE...
ARE YOU OK?
WHAT THE HELL DO YOU CARE?
BEFORE YOUR TRIAL I'D LIKE... I'D LIKE YOU TO HELP ME UNDERSTAND WHAT IT'S LIKE ON THE OUTSIDE...
WOW... YOU'RE REALLY SOMETHING, AREN'T YOU?

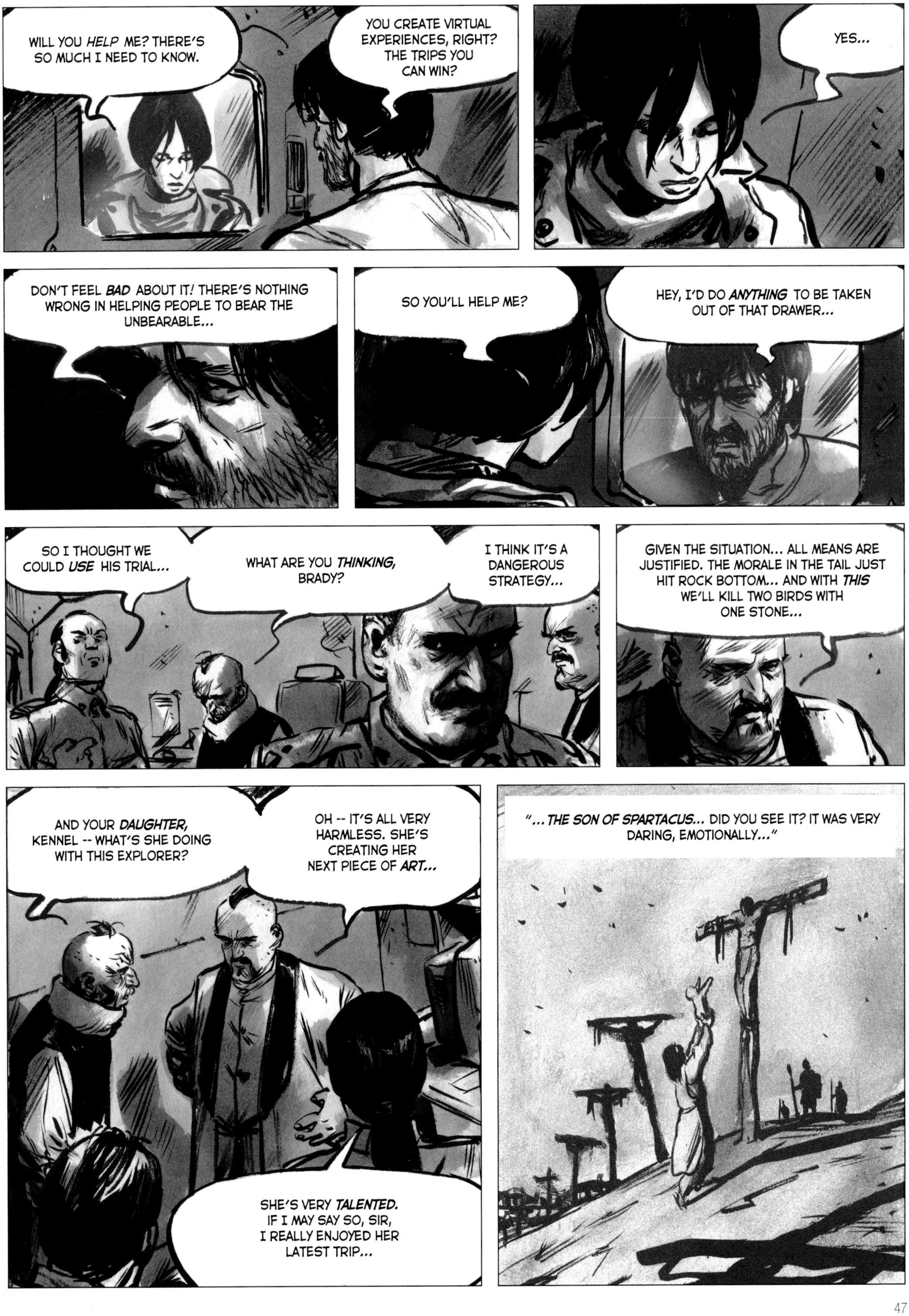
WILL YOU HELP ME? THERE'S SO MUCH I NEED TO KNOW.
YOU CREATE VIRTUAL EXPERIENCES, RIGHT? THE TRIPS YOU CAN WIN?
YES...
DON'T FEEL BAD ABOUT IT! THERE'S NOTHING WRONG IN HELPING PEOPLE TO BEAR THE UNBEARABLE...
SO YOU'LL HELP ME?
HEY, I'D DO ANYTHING TO BE TAKEN OUT OF THAT DRAWER...
SO I THOUGHT WE COULD USE HIS TRIAL...
WHAT ARE YOU THINKING, BRADY?
I THINK IT'S A DANGEROUS STRATEGY...
GIVEN THE SITUATION... ALL MEANS ARE JUSTIFIED. THE MORALE IN THE TAIL JUST HIT ROCK BOTTOM... AND WITH THIS WE'LL KILL TWO BIRDS WITH ONE STONE...
AND YOUR DAUGHTER, KENNEL -- WHAT'S SHE DOING WITH THIS EXPLORER?
OH -- IT'S ALL VERY HARMLESS. SHE'S CREATING HER NEXT PIECE OF ART...
SHE'S VERY TALENTED. IF I MAY SAY SO, SIR, I REALLY ENJOYED HER LATEST TRIP...
"...THE SON OF SPARTACUS... DID YOU SEE IT? IT WAS VERY DARING, EMOTIONALLY..."

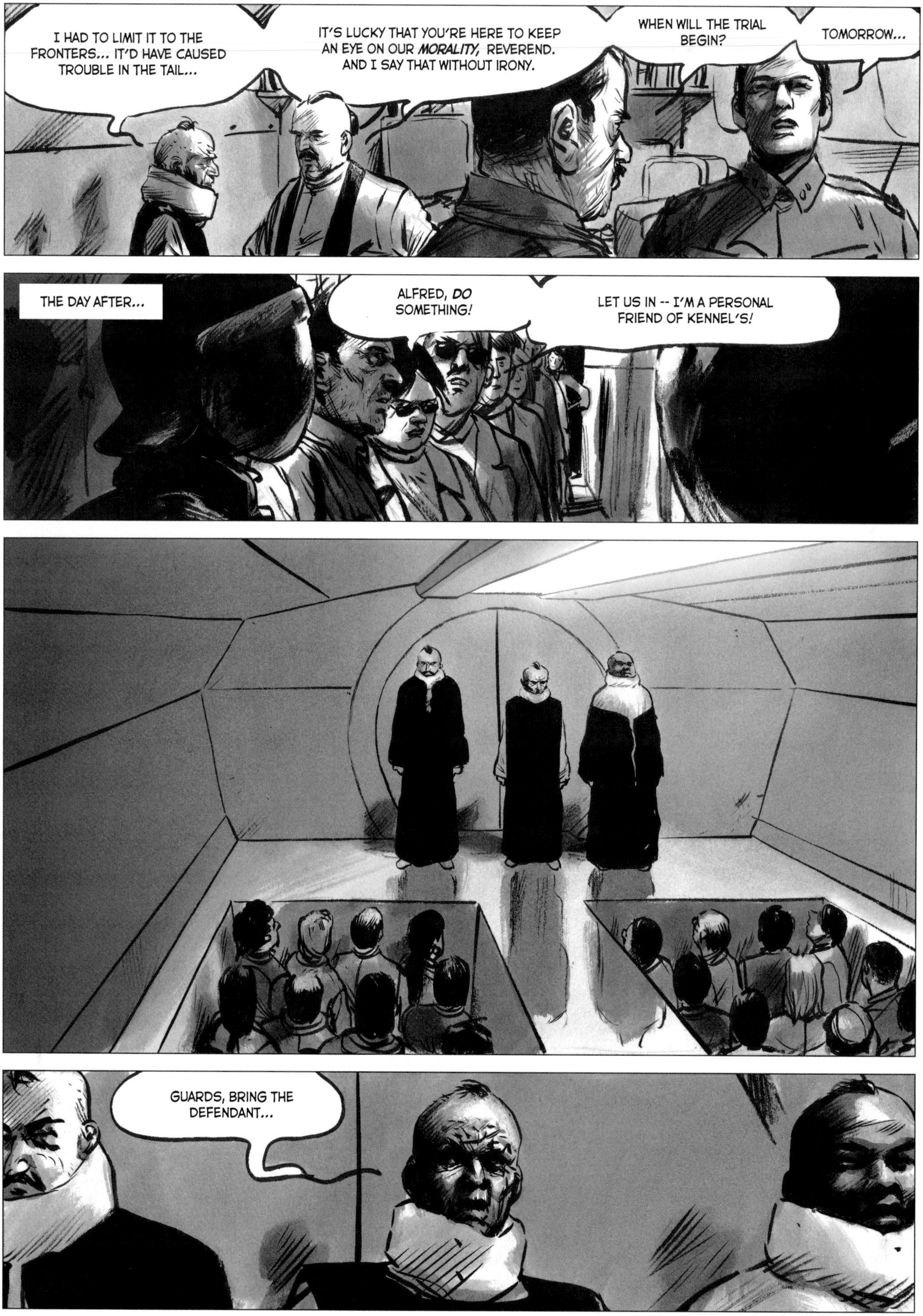
I HAD TO LIMIT IT TO THE FRONTERS... IT'D HAVE CAUSED TROUBLE IN THE TAIL...
IT'S LUCKY THAT YOU'RE HERE TO KEEP AN EYE ON OUR *MORALITY,* REVEREND. AND I SAY THAT WITHOUT IRONY.
WHEN WILL THE TRIAL BEGIN?
TOMORROW...
THE DAY AFTER...
ALFRED, **DO** SOMETHING!
LET US IN -- I'M A PERSONAL FRIEND OF KENNEL'S!
GUARDS, BRING THE DEFENDANT...

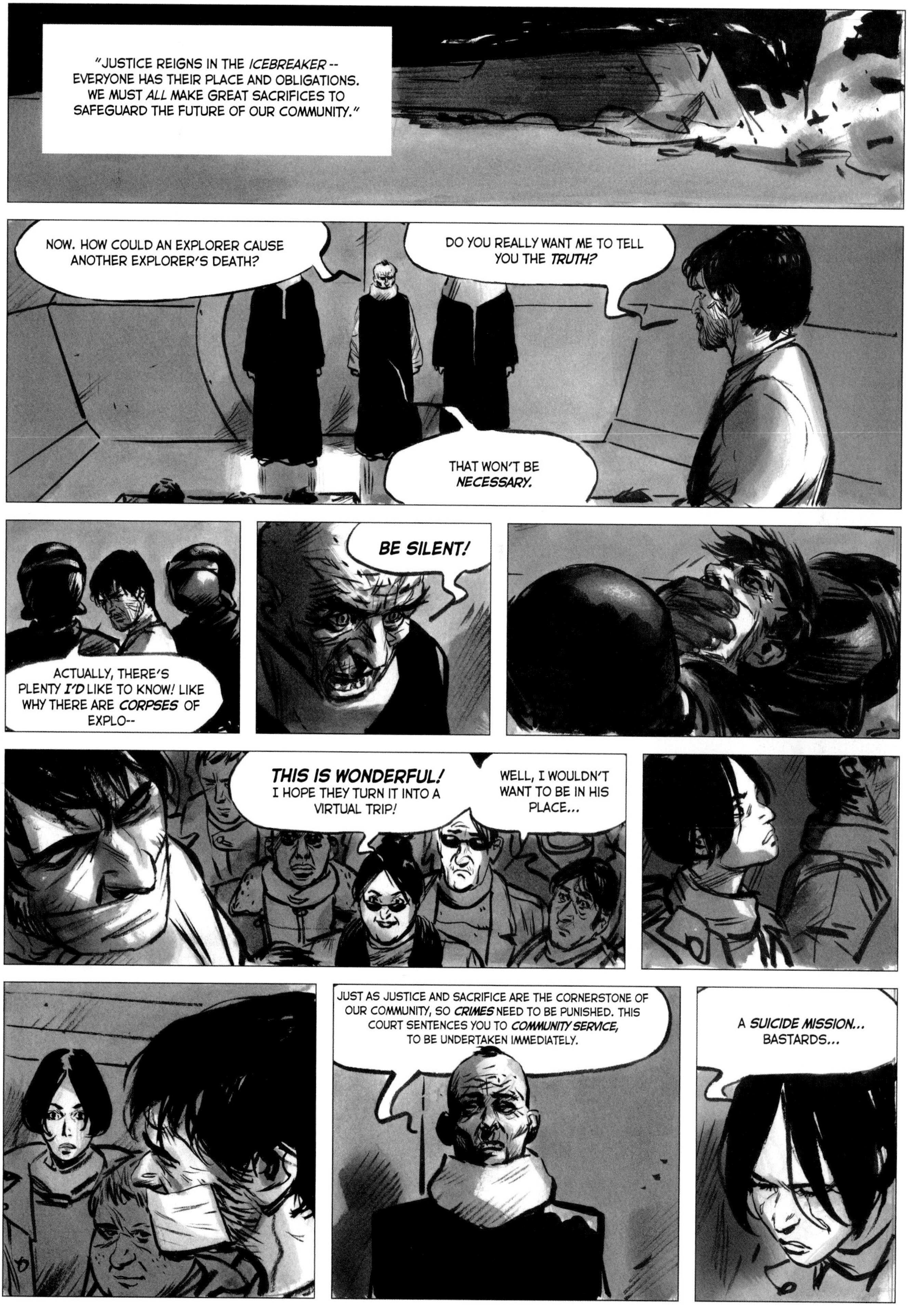
"JUSTICE REIGNS IN THE *ICEBREAKER* -- EVERYONE HAS THEIR PLACE AND OBLIGATIONS. WE MUST *ALL* MAKE GREAT SACRIFICES TO SAFEGUARD THE FUTURE OF OUR COMMUNITY."
NOW. HOW COULD AN EXPLORER CAUSE ANOTHER EXPLORER'S DEATH?
DO YOU REALLY WANT ME TO TELL YOU THE *TRUTH?*
THAT WON'T BE *NECESSARY.*
ACTUALLY, THERE'S PLENTY *I'D* LIKE TO KNOW! LIKE WHY THERE ARE *CORPSES* OF EXPLO--
BE SILENT!
THIS IS WONDERFUL! I HOPE THEY TURN IT INTO A VIRTUAL TRIP!
WELL, I WOULDN'T WANT TO BE IN HIS PLACE...
JUST AS JUSTICE AND SACRIFICE ARE THE CORNERSTONE OF OUR COMMUNITY, SO *CRIMES* NEED TO BE PUNISHED. THIS COURT SENTENCES YOU TO *COMMUNITY SERVICE,* TO BE UNDERTAKEN IMMEDIATELY.
A *SUICIDE MISSION...* BASTARDS...

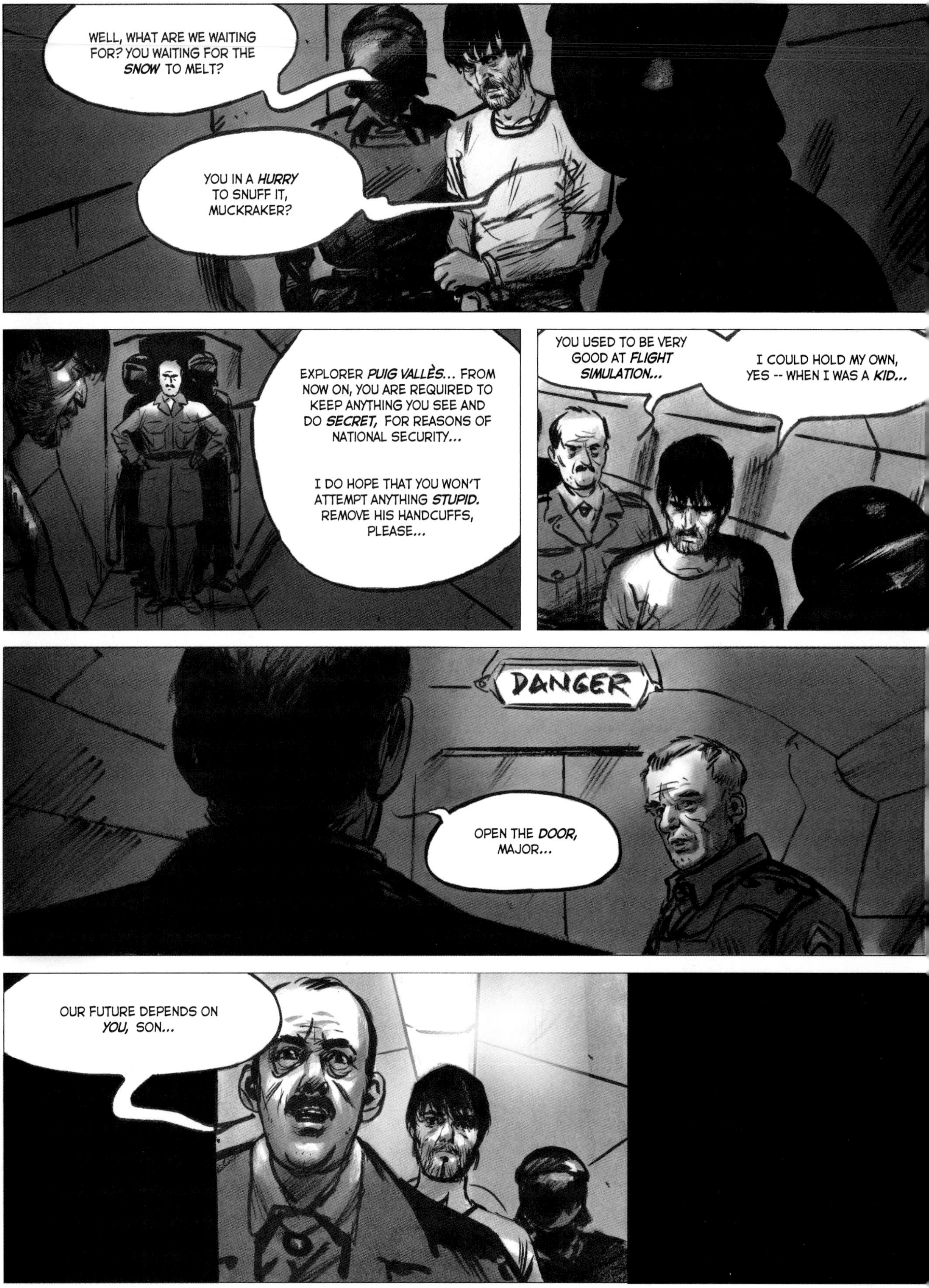

WELL, WHAT ARE WE WAITING FOR? YOU WAITING FOR THE SNOW TO MELT?
YOU IN A HURRY TO SNUFF IT, MUCKRAKER?
EXPLORER PUIG VALLÈS... FROM NOW ON, YOU ARE REQUIRED TO KEEP ANYTHING YOU SEE AND DO SECRET, FOR REASONS OF NATIONAL SECURITY...
I DO HOPE THAT YOU WON'T ATTEMPT ANYTHING STUPID. REMOVE HIS HANDCUFFS, PLEASE...
YOU USED TO BE VERY GOOD AT FLIGHT SIMULATION...
I COULD HOLD MY OWN, YES -- WHEN I WAS A KID...
DANGER
OPEN THE DOOR, MAJOR...
OUR FUTURE DEPENDS ON YOU, SON...

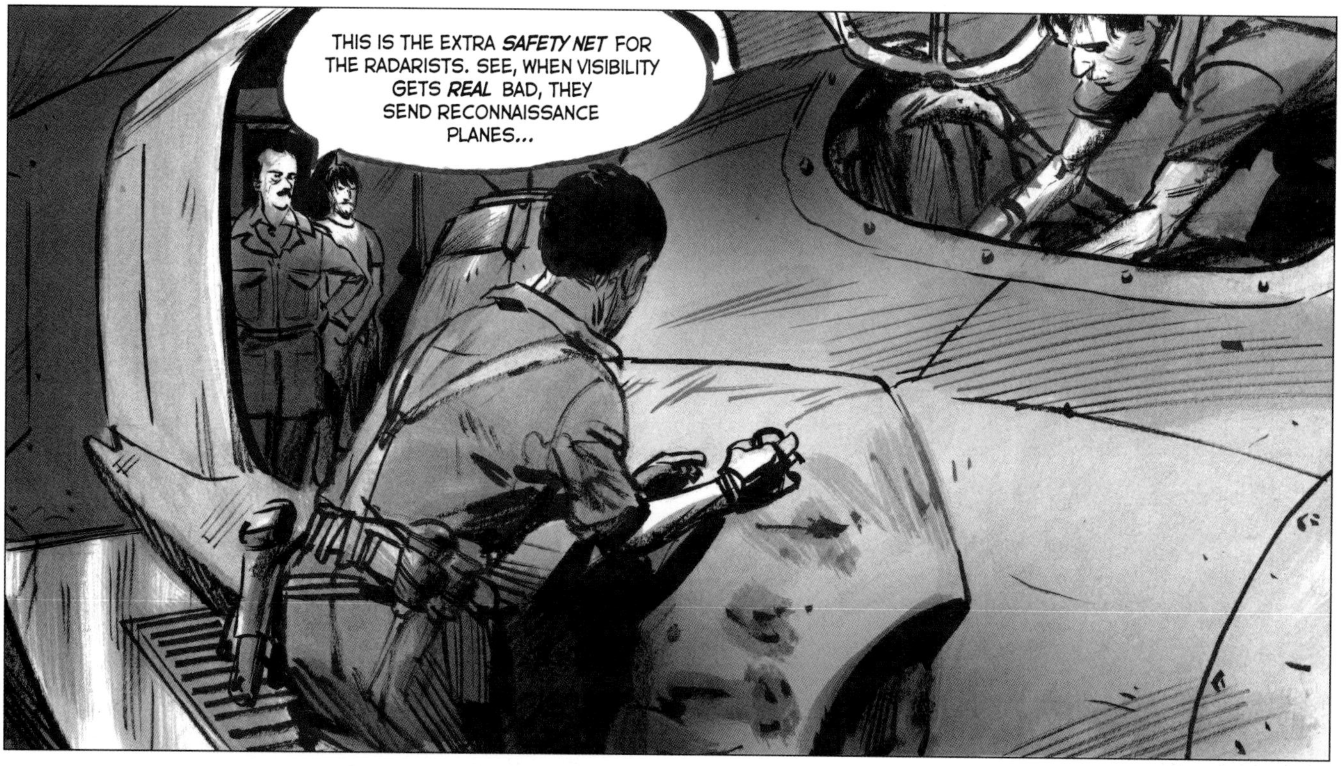
THIS IS THE EXTRA SAFETY NET FOR THE RADARISTS. SEE, WHEN VISIBILITY GETS REAL BAD, THEY SEND RECONNAISSANCE PLANES...

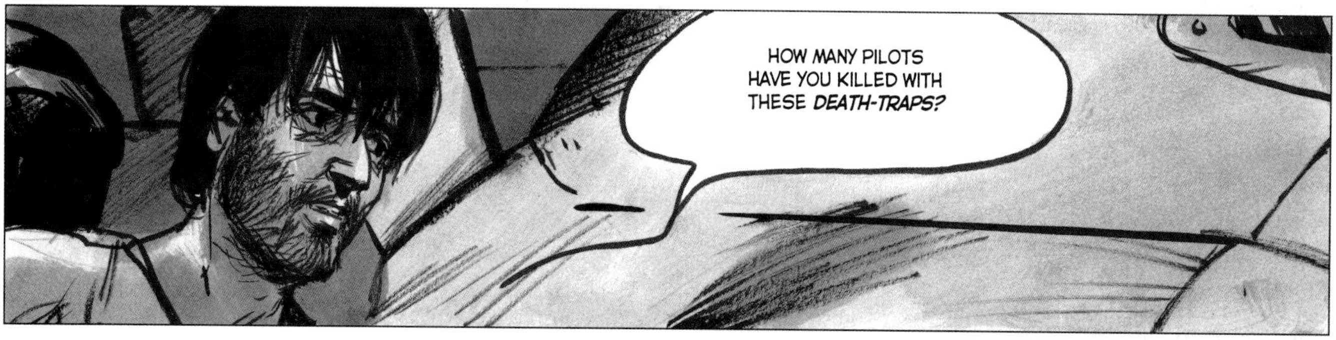
HOW MANY PILOTS HAVE YOU KILLED WITH THESE DEATH-TRAPS?

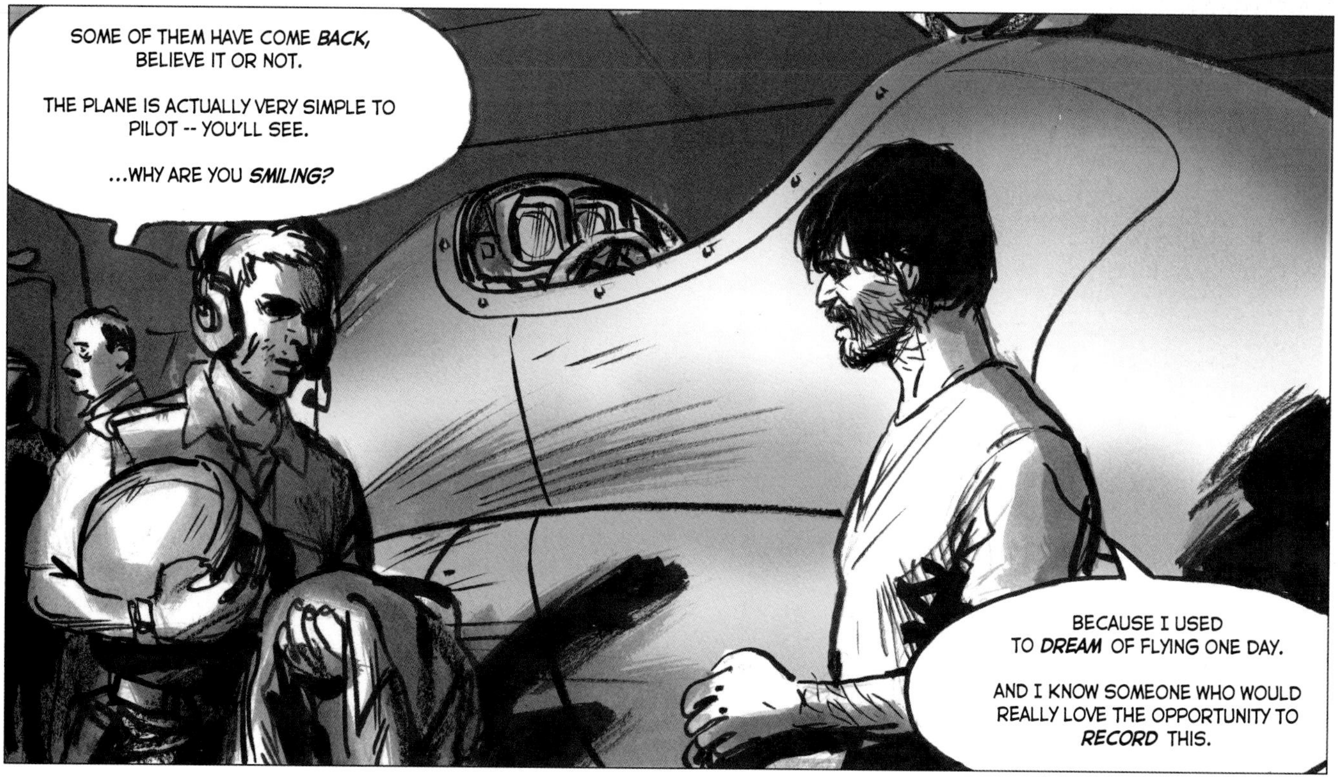
SOME OF THEM HAVE COME BACK, BELIEVE IT OR NOT.
THE PLANE IS ACTUALLY VERY SIMPLE TO PILOT -- YOU'LL SEE.
...WHY ARE YOU SMILING?
BECAUSE I USED TO DREAM OF FLYING ONE DAY.
AND I KNOW SOMEONE WHO WOULD REALLY LOVE THE OPPORTUNITY TO RECORD THIS.

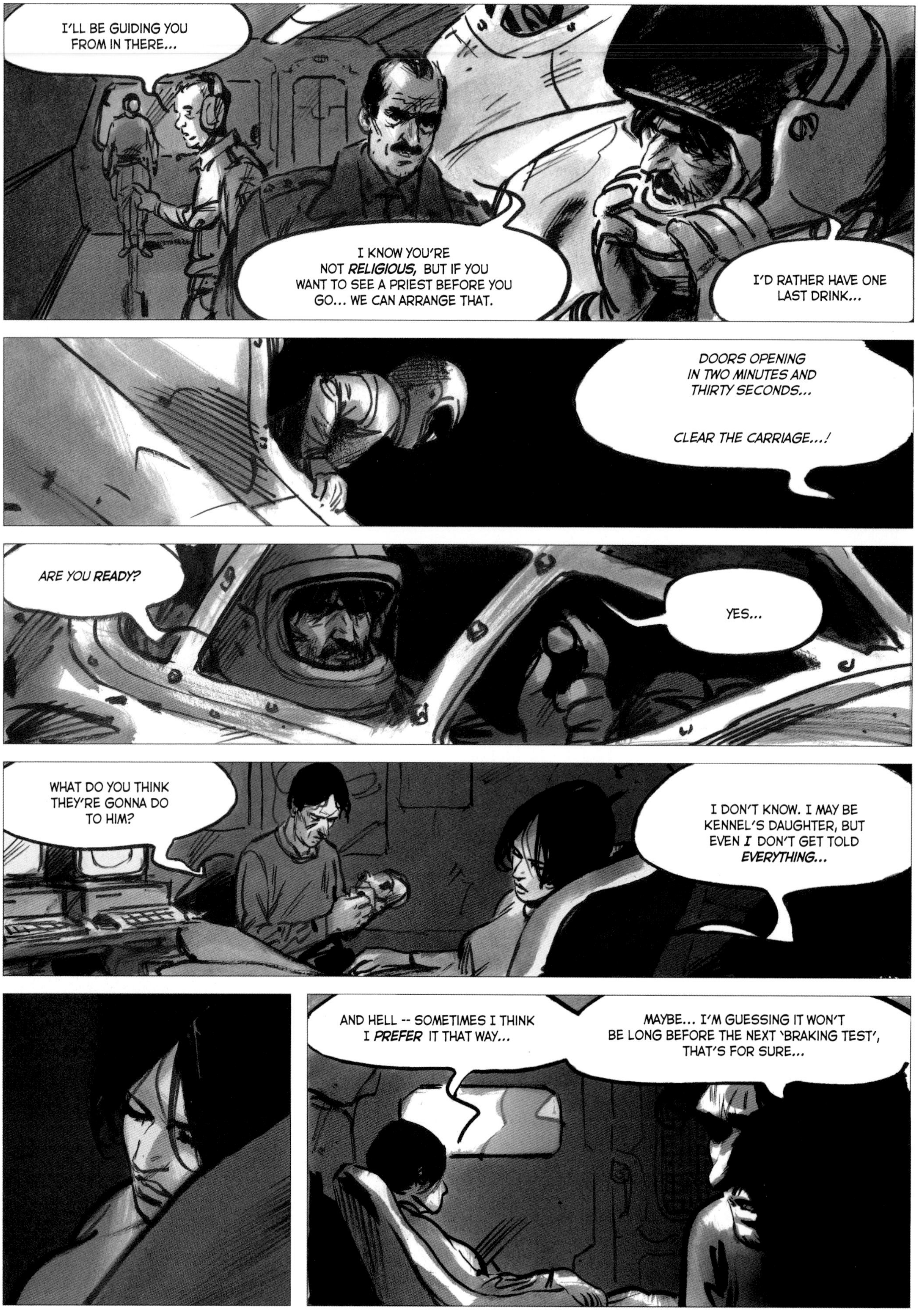
I'LL BE GUIDING YOU FROM IN THERE...
I KNOW YOU'RE NOT RELIGIOUS, BUT IF YOU WANT TO SEE A PRIEST BEFORE YOU GO... WE CAN ARRANGE THAT.
I'D RATHER HAVE ONE LAST DRINK...
DOORS OPENING IN TWO MINUTES AND THIRTY SECONDS...
CLEAR THE CARRIAGE...!
ARE YOU READY?
YES...
WHAT DO YOU THINK THEY'RE GONNA DO TO HIM?
I DON'T KNOW. I MAY BE KENNEL'S DAUGHTER, BUT EVEN I DON'T GET TOLD EVERYTHING...
AND HELL -- SOMETIMES I THINK I PREFER IT THAT WAY...
MAYBE... I'M GUESSING IT WON'T BE LONG BEFORE THE NEXT 'BRAKING TEST', THAT'S FOR SURE...

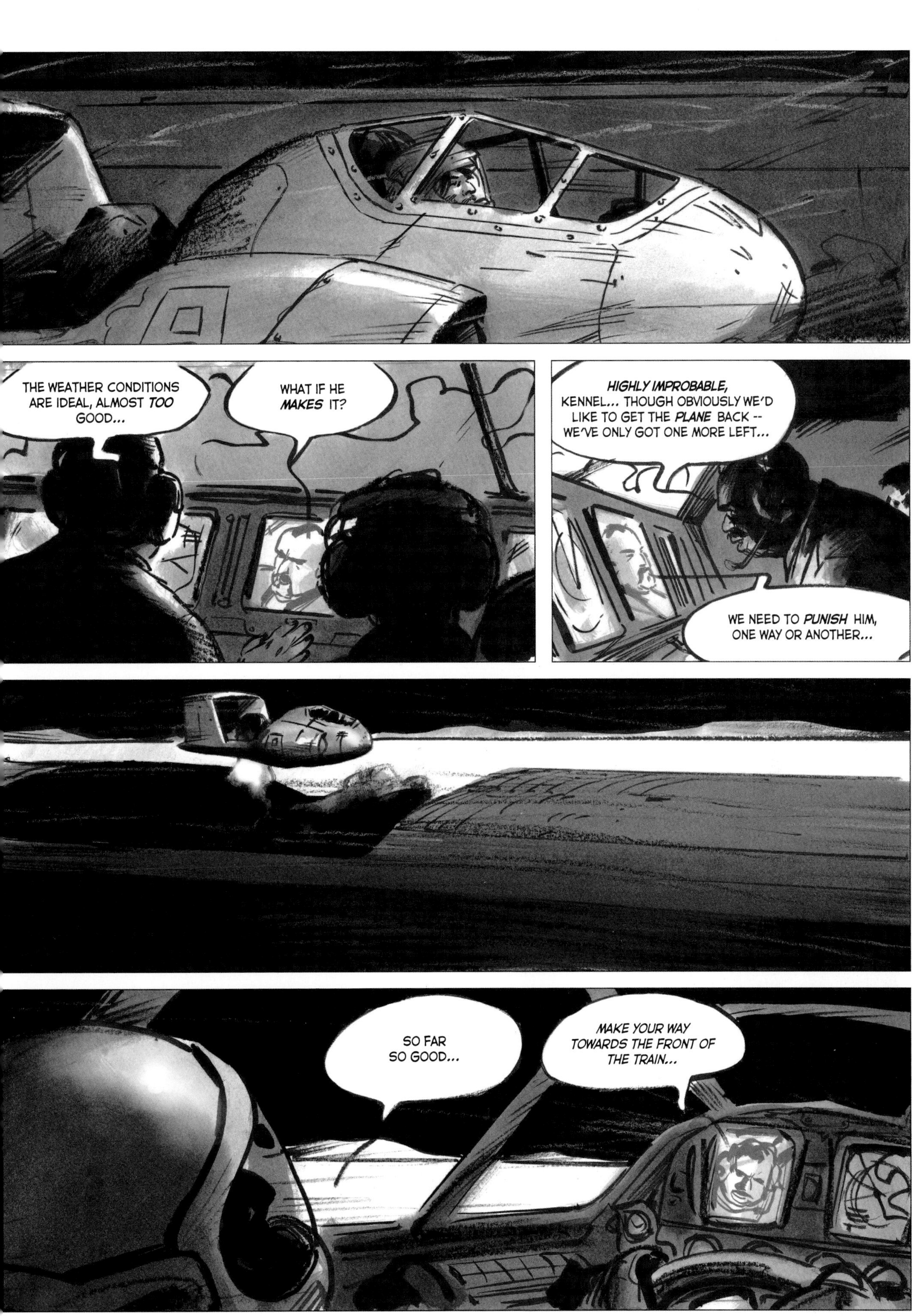
THE WEATHER CONDITIONS ARE IDEAL, ALMOST *TOO* GOOD...
WHAT IF HE *MAKES* IT?
HIGHLY IMPROBABLE, KENNEL... THOUGH OBVIOUSLY WE'D LIKE TO GET THE ***PLANE*** BACK -- WE'VE ONLY GOT ONE MORE LEFT...
WE NEED TO ***PUNISH*** HIM, ONE WAY OR ANOTHER...
SO FAR SO GOOD...
MAKE YOUR WAY TOWARDS THE FRONT OF THE TRAIN...

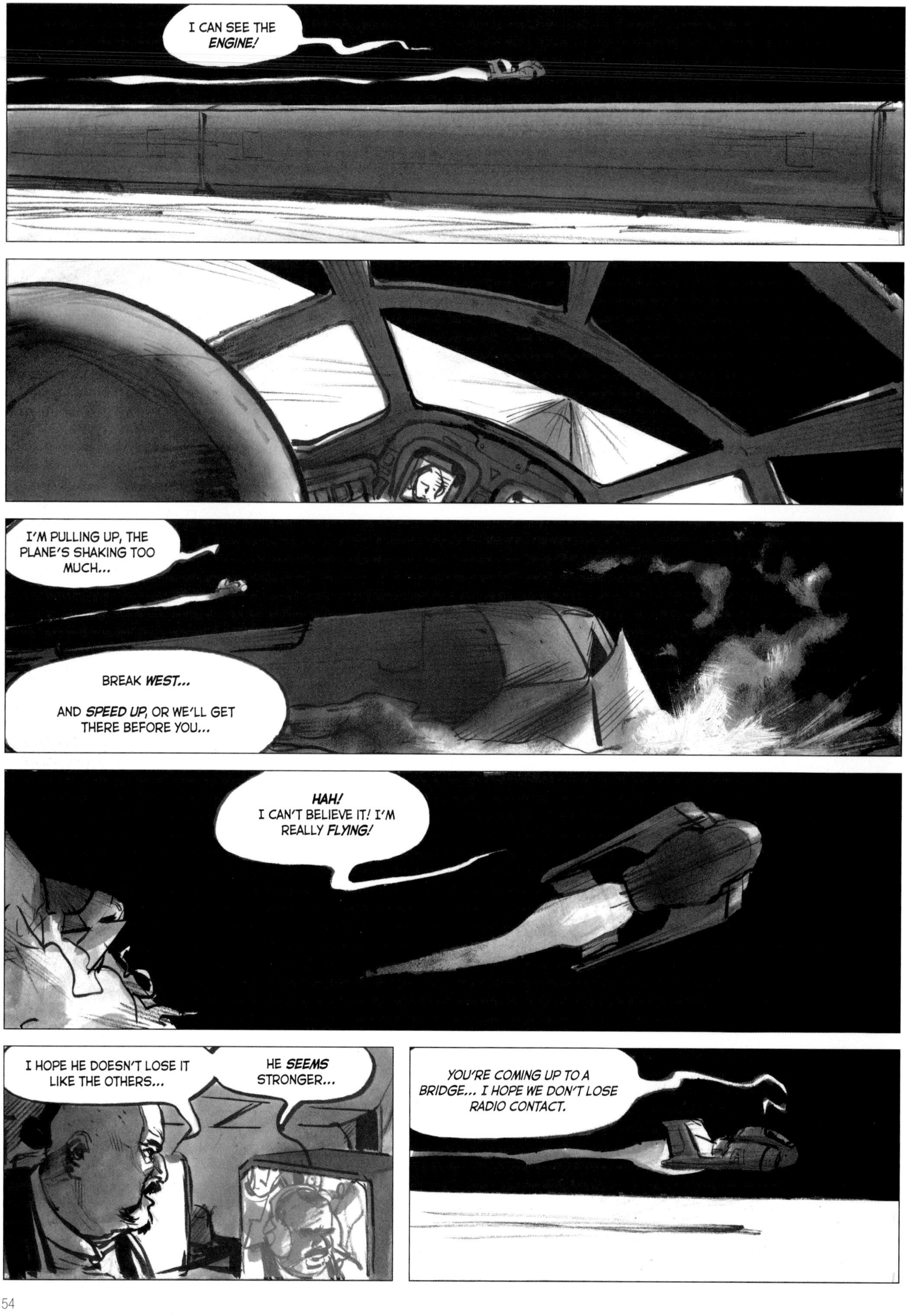
I CAN SEE THE ENGINE!
I'M PULLING UP, THE PLANE'S SHAKING TOO MUCH...
BREAK WEST...
AND SPEED UP, OR WE'LL GET THERE BEFORE YOU...
HAH! I CAN'T BELIEVE IT! I'M REALLY FLYING!
I HOPE HE DOESN'T LOSE IT LIKE THE OTHERS...
HE SEEMS STRONGER...
YOU'RE COMING UP TO A BRIDGE... I HOPE WE DON'T LOSE RADIO CONTACT.

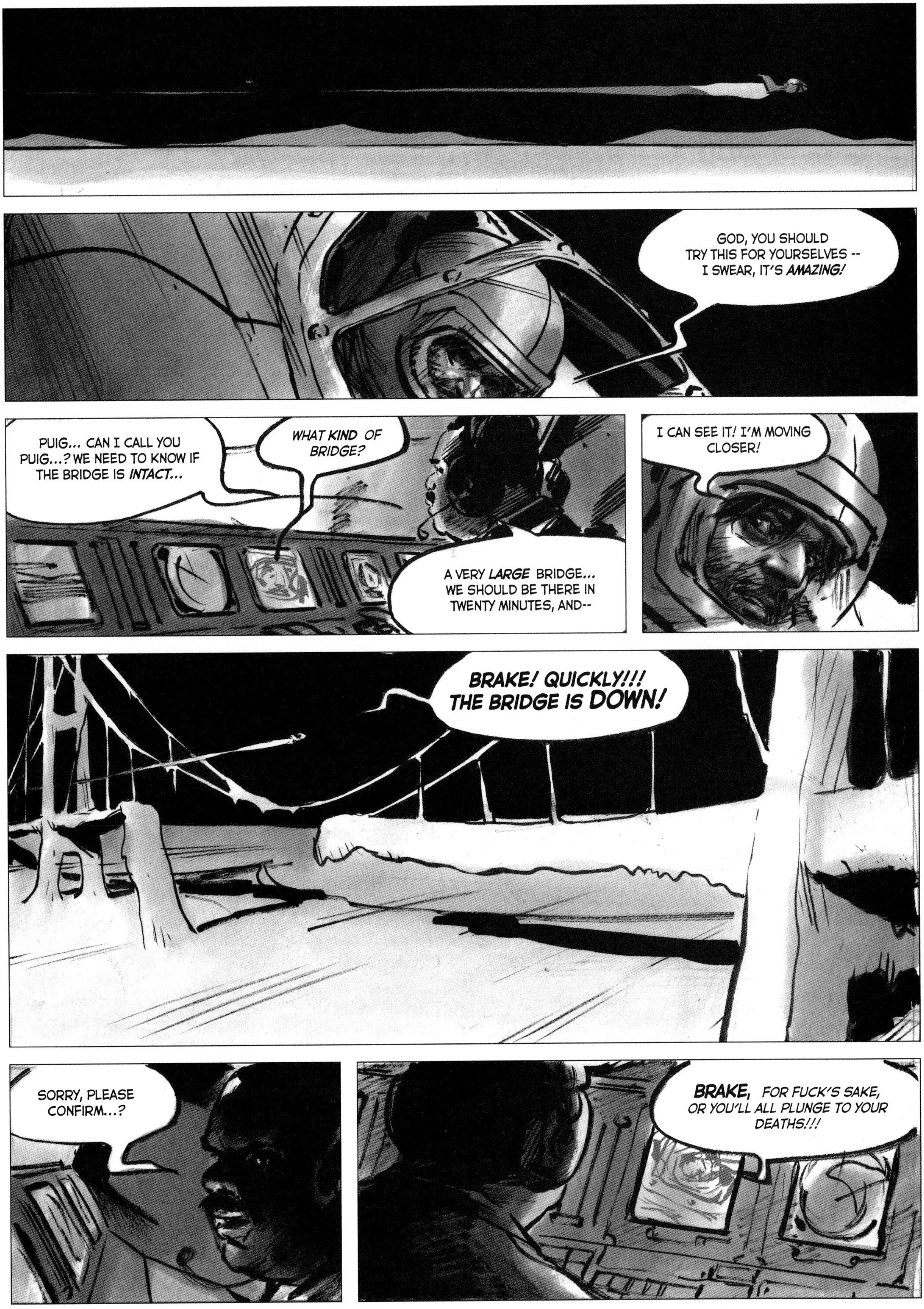
GOD, YOU SHOULD TRY THIS FOR YOURSELVES -- I SWEAR, IT'S *AMAZING!*
PUIG... CAN I CALL YOU PUIG...? WE NEED TO KNOW IF THE BRIDGE IS *INTACT...*
WHAT KIND OF BRIDGE?
A VERY *LARGE* BRIDGE... WE SHOULD BE THERE IN TWENTY MINUTES, AND--
I CAN SEE IT*!* I'M MOVING CLOSER*!*
BRAKE! QUICKLY!!! THE BRIDGE IS DOWN!
SORRY, PLEASE CONFIRM...?
BRAKE, FOR FUCK'S SAKE, OR YOU'LL ALL PLUNGE TO YOUR DEATHS!!!

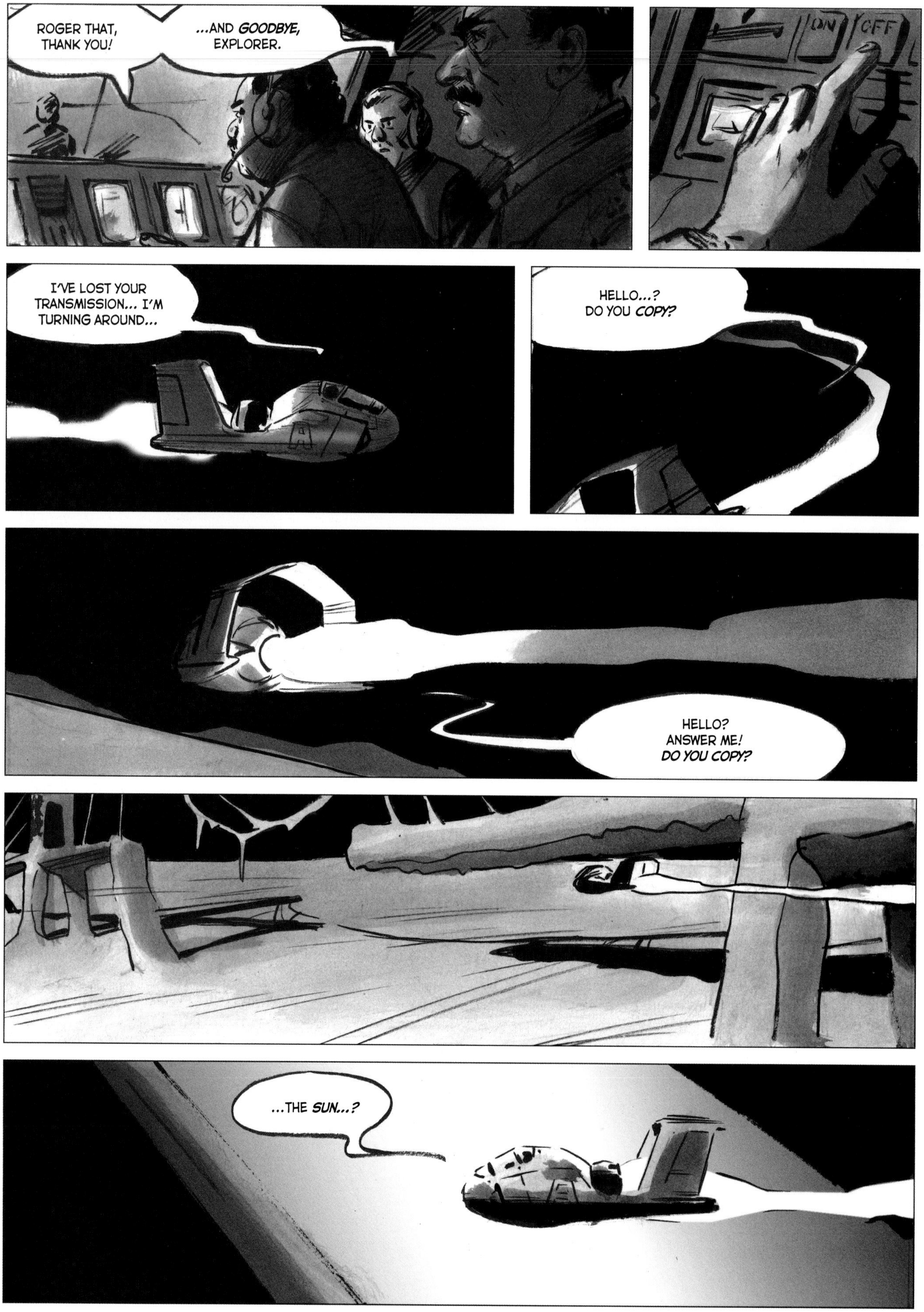
ROGER THAT, THANK YOU!
...AND GOODBYE, EXPLORER.
ON
OFF
I'VE LOST YOUR TRANSMISSION... I'M TURNING AROUND...
HELLO...? DO YOU COPY?
HELLO? ANSWER ME! DO YOU COPY?
...THE SUN...?

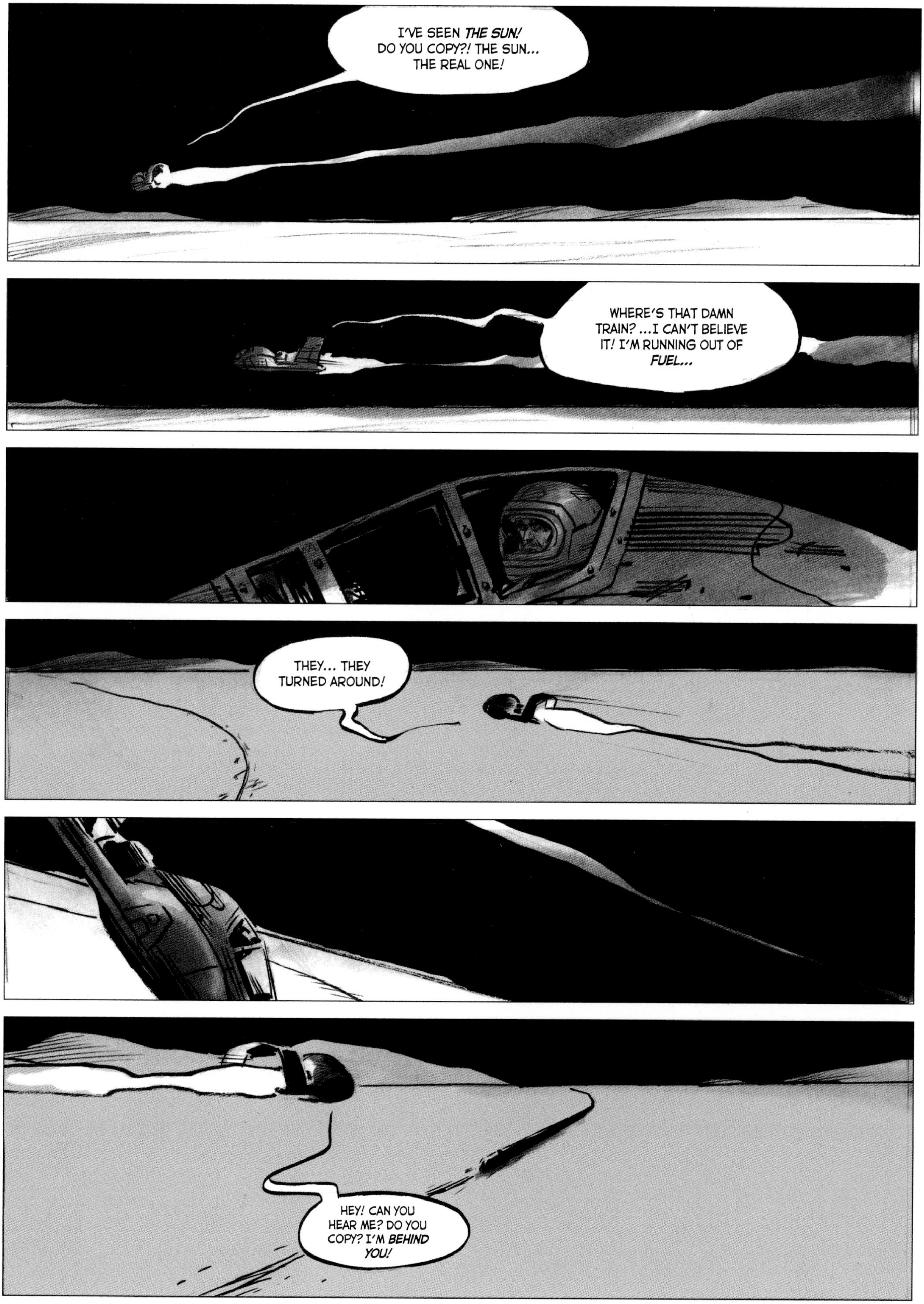
I'VE SEEN THE SUN! DO YOU COPY?! THE SUN... THE REAL ONE!
WHERE'S THAT DAMN TRAIN? ...I CAN'T BELIEVE IT! I'M RUNNING OUT OF FUEL...
THEY... THEY TURNED AROUND!
HEY! CAN YOU HEAR ME? DO YOU COPY? I'M BEHIND YOU!

HUH...? THEY NEVER TOLD US THERE WAS ANOTHER ENGINE AT THE *REAR*...
THE REAR GUARD HAS HIM IN SIGHT.
WELL THEN, WHAT THE FUCK ARE YOU *WAITING FOR?* SHOOT HIM!
RATATAT
BASTARDS! LIARS! YOU FUCKING SACKS OF SHIT!
RATATAT
RATA-
RATATAT
I KNOW YOU CAN *HEAR ME,* SO LISTEN TO ME, ALL OF YOU DOWN THERE...

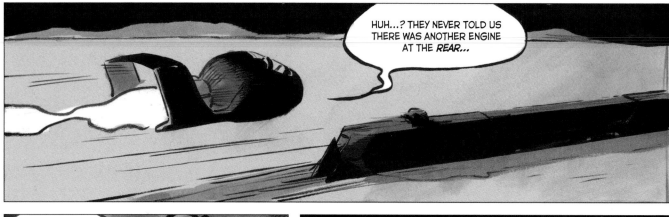

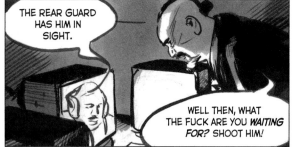

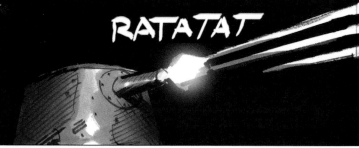

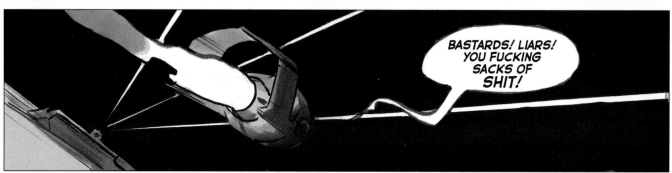

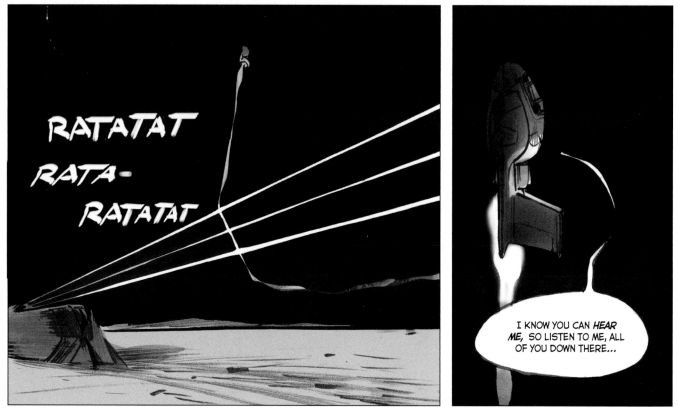

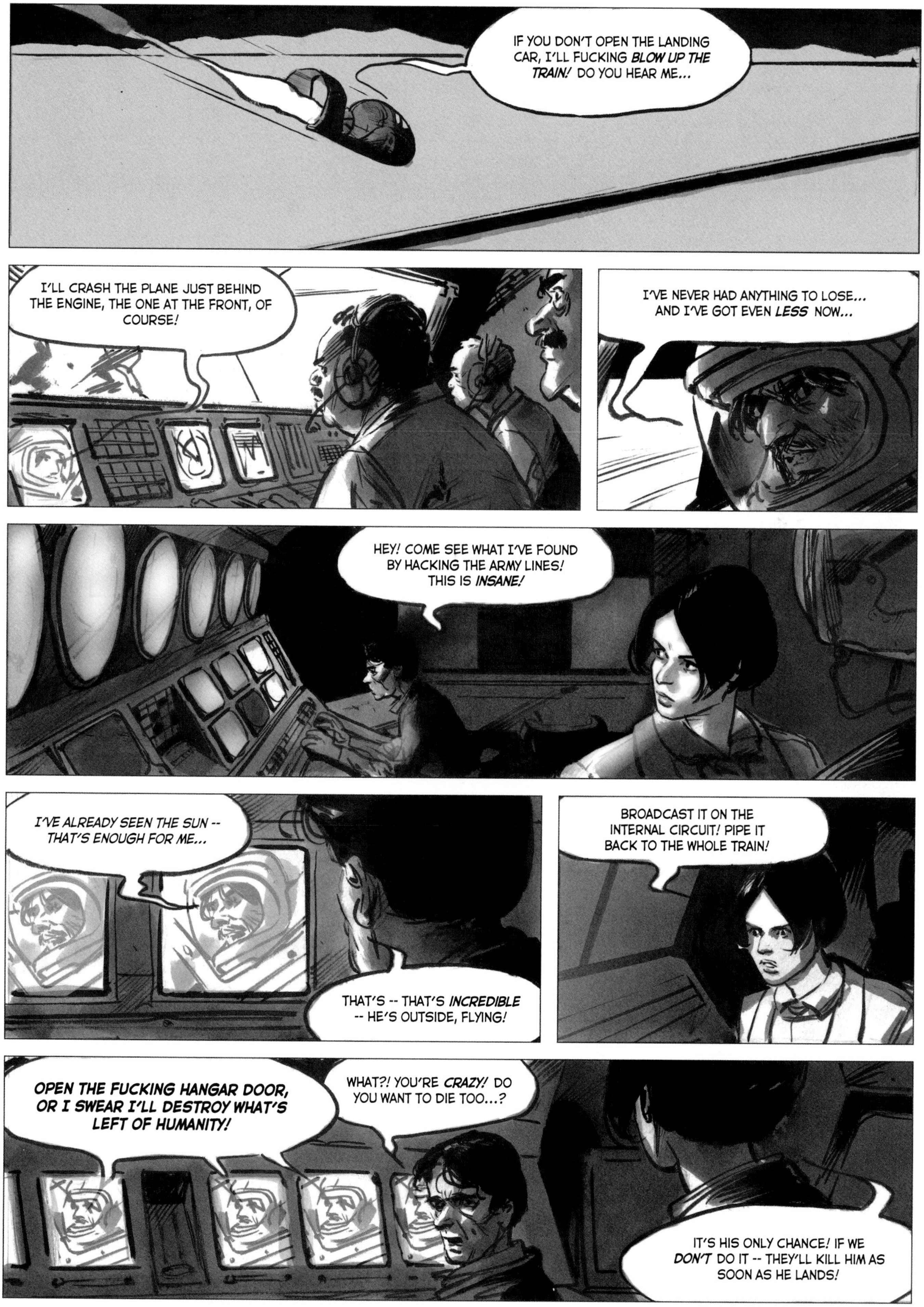
IF YOU DON'T OPEN THE LANDING CAR, I'LL FUCKING *BLOW UP THE TRAIN!* DO YOU HEAR ME...
I'LL CRASH THE PLANE JUST BEHIND THE ENGINE, THE ONE AT THE FRONT, OF COURSE!
I'VE NEVER HAD ANYTHING TO LOSE... AND I'VE GOT EVEN *LESS* NOW...
HEY! COME SEE WHAT I'VE FOUND BY HACKING THE ARMY LINES! THIS IS *INSANE!*
I'VE ALREADY SEEN THE SUN -- THAT'S ENOUGH FOR ME...
THAT'S -- THAT'S *INCREDIBLE* -- HE'S OUTSIDE, FLYING!
BROADCAST IT ON THE INTERNAL CIRCUIT! PIPE IT BACK TO THE WHOLE TRAIN!
OPEN THE FUCKING HANGAR DOOR, OR I SWEAR I'LL DESTROY WHAT'S LEFT OF HUMANITY!
WHAT?! YOU'RE *CRAZY!* DO YOU WANT TO DIE TOO...?
IT'S HIS ONLY CHANCE! IF WE *DON'T* DO IT -- THEY'LL KILL HIM AS SOON AS HE LANDS!

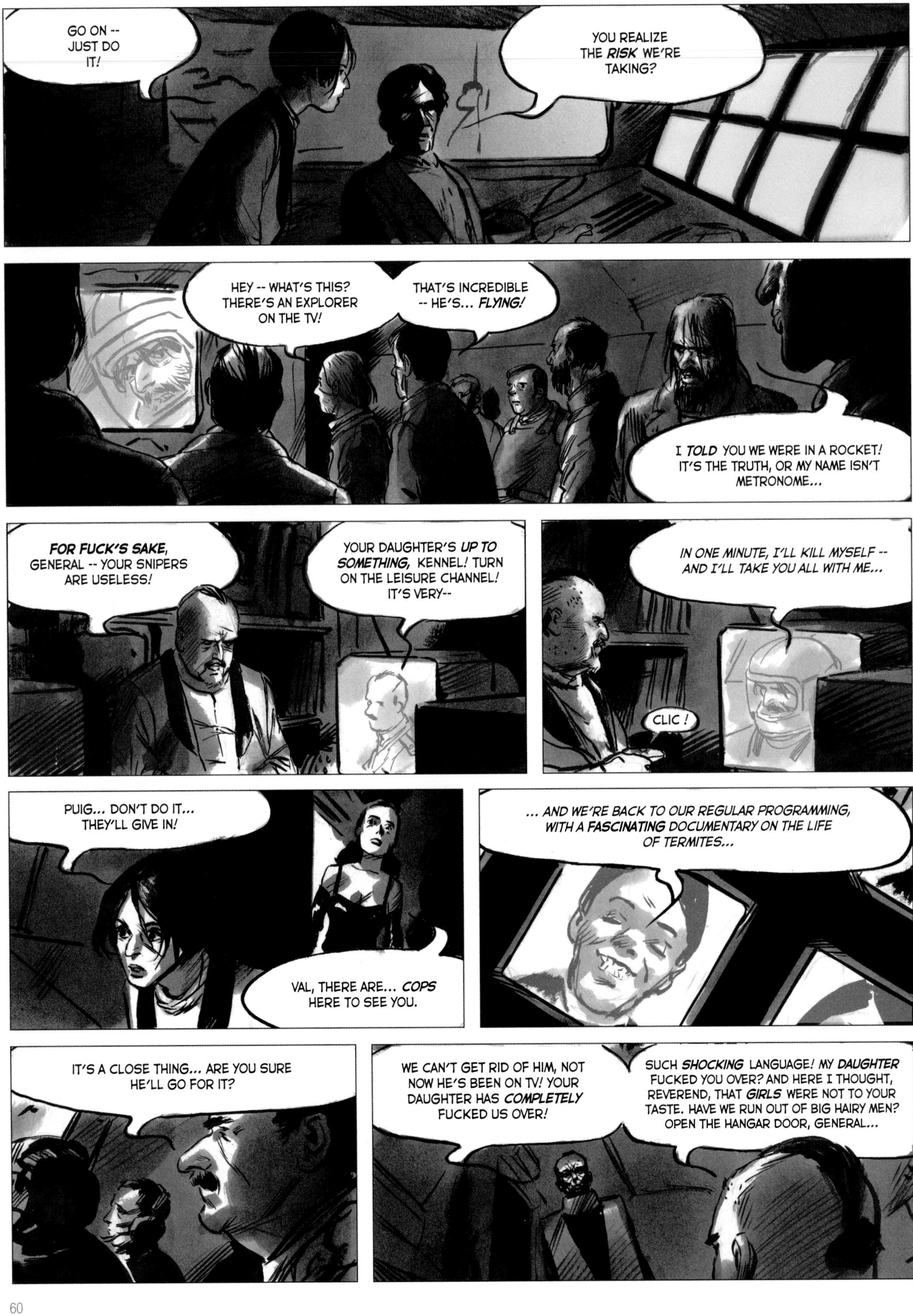
GO ON -- JUST DO IT!
YOU REALIZE THE RISK WE'RE TAKING?
HEY -- WHAT'S THIS? THERE'S AN EXPLORER ON THE TV!
THAT'S INCREDIBLE -- HE'S... FLYING!
I TOLD YOU WE WERE IN A ROCKET! IT'S THE TRUTH, OR MY NAME ISN'T METRONOME...
FOR FUCK'S SAKE, GENERAL -- YOUR SNIPERS ARE USELESS!
YOUR DAUGHTER'S UP TO SOMETHING, KENNEL! TURN ON THE LEISURE CHANNEL! IT'S VERY--
IN ONE MINUTE, I'LL KILL MYSELF -- AND I'LL TAKE YOU ALL WITH ME...
CLIC !
PUIG... DON'T DO IT... THEY'LL GIVE IN!
VAL, THERE ARE... COPS HERE TO SEE YOU.
... AND WE'RE BACK TO OUR REGULAR PROGRAMMING, WITH A FASCINATING DOCUMENTARY ON THE LIFE OF TERMITES...
IT'S A CLOSE THING... ARE YOU SURE HE'LL GO FOR IT?
WE CAN'T GET RID OF HIM, NOT NOW HE'S BEEN ON TV! YOUR DAUGHTER HAS COMPLETELY FUCKED US OVER!
SUCH SHOCKING LANGUAGE! MY DAUGHTER FUCKED YOU OVER? AND HERE I THOUGHT, REVEREND, THAT GIRLS WERE NOT TO YOUR TASTE. HAVE WE RUN OUT OF BIG HAIRY MEN? OPEN THE HANGAR DOOR, GENERAL...

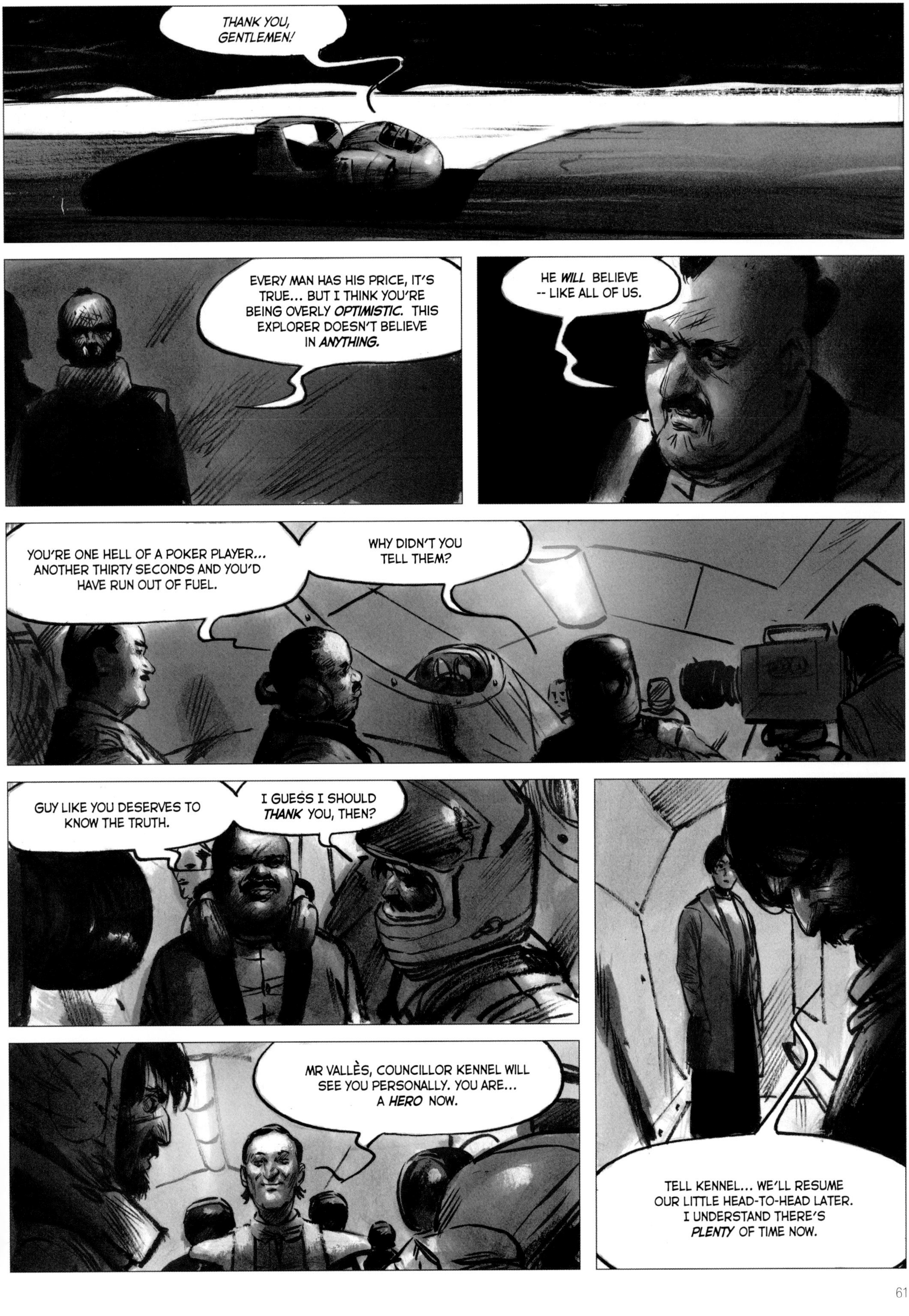
THANK YOU, GENTLEMEN!
EVERY MAN HAS HIS PRICE, IT'S TRUE... BUT I THINK YOU'RE BEING OVERLY OPTIMISTIC. THIS EXPLORER DOESN'T BELIEVE IN ANYTHING.
HE WILL BELIEVE -- LIKE ALL OF US.
YOU'RE ONE HELL OF A POKER PLAYER... ANOTHER THIRTY SECONDS AND YOU'D HAVE RUN OUT OF FUEL.
WHY DIDN'T YOU TELL THEM?
GUY LIKE YOU DESERVES TO KNOW THE TRUTH.
I GUESS I SHOULD THANK YOU, THEN?
MR VALLÈS, COUNCILLOR KENNEL WILL SEE YOU PERSONALLY. YOU ARE... A HERO NOW.
TELL KENNEL... WE'LL RESUME OUR LITTLE HEAD-TO-HEAD LATER. I UNDERSTAND THERE'S PLENTY OF TIME NOW.

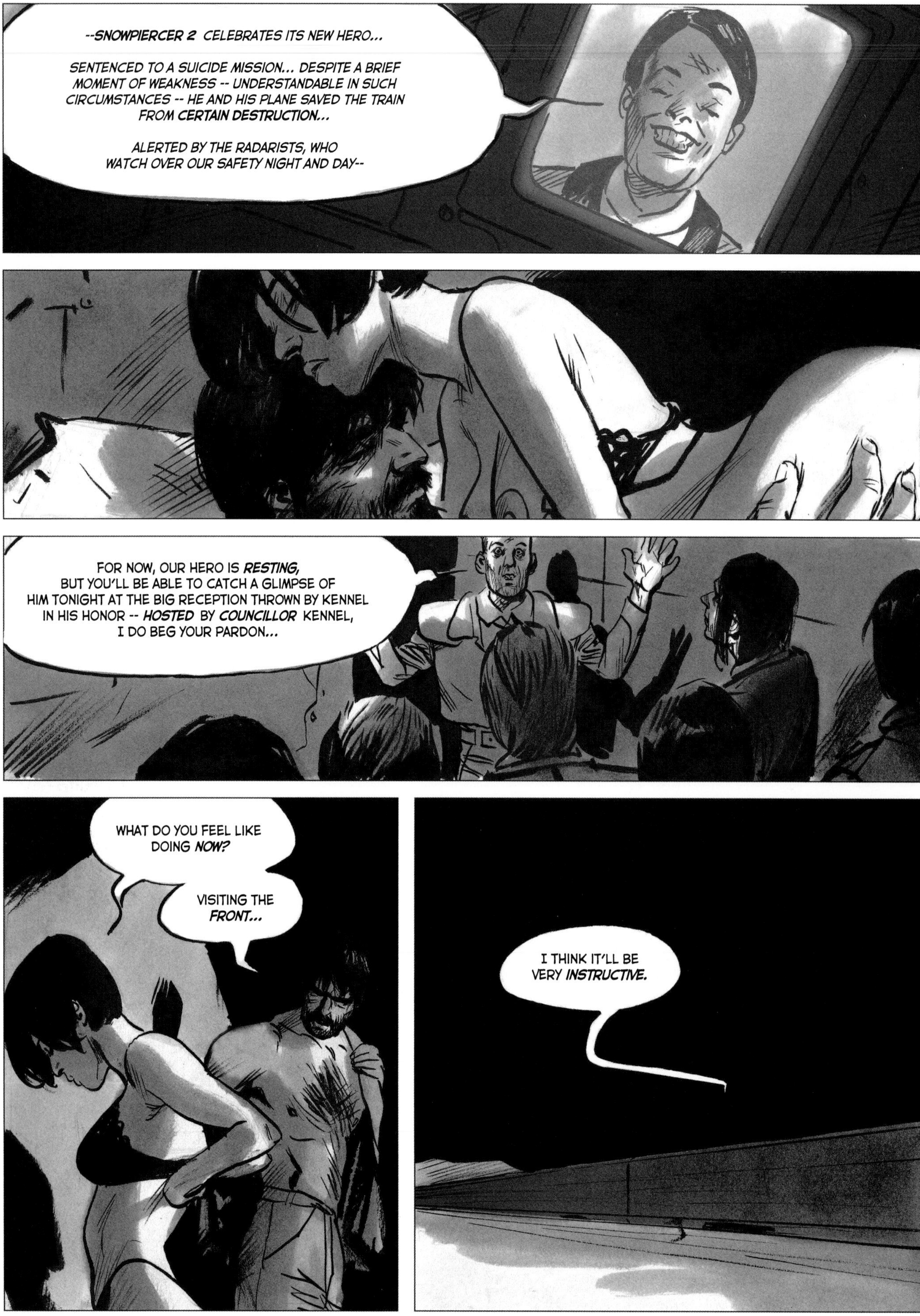
--SNOWPIERCER 2 CELEBRATES ITS NEW HERO...
SENTENCED TO A SUICIDE MISSION... DESPITE A BRIEF MOMENT OF WEAKNESS -- UNDERSTANDABLE IN SUCH CIRCUMSTANCES -- HE AND HIS PLANE SAVED THE TRAIN FROM CERTAIN DESTRUCTION...
ALERTED BY THE RADARISTS, WHO WATCH OVER OUR SAFETY NIGHT AND DAY--
FOR NOW, OUR HERO IS RESTING, BUT YOU'LL BE ABLE TO CATCH A GLIMPSE OF HIM TONIGHT AT THE BIG RECEPTION THROWN BY KENNEL IN HIS HONOR -- HOSTED BY COUNCILLOR KENNEL, I DO BEG YOUR PARDON...
WHAT DO YOU FEEL LIKE DOING NOW?
VISITING THE FRONT...
I THINK IT'LL BE VERY INSTRUCTIVE.

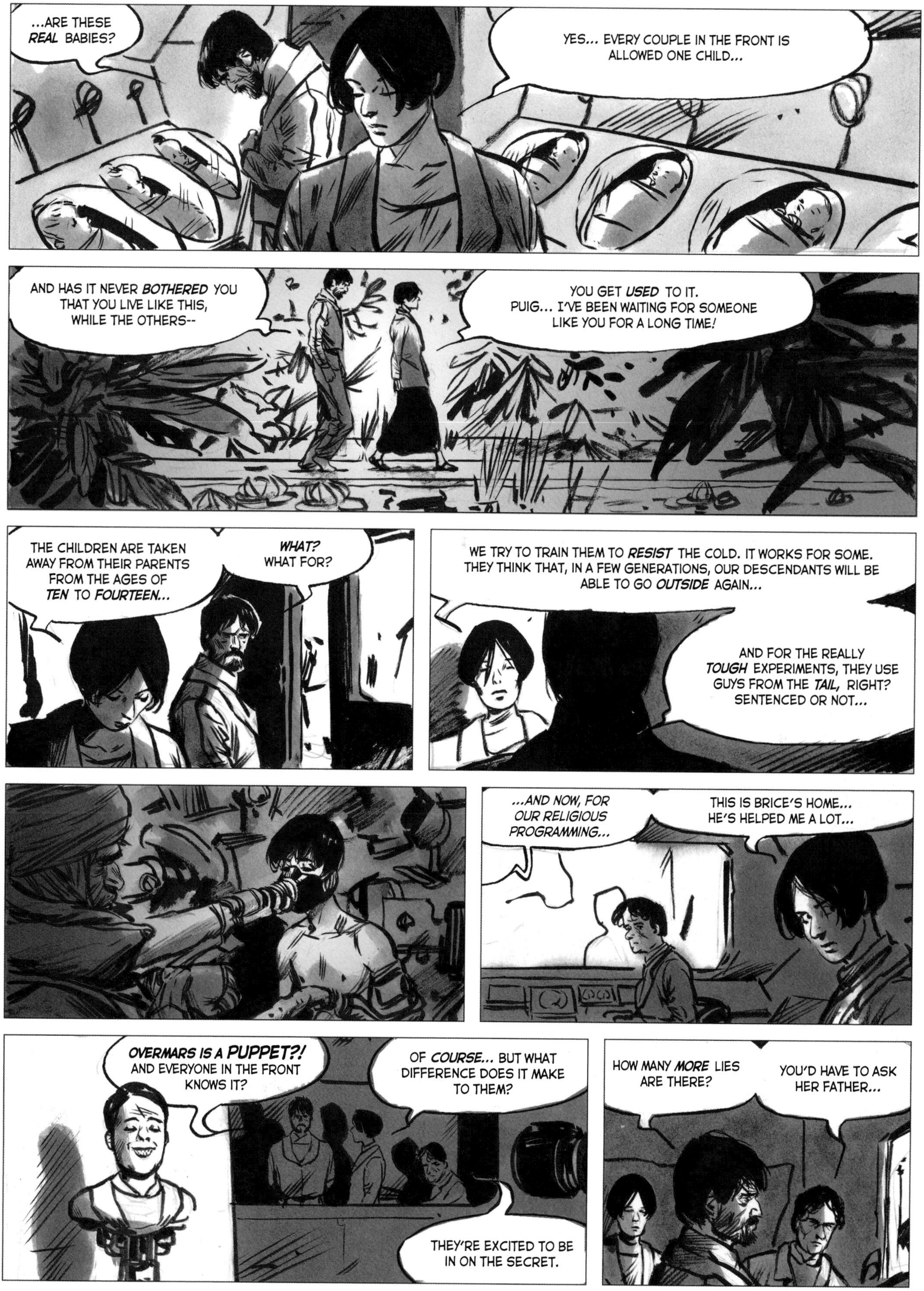
...ARE THESE REAL BABIES?
YES... EVERY COUPLE IN THE FRONT IS ALLOWED ONE CHILD...
AND HAS IT NEVER BOTHERED YOU THAT YOU LIVE LIKE THIS, WHILE THE OTHERS--
YOU GET USED TO IT. PUIG... I'VE BEEN WAITING FOR SOMEONE LIKE YOU FOR A LONG TIME!
THE CHILDREN ARE TAKEN AWAY FROM THEIR PARENTS FROM THE AGES OF TEN TO FOURTEEN...
WHAT? WHAT FOR?
WE TRY TO TRAIN THEM TO RESIST THE COLD. IT WORKS FOR SOME. THEY THINK THAT, IN A FEW GENERATIONS, OUR DESCENDANTS WILL BE ABLE TO GO OUTSIDE AGAIN...
AND FOR THE REALLY TOUGH EXPERIMENTS, THEY USE GUYS FROM THE TAIL, RIGHT? SENTENCED OR NOT...
...AND NOW, FOR OUR RELIGIOUS PROGRAMMING...
THIS IS BRICE'S HOME... HE'S HELPED ME A LOT...
OVERMARS IS A PUPPET?! AND EVERYONE IN THE FRONT KNOWS IT?
OF COURSE... BUT WHAT DIFFERENCE DOES IT MAKE TO THEM?
THEY'RE EXCITED TO BE IN ON THE SECRET.
HOW MANY MORE LIES ARE THERE?
YOU'D HAVE TO ASK HER FATHER...

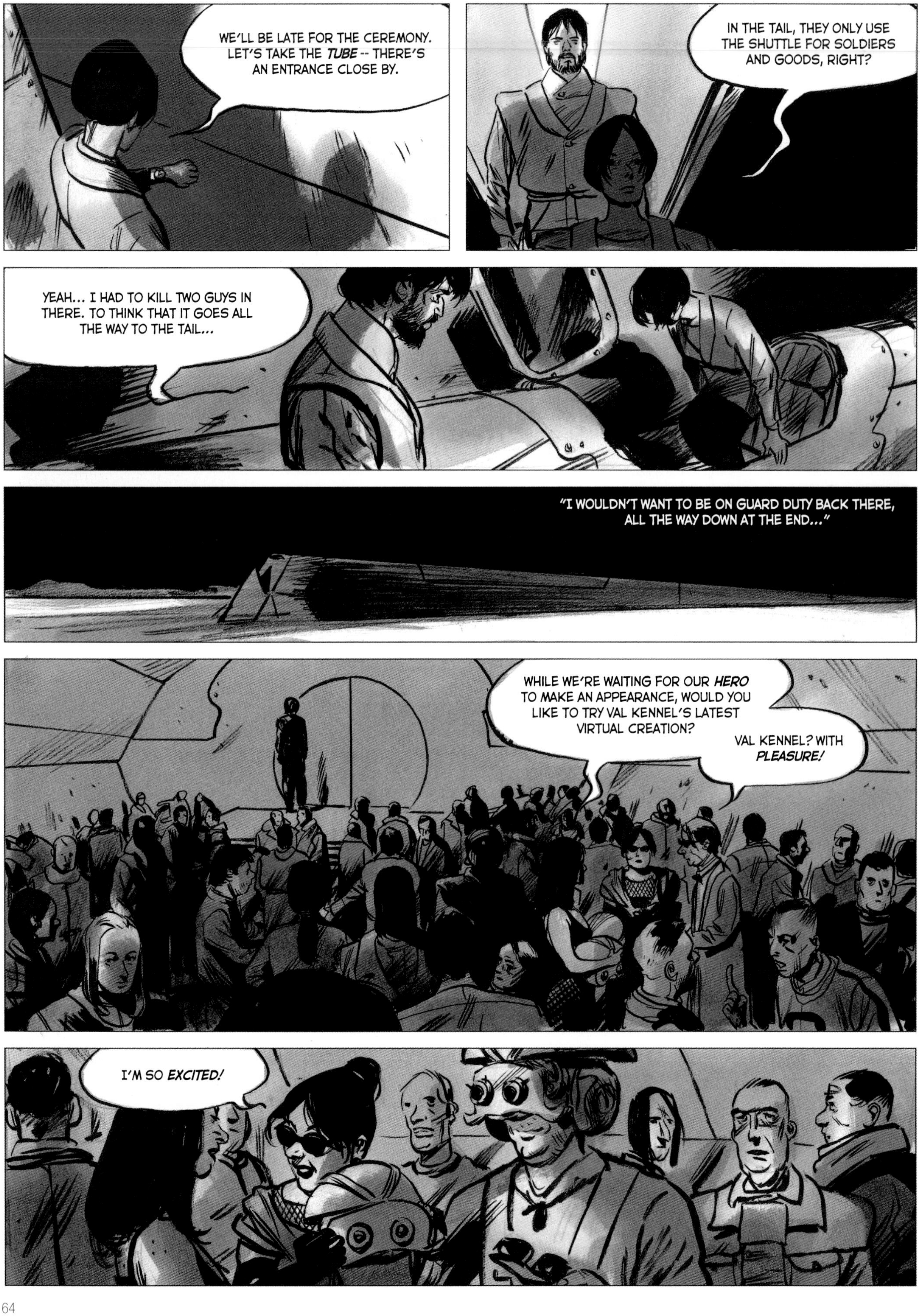

WE'LL BE LATE FOR THE CEREMONY. LET'S TAKE THE *TUBE* -- THERE'S AN ENTRANCE CLOSE BY.
IN THE TAIL, THEY ONLY USE THE SHUTTLE FOR SOLDIERS AND GOODS, RIGHT?
YEAH... I HAD TO KILL TWO GUYS IN THERE. TO THINK THAT IT GOES ALL THE WAY TO THE TAIL...
"I WOULDN'T WANT TO BE ON GUARD DUTY BACK THERE, ALL THE WAY DOWN AT THE END..."
WHILE WE'RE WAITING FOR OUR *HERO* TO MAKE AN APPEARANCE, WOULD YOU LIKE TO TRY VAL KENNEL'S LATEST VIRTUAL CREATION?
VAL KENNEL? WITH *PLEASURE!*
I'M SO *EXCITED!*

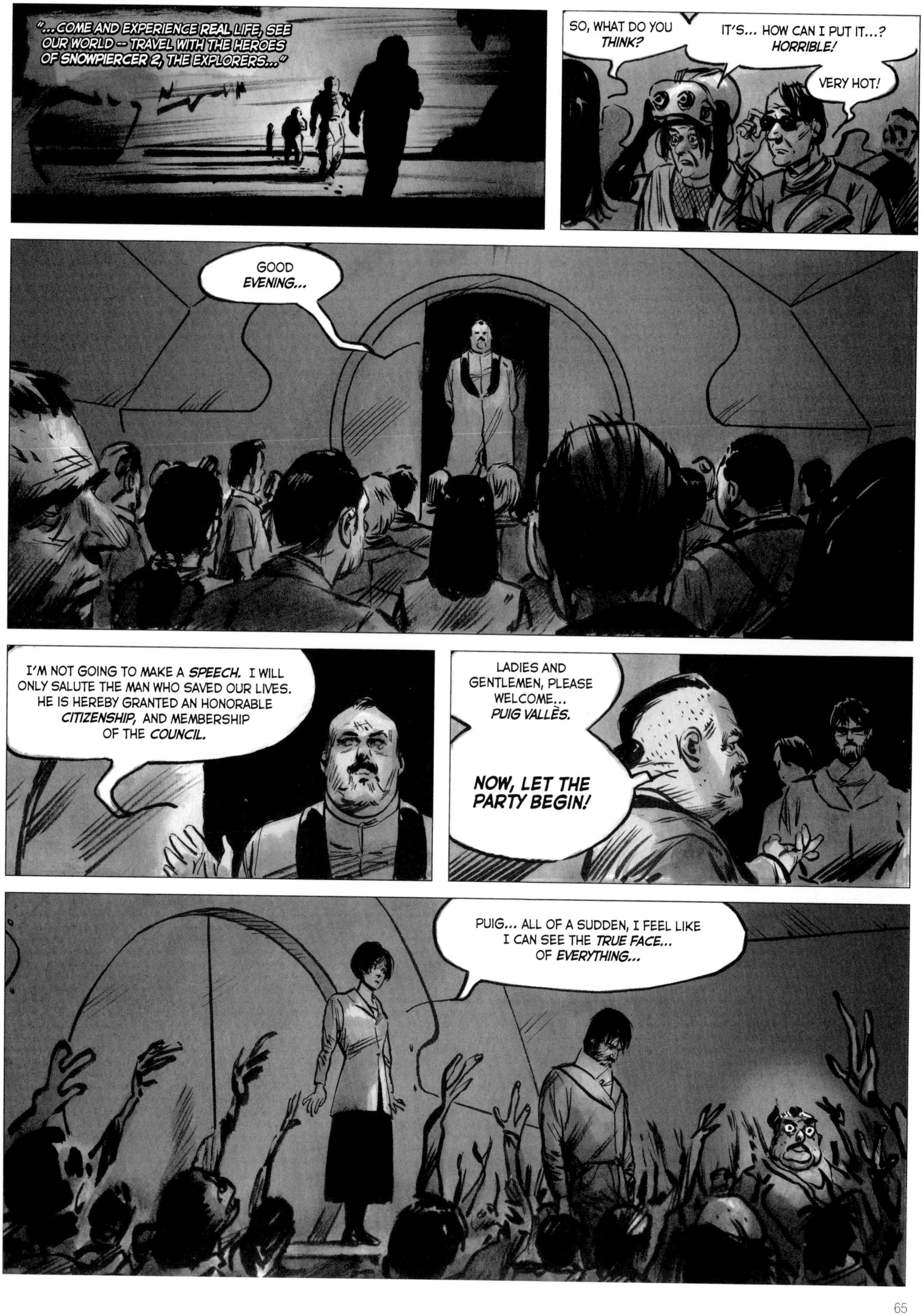
"...COME AND EXPERIENCE REAL LIFE, SEE OUR WORLD -- TRAVEL WITH THE HEROES OF SNOWPIERCER 2, THE EXPLORERS..."
SO, WHAT DO YOU THINK?
IT'S... HOW CAN I PUT IT...? HORRIBLE!
VERY HOT!
GOOD EVENING...
I'M NOT GOING TO MAKE A SPEECH. I WILL ONLY SALUTE THE MAN WHO SAVED OUR LIVES. HE IS HEREBY GRANTED AN HONORABLE CITIZENSHIP, AND MEMBERSHIP OF THE COUNCIL.
LADIES AND GENTLEMEN, PLEASE WELCOME... PUIG VALLÈS.
NOW, LET THE PARTY BEGIN!
PUIG... ALL OF A SUDDEN, I FEEL LIKE I CAN SEE THE TRUE FACE... OF EVERYTHING...

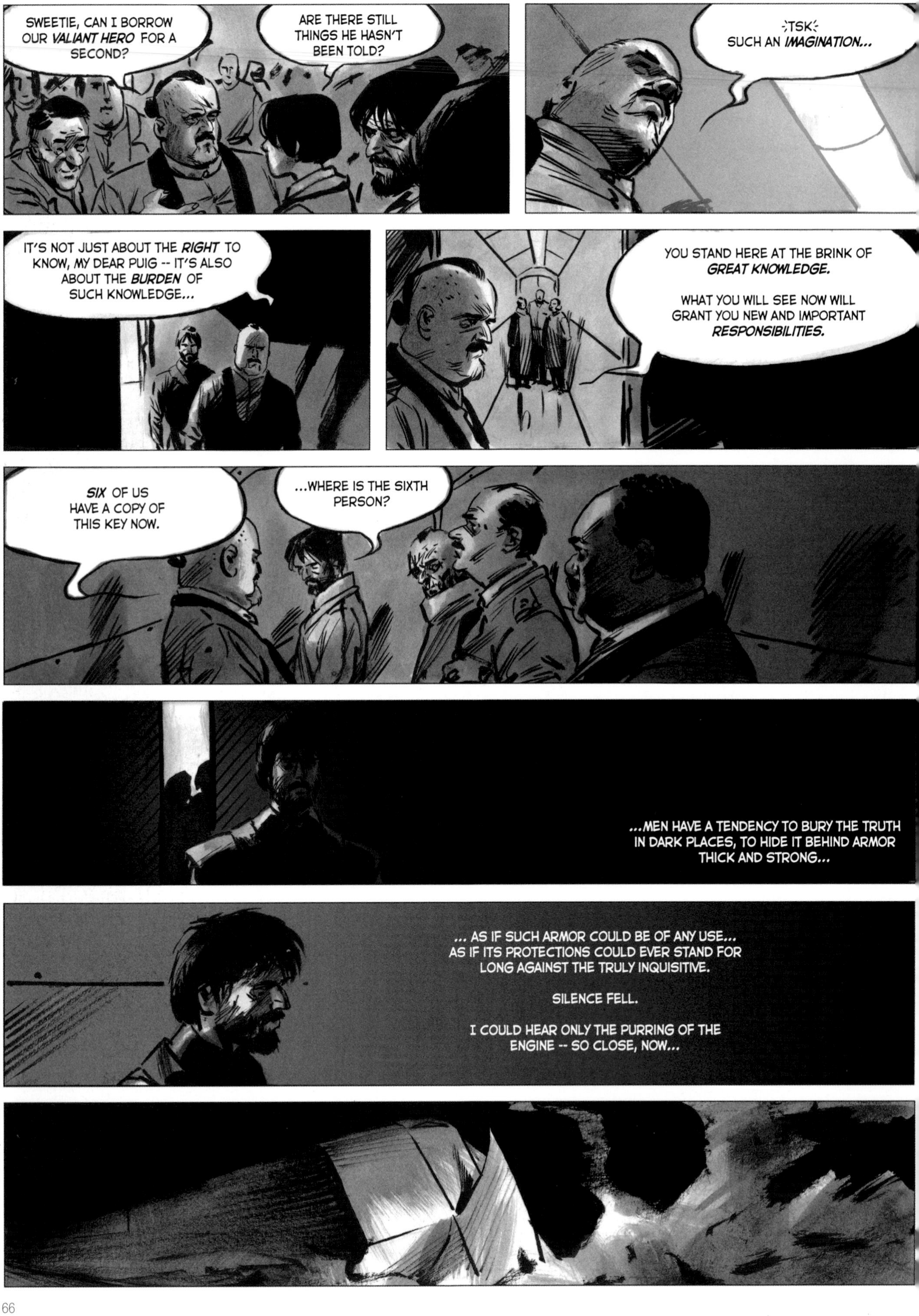
SWEETIE, CAN I BORROW OUR *VALIANT HERO* FOR A SECOND?
ARE THERE STILL THINGS HE HASN'T BEEN TOLD?
TSK
SUCH AN *IMAGINATION...*
IT'S NOT JUST ABOUT THE *RIGHT* TO KNOW, MY DEAR PUIG -- IT'S ALSO ABOUT THE *BURDEN* OF SUCH KNOWLEDGE...
YOU STAND HERE AT THE BRINK OF *GREAT KNOWLEDGE.*
WHAT YOU WILL SEE NOW WILL GRANT YOU NEW AND IMPORTANT *RESPONSIBILITIES.*
SIX OF US HAVE A COPY OF THIS KEY NOW.
...WHERE IS THE SIXTH PERSON?
...MEN HAVE A TENDENCY TO BURY THE TRUTH IN DARK PLACES, TO HIDE IT BEHIND ARMOR THICK AND STRONG...
... AS IF SUCH ARMOR COULD BE OF ANY USE... AS IF ITS PROTECTIONS COULD EVER STAND FOR LONG AGAINST THE TRULY INQUISITIVE.
SILENCE FELL.
I COULD HEAR ONLY THE PURRING OF THE ENGINE -- SO CLOSE, NOW...

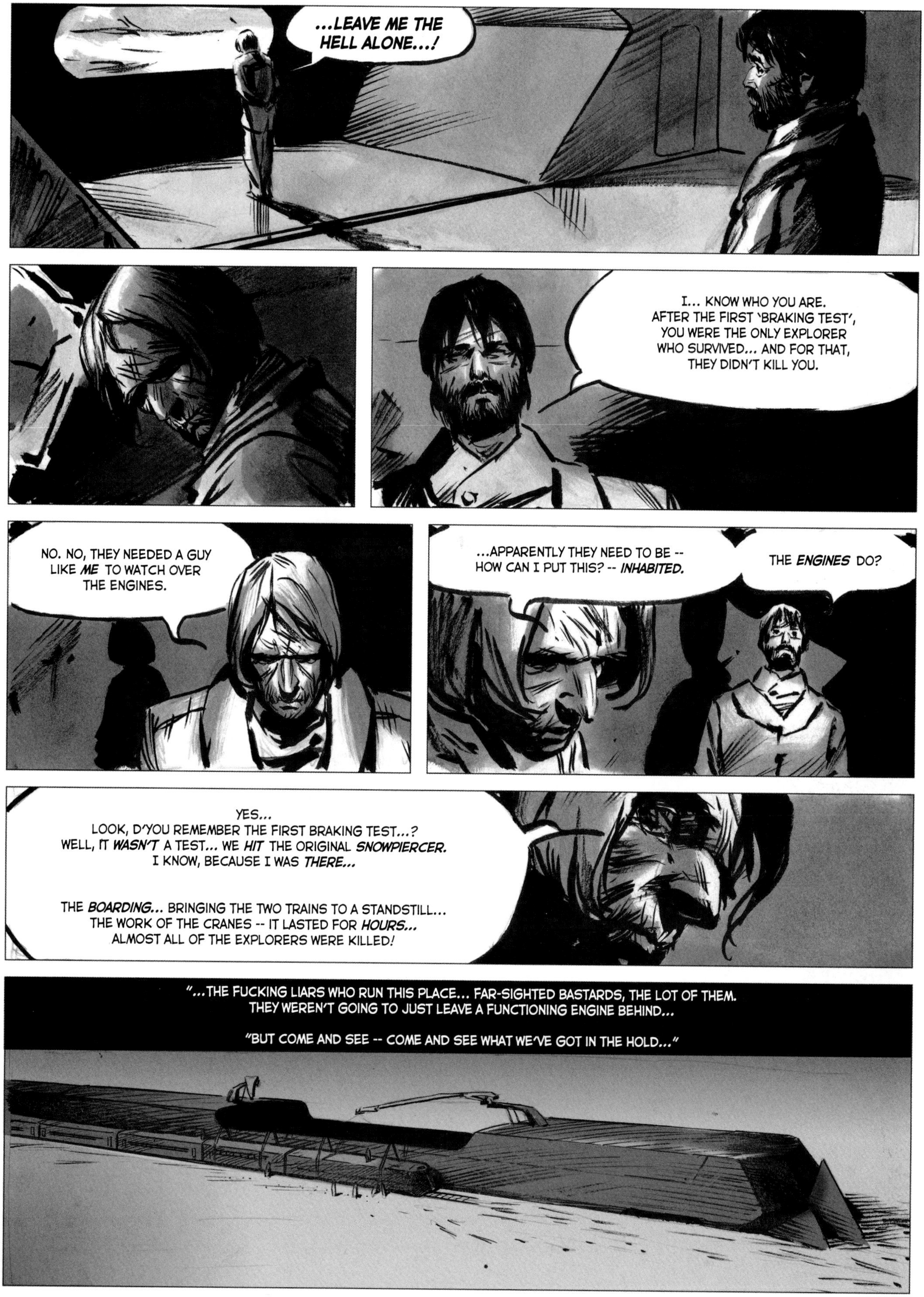
...LEAVE ME THE HELL ALONE...!
I... KNOW WHO YOU ARE. AFTER THE FIRST 'BRAKING TEST', YOU WERE THE ONLY EXPLORER WHO SURVIVED... AND FOR THAT, THEY DIDN'T KILL YOU.
NO. NO, THEY NEEDED A GUY LIKE *ME* TO WATCH OVER THE ENGINES.
...APPARENTLY THEY NEED TO BE -- HOW CAN I PUT THIS? -- *INHABITED.*
THE *ENGINES* DO?
YES... LOOK, D'YOU REMEMBER THE FIRST BRAKING TEST...? WELL, IT *WASN'T* A TEST... WE *HIT* THE ORIGINAL *SNOWPIERCER.* I KNOW, BECAUSE I WAS *THERE...*
THE *BOARDING...* BRINGING THE TWO TRAINS TO A STANDSTILL... THE WORK OF THE CRANES -- IT LASTED FOR *HOURS...* ALMOST ALL OF THE EXPLORERS WERE KILLED!
"...THE FUCKING LIARS WHO RUN THIS PLACE... FAR-SIGHTED BASTARDS, THE LOT OF THEM. THEY WEREN'T GOING TO JUST LEAVE A FUNCTIONING ENGINE BEHIND...
"BUT COME AND SEE -- COME AND SEE WHAT WE'VE GOT IN THE HOLD..."

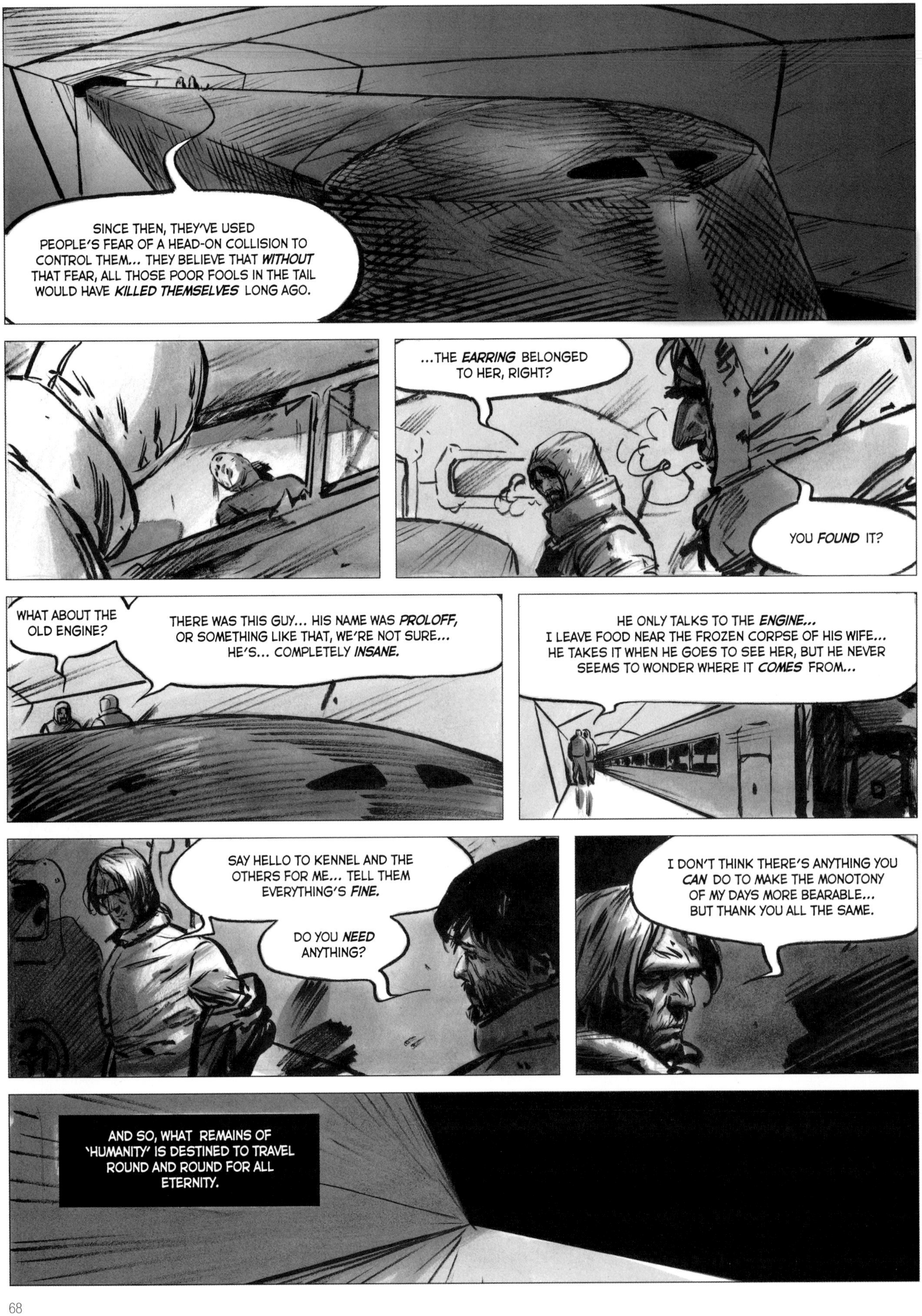
SINCE THEN, THEY'VE USED PEOPLE'S FEAR OF A HEAD-ON COLLISION TO CONTROL THEM... THEY BELIEVE THAT *WITHOUT* THAT FEAR, ALL THOSE POOR FOOLS IN THE TAIL WOULD HAVE *KILLED THEMSELVES* LONG AGO.
...THE *EARRING* BELONGED TO HER, RIGHT?
YOU *FOUND* IT?
WHAT ABOUT THE OLD ENGINE?
THERE WAS THIS GUY... HIS NAME WAS *PROLOFF,* OR SOMETHING LIKE THAT, WE'RE NOT SURE... HE'S... COMPLETELY *INSANE.*
HE ONLY TALKS TO THE *ENGINE...* I LEAVE FOOD NEAR THE FROZEN CORPSE OF HIS WIFE... HE TAKES IT WHEN HE GOES TO SEE HER, BUT HE NEVER SEEMS TO WONDER WHERE IT *COMES* FROM...
SAY HELLO TO KENNEL AND THE OTHERS FOR ME... TELL THEM EVERYTHING'S *FINE.*
DO YOU *NEED* ANYTHING?
I DON'T THINK THERE'S ANYTHING YOU *CAN* DO TO MAKE THE MONOTONY OF MY DAYS MORE BEARABLE... BUT THANK YOU ALL THE SAME.
AND SO, WHAT REMAINS OF 'HUMANITY' IS DESTINED TO TRAVEL ROUND AND ROUND FOR ALL ETERNITY.

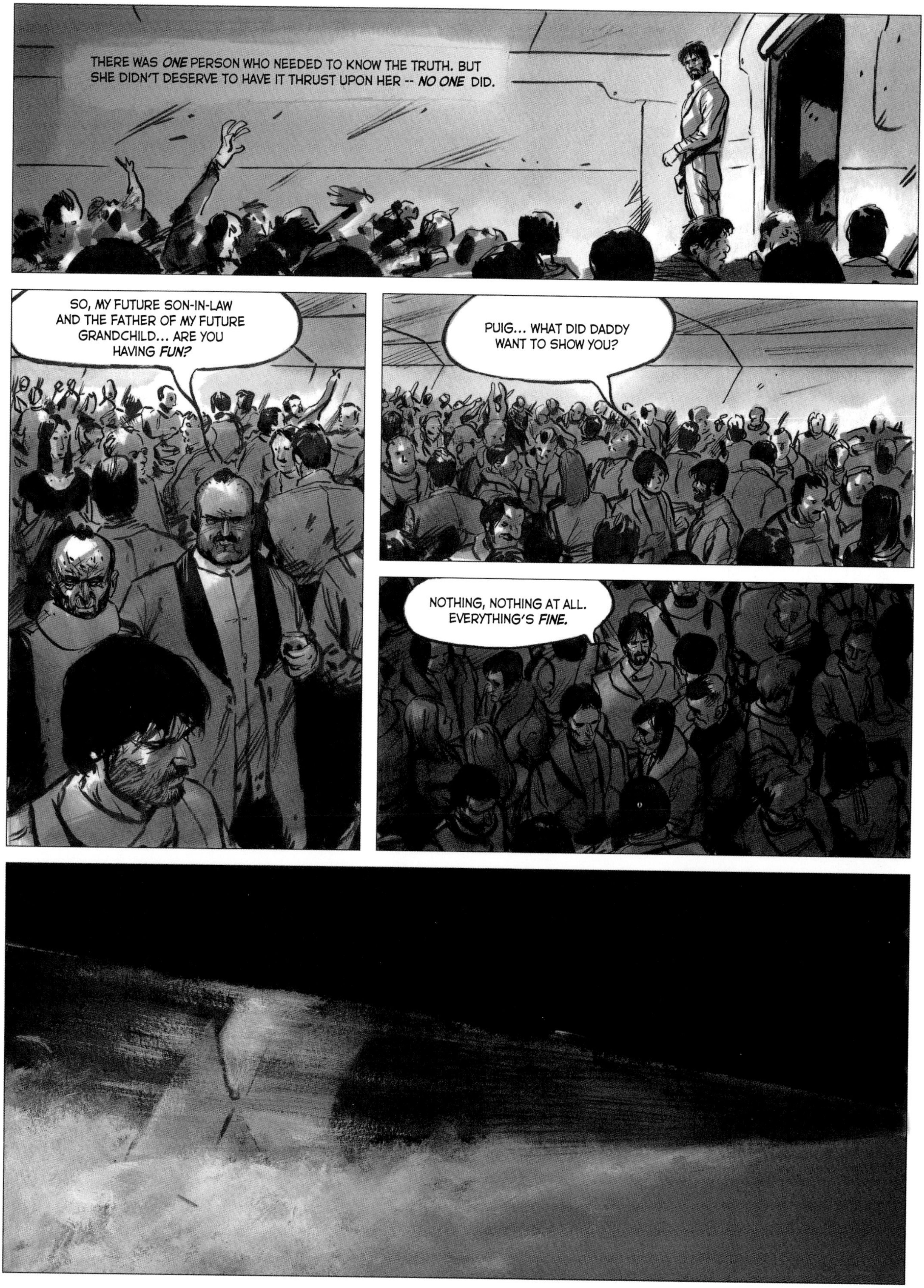
THERE WAS *ONE* PERSON WHO NEEDED TO KNOW THE TRUTH. BUT SHE DIDN'T DESERVE TO HAVE IT THRUST UPON HER -- ***NO ONE*** DID.
SO, MY FUTURE SON-IN-LAW AND THE FATHER OF MY FUTURE GRANDCHILD... ARE YOU HAVING *FUN?*
PUIG... WHAT DID DADDY WANT TO SHOW YOU?
NOTHING, NOTHING AT ALL. EVERYTHING'S ***FINE.***

SO ROUND AND ROUND *SNOWPIERCER*
GOES -- ROUND AND ROUND FOREVER.

ROUND AND ROUND THE FROZEN EARTH...

ROUND AND ROUND...

FOREVER.

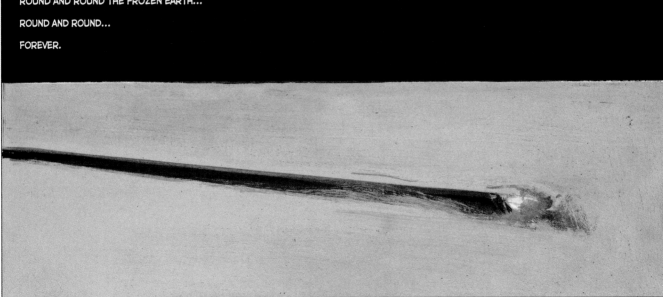

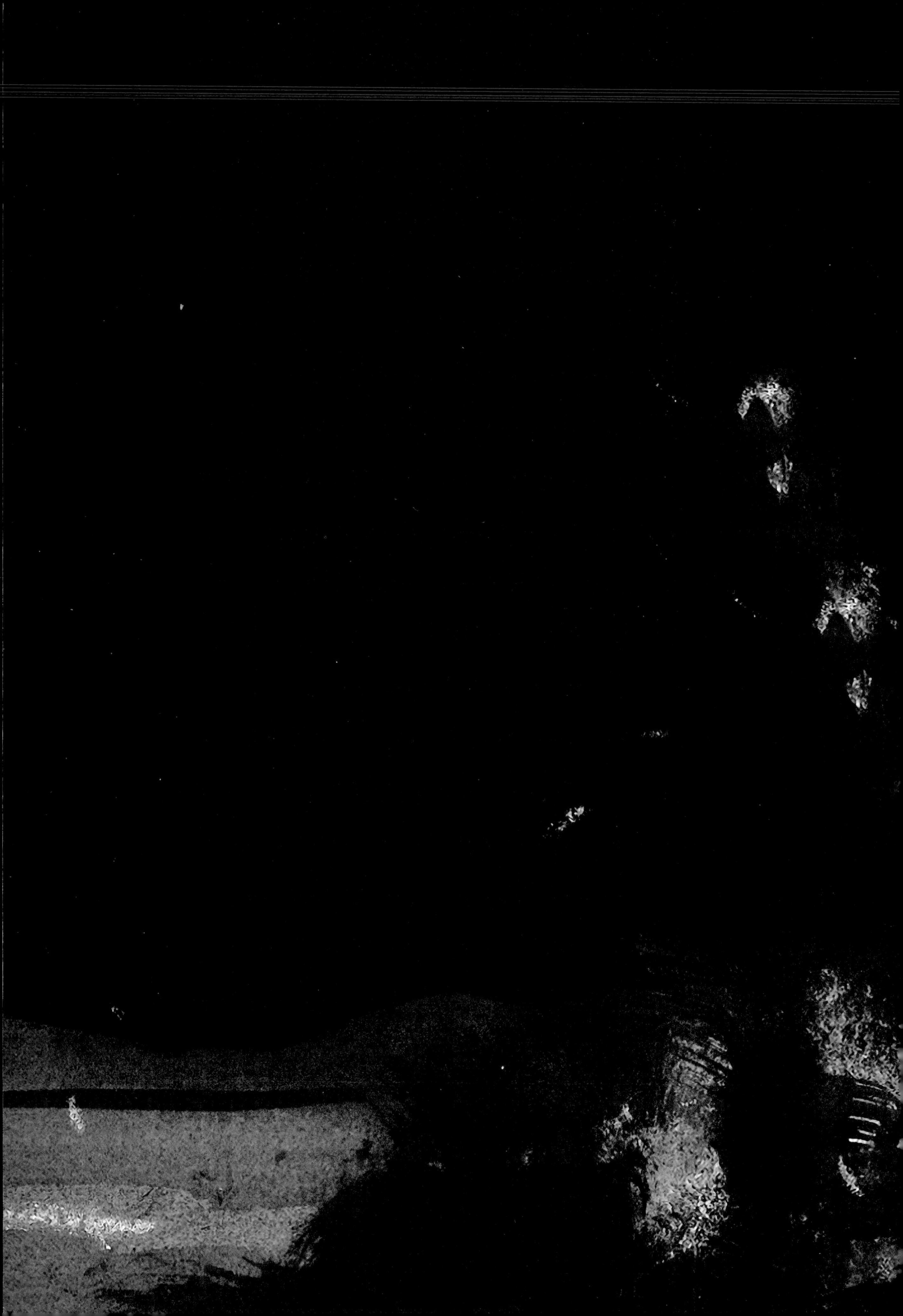

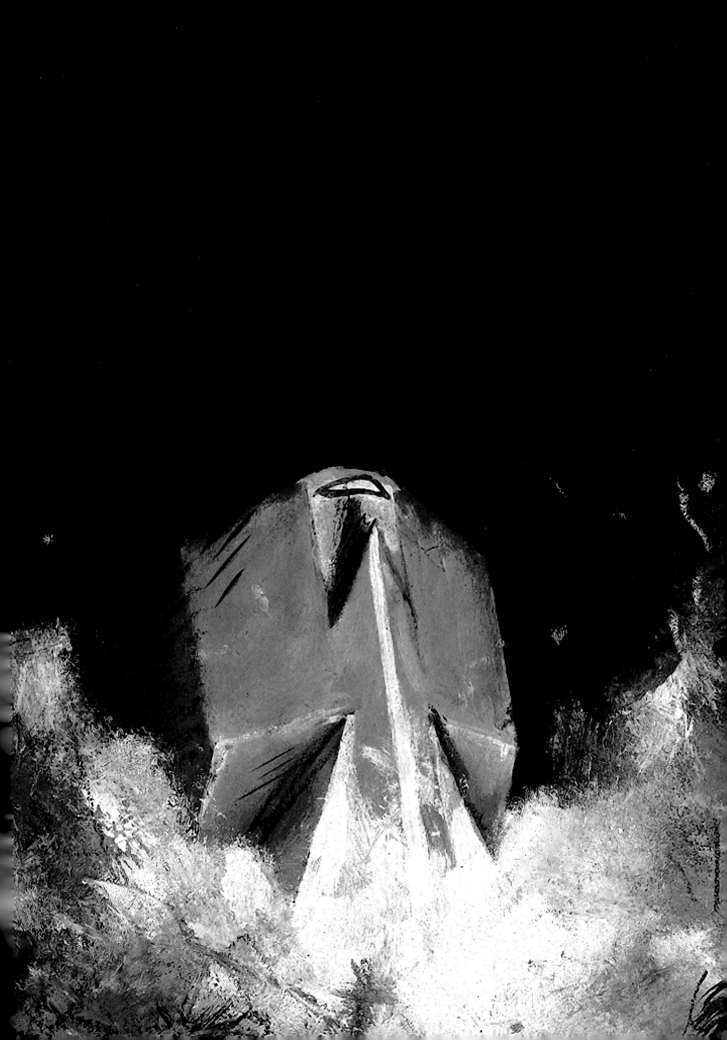

SNOWPIERCER

3: THE CROSSING

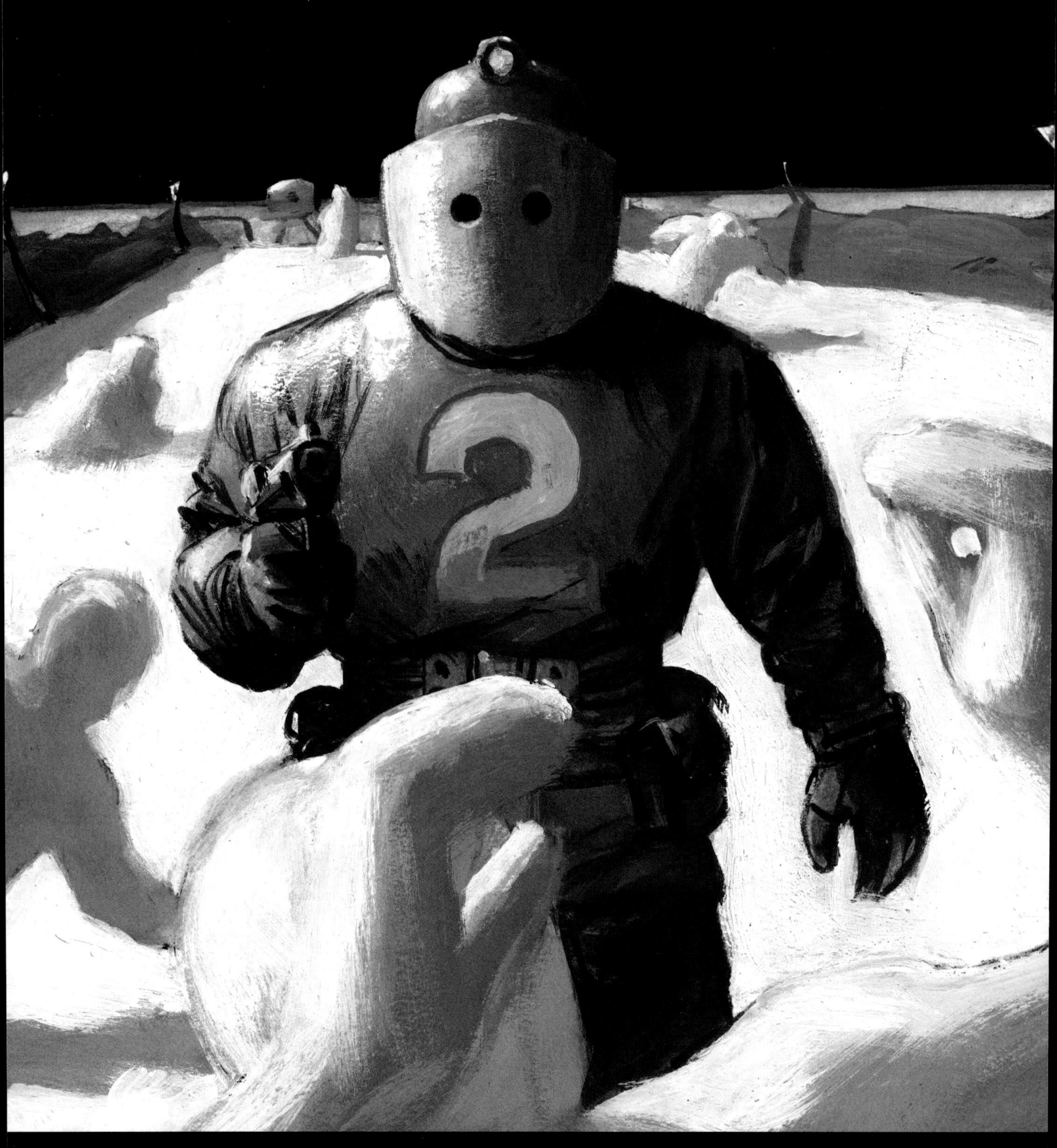

LEGRAND / ROCHETTE

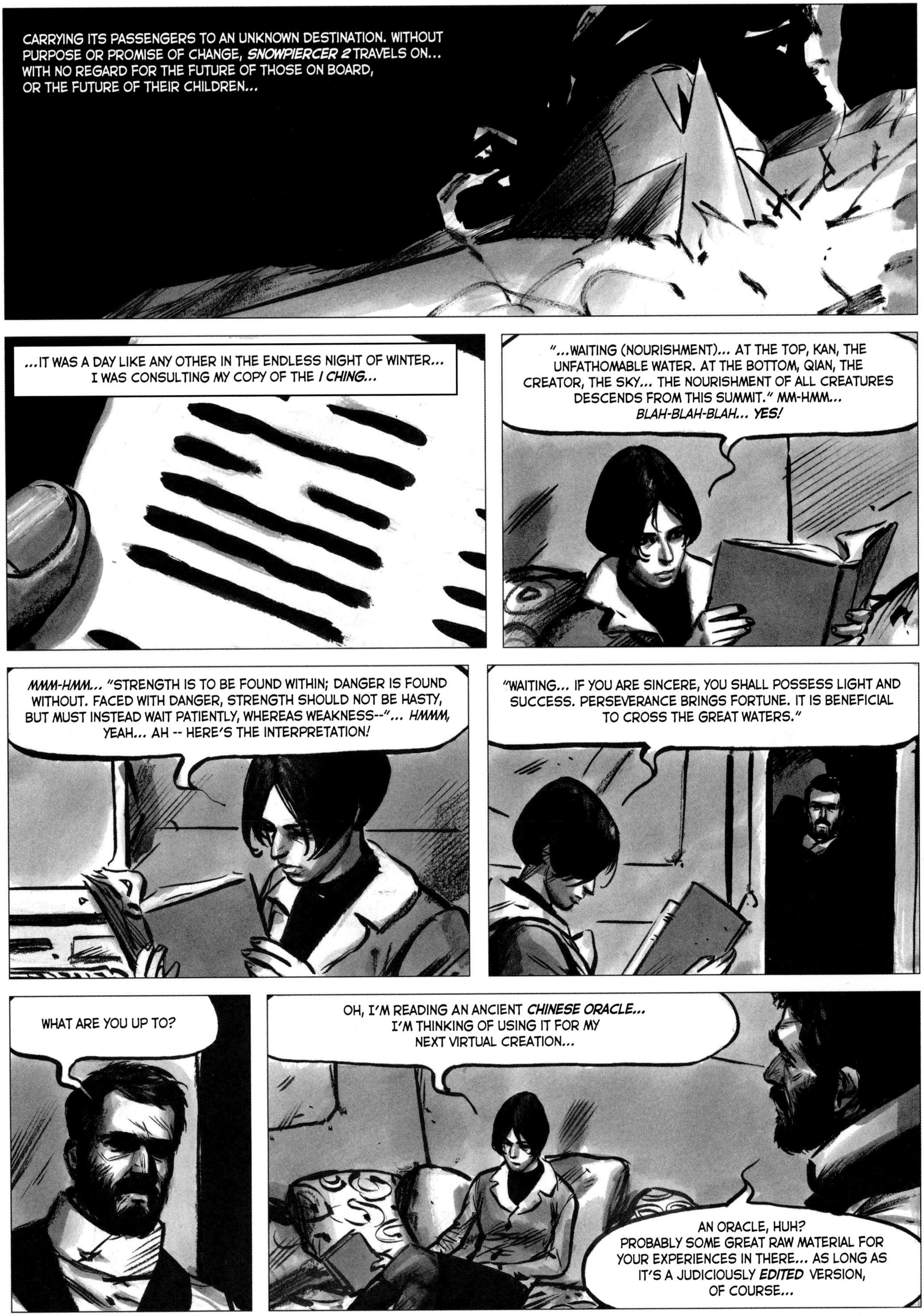
CARRYING ITS PASSENGERS TO AN UNKNOWN DESTINATION. WITHOUT PURPOSE OR PROMISE OF CHANGE, *SNOWPIERCER 2* TRAVELS ON... WITH NO REGARD FOR THE FUTURE OF THOSE ON BOARD, OR THE FUTURE OF THEIR CHILDREN...
...IT WAS A DAY LIKE ANY OTHER IN THE ENDLESS NIGHT OF WINTER... I WAS CONSULTING MY COPY OF THE *I CHING*...
"...WAITING (NOURISHMENT)... AT THE TOP, KAN, THE UNFATHOMABLE WATER. AT THE BOTTOM, QIAN, THE CREATOR, THE SKY... THE NOURISHMENT OF ALL CREATURES DESCENDS FROM THIS SUMMIT." MM-HMM... *BLAH-BLAH-BLAH... YES!*
MMM-HMM... "STRENGTH IS TO BE FOUND WITHIN; DANGER IS FOUND WITHOUT. FACED WITH DANGER, STRENGTH SHOULD NOT BE HASTY, BUT MUST INSTEAD WAIT PATIENTLY, WHEREAS WEAKNESS--"... *HMMM,* YEAH... AH -- HERE'S THE INTERPRETATION!
"WAITING... IF YOU ARE SINCERE, YOU SHALL POSSESS LIGHT AND SUCCESS. PERSEVERANCE BRINGS FORTUNE. IT IS BENEFICIAL TO CROSS THE GREAT WATERS."
WHAT ARE YOU UP TO?
OH, I'M READING AN ANCIENT *CHINESE ORACLE...* I'M THINKING OF USING IT FOR MY NEXT VIRTUAL CREATION...
AN ORACLE, HUH? PROBABLY SOME GREAT RAW MATERIAL FOR YOUR EXPERIENCES IN THERE... AS LONG AS IT'S A JUDICIOUSLY *EDITED* VERSION, OF COURSE...

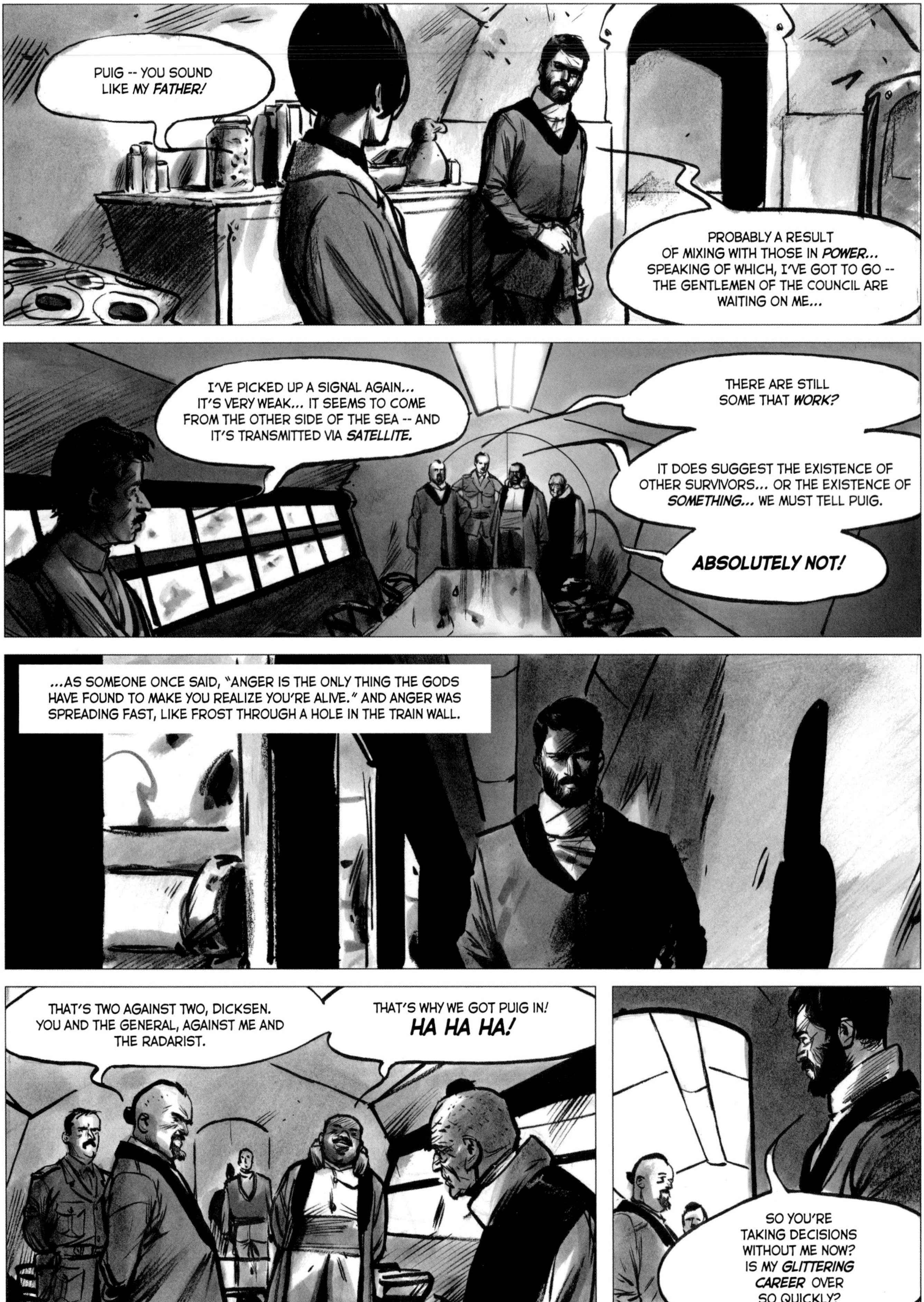
PUIG -- YOU SOUND LIKE MY *FATHER!*
PROBABLY A RESULT OF MIXING WITH THOSE IN *POWER...* SPEAKING OF WHICH, I'VE GOT TO GO -- THE GENTLEMEN OF THE COUNCIL ARE WAITING ON ME...
I'VE PICKED UP A SIGNAL AGAIN... IT'S VERY WEAK... IT SEEMS TO COME FROM THE OTHER SIDE OF THE SEA -- AND IT'S TRANSMITTED VIA *SATELLITE.*
THERE ARE STILL SOME THAT *WORK?*
IT DOES SUGGEST THE EXISTENCE OF OTHER SURVIVORS... OR THE EXISTENCE OF *SOMETHING...* WE MUST TELL PUIG.
ABSOLUTELY NOT!
...AS SOMEONE ONCE SAID, "ANGER IS THE ONLY THING THE GODS HAVE FOUND TO MAKE YOU REALIZE YOU'RE ALIVE." AND ANGER WAS SPREADING FAST, LIKE FROST THROUGH A HOLE IN THE TRAIN WALL.
THAT'S TWO AGAINST TWO, DICKSEN. YOU AND THE GENERAL, AGAINST ME AND THE RADARIST.
THAT'S WHY WE GOT PUIG IN! ***HA HA HA!***
SO YOU'RE TAKING DECISIONS WITHOUT ME NOW? IS MY *GLITTERING CAREER* OVER SO QUICKLY?

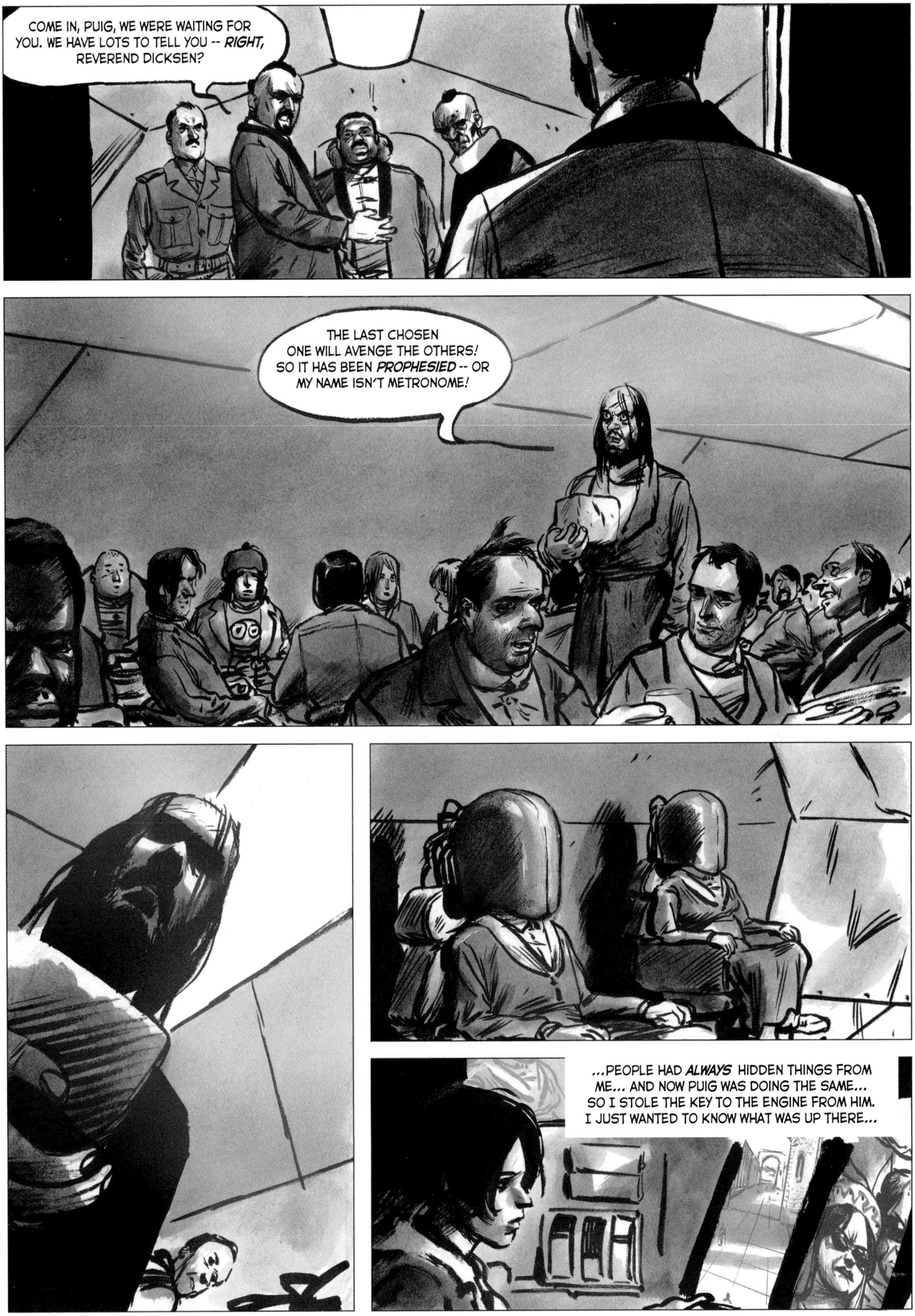
COME IN, PUIG, WE WERE WAITING FOR YOU. WE HAVE LOTS TO TELL YOU -- *RIGHT,* REVEREND DICKSEN?
THE LAST CHOSEN ONE WILL AVENGE THE OTHERS! SO IT HAS BEEN *PROPHESIED* -- OR MY NAME ISN'T METRONOME!
...PEOPLE HAD *ALWAYS* HIDDEN THINGS FROM ME... AND NOW PUIG WAS DOING THE SAME... SO I STOLE THE KEY TO THE ENGINE FROM HIM. I JUST WANTED TO KNOW WHAT WAS UP THERE...

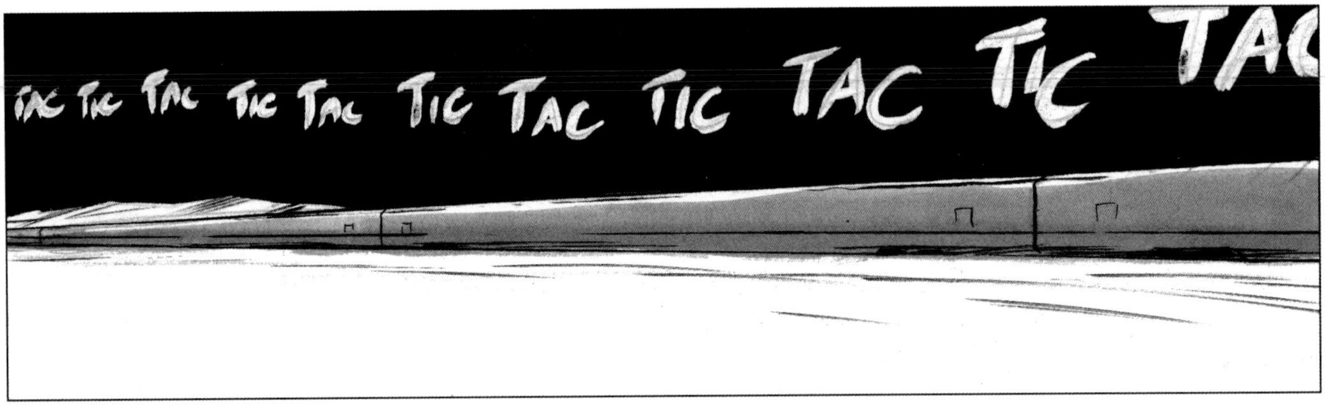
TAC TIC TAC TIC TAC TIC TAC TIC TAC TIC TAC

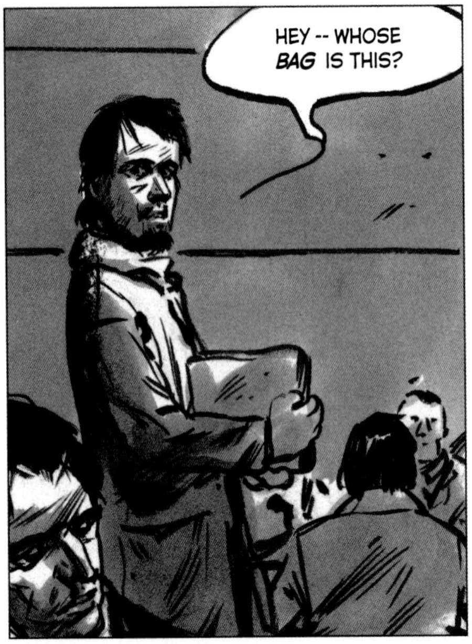
HEY -- WHOSE *BAG* IS THIS?

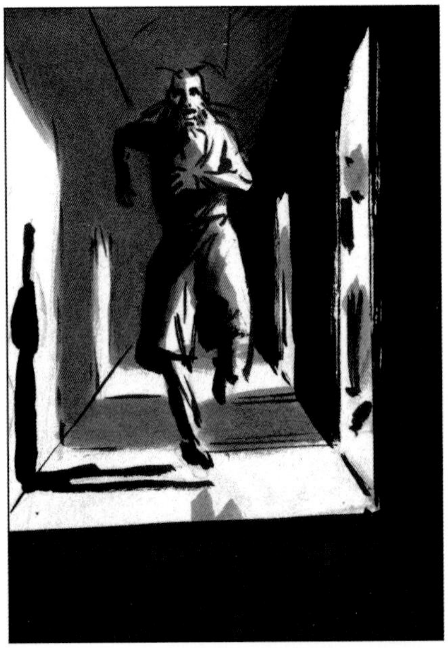

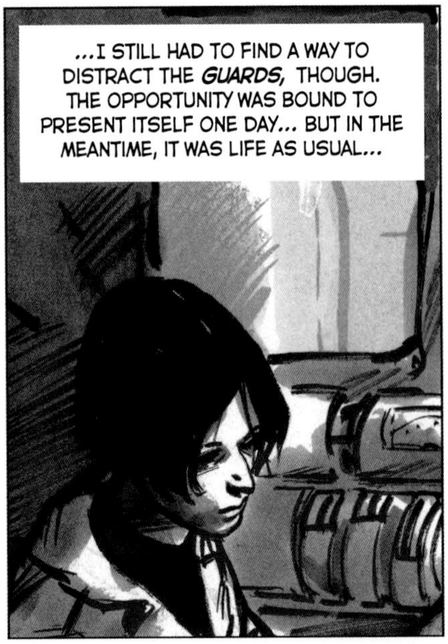
...I STILL HAD TO FIND A WAY TO DISTRACT THE *GUARDS,* THOUGH. THE OPPORTUNITY WAS BOUND TO PRESENT ITSELF ONE DAY... BUT IN THE MEANTIME, IT WAS LIFE AS USUAL...

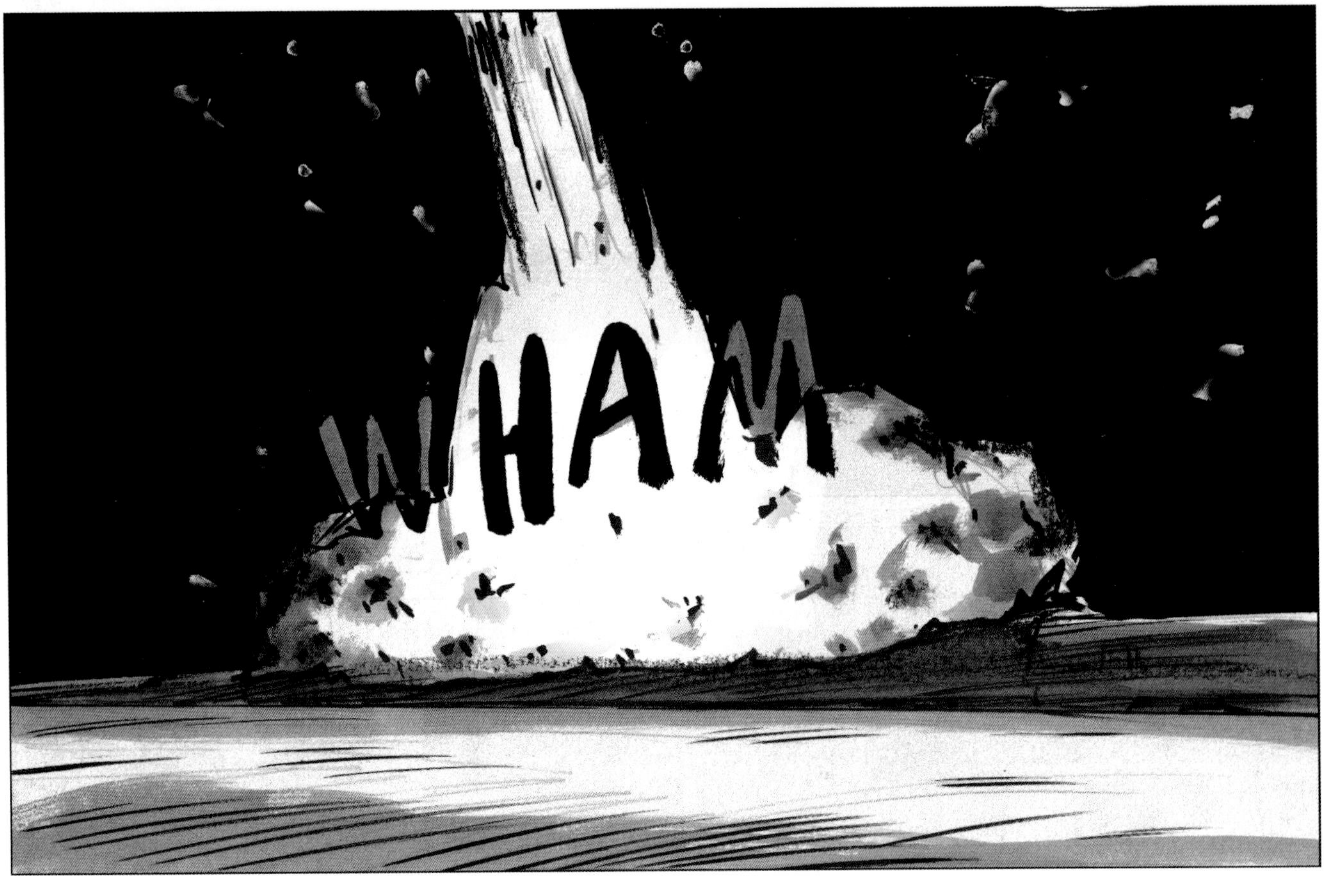
WHAM

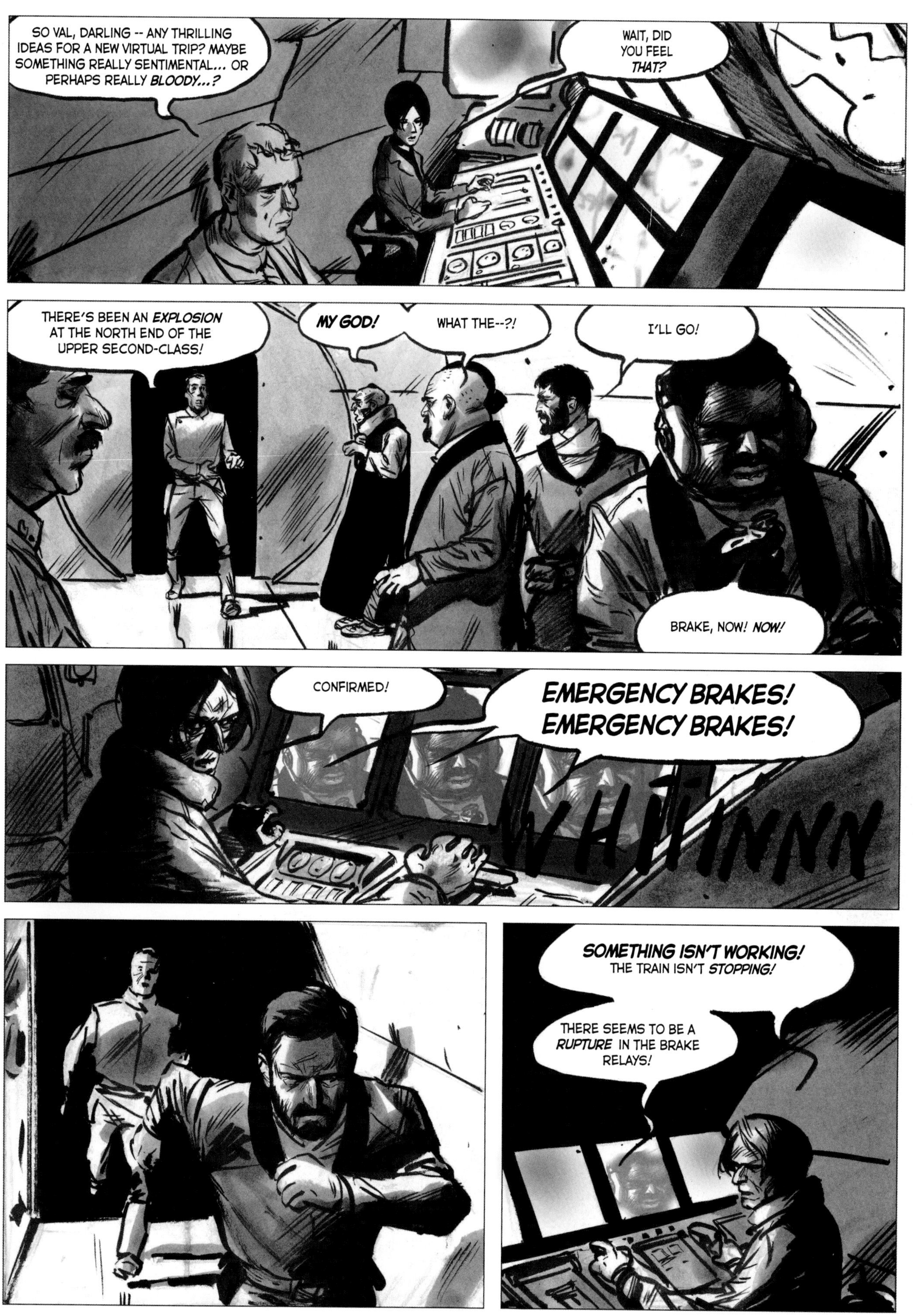
SO VAL, DARLING -- ANY THRILLING IDEAS FOR A NEW VIRTUAL TRIP? MAYBE SOMETHING REALLY SENTIMENTAL... OR PERHAPS REALLY *BLOODY...?*
WAIT, DID YOU FEEL *THAT?*
THERE'S BEEN AN *EXPLOSION* AT THE NORTH END OF THE UPPER SECOND-CLASS!
MY GOD!
WHAT THE--?!
I'LL GO!
BRAKE, NOW! ***NOW!***
CONFIRMED!
EMERGENCY BRAKES! EMERGENCY BRAKES!
WHIIINNNN
SOMETHING ISN'T WORKING! THE TRAIN ISN'T *STOPPING!*
THERE SEEMS TO BE A ***RUPTURE*** IN THE BRAKE RELAYS!

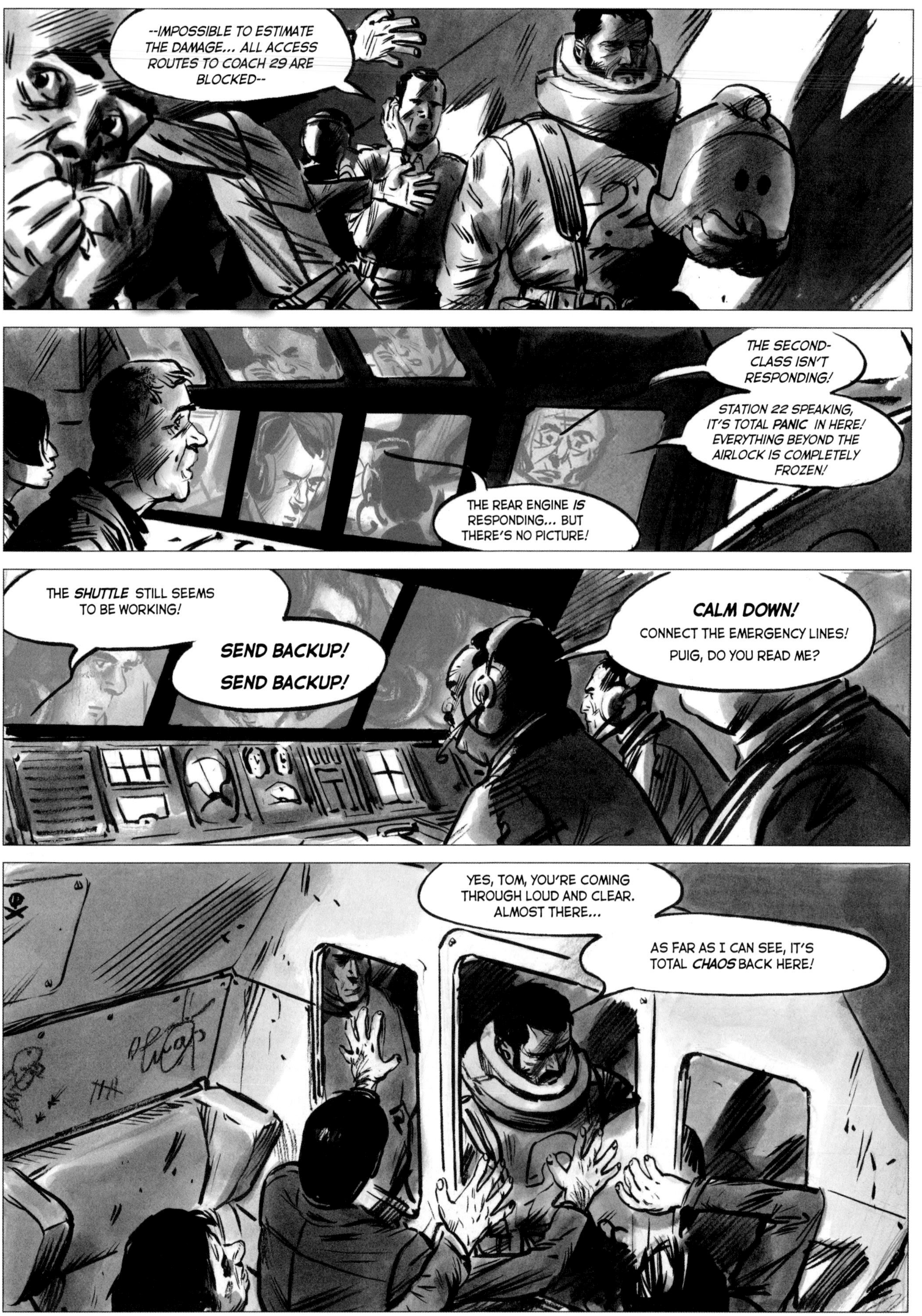
--IMPOSSIBLE TO ESTIMATE THE DAMAGE... ALL ACCESS ROUTES TO COACH 29 ARE BLOCKED--
THE SECOND-CLASS ISN'T RESPONDING!
STATION 22 SPEAKING, IT'S TOTAL PANIC IN HERE! EVERYTHING BEYOND THE AIRLOCK IS COMPLETELY FROZEN!
THE REAR ENGINE *IS* RESPONDING... BUT THERE'S NO PICTURE!
THE *SHUTTLE* STILL SEEMS TO BE WORKING!
SEND BACKUP! SEND BACKUP!
CALM DOWN!
CONNECT THE EMERGENCY LINES!
PUIG, DO YOU READ ME?
YES, TOM, YOU'RE COMING THROUGH LOUD AND CLEAR. ALMOST THERE...
AS FAR AS I CAN SEE, IT'S TOTAL *CHAOS* BACK HERE!

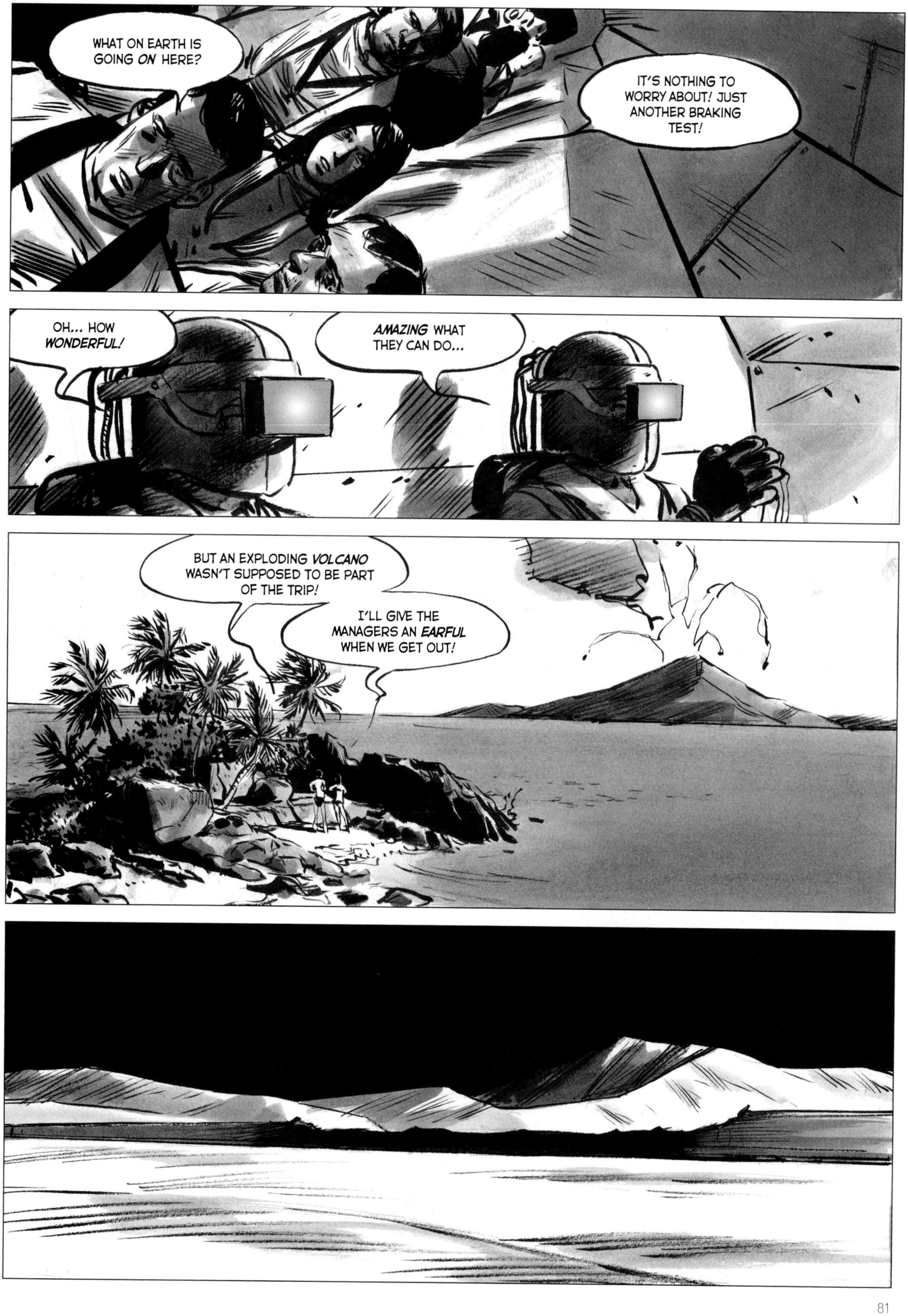
WHAT ON EARTH IS GOING *ON* HERE?
IT'S NOTHING TO WORRY ABOUT! JUST ANOTHER BRAKING TEST!
OH... HOW *WONDERFUL!*
AMAZING WHAT THEY CAN DO...
BUT AN EXPLODING *VOLCANO* WASN'T SUPPOSED TO BE PART OF THE TRIP!
I'LL GIVE THE MANAGERS AN *EARFUL* WHEN WE GET OUT!

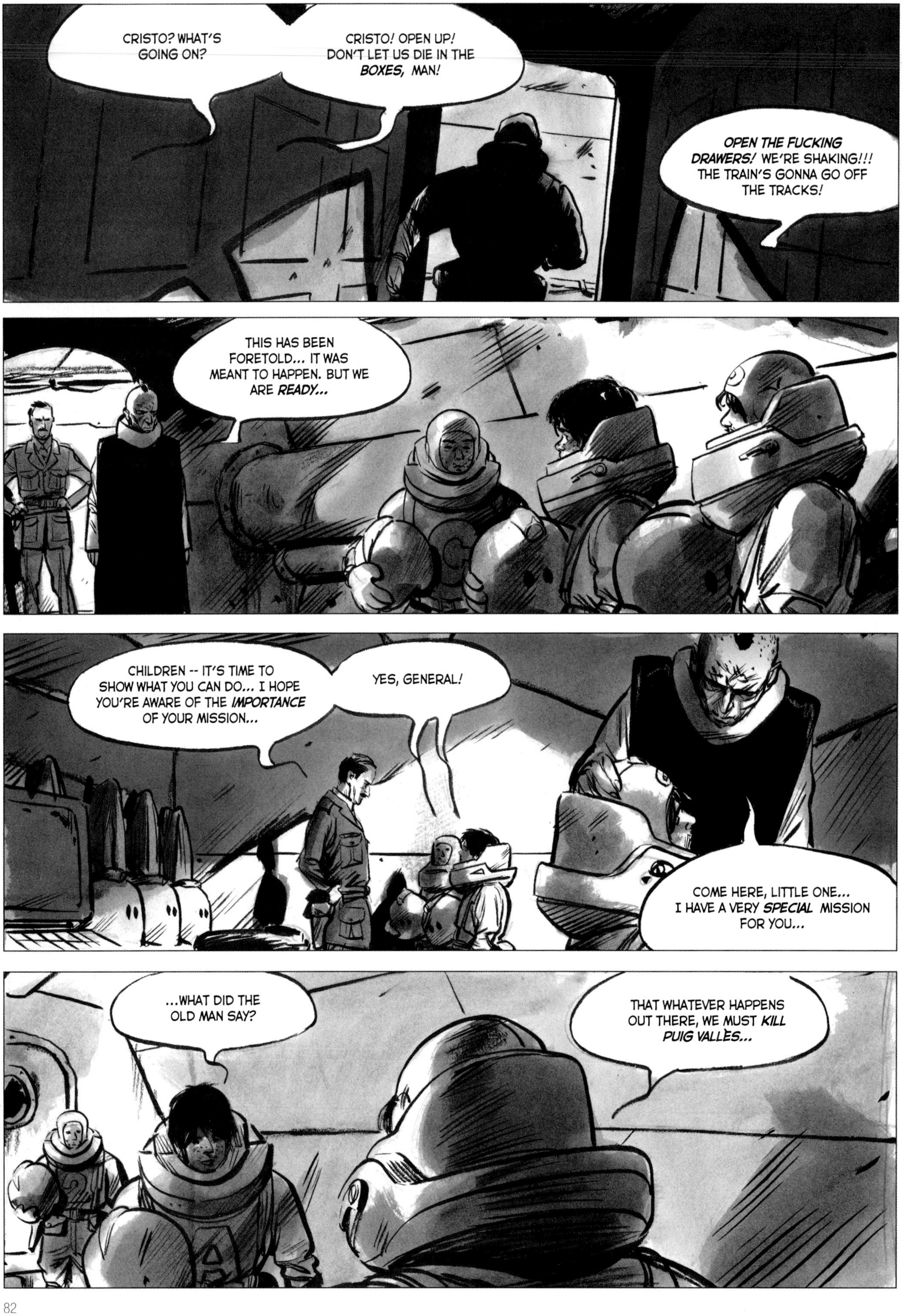
CRISTO? WHAT'S GOING ON?
CRISTO! OPEN UP! DON'T LET US DIE IN THE BOXES, MAN!
OPEN THE FUCKING DRAWERS! WE'RE SHAKING!!! THE TRAIN'S GONNA GO OFF THE TRACKS!
THIS HAS BEEN FORETOLD... IT WAS MEANT TO HAPPEN. BUT WE ARE READY...
CHILDREN -- IT'S TIME TO SHOW WHAT YOU CAN DO... I HOPE YOU'RE AWARE OF THE IMPORTANCE OF YOUR MISSION...
YES, GENERAL!
COME HERE, LITTLE ONE... I HAVE A VERY SPECIAL MISSION FOR YOU...
...WHAT DID THE OLD MAN SAY?
THAT WHATEVER HAPPENS OUT THERE, WE MUST KILL PUIG VALLÈS...

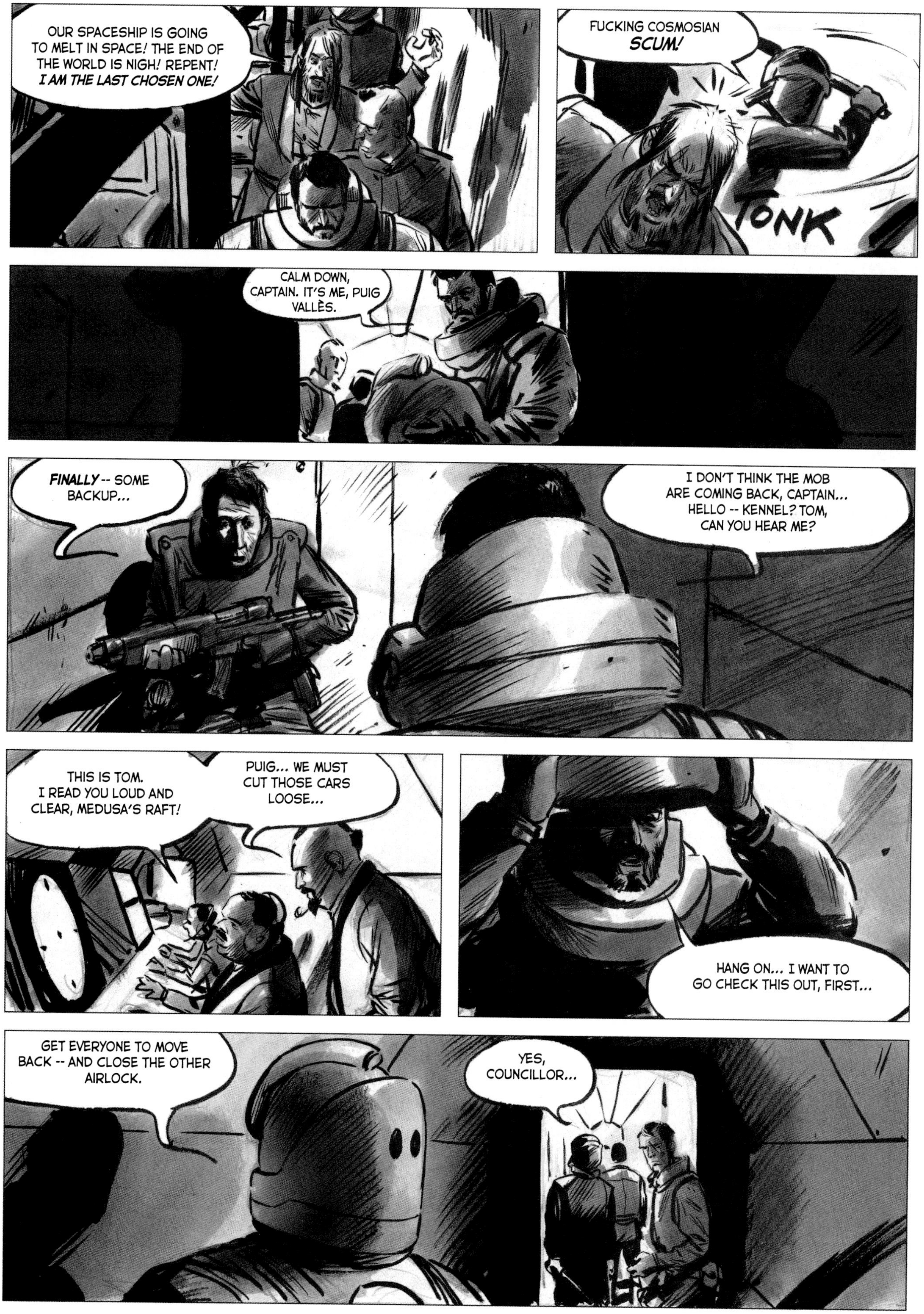
OUR SPACESHIP IS GOING TO MELT IN SPACE! THE END OF THE WORLD IS NIGH! REPENT! I AM THE LAST CHOSEN ONE!
FUCKING COSMOSIAN SCUM!
TONK
CALM DOWN, CAPTAIN. IT'S ME, PUIG VALLÈS.
FINALLY -- SOME BACKUP...
I DON'T THINK THE MOB ARE COMING BACK, CAPTAIN... HELLO -- KENNEL? TOM, CAN YOU HEAR ME?
THIS IS TOM. I READ YOU LOUD AND CLEAR, MEDUSA'S RAFT!
PUIG... WE MUST CUT THOSE CARS LOOSE...
HANG ON... I WANT TO GO CHECK THIS OUT, FIRST...
GET EVERYONE TO MOVE BACK -- AND CLOSE THE OTHER AIRLOCK.
YES, COUNCILLOR...

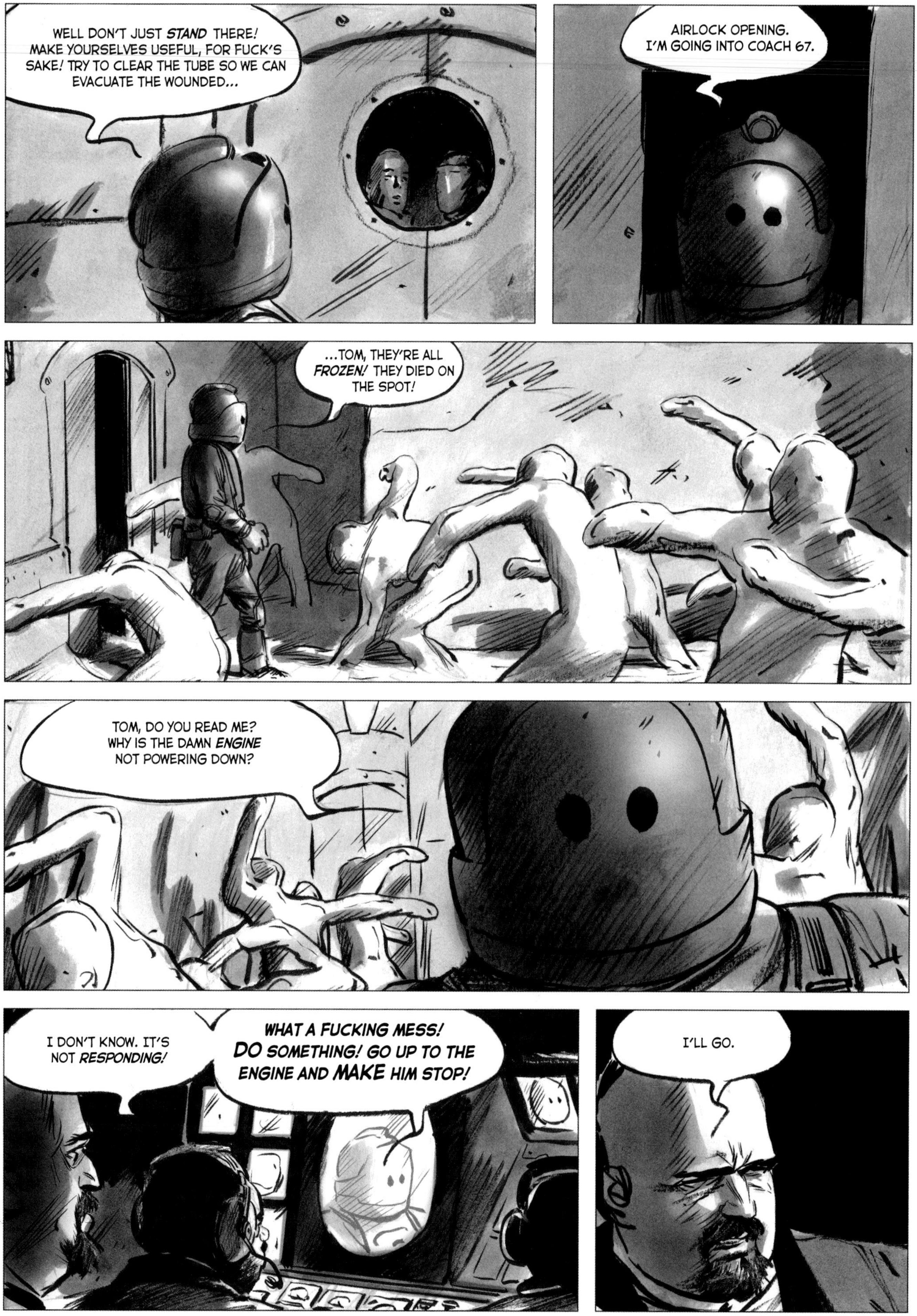
WELL DON'T JUST *STAND* THERE! MAKE YOURSELVES USEFUL, FOR FUCK'S SAKE! TRY TO CLEAR THE TUBE SO WE CAN EVACUATE THE WOUNDED...
AIRLOCK OPENING. I'M GOING INTO COACH 67.
...TOM, THEY'RE ALL *FROZEN!* THEY DIED ON THE SPOT!
TOM, DO YOU READ ME? WHY IS THE DAMN *ENGINE* NOT POWERING DOWN?
I DON'T KNOW. IT'S NOT *RESPONDING!*
WHAT A FUCKING MESS! DO SOMETHING! GO UP TO THE ENGINE AND MAKE HIM STOP!
I'LL GO.

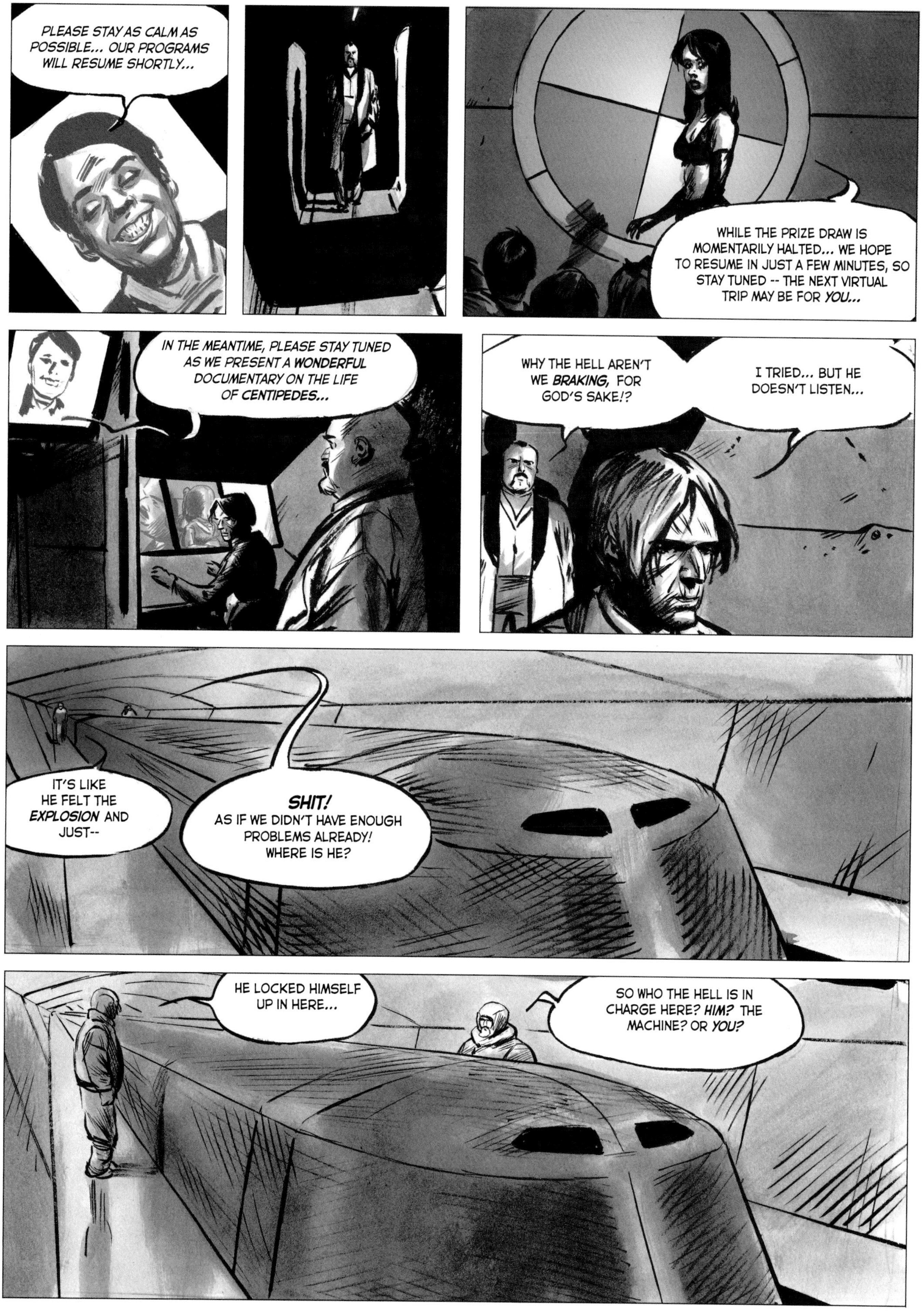

PLEASE STAY AS CALM AS POSSIBLE... OUR PROGRAMS WILL RESUME SHORTLY...
WHILE THE PRIZE DRAW IS MOMENTARILY HALTED... WE HOPE TO RESUME IN JUST A FEW MINUTES, SO STAY TUNED -- THE NEXT VIRTUAL TRIP MAY BE FOR YOU...
IN THE MEANTIME, PLEASE STAY TUNED AS WE PRESENT A WONDERFUL DOCUMENTARY ON THE LIFE OF CENTIPEDES...
WHY THE HELL AREN'T WE BRAKING, FOR GOD'S SAKE!?
I TRIED... BUT HE DOESN'T LISTEN...
IT'S LIKE HE FELT THE EXPLOSION AND JUST--
SHIT! AS IF WE DIDN'T HAVE ENOUGH PROBLEMS ALREADY! WHERE IS HE?
HE LOCKED HIMSELF UP IN HERE...
SO WHO THE HELL IS IN CHARGE HERE? HIM? THE MACHINE? OR YOU?

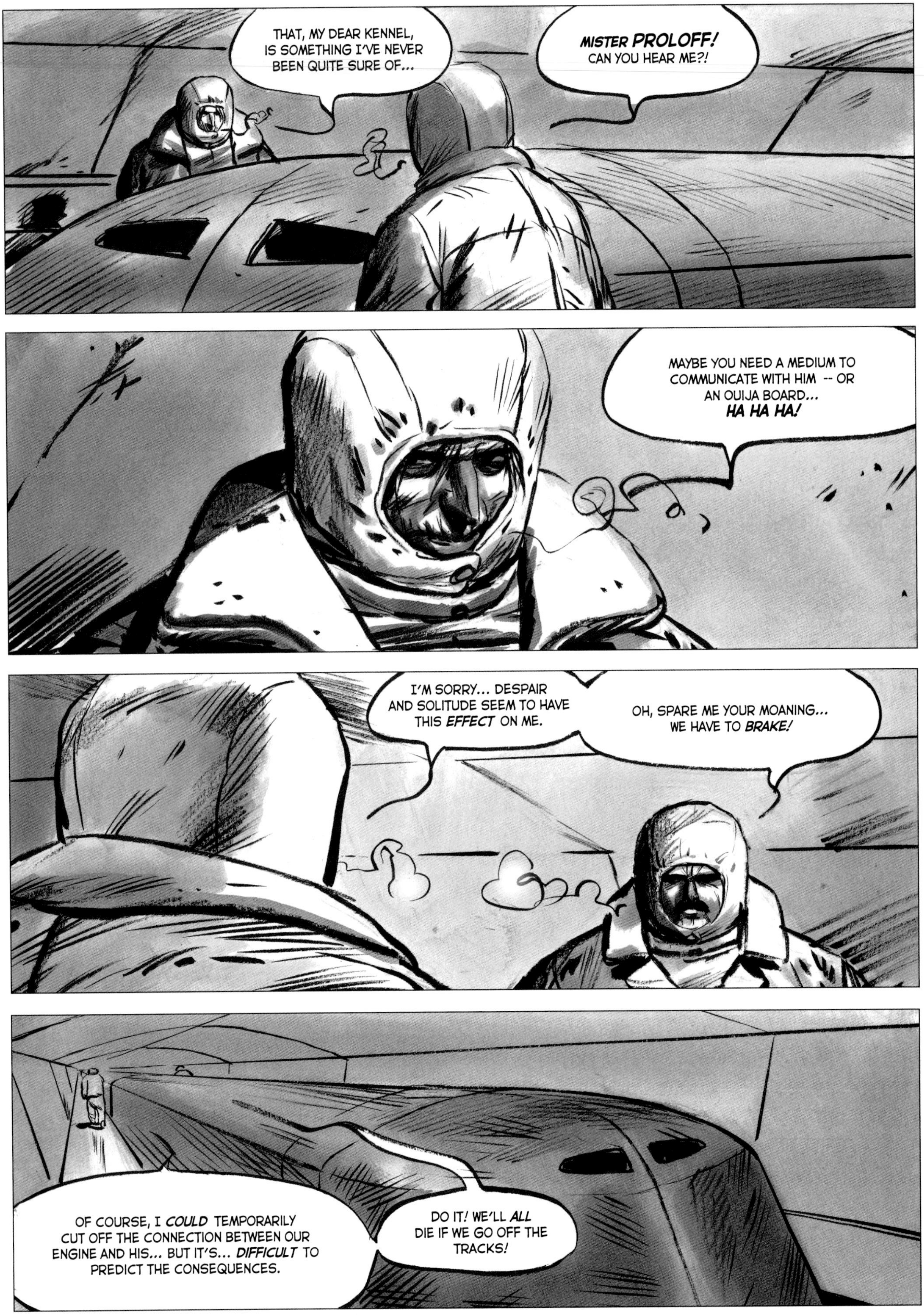
THAT, MY DEAR KENNEL, IS SOMETHING I'VE NEVER BEEN QUITE SURE OF...
MISTER PROLOFF! CAN YOU HEAR ME?!
MAYBE YOU NEED A MEDIUM TO COMMUNICATE WITH HIM -- OR AN OUIJA BOARD... HA HA HA!
I'M SORRY... DESPAIR AND SOLITUDE SEEM TO HAVE THIS EFFECT ON ME.
OH, SPARE ME YOUR MOANING... WE HAVE TO BRAKE!
OF COURSE, I COULD TEMPORARILY CUT OFF THE CONNECTION BETWEEN OUR ENGINE AND HIS... BUT IT'S... DIFFICULT TO PREDICT THE CONSEQUENCES.
DO IT! WE'LL ALL DIE IF WE GO OFF THE TRACKS!

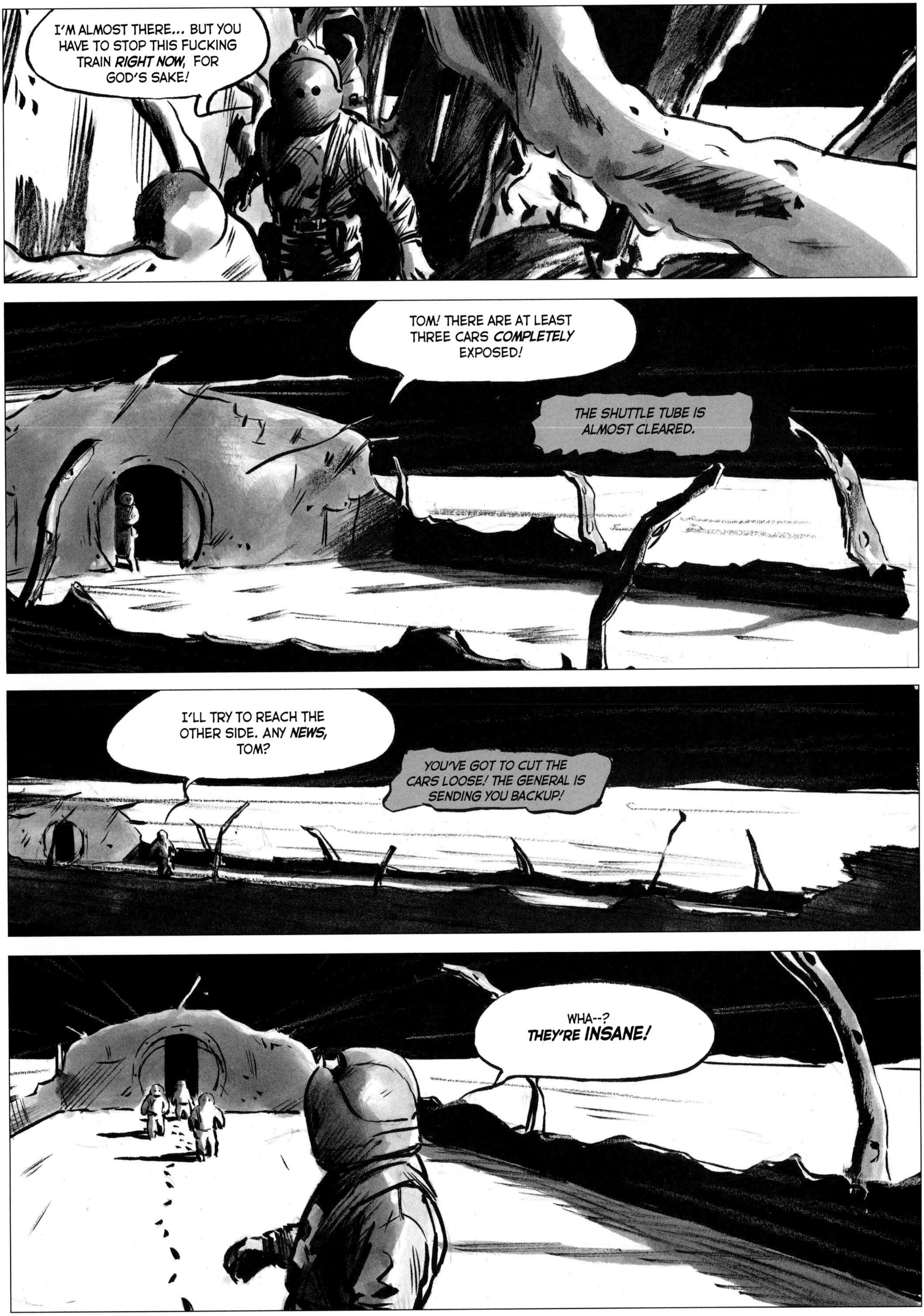
I'M ALMOST THERE... BUT YOU HAVE TO STOP THIS FUCKING TRAIN RIGHT NOW, FOR GOD'S SAKE!
TOM! THERE ARE AT LEAST THREE CARS COMPLETELY EXPOSED!
THE SHUTTLE TUBE IS ALMOST CLEARED.
I'LL TRY TO REACH THE OTHER SIDE. ANY NEWS, TOM?
YOU'VE GOT TO CUT THE CARS LOOSE! THE GENERAL IS SENDING YOU BACKUP!
WHA--? THEY'RE INSANE!

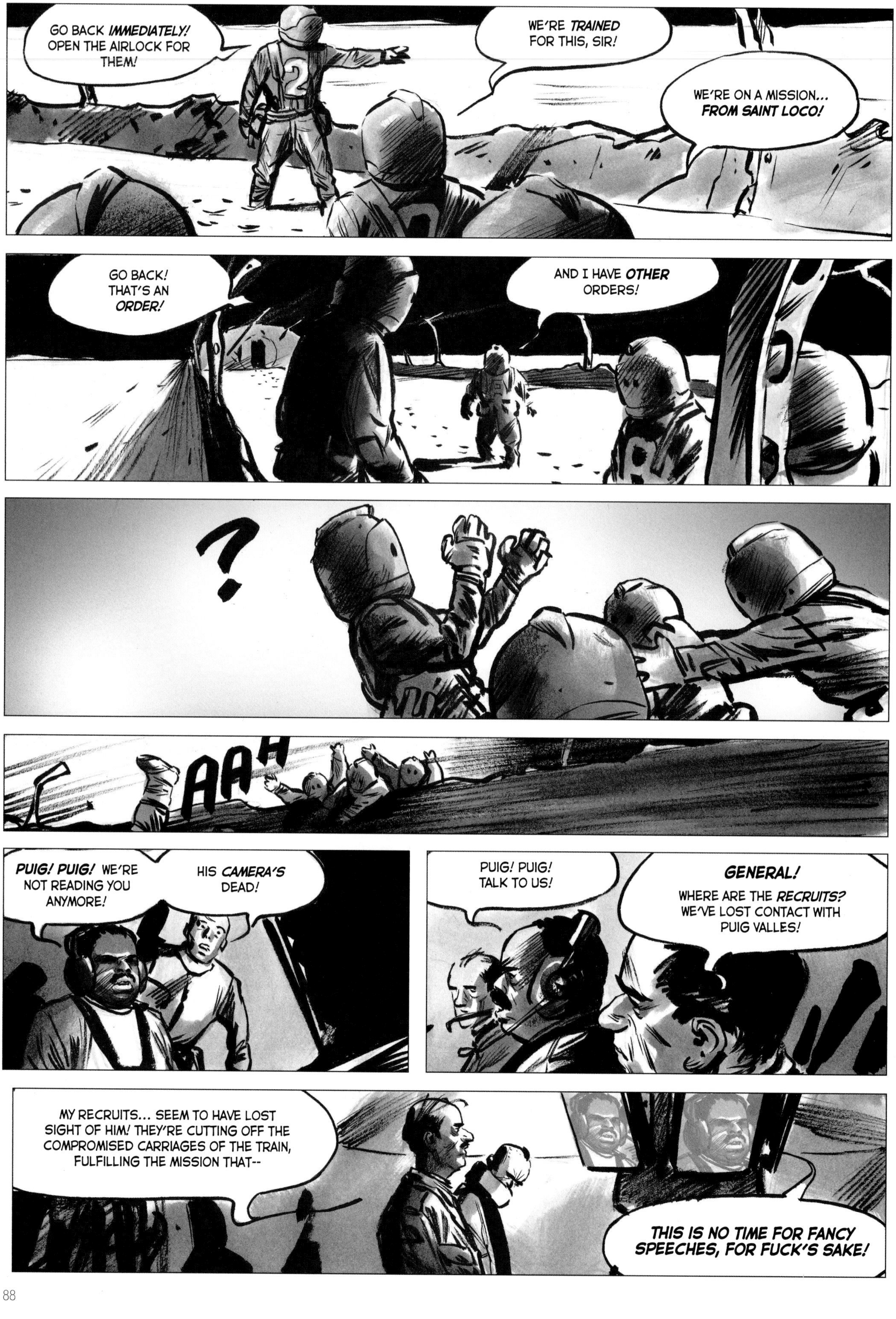
GO BACK *IMMEDIATELY!* OPEN THE AIRLOCK FOR THEM!
WE'RE *TRAINED* FOR THIS, SIR!
WE'RE ON A MISSION... **FROM SAINT LOCO!**
GO BACK! THAT'S AN *ORDER!*
AND I HAVE **OTHER** ORDERS!
?
AAH
PUIG! PUIG! WE'RE NOT READING YOU ANYMORE!
HIS *CAMERA'S* DEAD!
PUIG! PUIG! TALK TO US!
GENERAL!
WHERE ARE THE *RECRUITS?* WE'VE LOST CONTACT WITH PUIG VALLES!
MY RECRUITS... SEEM TO HAVE LOST SIGHT OF HIM! THEY'RE CUTTING OFF THE COMPROMISED CARRIAGES OF THE TRAIN, FULFILLING THE MISSION THAT--
THIS IS NO TIME FOR FANCY SPEECHES, FOR FUCK'S SAKE!

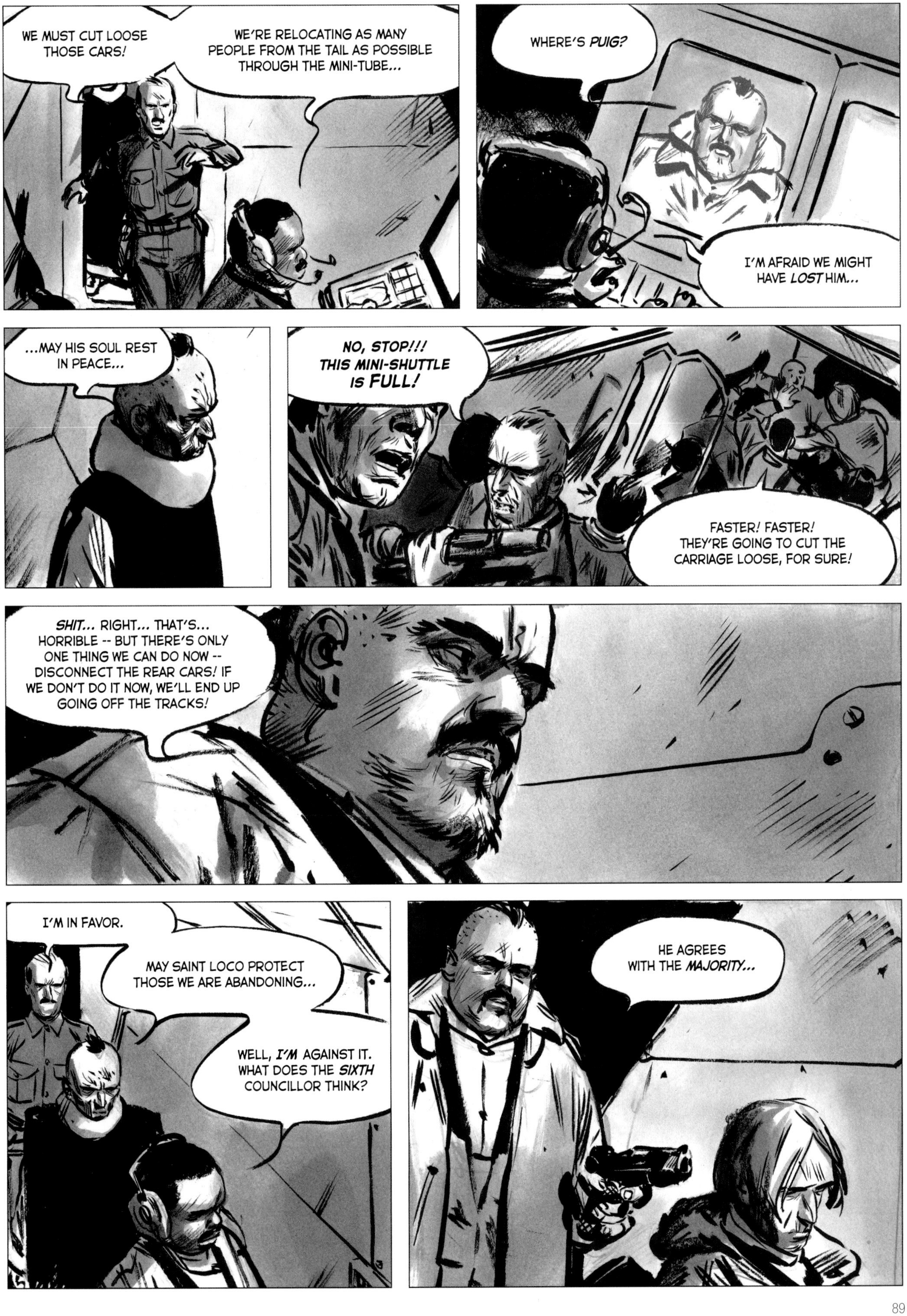
WE MUST CUT LOOSE THOSE CARS!
WE'RE RELOCATING AS MANY PEOPLE FROM THE TAIL AS POSSIBLE THROUGH THE MINI-TUBE...
WHERE'S PUIG?
I'M AFRAID WE MIGHT HAVE LOST HIM...
...MAY HIS SOUL REST IN PEACE...
NO, STOP!!! THIS MINI-SHUTTLE IS FULL!
FASTER! FASTER! THEY'RE GOING TO CUT THE CARRIAGE LOOSE, FOR SURE!
SHIT... RIGHT... THAT'S... HORRIBLE -- BUT THERE'S ONLY ONE THING WE CAN DO NOW -- DISCONNECT THE REAR CARS! IF WE DON'T DO IT NOW, WE'LL END UP GOING OFF THE TRACKS!
I'M IN FAVOR.
MAY SAINT LOCO PROTECT THOSE WE ARE ABANDONING...
WELL, I'M AGAINST IT. WHAT DOES THE SIXTH COUNCILLOR THINK?
HE AGREES WITH THE MAJORITY...

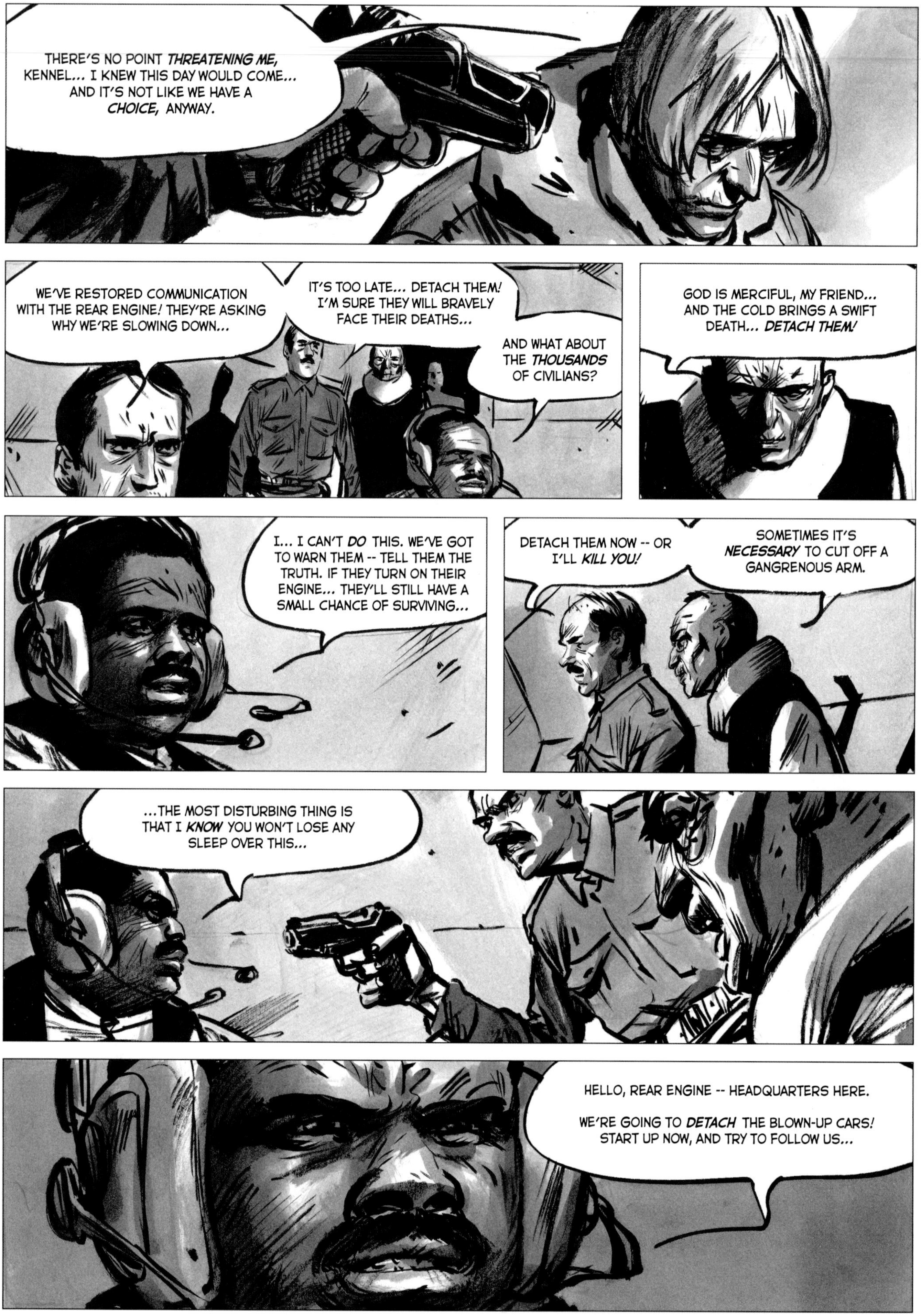

THERE'S NO POINT THREATENING ME, KENNEL... I KNEW THIS DAY WOULD COME... AND IT'S NOT LIKE WE HAVE A CHOICE, ANYWAY.
WE'VE RESTORED COMMUNICATION WITH THE REAR ENGINE! THEY'RE ASKING WHY WE'RE SLOWING DOWN...
IT'S TOO LATE... DETACH THEM! I'M SURE THEY WILL BRAVELY FACE THEIR DEATHS...
AND WHAT ABOUT THE THOUSANDS OF CIVILIANS?
GOD IS MERCIFUL, MY FRIEND... AND THE COLD BRINGS A SWIFT DEATH... DETACH THEM!
I... I CAN'T DO THIS. WE'VE GOT TO WARN THEM -- TELL THEM THE TRUTH. IF THEY TURN ON THEIR ENGINE... THEY'LL STILL HAVE A SMALL CHANCE OF SURVIVING...
DETACH THEM NOW -- OR I'LL KILL YOU!
SOMETIMES IT'S NECESSARY TO CUT OFF A GANGRENOUS ARM.
...THE MOST DISTURBING THING IS THAT I KNOW YOU WON'T LOSE ANY SLEEP OVER THIS...
HELLO, REAR ENGINE -- HEADQUARTERS HERE.
WE'RE GOING TO DETACH THE BLOWN-UP CARS! START UP NOW, AND TRY TO FOLLOW US...

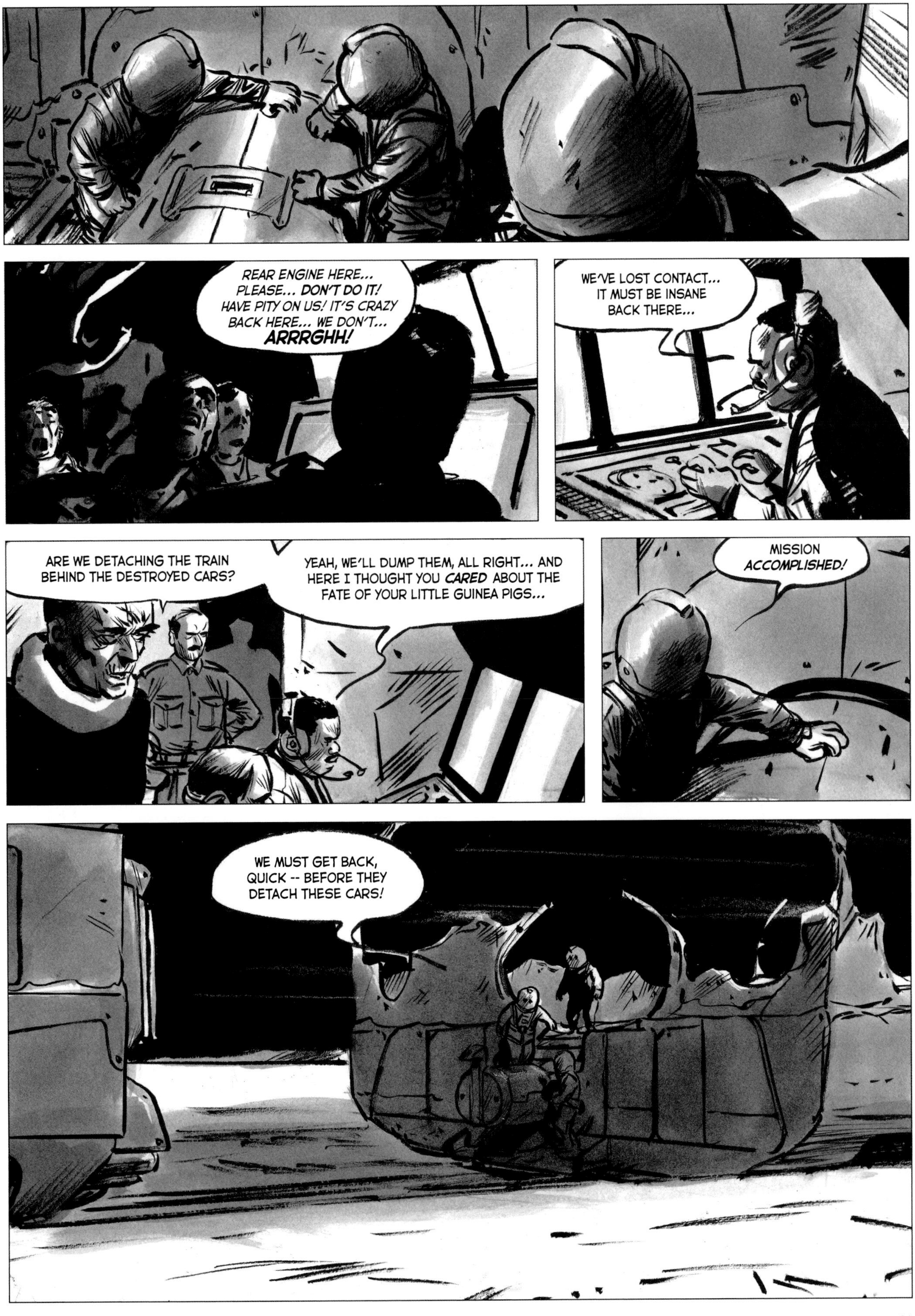
REAR ENGINE HERE... PLEASE... DON'T DO IT! HAVE PITY ON US! IT'S CRAZY BACK HERE... WE DON'T... ARRRGHH!
WE'VE LOST CONTACT... IT MUST BE INSANE BACK THERE...
ARE WE DETACHING THE TRAIN BEHIND THE DESTROYED CARS?
YEAH, WE'LL DUMP THEM, ALL RIGHT... AND HERE I THOUGHT YOU CARED ABOUT THE FATE OF YOUR LITTLE GUINEA PIGS...
MISSION ACCOMPLISHED!
WE MUST GET BACK, QUICK -- BEFORE THEY DETACH THESE CARS!

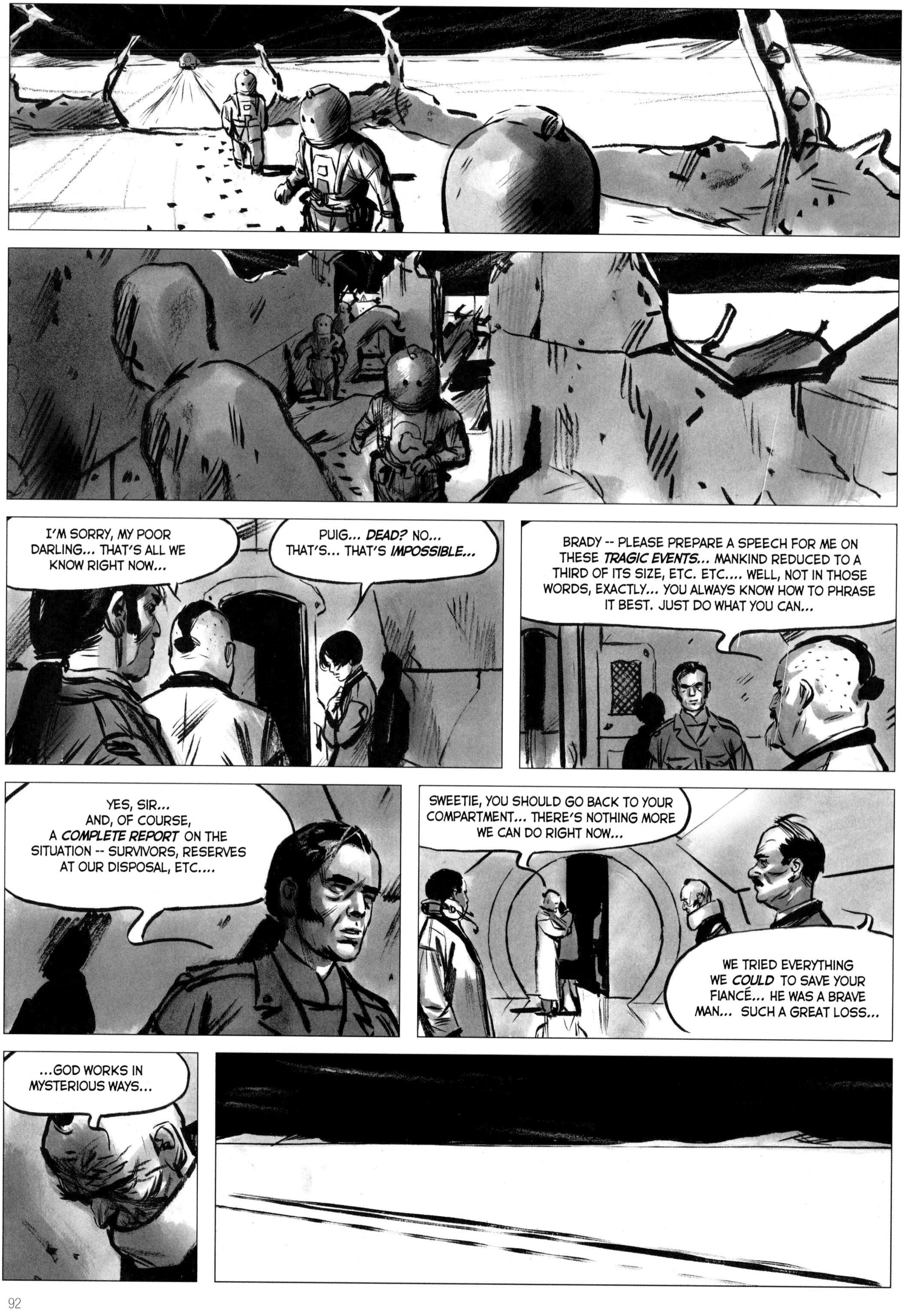
I'M SORRY, MY POOR DARLING... THAT'S ALL WE KNOW RIGHT NOW...
PUIG... DEAD? NO... THAT'S... THAT'S IMPOSSIBLE...
BRADY -- PLEASE PREPARE A SPEECH FOR ME ON THESE TRAGIC EVENTS... MANKIND REDUCED TO A THIRD OF ITS SIZE, ETC. ETC.... WELL, NOT IN THOSE WORDS, EXACTLY... YOU ALWAYS KNOW HOW TO PHRASE IT BEST. JUST DO WHAT YOU CAN...
YES, SIR... AND, OF COURSE, A COMPLETE REPORT ON THE SITUATION -- SURVIVORS, RESERVES AT OUR DISPOSAL, ETC....
SWEETIE, YOU SHOULD GO BACK TO YOUR COMPARTMENT... THERE'S NOTHING MORE WE CAN DO RIGHT NOW...
WE TRIED EVERYTHING WE COULD TO SAVE YOUR FIANCÉ... HE WAS A BRAVE MAN... SUCH A GREAT LOSS...
...GOD WORKS IN MYSTERIOUS WAYS...

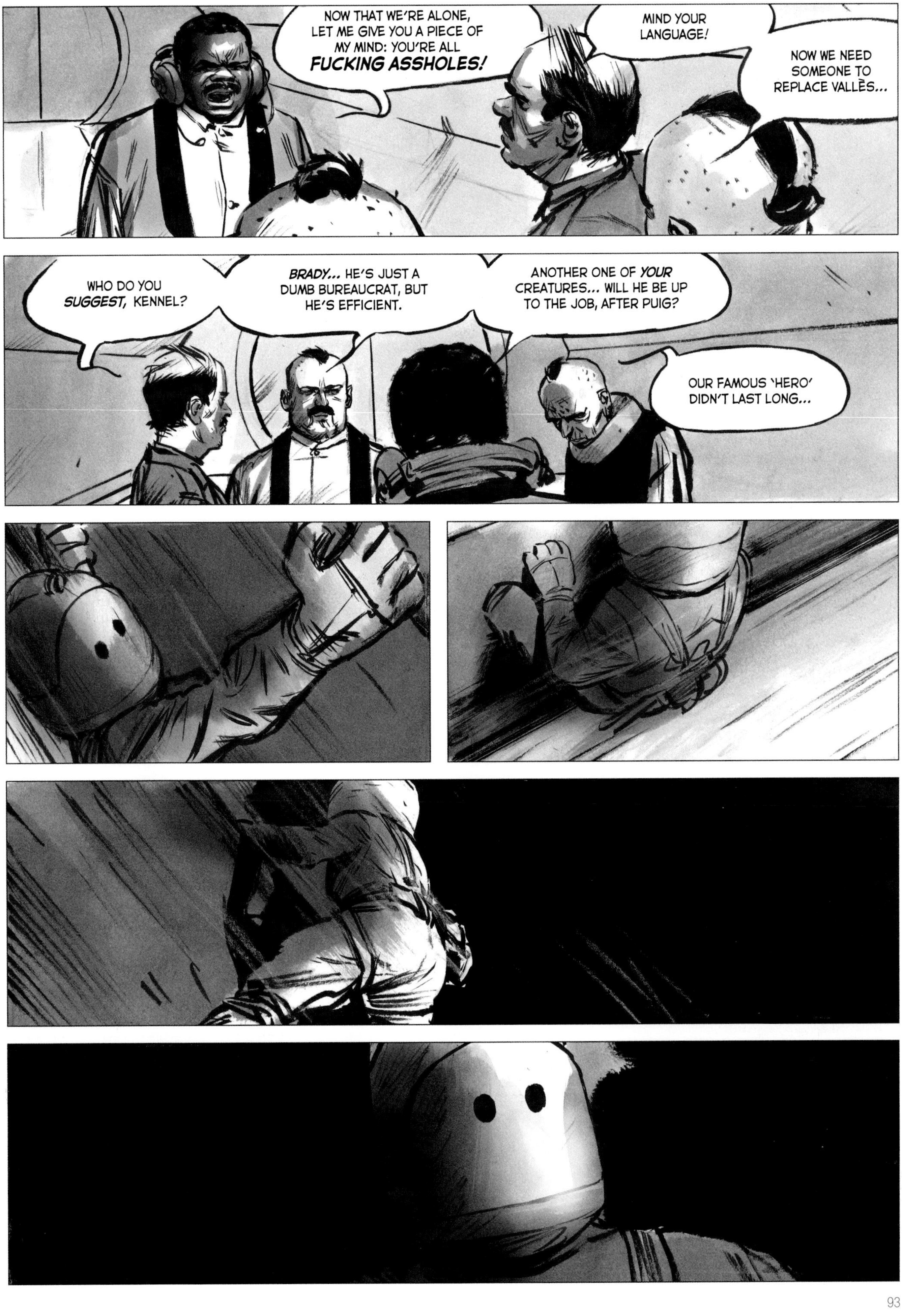
NOW THAT WE'RE ALONE, LET ME GIVE YOU A PIECE OF MY MIND: YOU'RE ALL **FUCKING ASSHOLES!**
MIND YOUR LANGUAGE!
NOW WE NEED SOMEONE TO REPLACE VALLÈS...
WHO DO YOU *SUGGEST,* KENNEL?
BRADY... HE'S JUST A DUMB BUREAUCRAT, BUT HE'S EFFICIENT.
ANOTHER ONE OF *YOUR* CREATURES... WILL HE BE UP TO THE JOB, AFTER PUIG?
OUR FAMOUS 'HERO' DIDN'T LAST LONG...

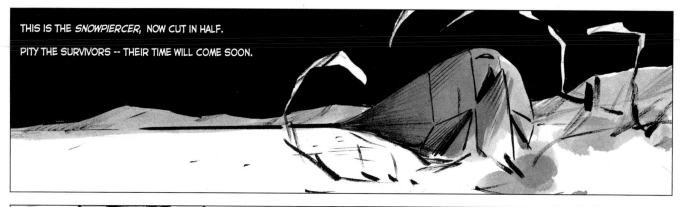

THIS IS THE *SNOWPIERCER*, NOW CUT IN HALF.

PITY THE SURVIVORS -- THEIR TIME WILL COME SOON.

COUNCILLOR *PUIG!* WE THOUGHT YOU WERE *DEAD!*

ME TOO... SO TELL *NO ONE.* FIND ME TWENTY LOYAL GUYS -- SOLDIERS AND EXPLORERS...

"BY *RETURNING,* WE BECOME EXEMPT FROM GUILT, REACHING A STATE OF *INNOCENCE.* UNEXPECTED MISFORTUNE COMES FROM WITHOUT. FIRMNESS ALSO COMES FROM WITHOUT, UNTIL IT MASTERS WHAT LIES WITHIN: *MOVEMENT AND STRENGTH.* SUCCESS WILL ONLY COME WITH THE RIGHT ATTITUDE. IF SOMEONE HAS NOT YET ATTAINED THE SELF THEY SHOULD BE, THEY WILL FACE ONLY *MISFORTUNE.* WHEN INNOCENCE IS LOST, WHERE THEN CAN WE GO...?"

YES... WHERE *CAN* WE GO?

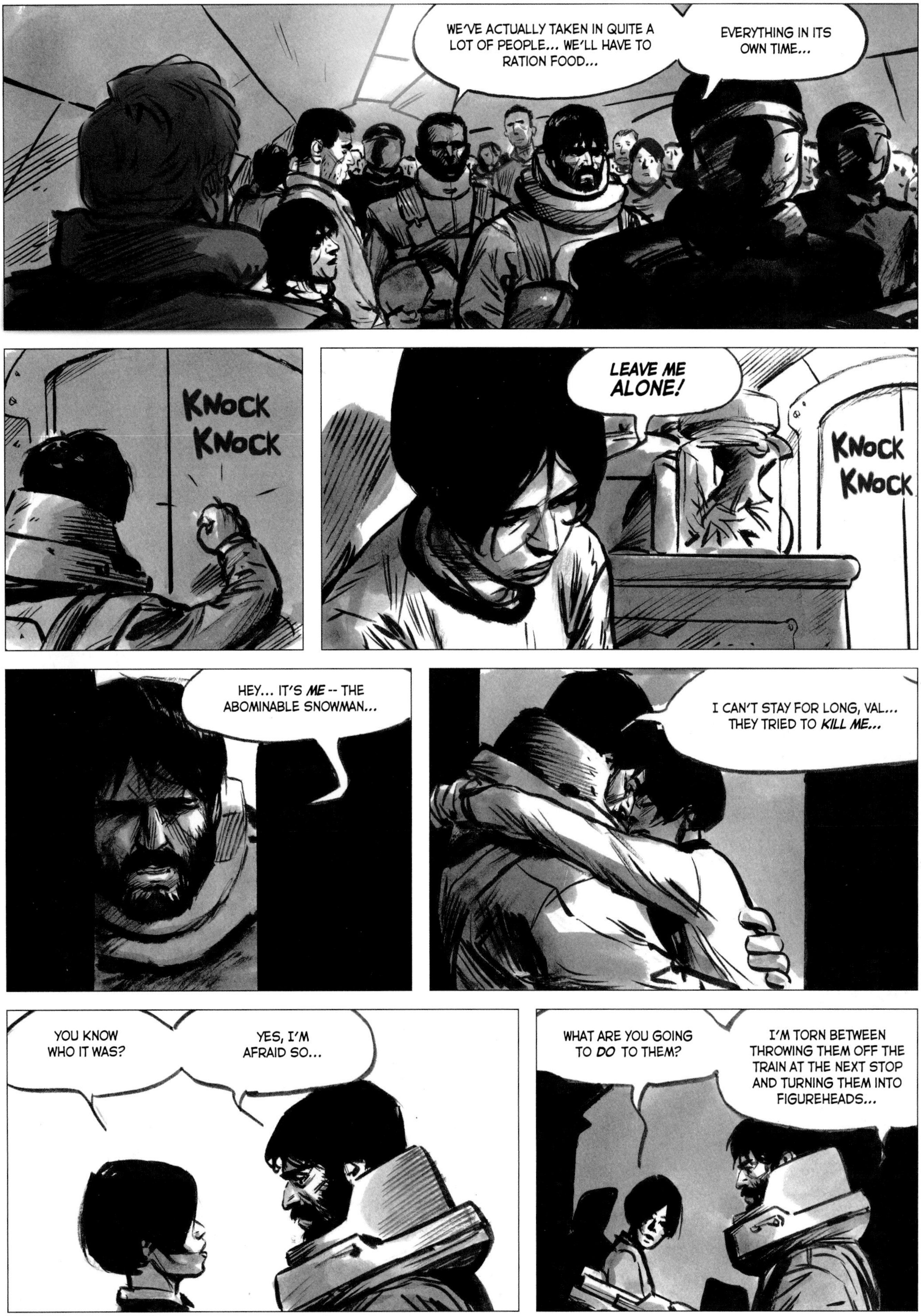
WE'VE ACTUALLY TAKEN IN QUITE A LOT OF PEOPLE... WE'LL HAVE TO RATION FOOD...
EVERYTHING IN ITS OWN TIME...
KNOCK KNOCK
LEAVE ME ALONE!
KNOCK KNOCK
HEY... IT'S *ME* -- THE ABOMINABLE SNOWMAN...
I CAN'T STAY FOR LONG, VAL... THEY TRIED TO *KILL ME...*
YOU KNOW WHO IT WAS?
YES, I'M AFRAID SO...
WHAT ARE YOU GOING TO *DO* TO THEM?
I'M TORN BETWEEN THROWING THEM OFF THE TRAIN AT THE NEXT STOP AND TURNING THEM INTO FIGUREHEADS...

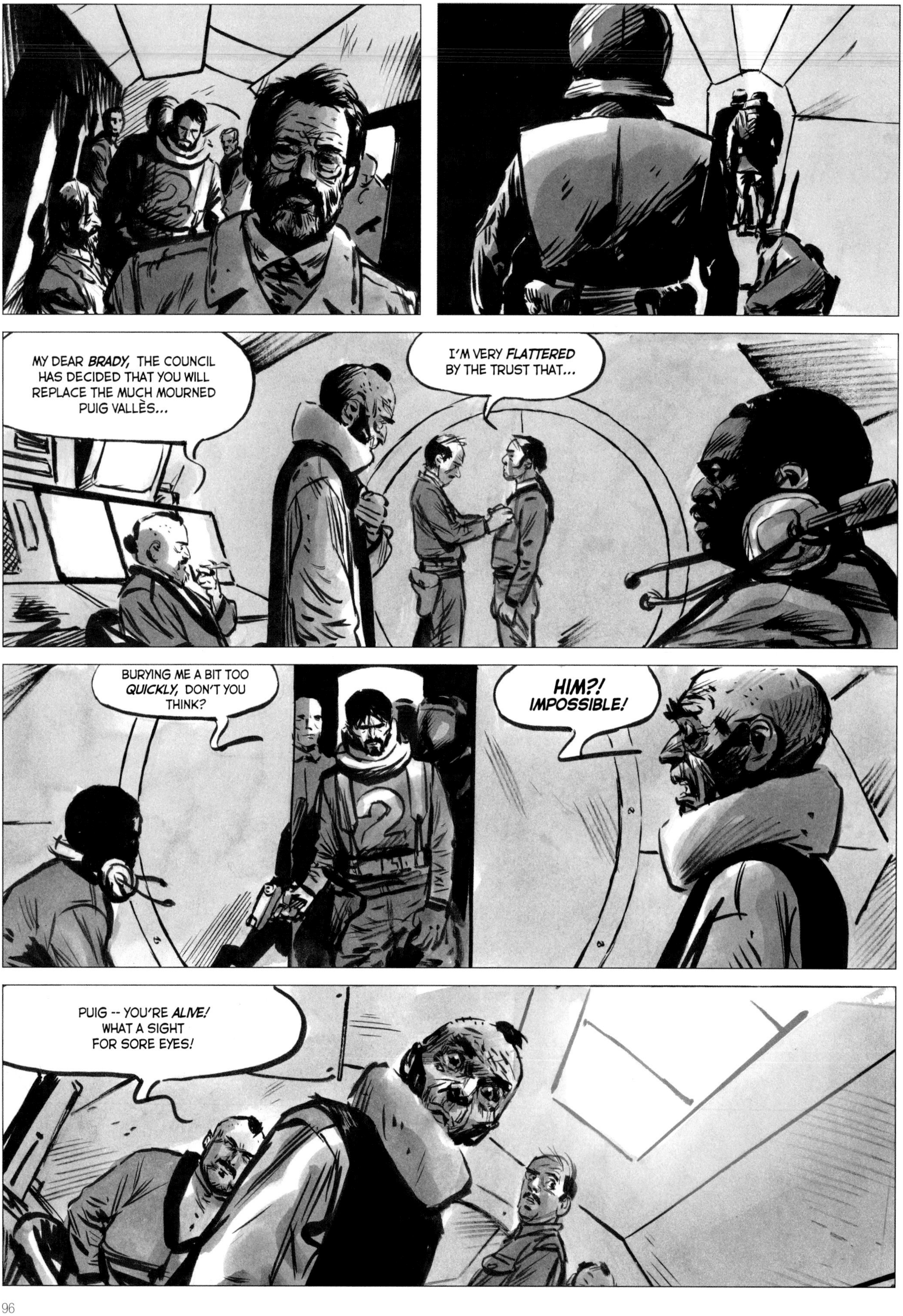
MY DEAR BRADY, THE COUNCIL HAS DECIDED THAT YOU WILL REPLACE THE MUCH MOURNED PUIG VALLÈS...
I'M VERY FLATTERED BY THE TRUST THAT...
BURYING ME A BIT TOO QUICKLY, DON'T YOU THINK?
HIM?! IMPOSSIBLE!
PUIG -- YOU'RE ALIVE! WHAT A SIGHT FOR SORE EYES!

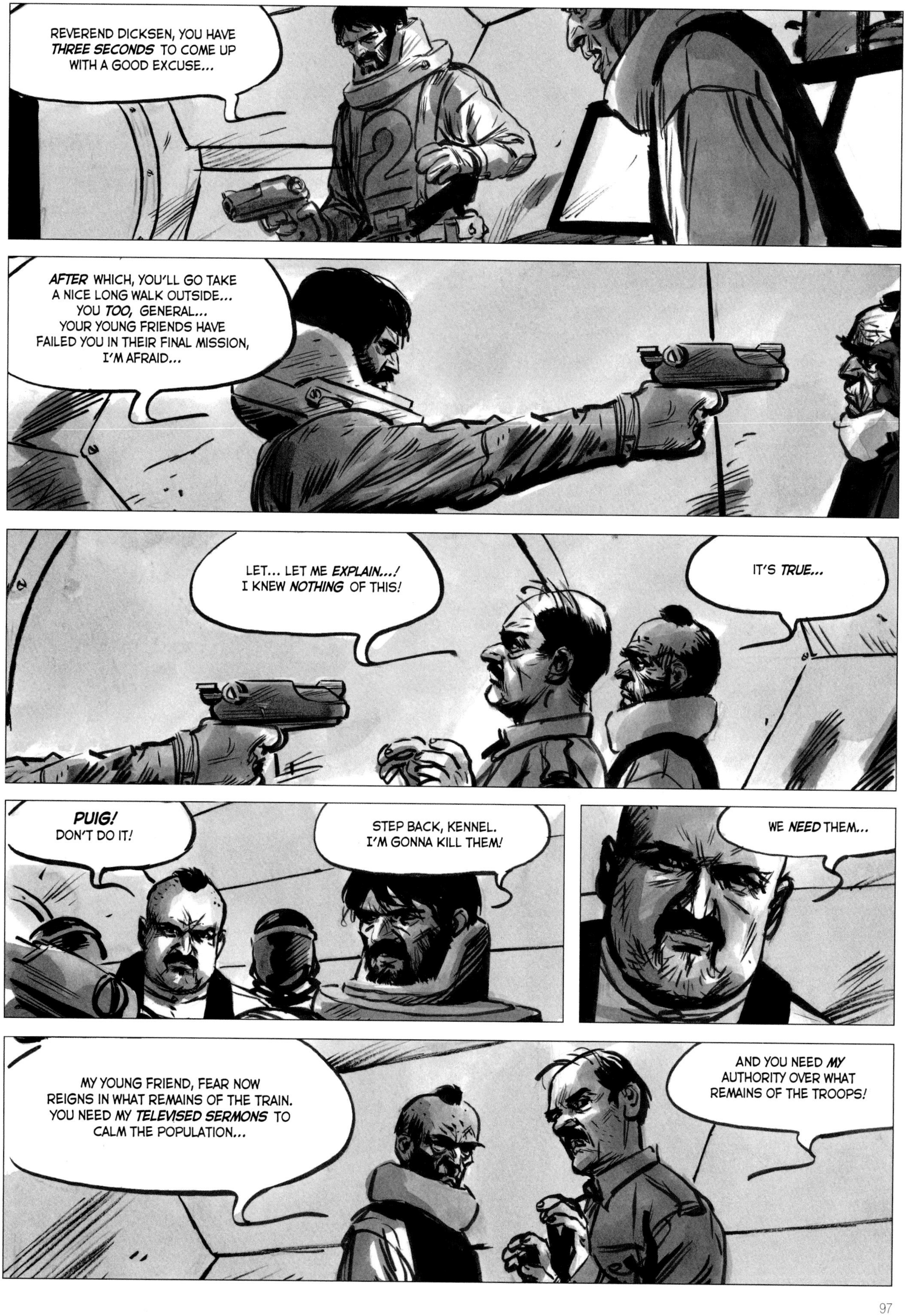

REVEREND DICKSEN, YOU HAVE THREE SECONDS TO COME UP WITH A GOOD EXCUSE...
AFTER WHICH, YOU'LL GO TAKE A NICE LONG WALK OUTSIDE... YOU TOO, GENERAL... YOUR YOUNG FRIENDS HAVE FAILED YOU IN THEIR FINAL MISSION, I'M AFRAID...
LET... LET ME EXPLAIN...! I KNEW NOTHING OF THIS!
IT'S TRUE...
PUIG! DON'T DO IT!
STEP BACK, KENNEL. I'M GONNA KILL THEM!
WE NEED THEM...
MY YOUNG FRIEND, FEAR NOW REIGNS IN WHAT REMAINS OF THE TRAIN. YOU NEED MY TELEVISED SERMONS TO CALM THE POPULATION...
AND YOU NEED MY AUTHORITY OVER WHAT REMAINS OF THE TROOPS!

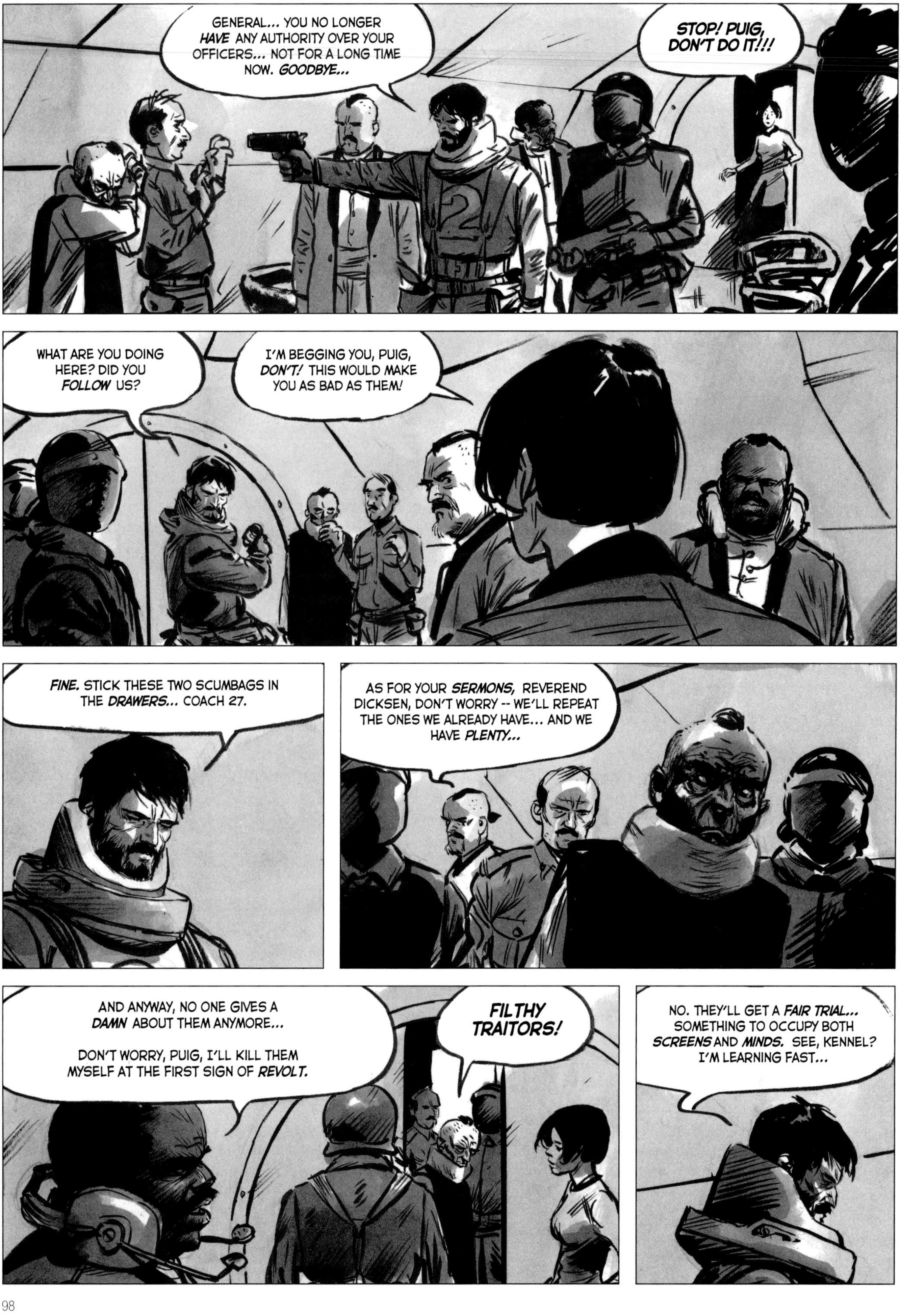
GENERAL... YOU NO LONGER HAVE ANY AUTHORITY OVER YOUR OFFICERS... NOT FOR A LONG TIME NOW. GOODBYE...
STOP! PUIG, DON'T DO IT!!!
WHAT ARE YOU DOING HERE? DID YOU FOLLOW US?
I'M BEGGING YOU, PUIG, DON'T! THIS WOULD MAKE YOU AS BAD AS THEM!
FINE. STICK THESE TWO SCUMBAGS IN THE DRAWERS... COACH 27.
AS FOR YOUR SERMONS, REVEREND DICKSEN, DON'T WORRY -- WE'LL REPEAT THE ONES WE ALREADY HAVE... AND WE HAVE PLENTY...
AND ANYWAY, NO ONE GIVES A DAMN ABOUT THEM ANYMORE...
DON'T WORRY, PUIG, I'LL KILL THEM MYSELF AT THE FIRST SIGN OF REVOLT.
FILTHY TRAITORS!
NO. THEY'LL GET A FAIR TRIAL... SOMETHING TO OCCUPY BOTH SCREENS AND MINDS. SEE, KENNEL? I'M LEARNING FAST...

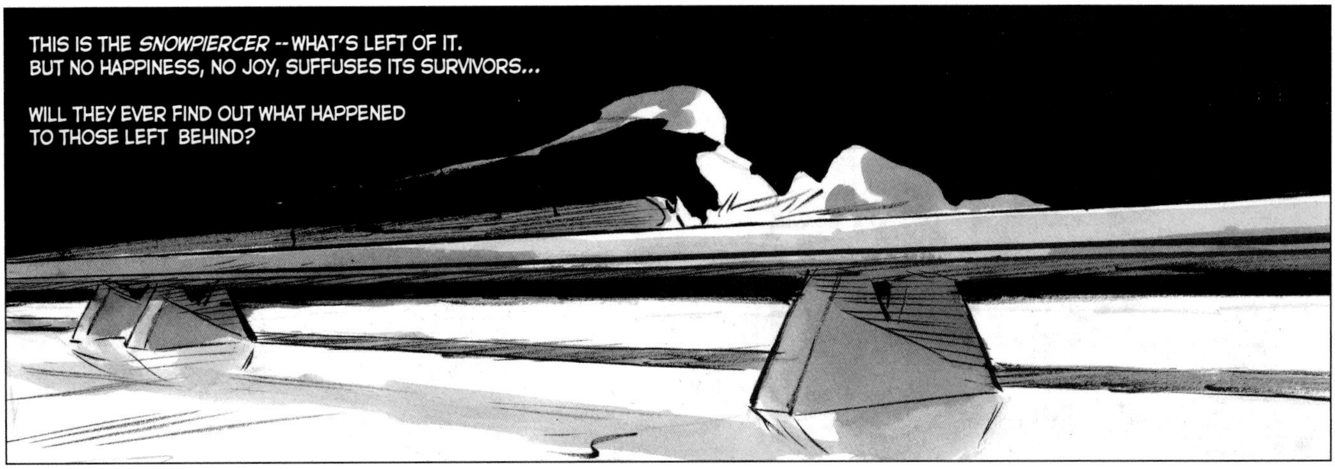
THIS IS THE *SNOWPIERCER* -- WHAT'S LEFT OF IT.
BUT NO HAPPINESS, NO JOY, SUFFUSES ITS SURVIVORS...
WILL THEY EVER FIND OUT WHAT HAPPENED TO THOSE LEFT BEHIND?

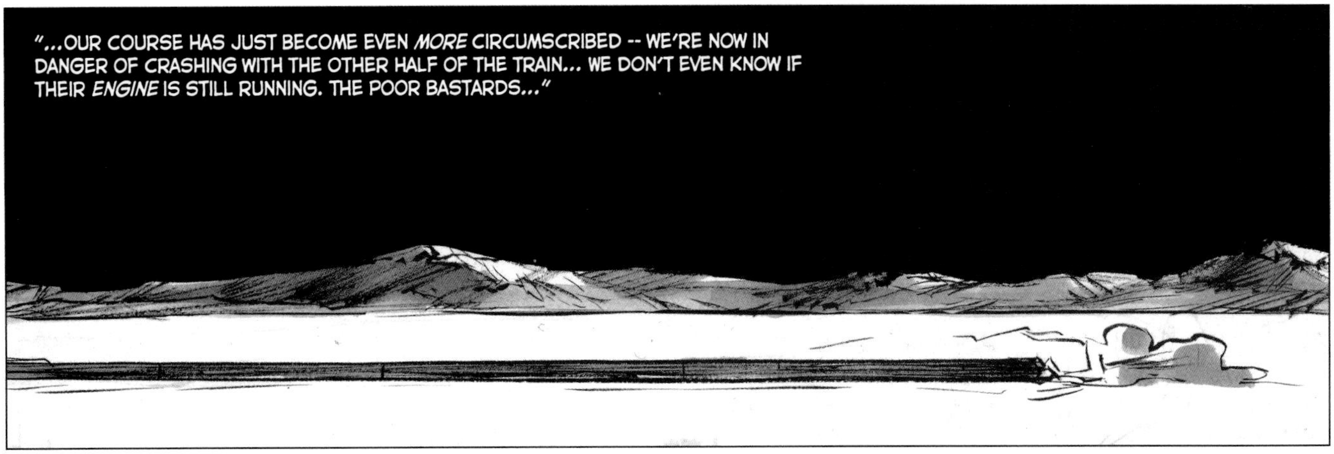
"...OUR COURSE HAS JUST BECOME EVEN *MORE* CIRCUMSCRIBED -- WE'RE NOW IN DANGER OF CRASHING WITH THE OTHER HALF OF THE TRAIN... WE DON'T EVEN KNOW IF THEIR *ENGINE* IS STILL RUNNING. THE POOR BASTARDS..."

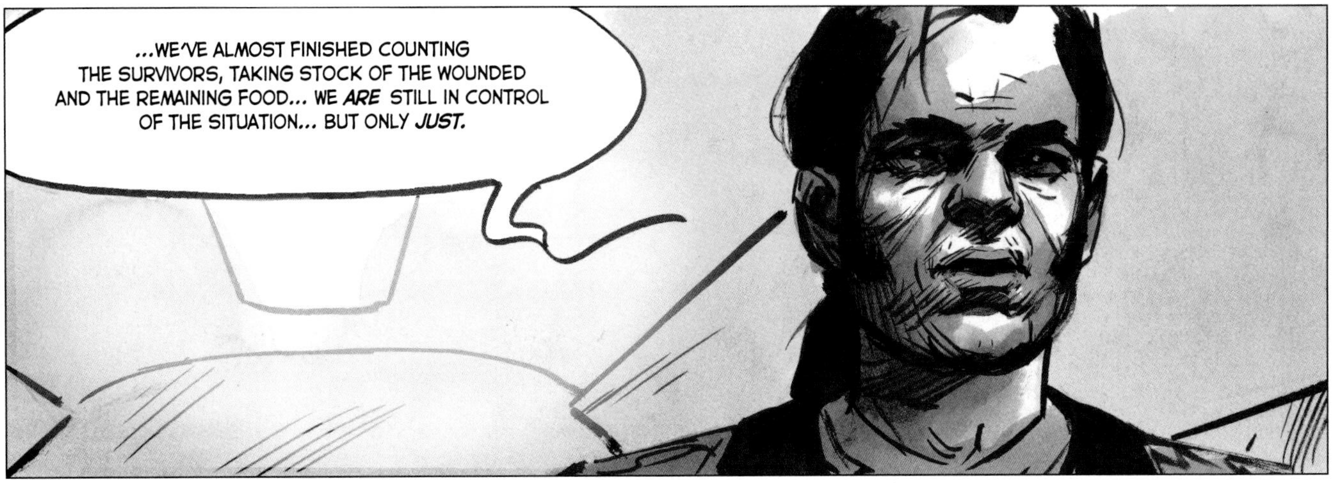
...WE'VE ALMOST FINISHED COUNTING THE SURVIVORS, TAKING STOCK OF THE WOUNDED AND THE REMAINING FOOD... WE *ARE* STILL IN CONTROL OF THE SITUATION... BUT ONLY *JUST.*

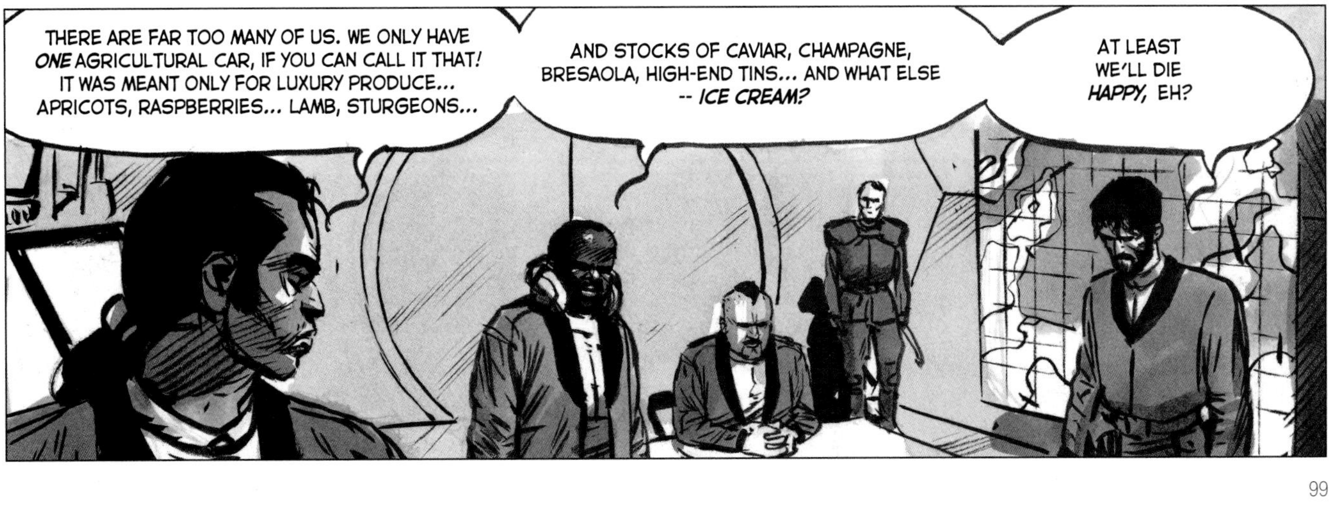
THERE ARE FAR TOO MANY OF US. WE ONLY HAVE *ONE* AGRICULTURAL CAR, IF YOU CAN CALL IT THAT! IT WAS MEANT ONLY FOR LUXURY PRODUCE... APRICOTS, RASPBERRIES... LAMB, STURGEONS...
AND STOCKS OF CAVIAR, CHAMPAGNE, BRESAOLA, HIGH-END TINS... AND WHAT ELSE -- *ICE CREAM?*
AT LEAST WE'LL DIE *HAPPY,* EH?

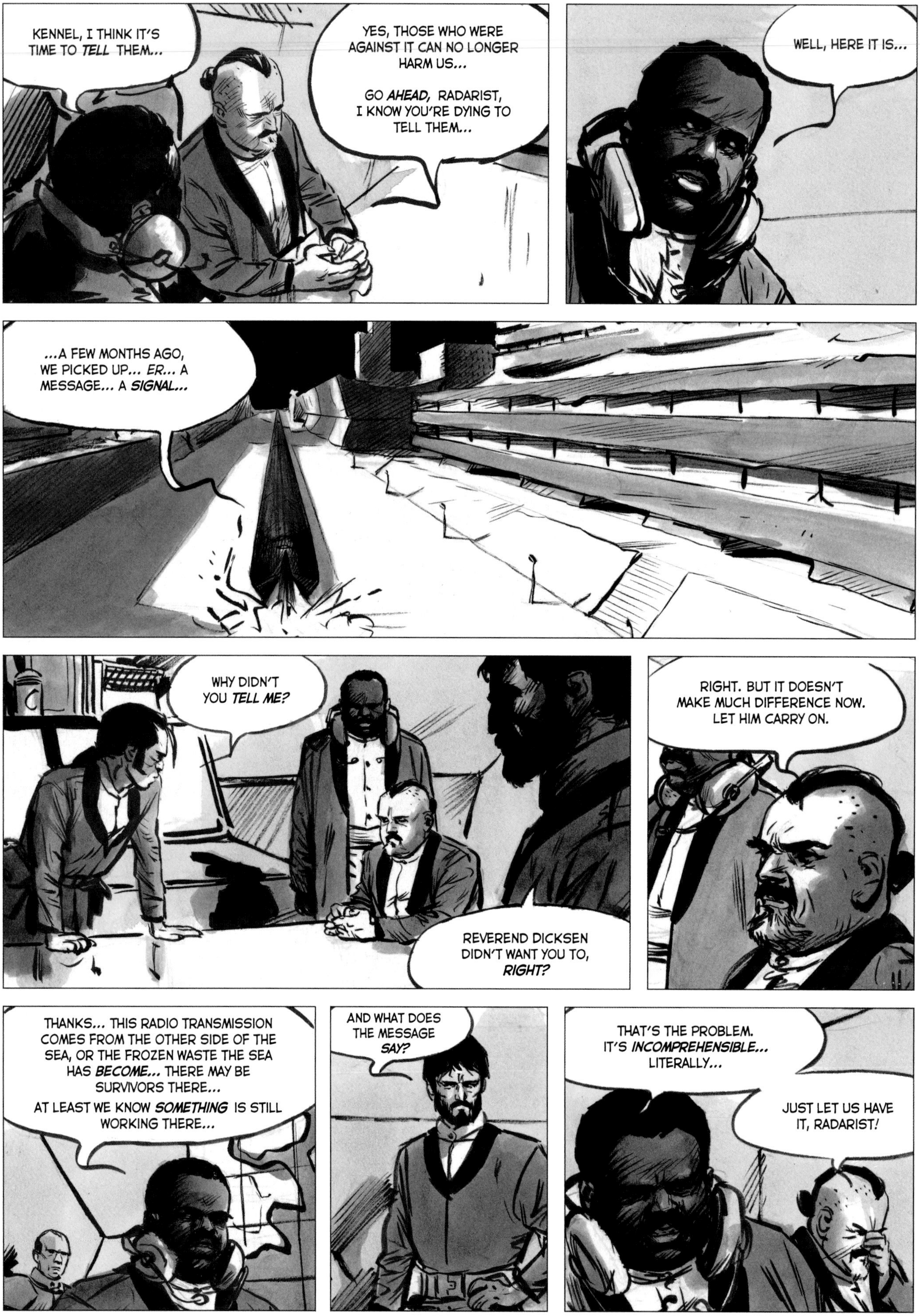
KENNEL, I THINK IT'S TIME TO *TELL* THEM...
YES, THOSE WHO WERE AGAINST IT CAN NO LONGER HARM US...
GO *AHEAD,* RADARIST, I KNOW YOU'RE DYING TO TELL THEM...
WELL, HERE IT IS...
...A FEW MONTHS AGO, WE PICKED UP... *ER...* A MESSAGE... A *SIGNAL...*
WHY DIDN'T YOU *TELL ME?*
REVEREND DICKSEN DIDN'T WANT YOU TO, *RIGHT?*
RIGHT. BUT IT DOESN'T MAKE MUCH DIFFERENCE NOW. LET HIM CARRY ON.
THANKS... THIS RADIO TRANSMISSION COMES FROM THE OTHER SIDE OF THE SEA, OR THE FROZEN WASTE THE SEA HAS *BECOME...* THERE MAY BE SURVIVORS THERE...
AT LEAST WE KNOW *SOMETHING* IS STILL WORKING THERE...
AND WHAT DOES THE MESSAGE *SAY?*
THAT'S THE PROBLEM. IT'S *INCOMPREHENSIBLE...* LITERALLY...
JUST LET US HAVE IT, RADARIST!

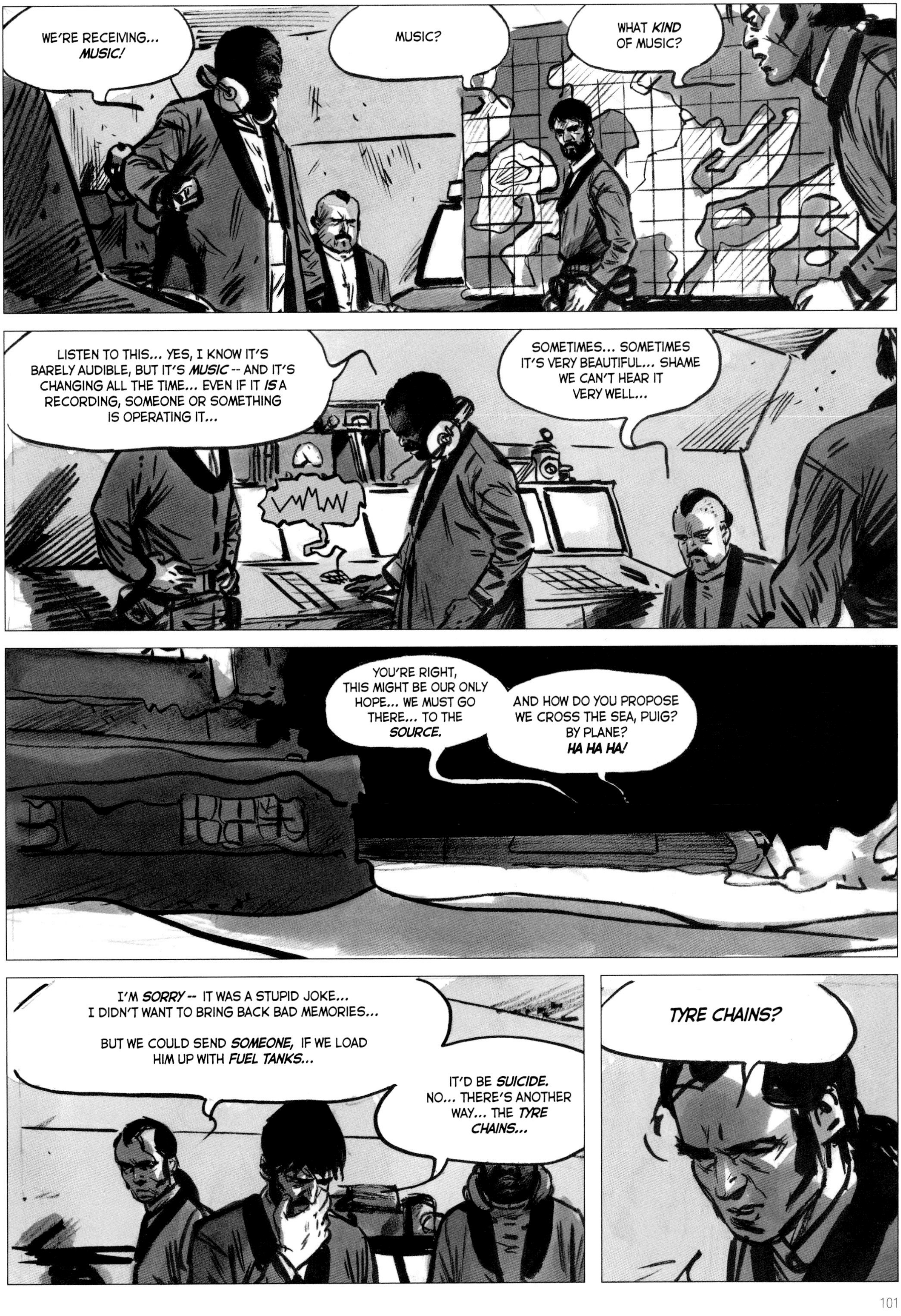
WE'RE RECEIVING... *MUSIC!*
MUSIC?
WHAT *KIND* OF MUSIC?
LISTEN TO THIS... YES, I KNOW IT'S BARELY AUDIBLE, BUT IT'S *MUSIC* -- AND IT'S CHANGING ALL THE TIME... EVEN IF IT *IS* A RECORDING, SOMEONE OR SOMETHING IS OPERATING IT...
SOMETIMES... SOMETIMES IT'S VERY BEAUTIFUL... SHAME WE CAN'T HEAR IT VERY WELL...
YOU'RE RIGHT, THIS MIGHT BE OUR ONLY HOPE... WE MUST GO THERE... TO THE *SOURCE.*
AND HOW DO YOU PROPOSE WE CROSS THE SEA, PUIG? BY PLANE? *HA HA HA!*
I'M *SORRY* -- IT WAS A STUPID JOKE... I DIDN'T WANT TO BRING BACK BAD MEMORIES...
BUT WE COULD SEND *SOMEONE,* IF WE LOAD HIM UP WITH *FUEL TANKS...*
IT'D BE *SUICIDE.* NO... THERE'S ANOTHER WAY... THE *TYRE CHAINS...*
TYRE CHAINS?

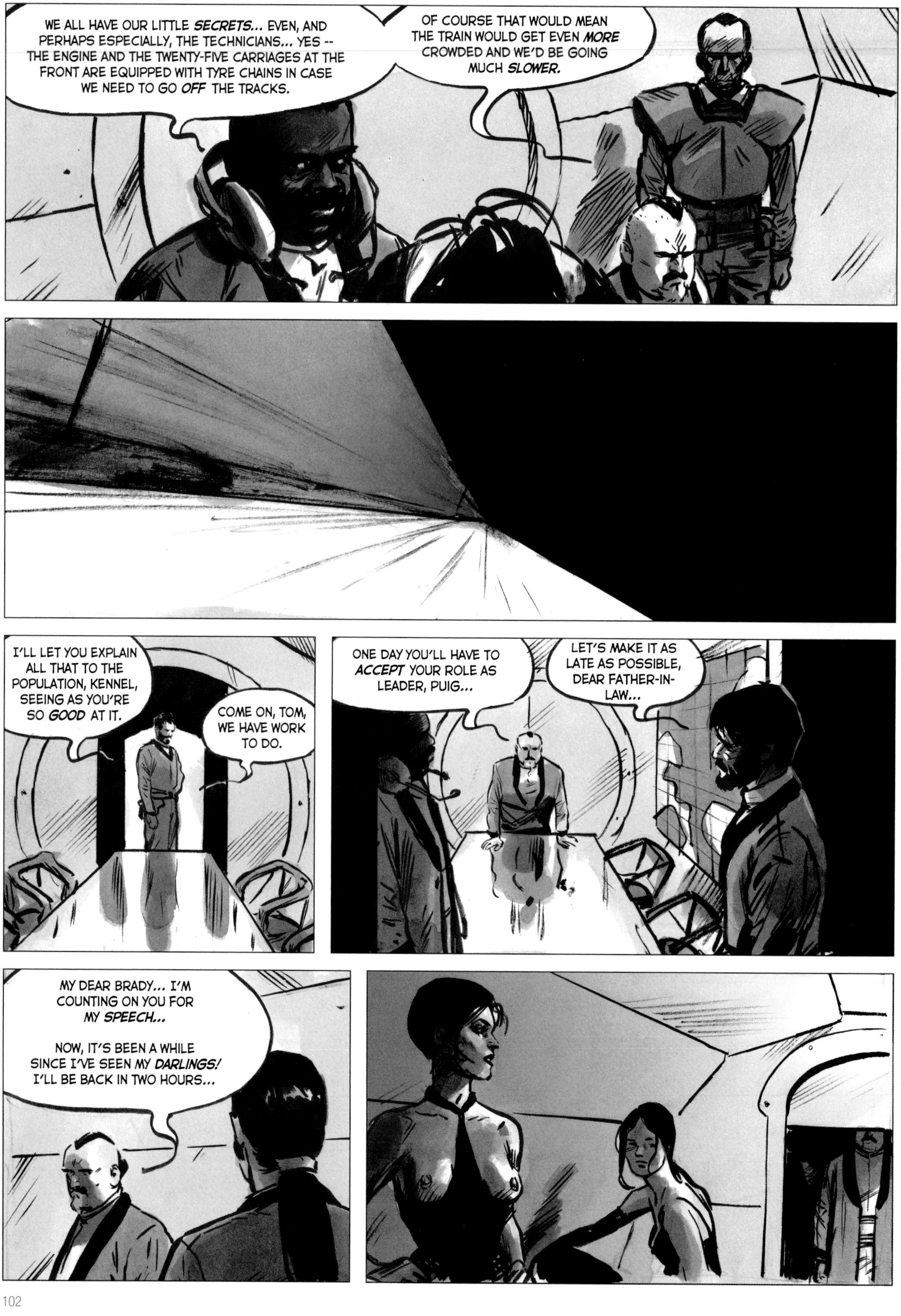
WE ALL HAVE OUR LITTLE SECRETS... EVEN, AND PERHAPS ESPECIALLY, THE TECHNICIANS... YES -- THE ENGINE AND THE TWENTY-FIVE CARRIAGES AT THE FRONT ARE EQUIPPED WITH TYRE CHAINS IN CASE WE NEED TO GO OFF THE TRACKS.
OF COURSE THAT WOULD MEAN THE TRAIN WOULD GET EVEN MORE CROWDED AND WE'D BE GOING MUCH SLOWER.
I'LL LET YOU EXPLAIN ALL THAT TO THE POPULATION, KENNEL, SEEING AS YOU'RE SO GOOD AT IT.
COME ON, TOM, WE HAVE WORK TO DO.
ONE DAY YOU'LL HAVE TO ACCEPT YOUR ROLE AS LEADER, PUIG...
LET'S MAKE IT AS LATE AS POSSIBLE, DEAR FATHER-IN-LAW...
MY DEAR BRADY... I'M COUNTING ON YOU FOR MY SPEECH...
NOW, IT'S BEEN A WHILE SINCE I'VE SEEN MY DARLINGS! I'LL BE BACK IN TWO HOURS...

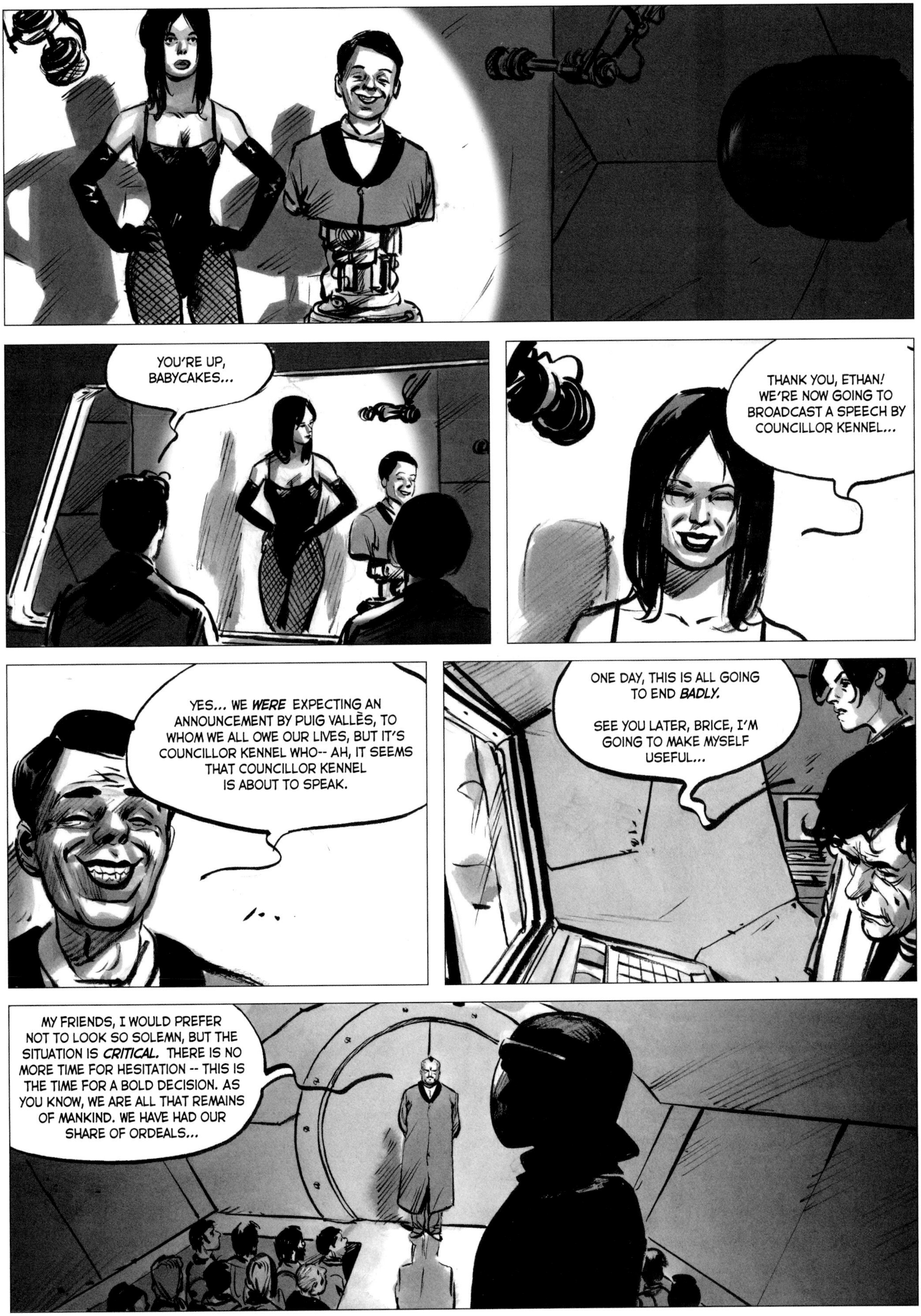
YOU'RE UP, BABYCAKES...
THANK YOU, ETHAN! WE'RE NOW GOING TO BROADCAST A SPEECH BY COUNCILLOR KENNEL...
YES... WE *WERE* EXPECTING AN ANNOUNCEMENT BY PUIG VALLÈS, TO WHOM WE ALL OWE OUR LIVES, BUT IT'S COUNCILLOR KENNEL WHO-- AH, IT SEEMS THAT COUNCILLOR KENNEL IS ABOUT TO SPEAK.
ONE DAY, THIS IS ALL GOING TO END *BADLY.*
SEE YOU LATER, BRICE, I'M GOING TO MAKE MYSELF USEFUL...
MY FRIENDS, I WOULD PREFER NOT TO LOOK SO SOLEMN, BUT THE SITUATION IS *CRITICAL.* THERE IS NO MORE TIME FOR HESITATION -- THIS IS THE TIME FOR A BOLD DECISION. AS YOU KNOW, WE ARE ALL THAT REMAINS OF MANKIND. WE HAVE HAD OUR SHARE OF ORDEALS...

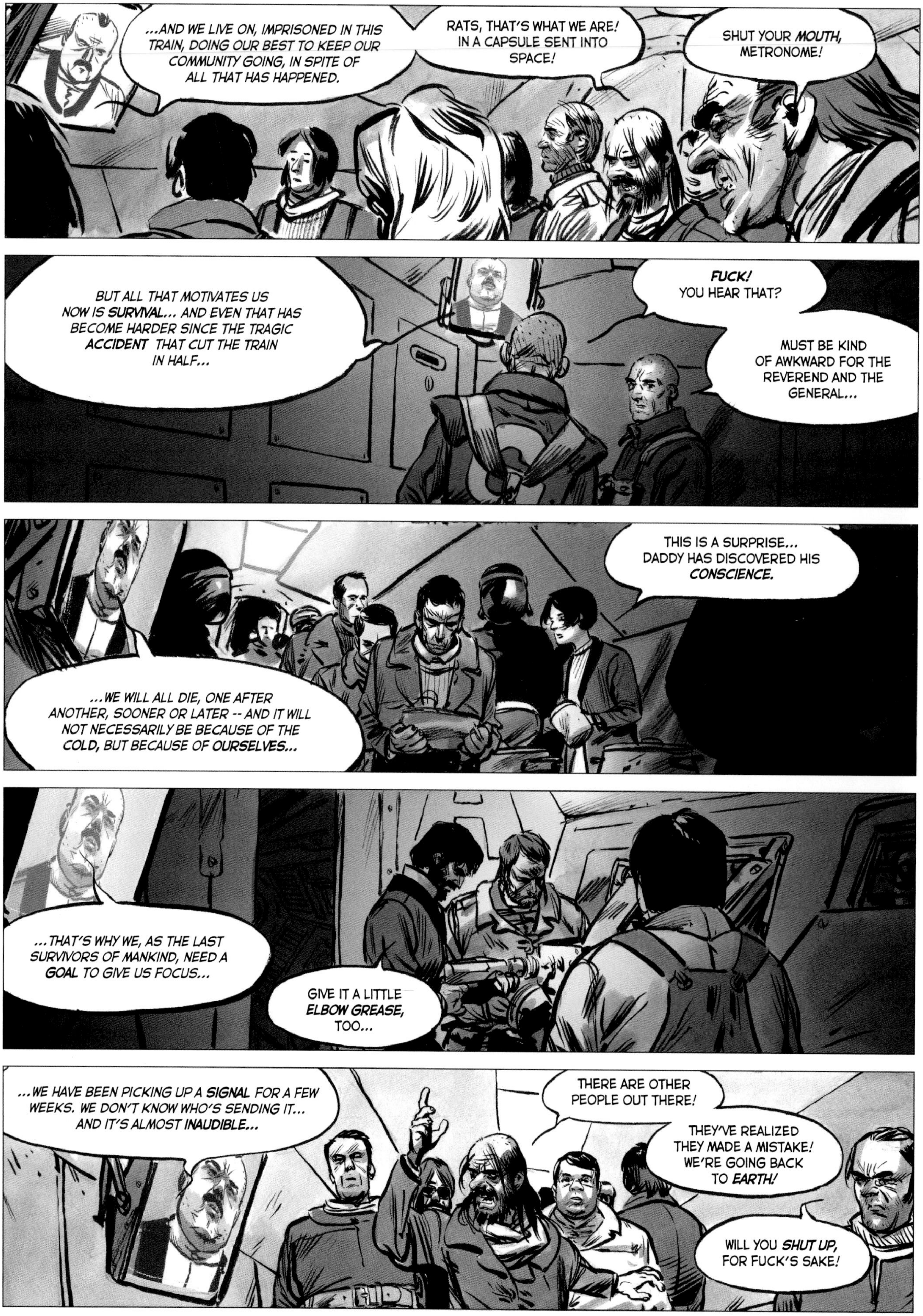
...AND WE LIVE ON, IMPRISONED IN THIS TRAIN, DOING OUR BEST TO KEEP OUR COMMUNITY GOING, IN SPITE OF ALL THAT HAS HAPPENED.
RATS, THAT'S WHAT WE ARE! IN A CAPSULE SENT INTO SPACE!
SHUT YOUR MOUTH, METRONOME!
BUT ALL THAT MOTIVATES US NOW IS SURVIVAL... AND EVEN THAT HAS BECOME HARDER SINCE THE TRAGIC ACCIDENT THAT CUT THE TRAIN IN HALF...
FUCK! YOU HEAR THAT?
MUST BE KIND OF AWKWARD FOR THE REVEREND AND THE GENERAL...
THIS IS A SURPRISE... DADDY HAS DISCOVERED HIS CONSCIENCE.
...WE WILL ALL DIE, ONE AFTER ANOTHER, SOONER OR LATER -- AND IT WILL NOT NECESSARILY BE BECAUSE OF THE COLD, BUT BECAUSE OF OURSELVES...
...THAT'S WHY WE, AS THE LAST SURVIVORS OF MANKIND, NEED A GOAL TO GIVE US FOCUS...
GIVE IT A LITTLE ELBOW GREASE, TOO...
...WE HAVE BEEN PICKING UP A SIGNAL FOR A FEW WEEKS. WE DON'T KNOW WHO'S SENDING IT... AND IT'S ALMOST INAUDIBLE...
THERE ARE OTHER PEOPLE OUT THERE!
THEY'VE REALIZED THEY MADE A MISTAKE! WE'RE GOING BACK TO EARTH!
WILL YOU SHUT UP, FOR FUCK'S SAKE!

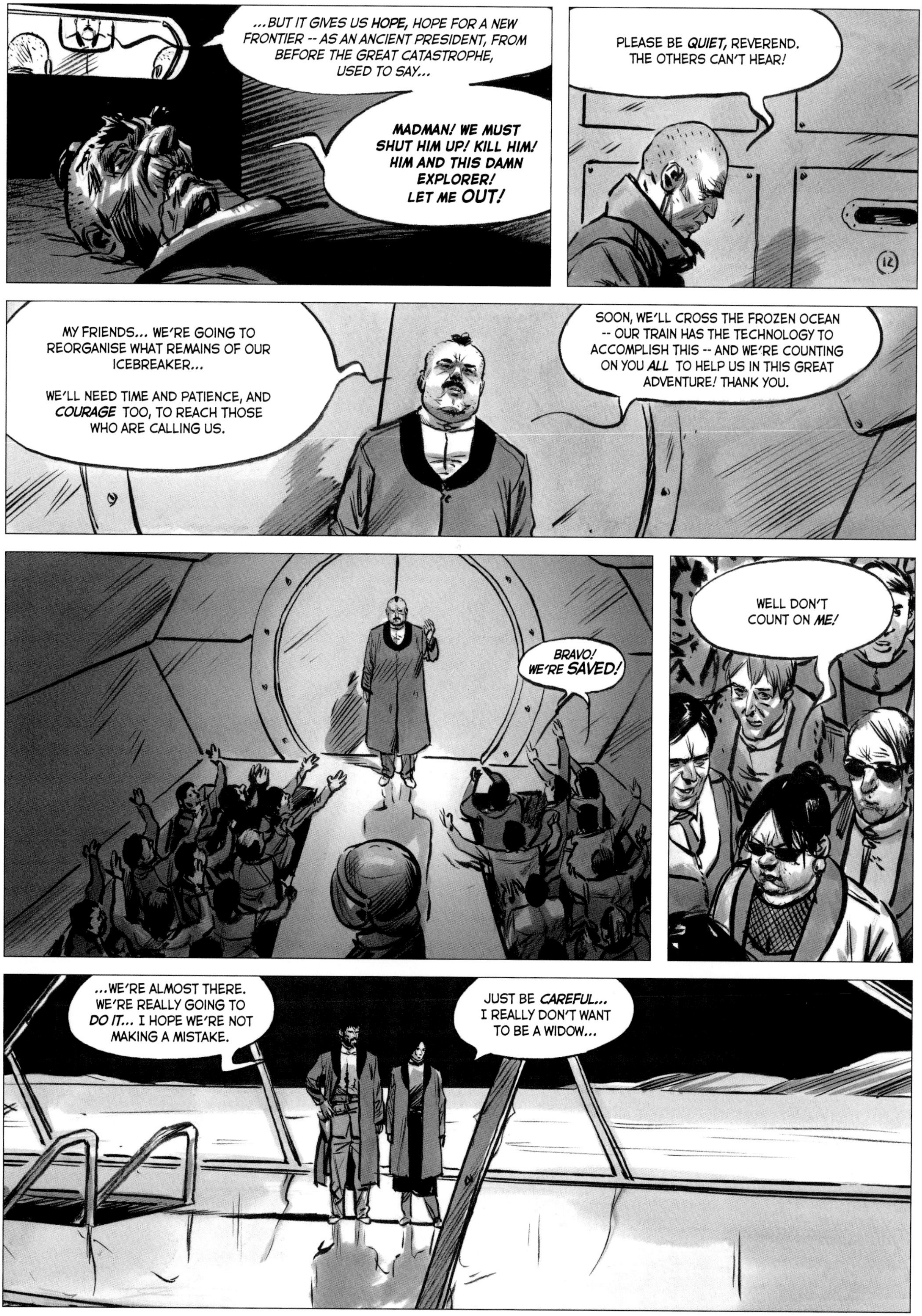
...BUT IT GIVES US HOPE, HOPE FOR A NEW FRONTIER -- AS AN ANCIENT PRESIDENT, FROM BEFORE THE GREAT CATASTROPHE, USED TO SAY...
MADMAN! WE MUST SHUT HIM UP! KILL HIM! HIM AND THIS DAMN EXPLORER! LET ME OUT!
PLEASE BE QUIET, REVEREND. THE OTHERS CAN'T HEAR!
12
MY FRIENDS... WE'RE GOING TO REORGANISE WHAT REMAINS OF OUR ICEBREAKER...
WE'LL NEED TIME AND PATIENCE, AND COURAGE TOO, TO REACH THOSE WHO ARE CALLING US.
SOON, WE'LL CROSS THE FROZEN OCEAN -- OUR TRAIN HAS THE TECHNOLOGY TO ACCOMPLISH THIS -- AND WE'RE COUNTING ON YOU ALL TO HELP US IN THIS GREAT ADVENTURE! THANK YOU.
BRAVO! WE'RE SAVED!
WELL DON'T COUNT ON ME!
...WE'RE ALMOST THERE. WE'RE REALLY GOING TO DO IT... I HOPE WE'RE NOT MAKING A MISTAKE.
JUST BE CAREFUL... I REALLY DON'T WANT TO BE A WIDOW...

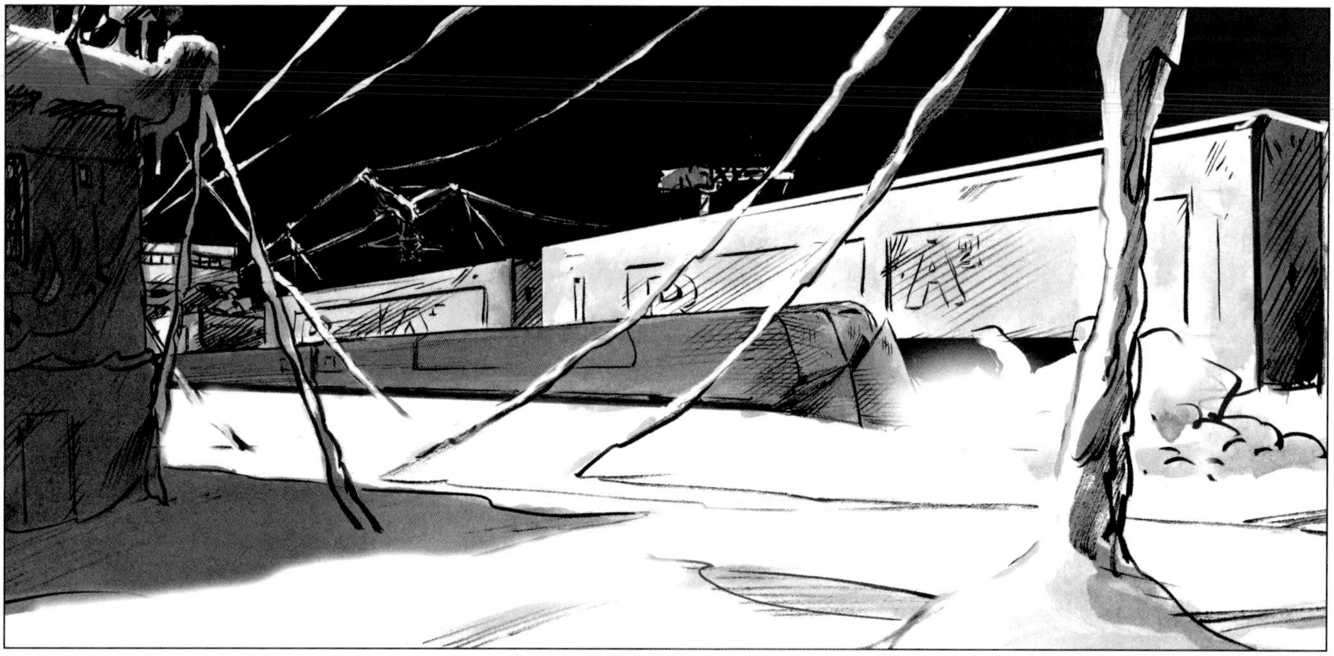

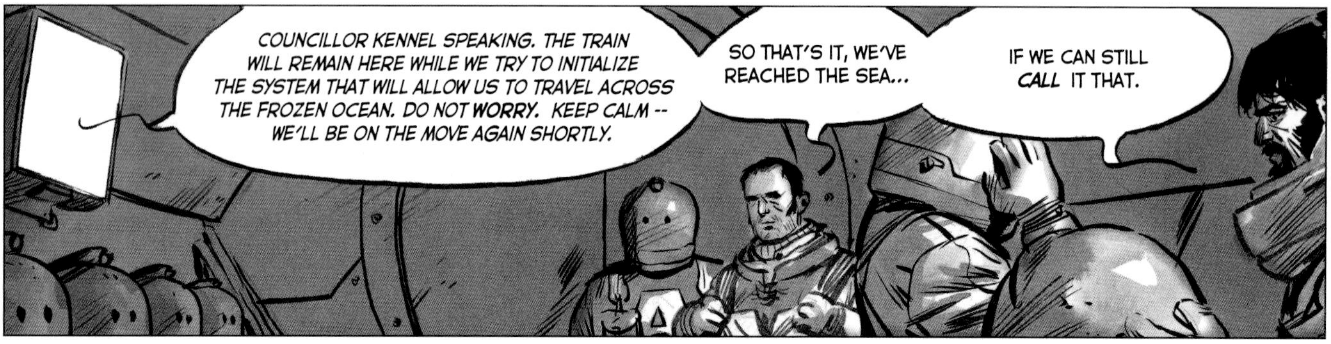
COUNCILLOR KENNEL SPEAKING. THE TRAIN WILL REMAIN HERE WHILE WE TRY TO INITIALIZE THE SYSTEM THAT WILL ALLOW US TO TRAVEL ACROSS THE FROZEN OCEAN. DO NOT WORRY. KEEP CALM -- WE'LL BE ON THE MOVE AGAIN SHORTLY.
SO THAT'S IT, WE'VE REACHED THE SEA...
IF WE CAN STILL CALL IT THAT.

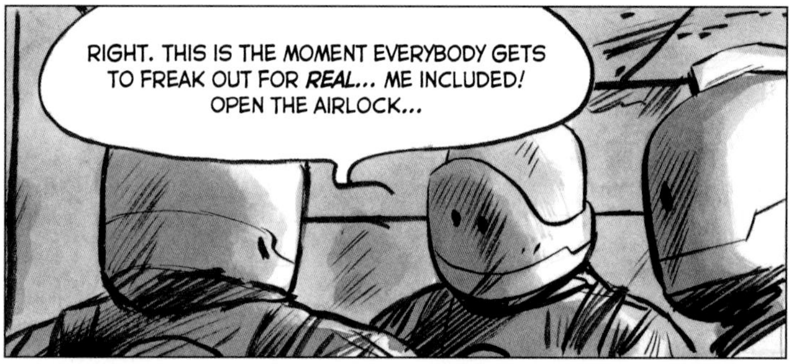
RIGHT. THIS IS THE MOMENT EVERYBODY GETS TO FREAK OUT FOR REAL... ME INCLUDED! OPEN THE AIRLOCK...

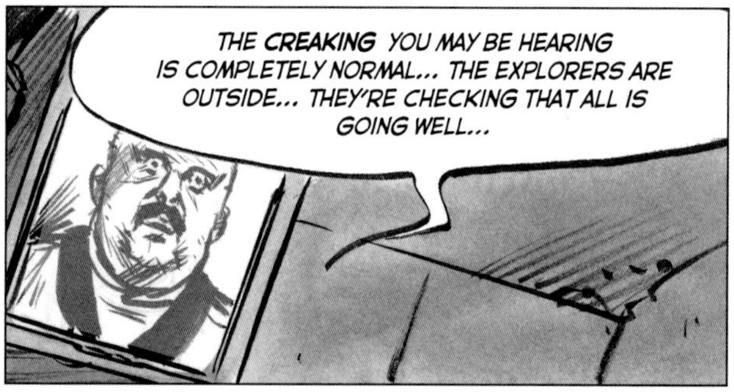
THE CREAKING YOU MAY BE HEARING IS COMPLETELY NORMAL... THE EXPLORERS ARE OUTSIDE... THEY'RE CHECKING THAT ALL IS GOING WELL...

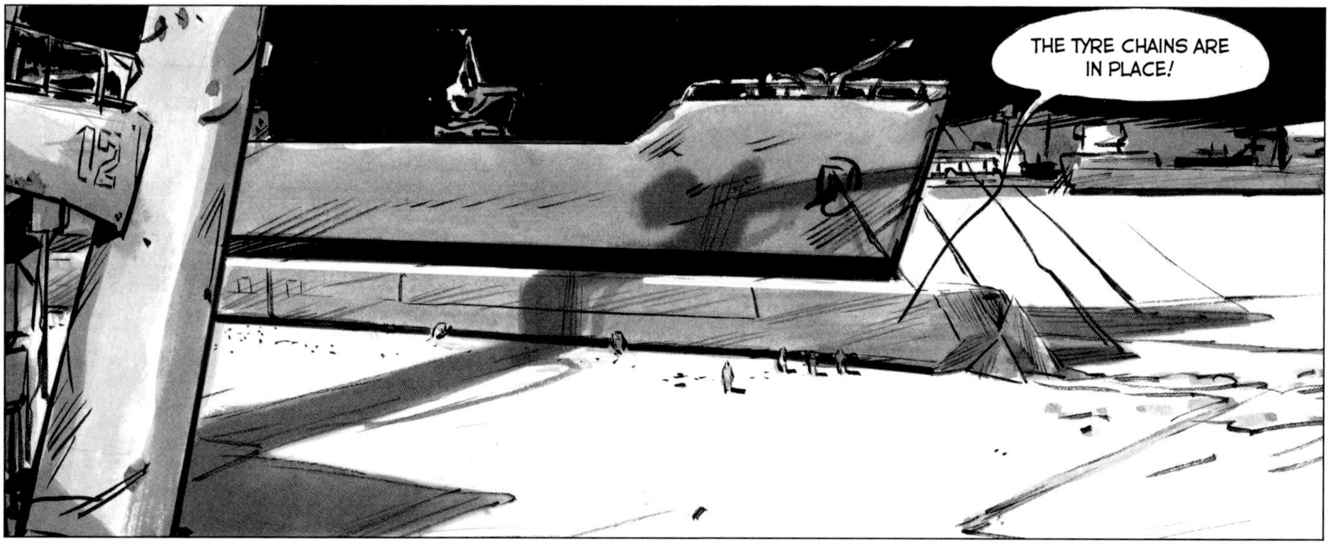
THE TYRE CHAINS ARE IN PLACE!

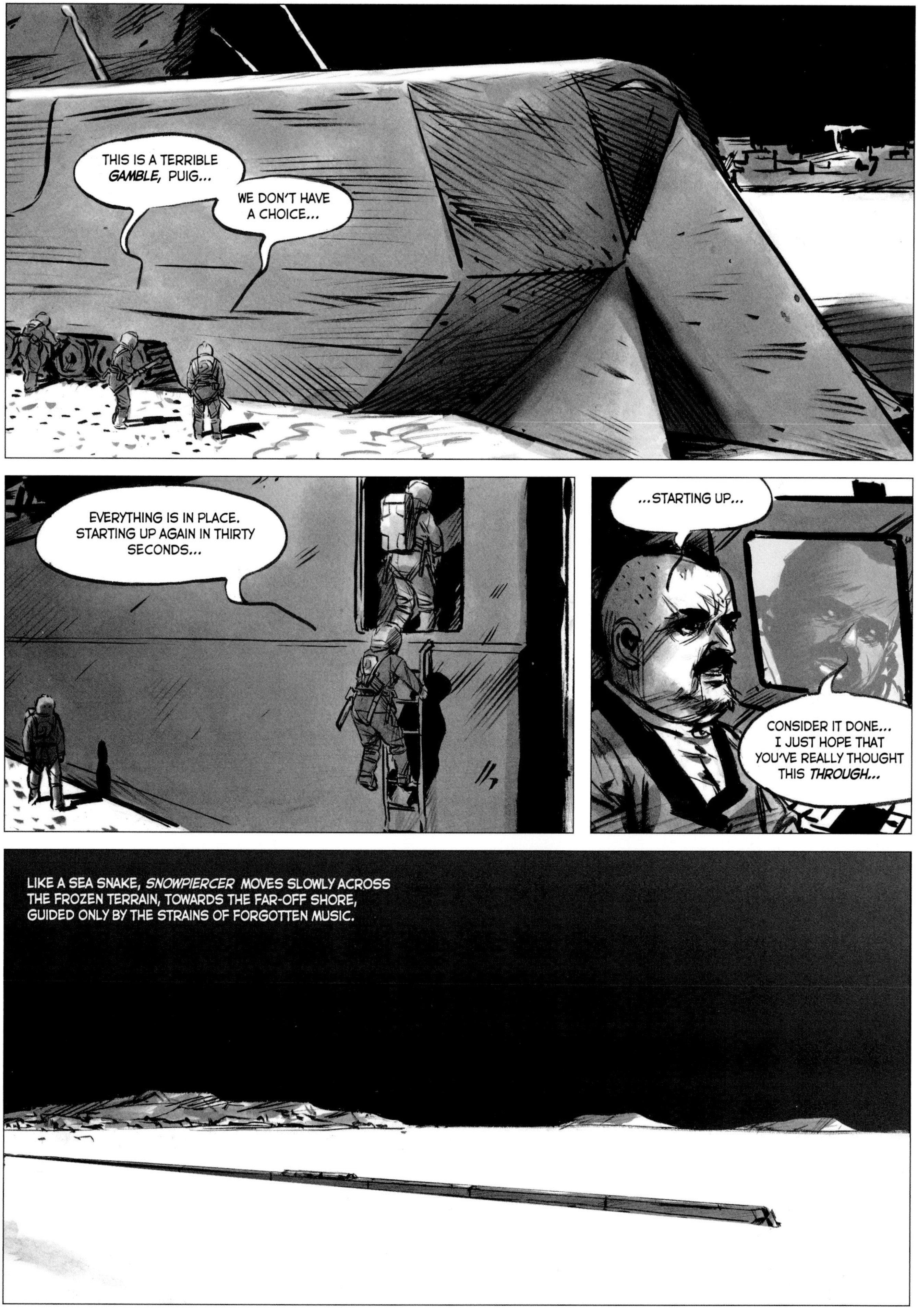
THIS IS A TERRIBLE *GAMBLE,* PUIG...
WE DON'T HAVE A CHOICE...
EVERYTHING IS IN PLACE. STARTING UP AGAIN IN THIRTY SECONDS...
...STARTING UP...
CONSIDER IT DONE... I JUST HOPE THAT YOU'VE REALLY THOUGHT THIS *THROUGH...*
LIKE A SEA SNAKE, *SNOWPIERCER* MOVES SLOWLY ACROSS THE FROZEN TERRAIN, TOWARDS THE FAR-OFF SHORE, GUIDED ONLY BY THE STRAINS OF FORGOTTEN MUSIC.

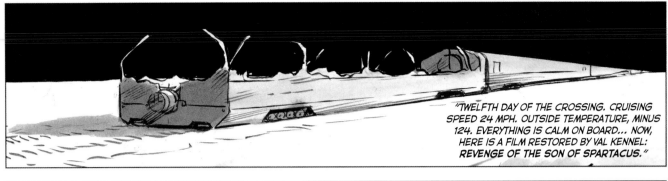

"TWELFTH DAY OF THE CROSSING. CRUISING SPEED 24 MPH. OUTSIDE TEMPERATURE, MINUS 124. EVERYTHING IS CALM ON BOARD... NOW, HERE IS A FILM RESTORED BY VAL KENNEL: *REVENGE OF THE SON OF SPARTACUS.*"

WHY DON'T THEY RUN THE *GAME* AGAIN? I'M FED UP WITH TV, IT'S ALWAYS THE SAME RUBBISH!

IT'S THIS *PUIG VALLÈS!* SINCE HE TOOK OVER, EVERYTHING'S GONE WRONG -- AND WE'RE FREEZING TO *DEATH* IN HERE!

THEY COULD AT LEAST TURN ON SOME *LIGHTS...*

NOTHING I CAN DO... AND I LIKED IT BETTER BEFORE AS WELL. UNDER THE GENERAL, WE AT LEAST HAD SOME *ORDER.* I EVEN WON A VIRTUAL VACATION ONCE...

WE COULDN'T FIND THE THREE KIDS... AND PEOPLE ARE ALREADY FED UP... THEY DON'T LIKE A LOT OF YOUR *DECISIONS.*

I DIDN'T *ASK* TO BE IN CHARGE. BUT I WILL NEVER LET *ANYONE* PUT THE TRAIN IN DANGER.

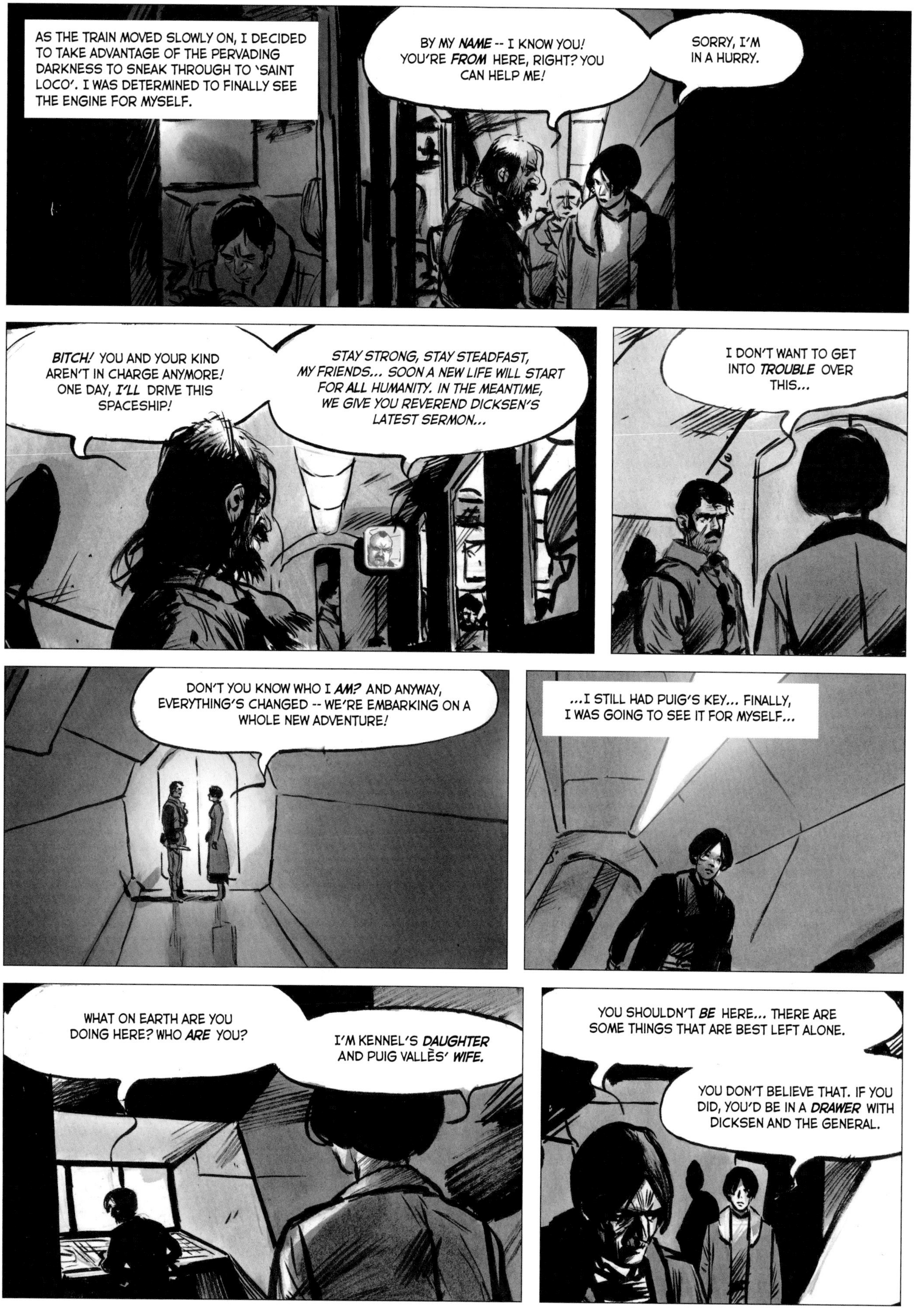

AS THE TRAIN MOVED SLOWLY ON, I DECIDED TO TAKE ADVANTAGE OF THE PERVADING DARKNESS TO SNEAK THROUGH TO 'SAINT LOCO'. I WAS DETERMINED TO FINALLY SEE THE ENGINE FOR MYSELF.
BY MY *NAME* -- I KNOW YOU! YOU'RE *FROM* HERE, RIGHT? YOU CAN HELP ME!
SORRY, I'M IN A HURRY.
BITCH! YOU AND YOUR KIND AREN'T IN CHARGE ANYMORE! ONE DAY, *I'LL* DRIVE THIS SPACESHIP!
STAY STRONG, STAY STEADFAST, MY FRIENDS... SOON A NEW LIFE WILL START FOR ALL *HUMANITY. IN THE MEANTIME, WE GIVE YOU REVEREND DICKSEN'S LATEST SERMON...*
I DON'T WANT TO GET INTO *TROUBLE* OVER THIS...
DON'T YOU KNOW WHO I *AM?* AND ANYWAY, EVERYTHING'S CHANGED -- WE'RE EMBARKING ON A WHOLE NEW ADVENTURE!
...I STILL HAD PUIG'S KEY... FINALLY, I WAS GOING TO SEE IT FOR MYSELF...
WHAT ON EARTH ARE YOU DOING HERE? WHO *ARE* YOU?
I'M KENNEL'S *DAUGHTER* AND PUIG VALLÈS' *WIFE.*
YOU SHOULDN'T *BE* HERE... THERE ARE SOME THINGS THAT ARE BEST LEFT ALONE.
YOU DON'T BELIEVE THAT. IF YOU DID, YOU'D BE IN A *DRAWER* WITH DICKSEN AND THE GENERAL.

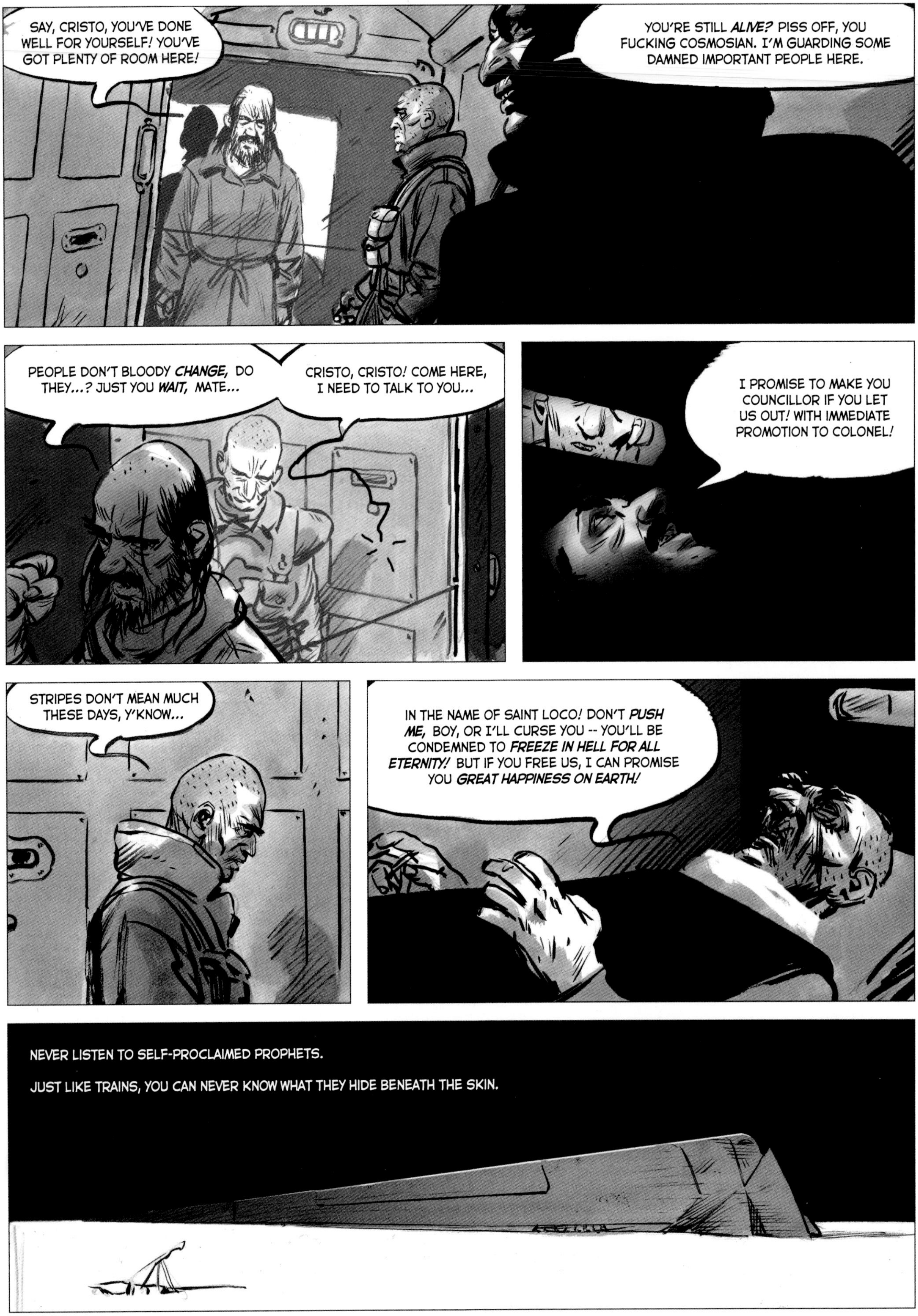
SAY, CRISTO, YOU'VE DONE WELL FOR YOURSELF! YOU'VE GOT PLENTY OF ROOM HERE!
YOU'RE STILL *ALIVE?* PISS OFF, YOU FUCKING COSMOSIAN. I'M GUARDING SOME DAMNED IMPORTANT PEOPLE HERE.
PEOPLE DON'T BLOODY *CHANGE,* DO THEY...? JUST YOU *WAIT,* MATE...
CRISTO, CRISTO! COME HERE, I NEED TO TALK TO YOU...
I PROMISE TO MAKE YOU COUNCILLOR IF YOU LET US OUT! WITH IMMEDIATE PROMOTION TO COLONEL!
STRIPES DON'T MEAN MUCH THESE DAYS, Y'KNOW...
IN THE NAME OF SAINT LOCO! DON'T *PUSH ME,* BOY, OR I'LL CURSE YOU -- YOU'LL BE CONDEMNED TO *FREEZE IN HELL FOR ALL ETERNITY!* BUT IF YOU FREE US, I CAN PROMISE YOU *GREAT HAPPINESS ON EARTH!*
NEVER LISTEN TO SELF-PROCLAIMED PROPHETS.
JUST LIKE TRAINS, YOU CAN NEVER KNOW WHAT THEY HIDE BENEATH THE SKIN.

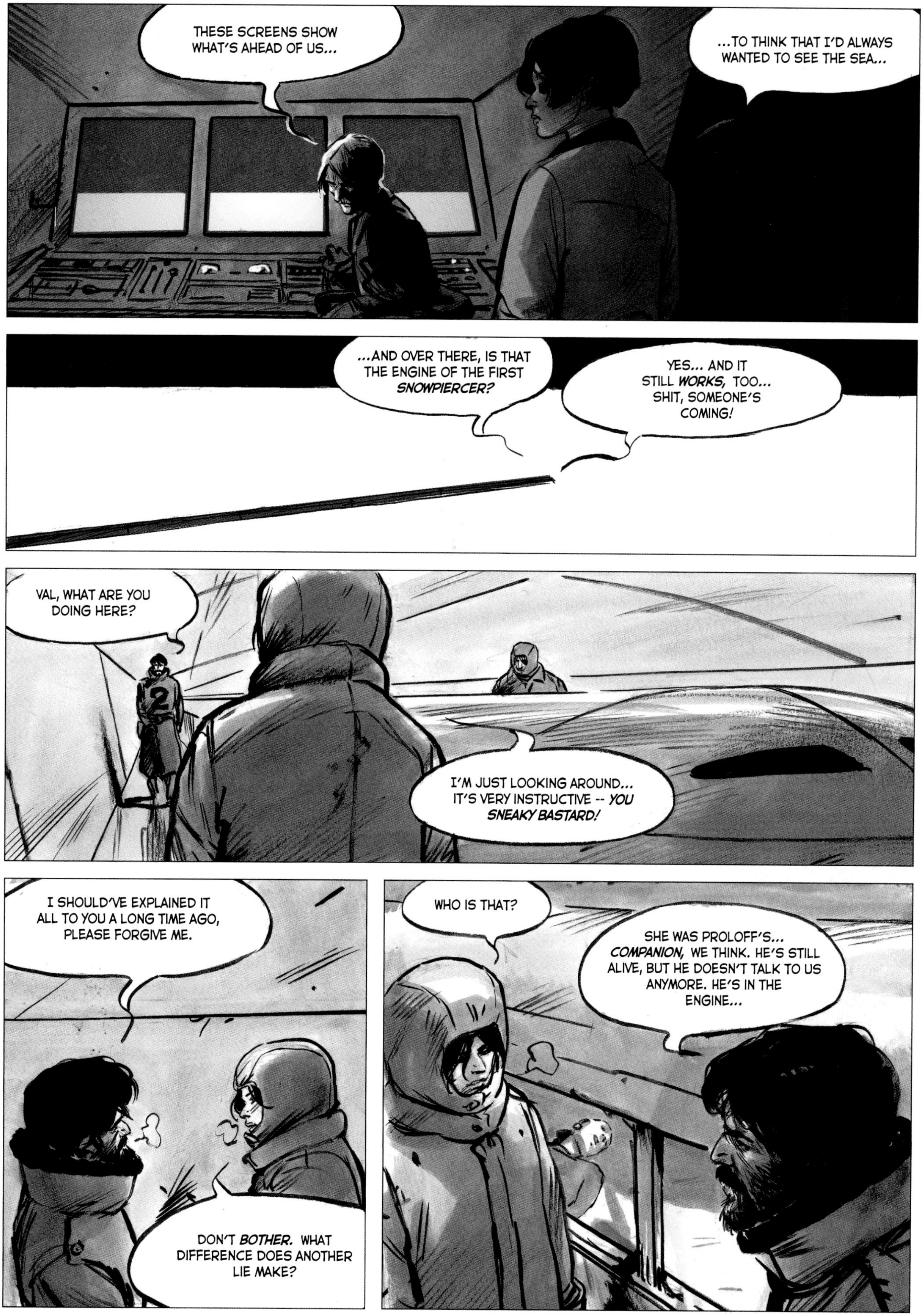
THESE SCREENS SHOW WHAT'S AHEAD OF US...
...TO THINK THAT I'D ALWAYS WANTED TO SEE THE SEA...
...AND OVER THERE, IS THAT THE ENGINE OF THE FIRST SNOWPIERCER?
YES... AND IT STILL WORKS, TOO... SHIT, SOMEONE'S COMING!
VAL, WHAT ARE YOU DOING HERE?
I'M JUST LOOKING AROUND... IT'S VERY INSTRUCTIVE -- YOU SNEAKY BASTARD!
I SHOULD'VE EXPLAINED IT ALL TO YOU A LONG TIME AGO, PLEASE FORGIVE ME.
DON'T BOTHER. WHAT DIFFERENCE DOES ANOTHER LIE MAKE?
WHO IS THAT?
SHE WAS PROLOFF'S... COMPANION, WE THINK. HE'S STILL ALIVE, BUT HE DOESN'T TALK TO US ANYMORE. HE'S IN THE ENGINE...

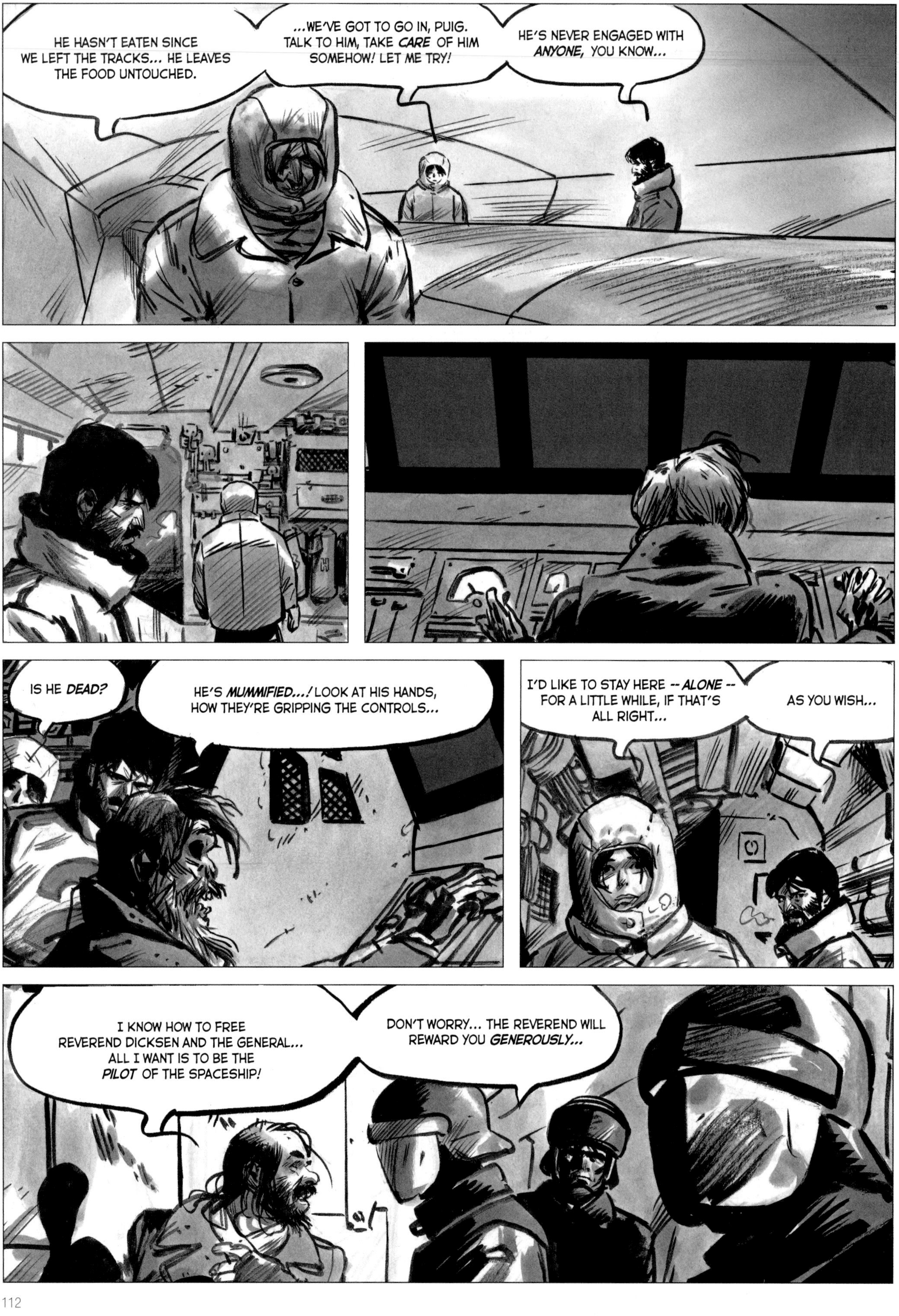
HE HASN'T EATEN SINCE WE LEFT THE TRACKS... HE LEAVES THE FOOD UNTOUCHED.
...WE'VE GOT TO GO IN, PUIG. TALK TO HIM, TAKE *CARE* OF HIM SOMEHOW! LET ME TRY!
HE'S NEVER ENGAGED WITH *ANYONE,* YOU KNOW...
IS HE *DEAD?*
HE'S *MUMMIFIED...!* LOOK AT HIS HANDS, HOW THEY'RE GRIPPING THE CONTROLS...
I'D LIKE TO STAY HERE -- *ALONE* -- FOR A LITTLE WHILE, IF THAT'S ALL RIGHT...
AS YOU WISH...
I KNOW HOW TO FREE REVEREND DICKSEN AND THE GENERAL... ALL I WANT IS TO BE THE *PILOT* OF THE SPACESHIP!
DON'T WORRY... THE REVEREND WILL REWARD YOU *GENEROUSLY...*

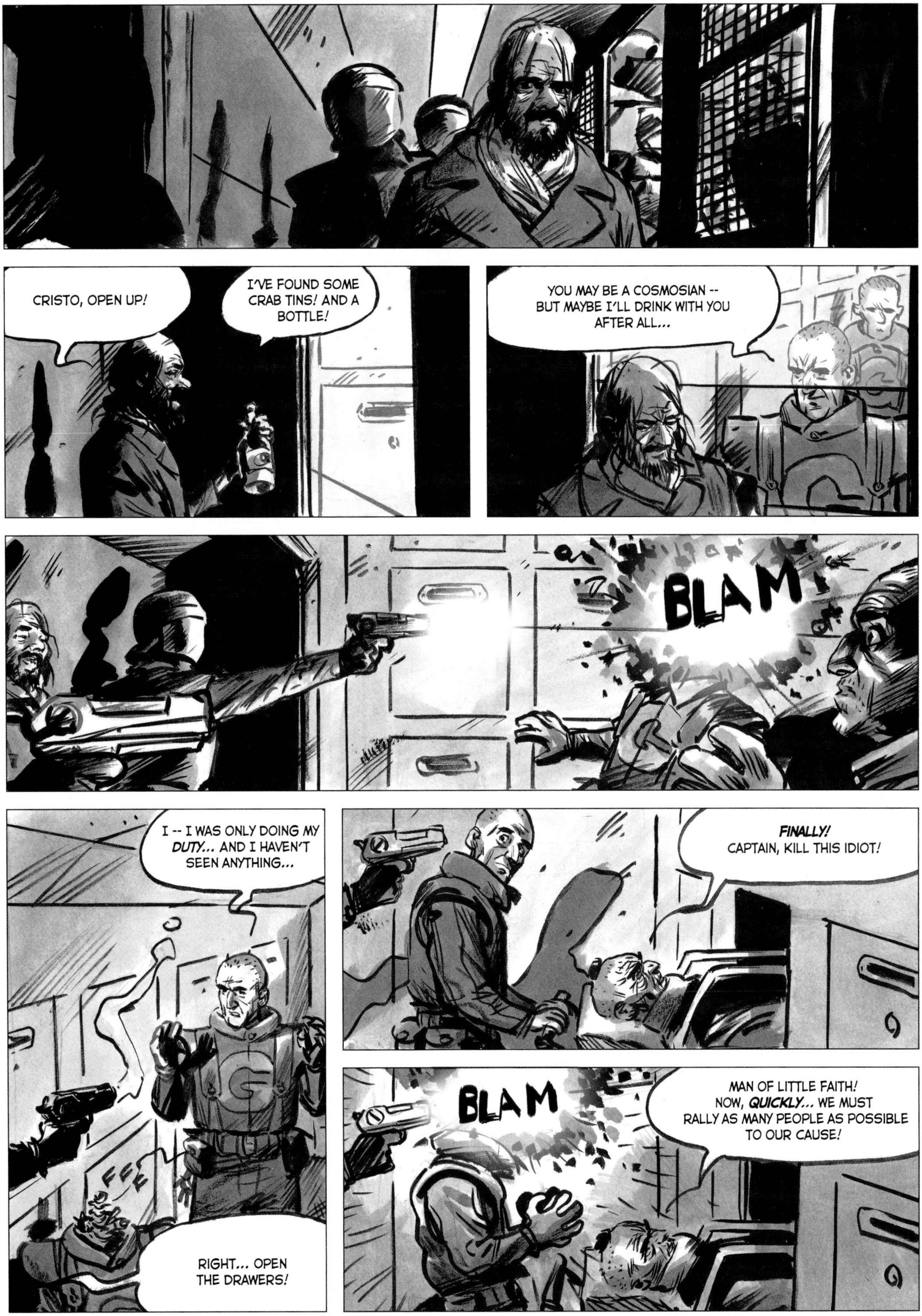
CRISTO, OPEN UP!
I'VE FOUND SOME CRAB TINS! AND A BOTTLE!
YOU MAY BE A COSMOSIAN -- BUT MAYBE I'LL DRINK WITH YOU AFTER ALL...
BLAM
I -- I WAS ONLY DOING MY *DUTY*... AND I HAVEN'T SEEN ANYTHING...
RIGHT... OPEN THE DRAWERS!
FINALLY!
CAPTAIN, KILL THIS IDIOT!
BLAM
MAN OF LITTLE FAITH! NOW, ***QUICKLY***... WE MUST RALLY AS MANY PEOPLE AS POSSIBLE TO OUR CAUSE!

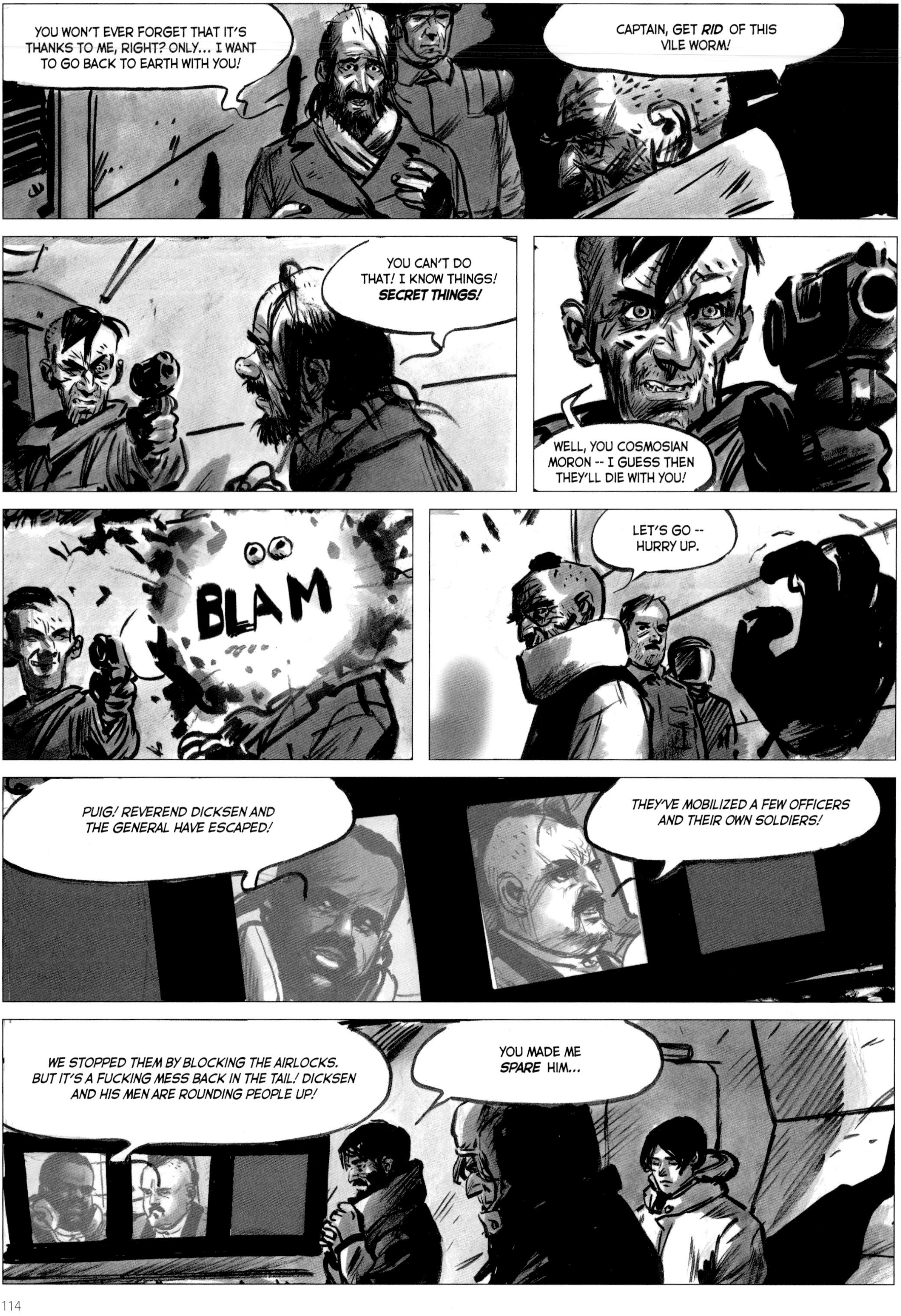
YOU WON'T EVER FORGET THAT IT'S THANKS TO ME, RIGHT? ONLY... I WANT TO GO BACK TO EARTH WITH YOU!
CAPTAIN, GET *RID* OF THIS VILE WORM!
YOU CAN'T DO THAT! I KNOW THINGS! *SECRET THINGS!*
WELL, YOU COSMOSIAN MORON -- I GUESS THEN THEY'LL DIE WITH YOU!
BLAM
LET'S GO -- HURRY UP.
PUIG! REVEREND DICKSEN AND THE GENERAL HAVE ESCAPED!
THEY'VE MOBILIZED A FEW OFFICERS AND THEIR OWN SOLDIERS!
WE STOPPED THEM BY BLOCKING THE AIRLOCKS. BUT IT'S A FUCKING MESS BACK IN THE TAIL! DICKSEN AND HIS MEN ARE ROUNDING PEOPLE UP!
YOU MADE ME *SPARE* HIM...

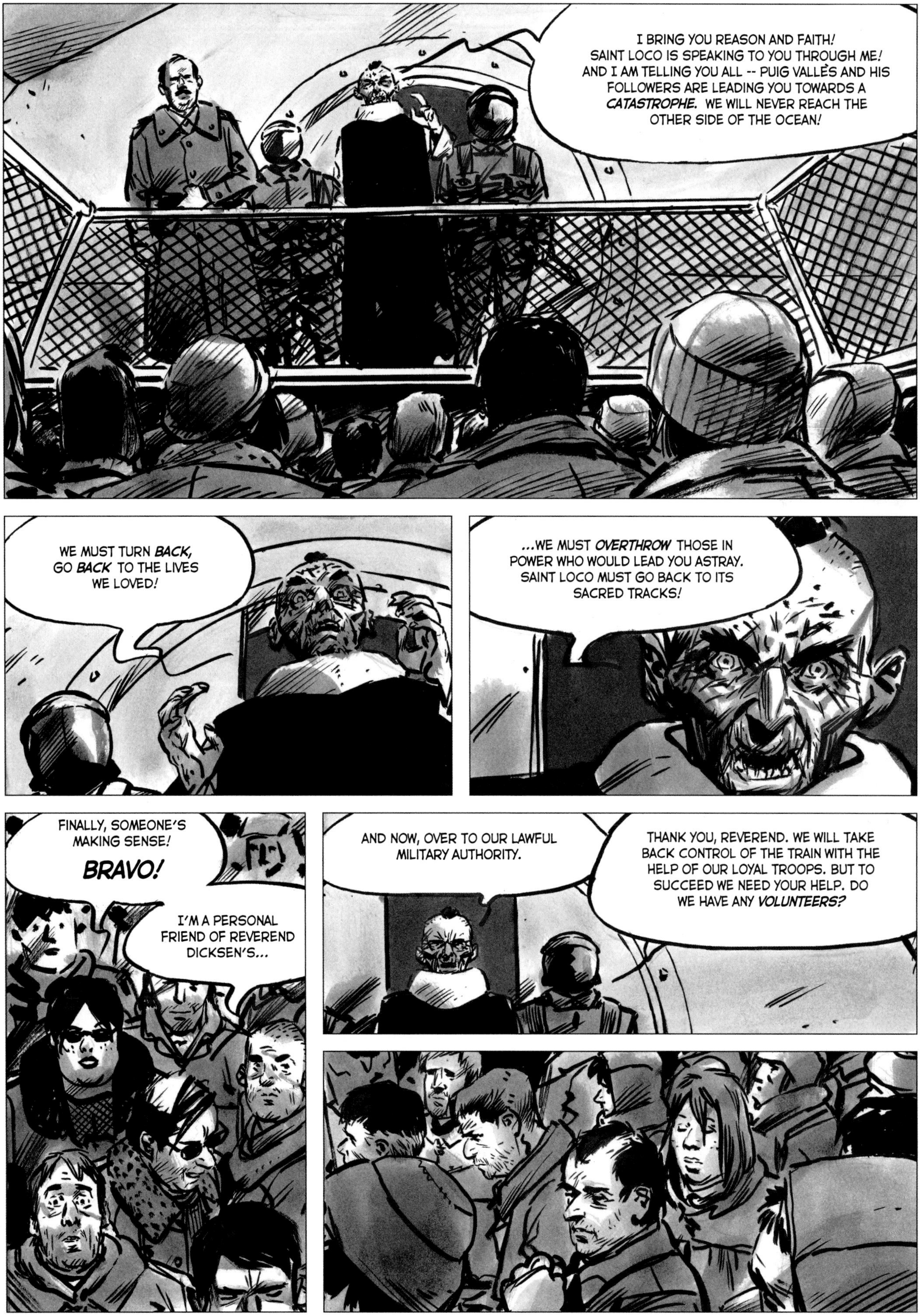

I BRING YOU REASON AND FAITH! SAINT LOCO IS SPEAKING TO YOU THROUGH ME! AND I AM TELLING YOU ALL -- PUIG VALLÈS AND HIS FOLLOWERS ARE LEADING YOU TOWARDS A *CATASTROPHE.* WE WILL NEVER REACH THE OTHER SIDE OF THE OCEAN!
WE MUST TURN *BACK,* GO *BACK* TO THE LIVES WE LOVED!
...WE MUST *OVERTHROW* THOSE IN POWER WHO WOULD LEAD YOU ASTRAY. SAINT LOCO MUST GO BACK TO ITS SACRED TRACKS!
FINALLY, SOMEONE'S MAKING SENSE! **BRAVO!**
I'M A PERSONAL FRIEND OF REVEREND DICKSEN'S...
AND NOW, OVER TO OUR LAWFUL MILITARY AUTHORITY.
THANK YOU, REVEREND. WE WILL TAKE BACK CONTROL OF THE TRAIN WITH THE HELP OF OUR LOYAL TROOPS. BUT TO SUCCEED WE NEED YOUR HELP. DO WE HAVE ANY *VOLUNTEERS?*

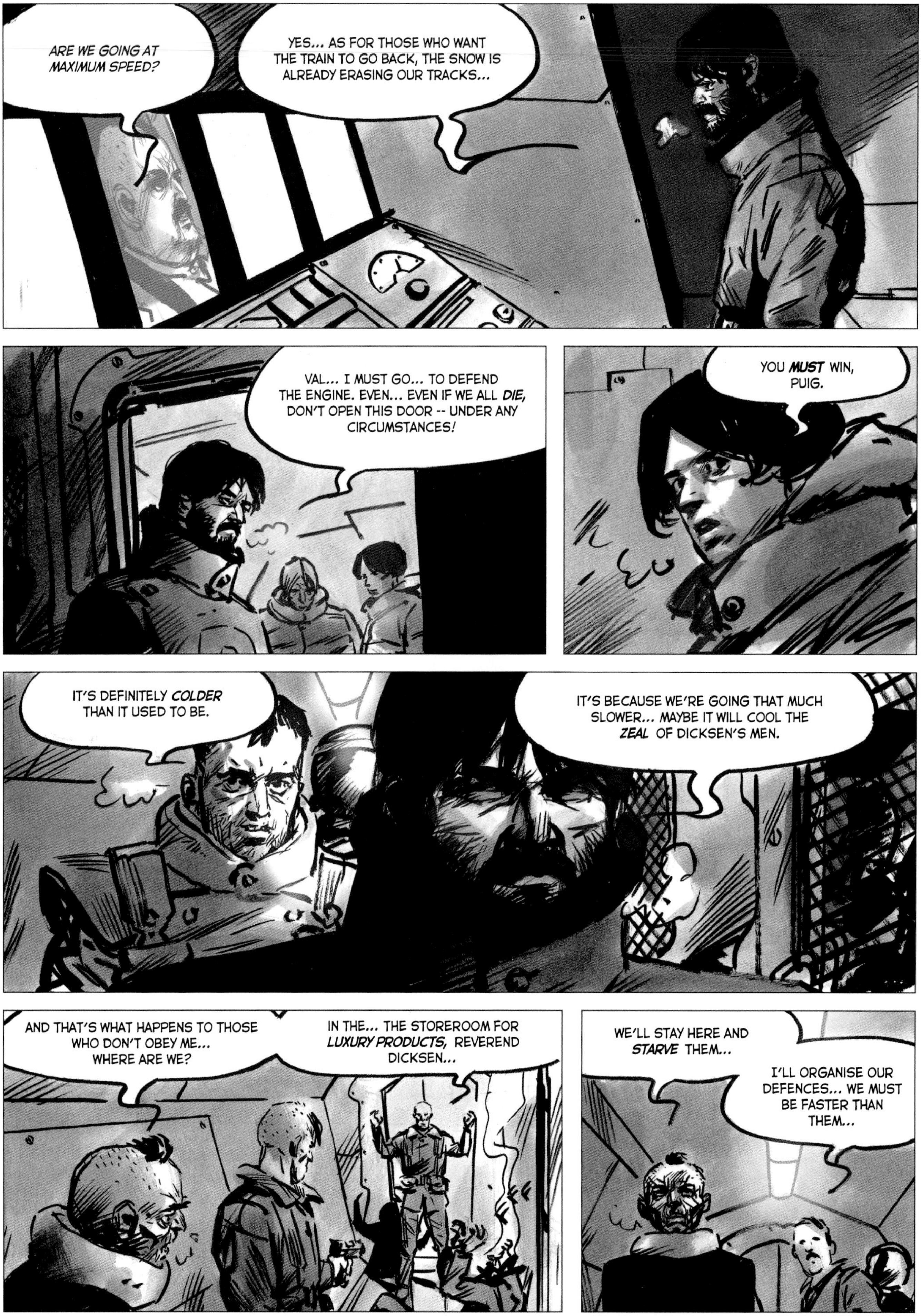

ARE WE GOING AT MAXIMUM SPEED?
YES... AS FOR THOSE WHO WANT THE TRAIN TO GO BACK, THE SNOW IS ALREADY ERASING OUR TRACKS...
VAL... I MUST GO... TO DEFEND THE ENGINE. EVEN... EVEN IF WE ALL DIE, DON'T OPEN THIS DOOR -- UNDER ANY CIRCUMSTANCES!
YOU MUST WIN, PUIG.
IT'S DEFINITELY COLDER THAN IT USED TO BE.
IT'S BECAUSE WE'RE GOING THAT MUCH SLOWER... MAYBE IT WILL COOL THE ZEAL OF DICKSEN'S MEN.
AND THAT'S WHAT HAPPENS TO THOSE WHO DON'T OBEY ME... WHERE ARE WE?
IN THE... THE STOREROOM FOR LUXURY PRODUCTS, REVEREND DICKSEN...
WE'LL STAY HERE AND STARVE THEM...
I'LL ORGANISE OUR DEFENCES... WE MUST BE FASTER THAN THEM...

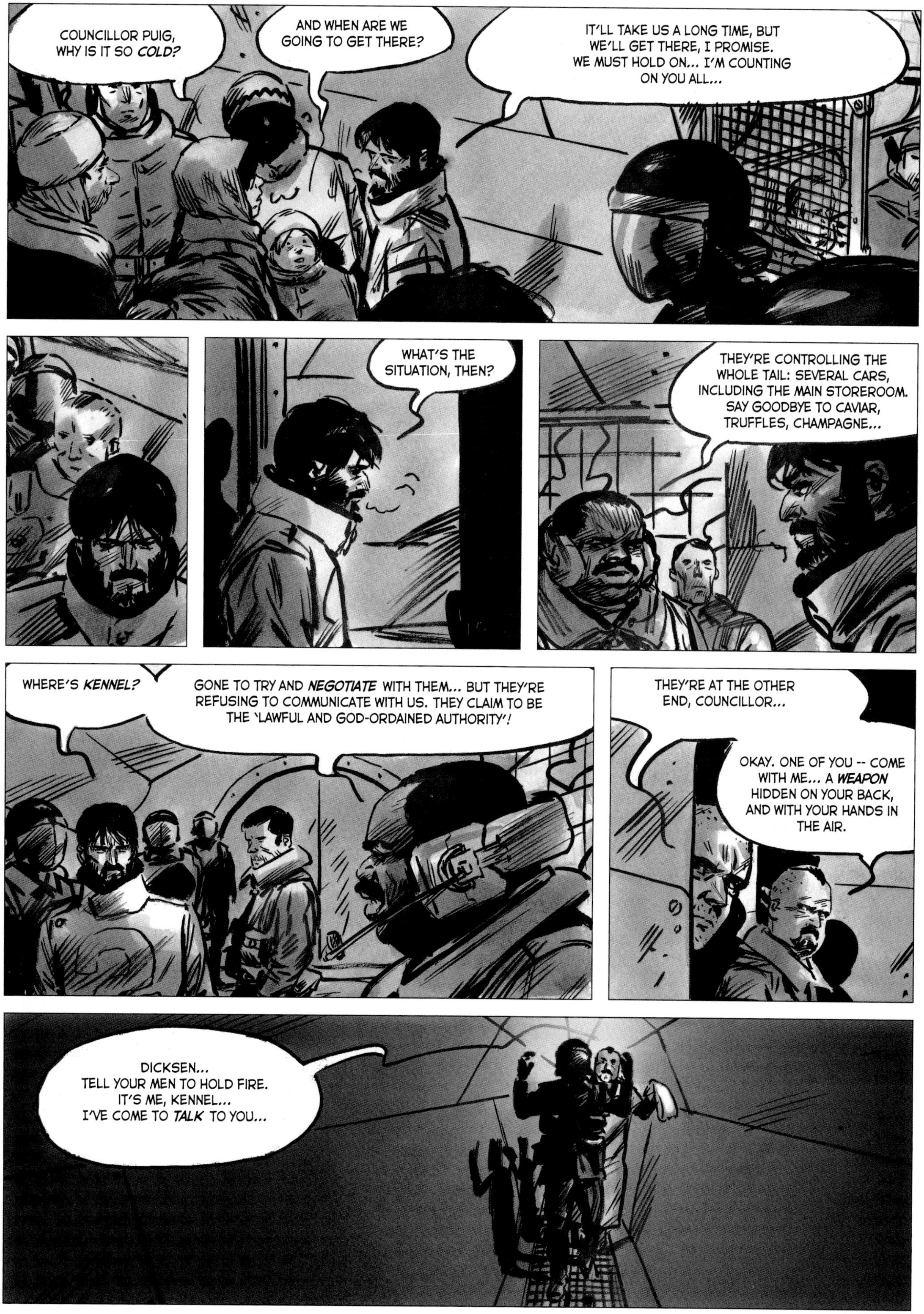
COUNCILLOR PUIG, WHY IS IT SO *COLD?*
AND WHEN ARE WE GOING TO GET THERE?
IT'LL TAKE US A LONG TIME, BUT WE'LL GET THERE, I PROMISE. WE MUST HOLD ON... I'M COUNTING ON YOU ALL...
WHAT'S THE SITUATION, THEN?
THEY'RE CONTROLLING THE WHOLE TAIL: SEVERAL CARS, INCLUDING THE MAIN STOREROOM. SAY GOODBYE TO CAVIAR, TRUFFLES, CHAMPAGNE...
WHERE'S *KENNEL?*
GONE TO TRY AND *NEGOTIATE* WITH THEM... BUT THEY'RE REFUSING TO COMMUNICATE WITH US. THEY CLAIM TO BE THE 'LAWFUL AND GOD-ORDAINED AUTHORITY'!
THEY'RE AT THE OTHER END, COUNCILLOR...
OKAY. ONE OF YOU -- COME WITH ME... A *WEAPON* HIDDEN ON YOUR BACK, AND WITH YOUR HANDS IN THE AIR.
DICKSEN... TELL YOUR MEN TO HOLD FIRE. IT'S ME, KENNEL... I'VE COME TO *TALK* TO YOU...

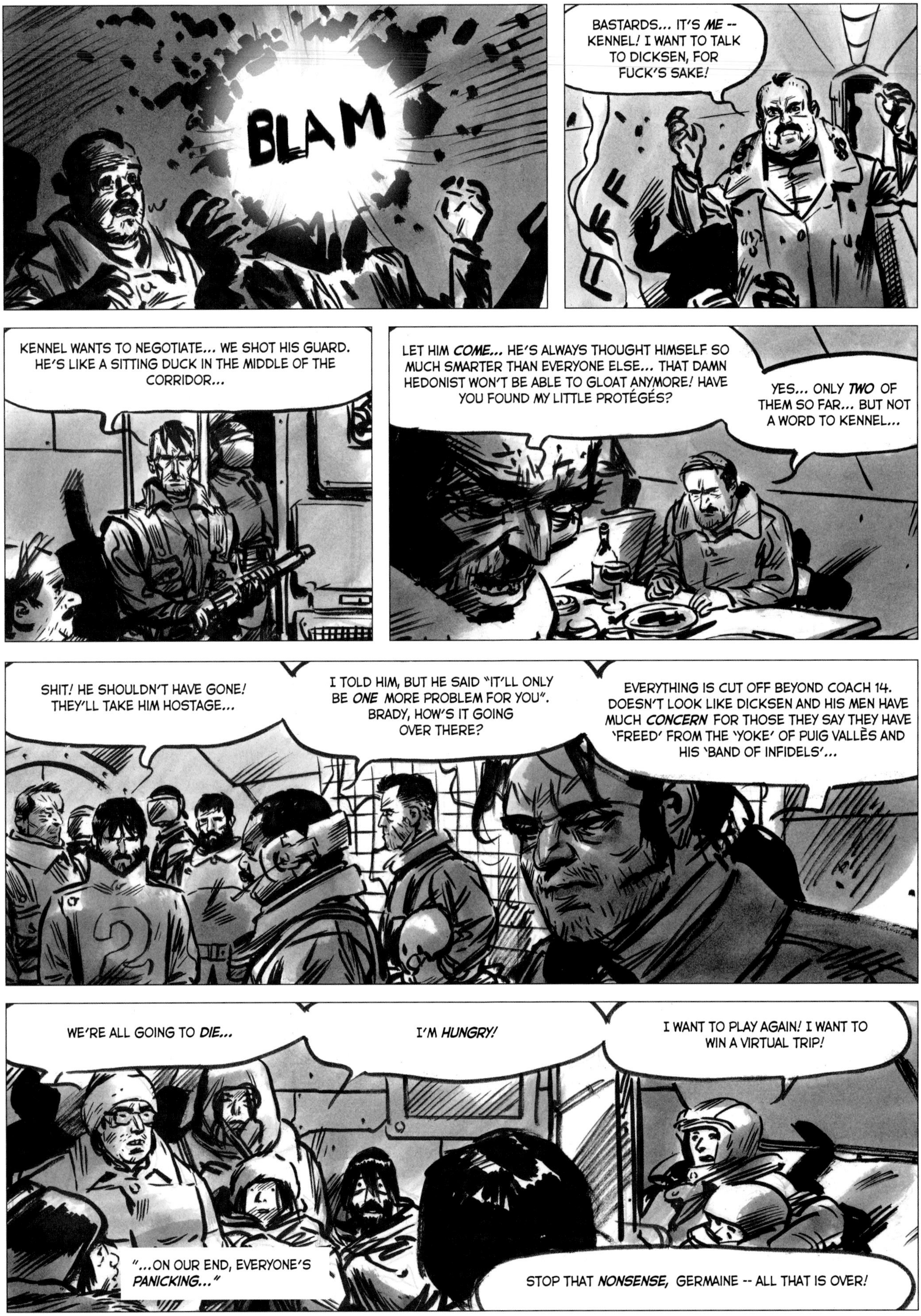
BLAM
BASTARDS... IT'S *ME* -- KENNEL! I WANT TO TALK TO DICKSEN, FOR FUCK'S SAKE!
KENNEL WANTS TO NEGOTIATE... WE SHOT HIS GUARD. HE'S LIKE A SITTING DUCK IN THE MIDDLE OF THE CORRIDOR...
LET HIM *COME...* HE'S ALWAYS THOUGHT HIMSELF SO MUCH SMARTER THAN EVERYONE ELSE... THAT DAMN HEDONIST WON'T BE ABLE TO GLOAT ANYMORE! HAVE YOU FOUND MY LITTLE PROTÉGÉS?
YES... ONLY *TWO* OF THEM SO FAR... BUT NOT A WORD TO KENNEL...
SHIT! HE SHOULDN'T HAVE GONE! THEY'LL TAKE HIM HOSTAGE...
I TOLD HIM, BUT HE SAID "IT'LL ONLY BE *ONE* MORE PROBLEM FOR YOU". BRADY, HOW'S IT GOING OVER THERE?
EVERYTHING IS CUT OFF BEYOND COACH 14. DOESN'T LOOK LIKE DICKSEN AND HIS MEN HAVE MUCH *CONCERN* FOR THOSE THEY SAY THEY HAVE 'FREED' FROM THE 'YOKE' OF PUIG VALLÈS AND HIS 'BAND OF INFIDELS'...
WE'RE ALL GOING TO *DIE...*
I'M *HUNGRY!*
I WANT TO PLAY AGAIN! I WANT TO WIN A VIRTUAL TRIP!
"...ON OUR END, EVERYONE'S *PANICKING...*"
STOP THAT *NONSENSE,* GERMAINE -- ALL THAT IS OVER!

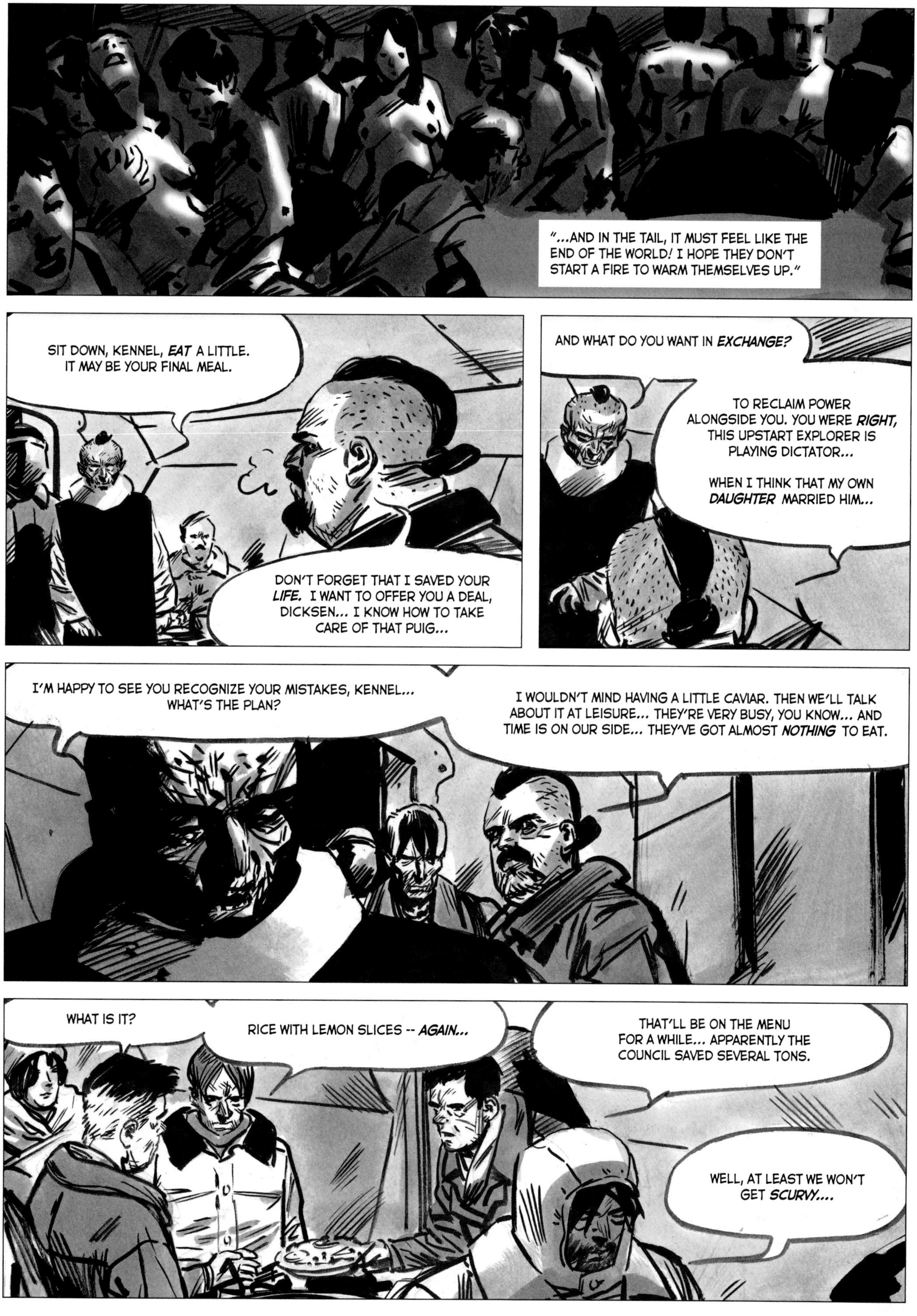
"...AND IN THE TAIL, IT MUST FEEL LIKE THE END OF THE WORLD! I HOPE THEY DON'T START A FIRE TO WARM THEMSELVES UP."
SIT DOWN, KENNEL, *EAT* A LITTLE. IT MAY BE YOUR FINAL MEAL.
DON'T FORGET THAT I SAVED YOUR *LIFE.* I WANT TO OFFER YOU A DEAL, DICKSEN... I KNOW HOW TO TAKE CARE OF THAT PUIG...
AND WHAT DO YOU WANT IN *EXCHANGE?*
TO RECLAIM POWER ALONGSIDE YOU. YOU WERE *RIGHT,* THIS UPSTART EXPLORER IS PLAYING DICTATOR...
WHEN I THINK THAT MY OWN *DAUGHTER* MARRIED HIM...
I'M HAPPY TO SEE YOU RECOGNIZE YOUR MISTAKES, KENNEL... WHAT'S THE PLAN?
I WOULDN'T MIND HAVING A LITTLE CAVIAR. THEN WE'LL TALK ABOUT IT AT LEISURE... THEY'RE VERY BUSY, YOU KNOW... AND TIME IS ON OUR SIDE... THEY'VE GOT ALMOST *NOTHING* TO EAT.
WHAT IS IT?
RICE WITH LEMON SLICES -- *AGAIN...*
THAT'LL BE ON THE MENU FOR A WHILE... APPARENTLY THE COUNCIL SAVED SEVERAL TONS.
WELL, AT LEAST WE WON'T GET *SCURVY....*

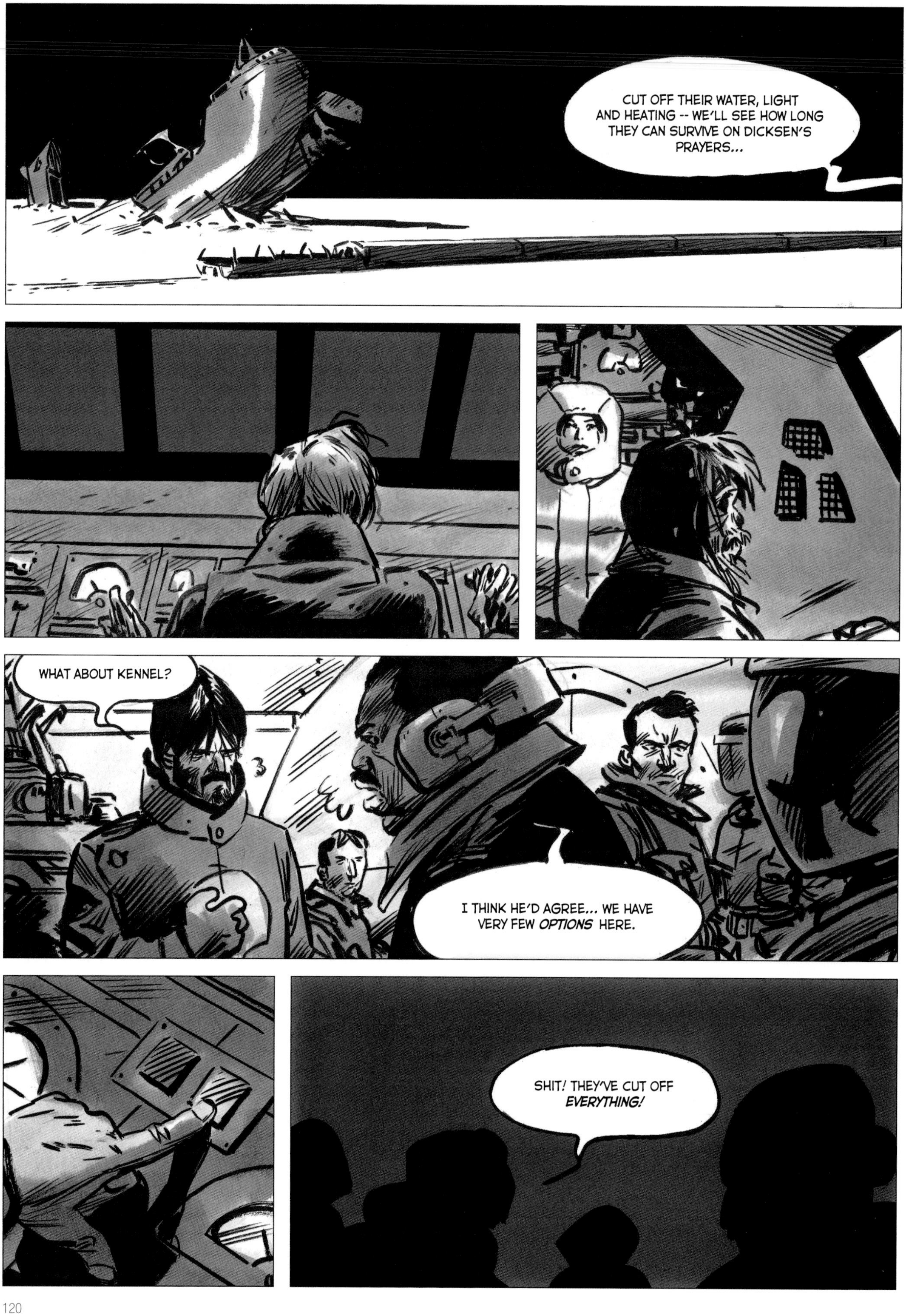
CUT OFF THEIR WATER, LIGHT AND HEATING -- WE'LL SEE HOW LONG THEY CAN SURVIVE ON DICKSEN'S PRAYERS...
WHAT ABOUT KENNEL?
I THINK HE'D AGREE... WE HAVE VERY FEW *OPTIONS* HERE.
SHIT! THEY'VE CUT OFF *EVERYTHING!*

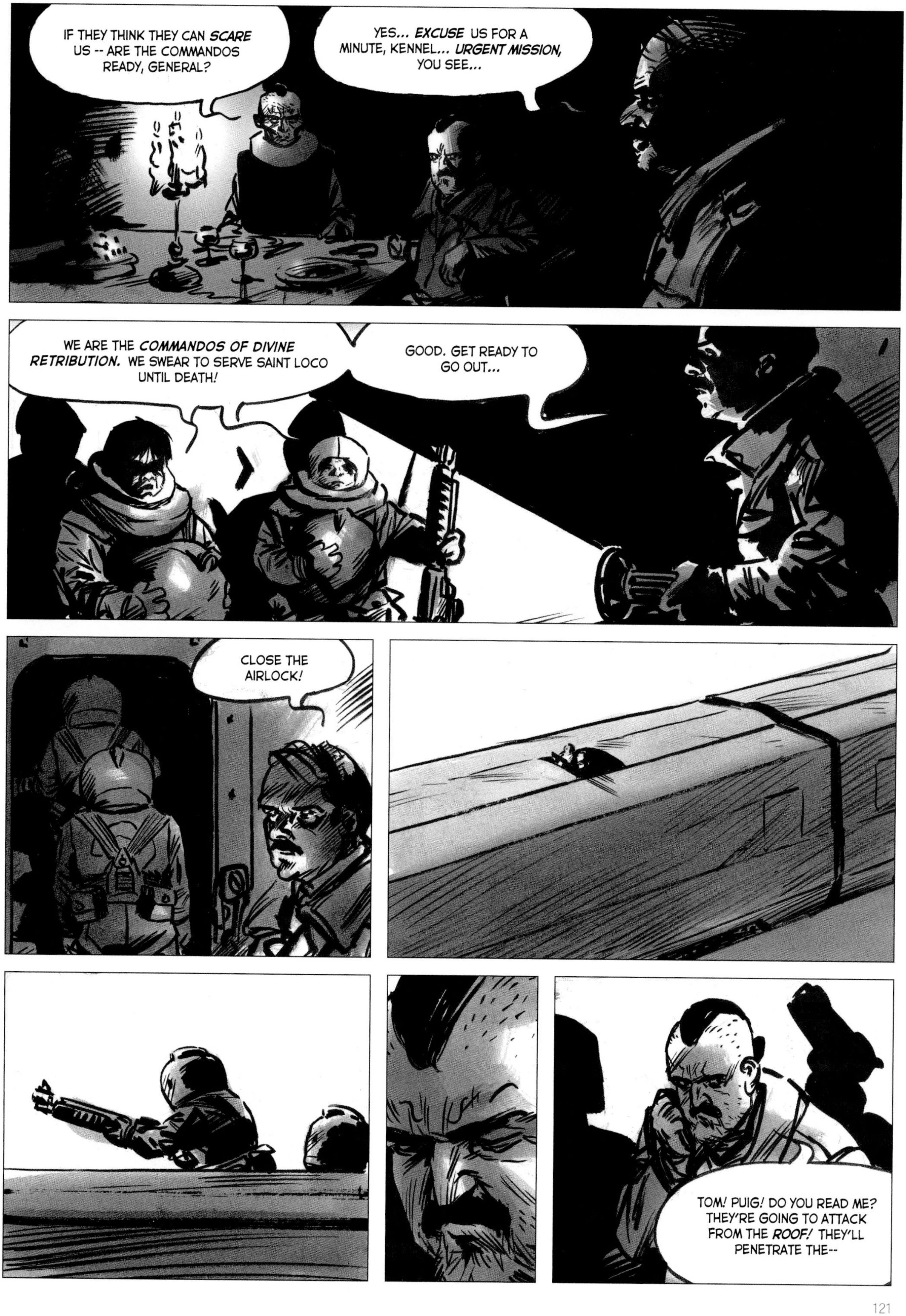
IF THEY THINK THEY CAN SCARE US -- ARE THE COMMANDOS READY, GENERAL?
YES... EXCUSE US FOR A MINUTE, KENNEL... URGENT MISSION, YOU SEE...
WE ARE THE COMMANDOS OF DIVINE RETRIBUTION. WE SWEAR TO SERVE SAINT LOCO UNTIL DEATH!
GOOD. GET READY TO GO OUT...
CLOSE THE AIRLOCK!
TOM! PUIG! DO YOU READ ME? THEY'RE GOING TO ATTACK FROM THE ROOF! THEY'LL PENETRATE THE--

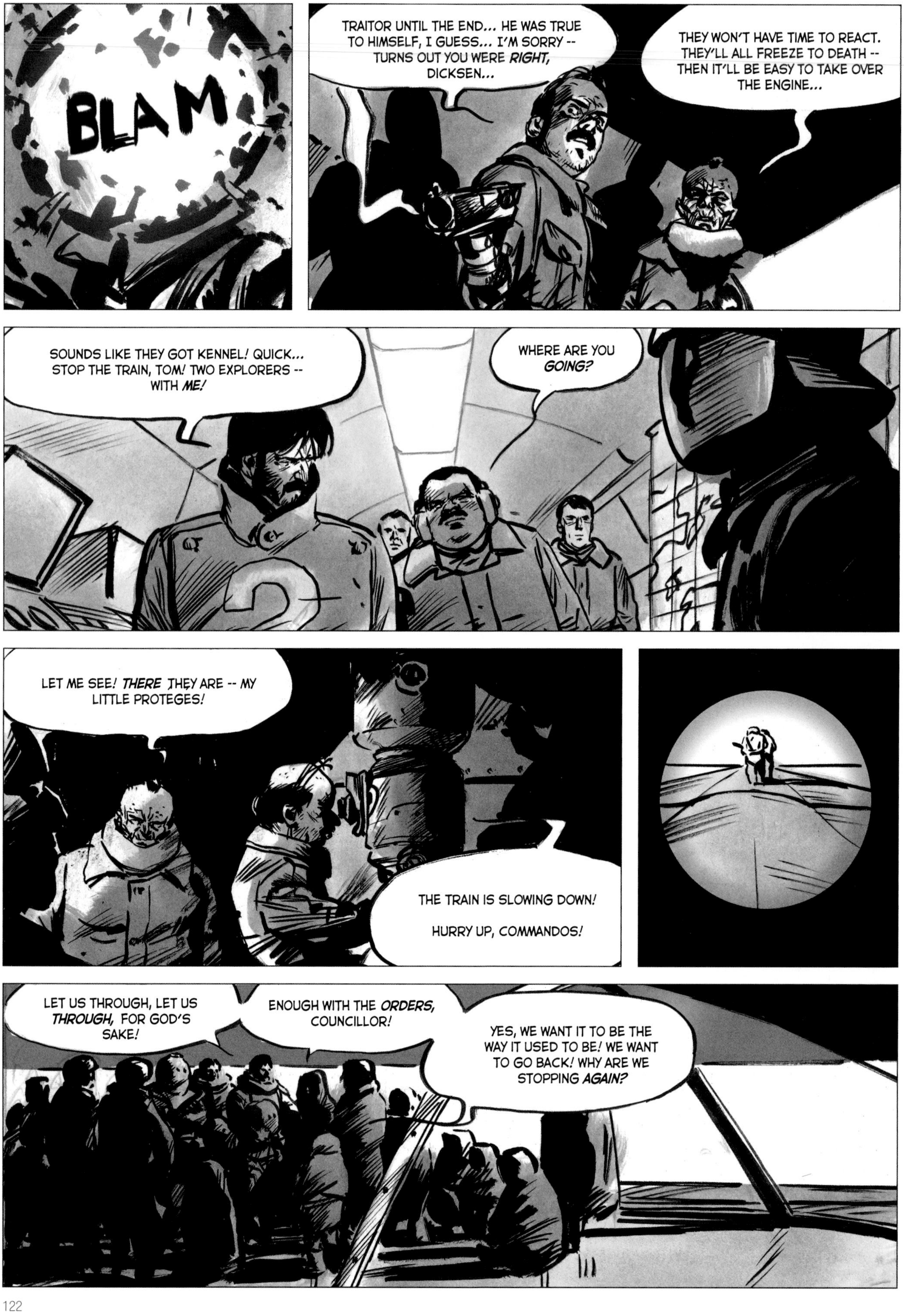
BLAM
TRAITOR UNTIL THE END... HE WAS TRUE TO HIMSELF, I GUESS... I'M SORRY -- TURNS OUT YOU WERE RIGHT, DICKSEN...
THEY WON'T HAVE TIME TO REACT. THEY'LL ALL FREEZE TO DEATH -- THEN IT'LL BE EASY TO TAKE OVER THE ENGINE...
SOUNDS LIKE THEY GOT KENNEL! QUICK... STOP THE TRAIN, TOM! TWO EXPLORERS -- WITH ME!
WHERE ARE YOU GOING?
LET ME SEE! THERE THEY ARE -- MY LITTLE PROTEGES!
THE TRAIN IS SLOWING DOWN!
HURRY UP, COMMANDOS!
LET US THROUGH, LET US THROUGH, FOR GOD'S SAKE!
ENOUGH WITH THE ORDERS, COUNCILLOR!
YES, WE WANT IT TO BE THE WAY IT USED TO BE! WE WANT TO GO BACK! WHY ARE WE STOPPING AGAIN?

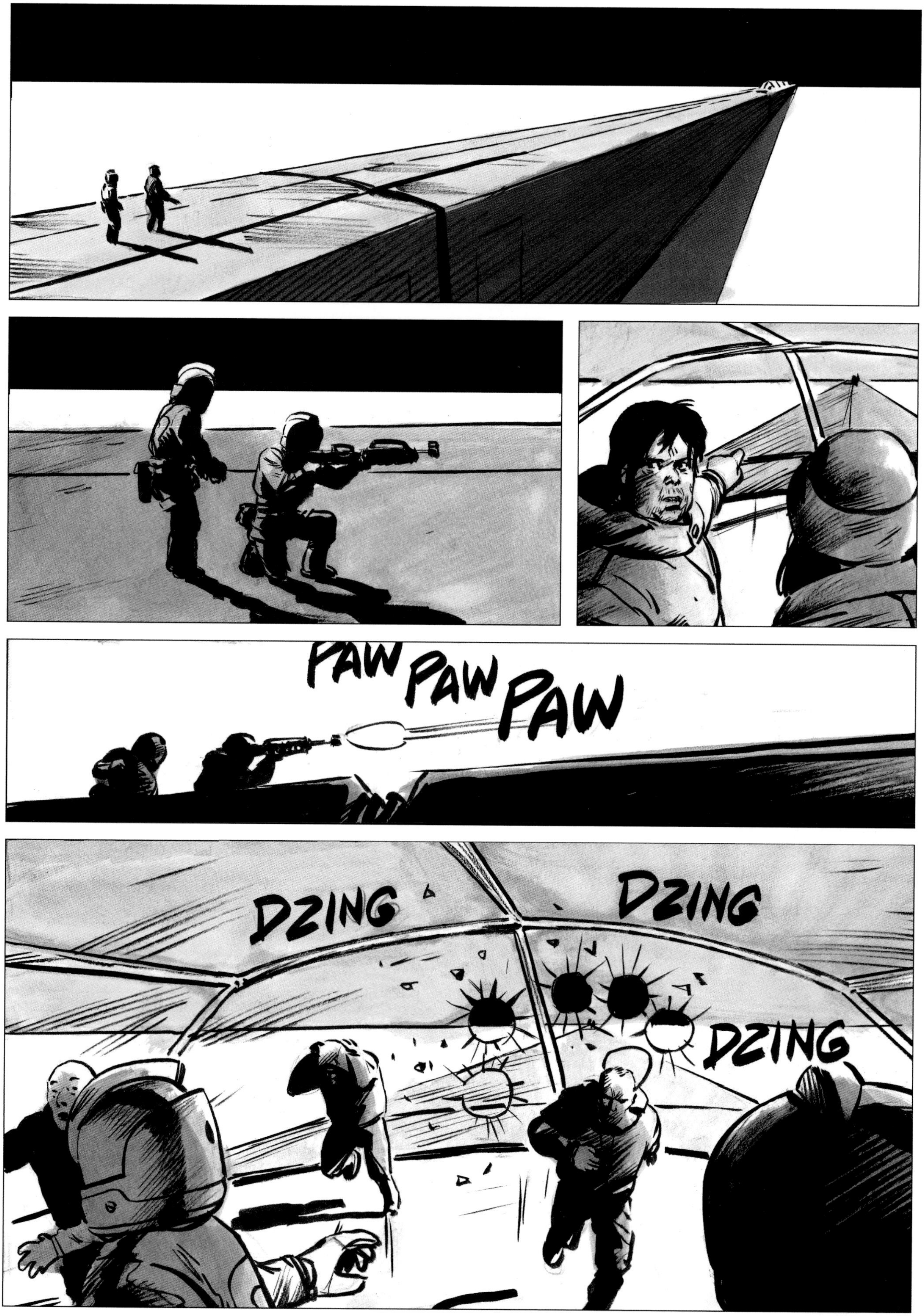
PAW PAW PAW
DZING
DZING
DZING

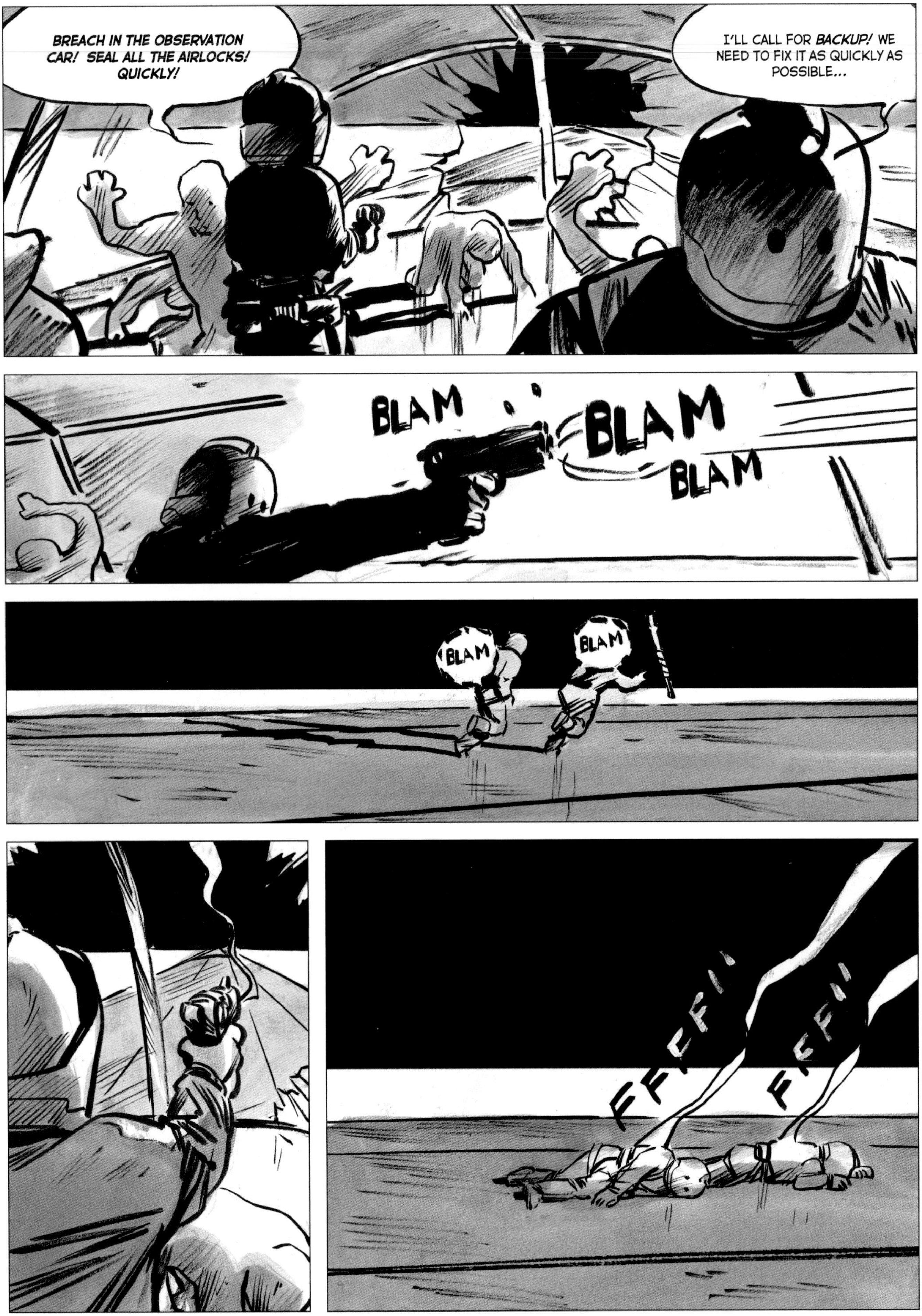
BREACH IN THE OBSERVATION CAR! SEAL ALL THE AIRLOCKS! QUICKLY!
I'LL CALL FOR BACKUP! WE NEED TO FIX IT AS QUICKLY AS POSSIBLE...
BLAM
BLAM
BLAM
BLAM
BLAM

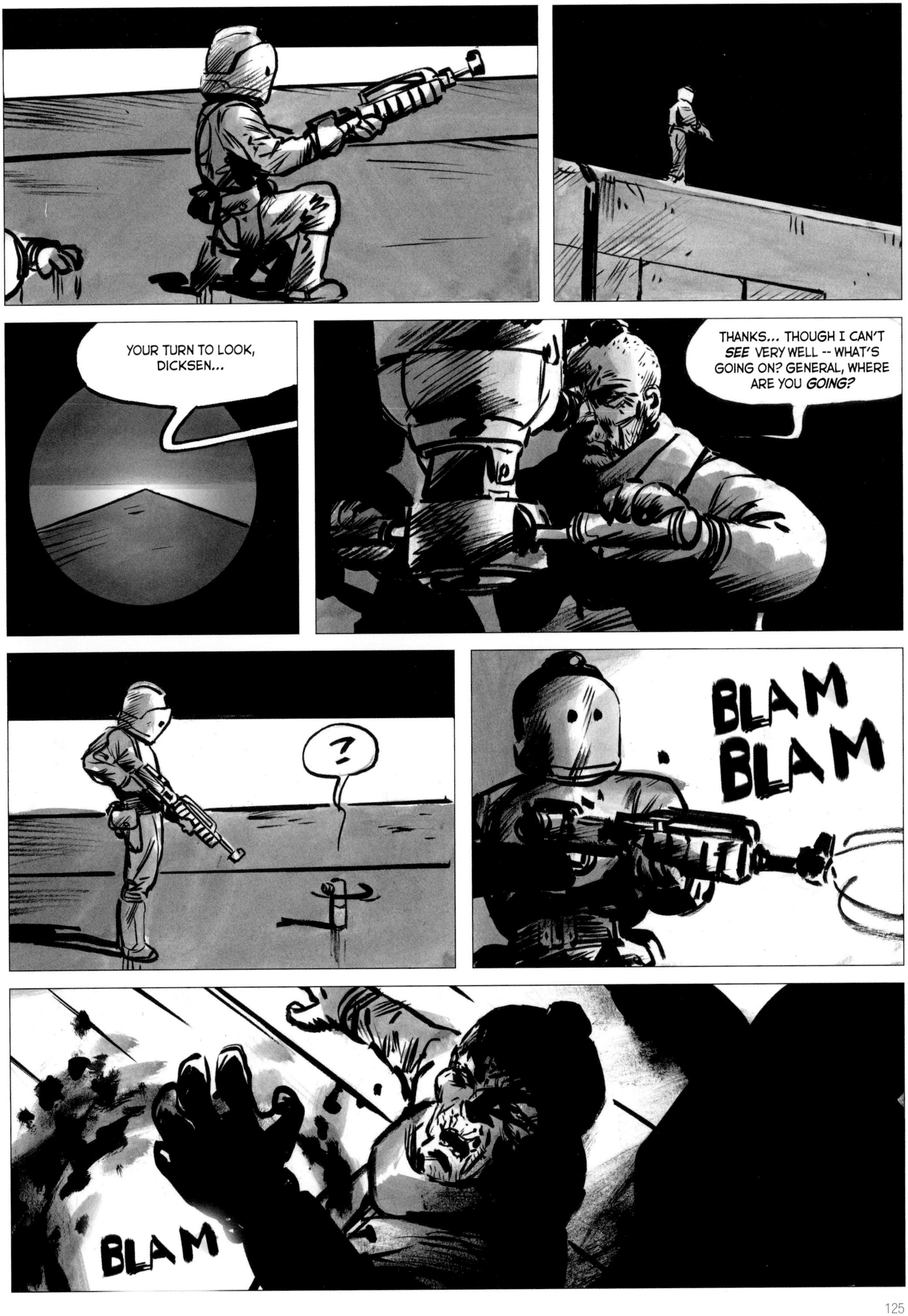
YOUR TURN TO LOOK, DICKSEN...
THANKS... THOUGH I CAN'T *SEE* VERY WELL -- WHAT'S GOING ON? GENERAL, WHERE ARE YOU *GOING?*
?
BLAM BLAM
BLAM

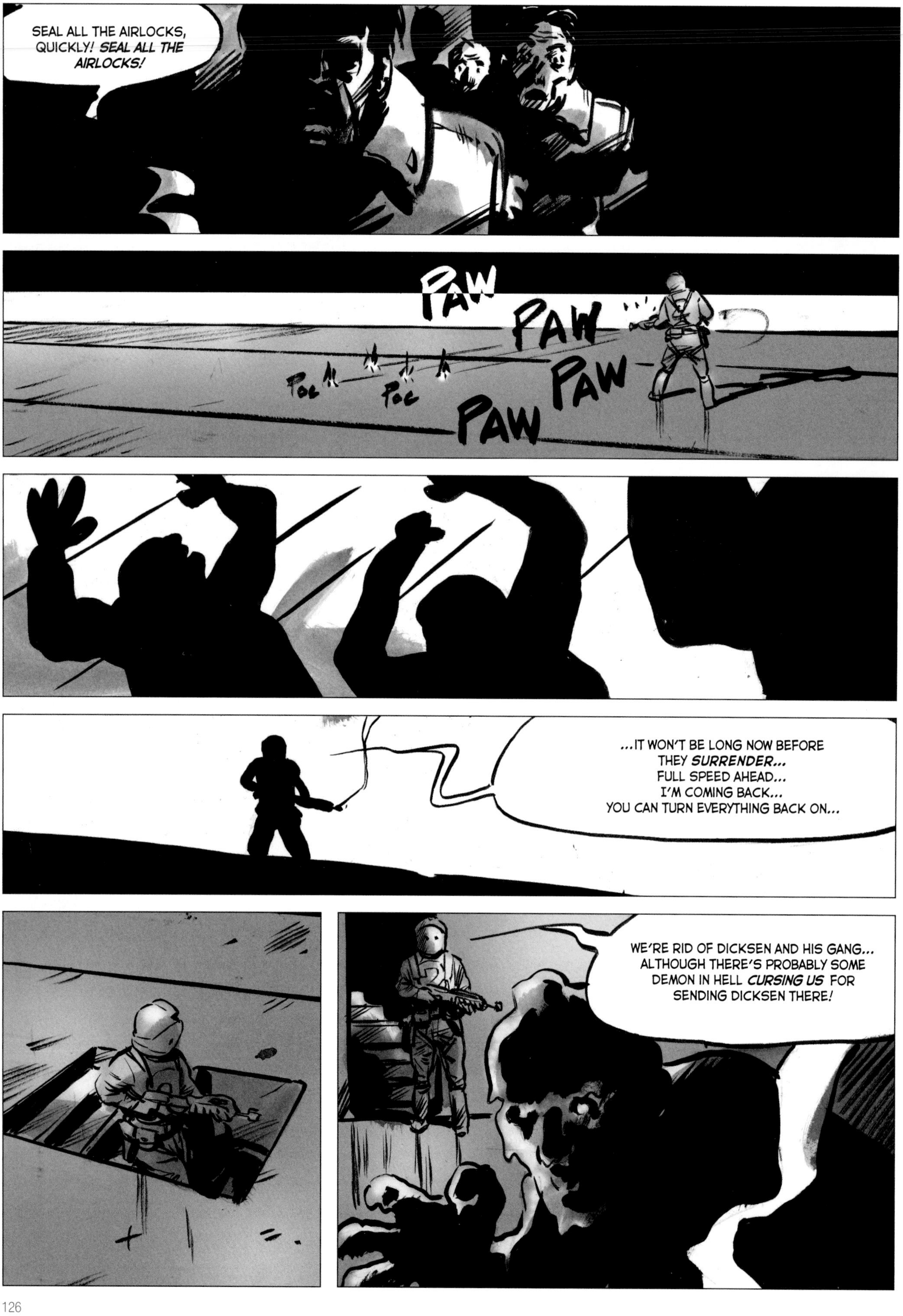
SEAL ALL THE AIRLOCKS, QUICKLY! *SEAL ALL THE AIRLOCKS!*
PAW PAW PAW PAW
POC POC
...IT WON'T BE LONG NOW BEFORE THEY *SURRENDER...* FULL SPEED AHEAD... I'M COMING BACK... YOU CAN TURN EVERYTHING BACK ON...
WE'RE RID OF DICKSEN AND HIS GANG... ALTHOUGH THERE'S PROBABLY SOME DEMON IN HELL *CURSING US* FOR SENDING DICKSEN THERE!

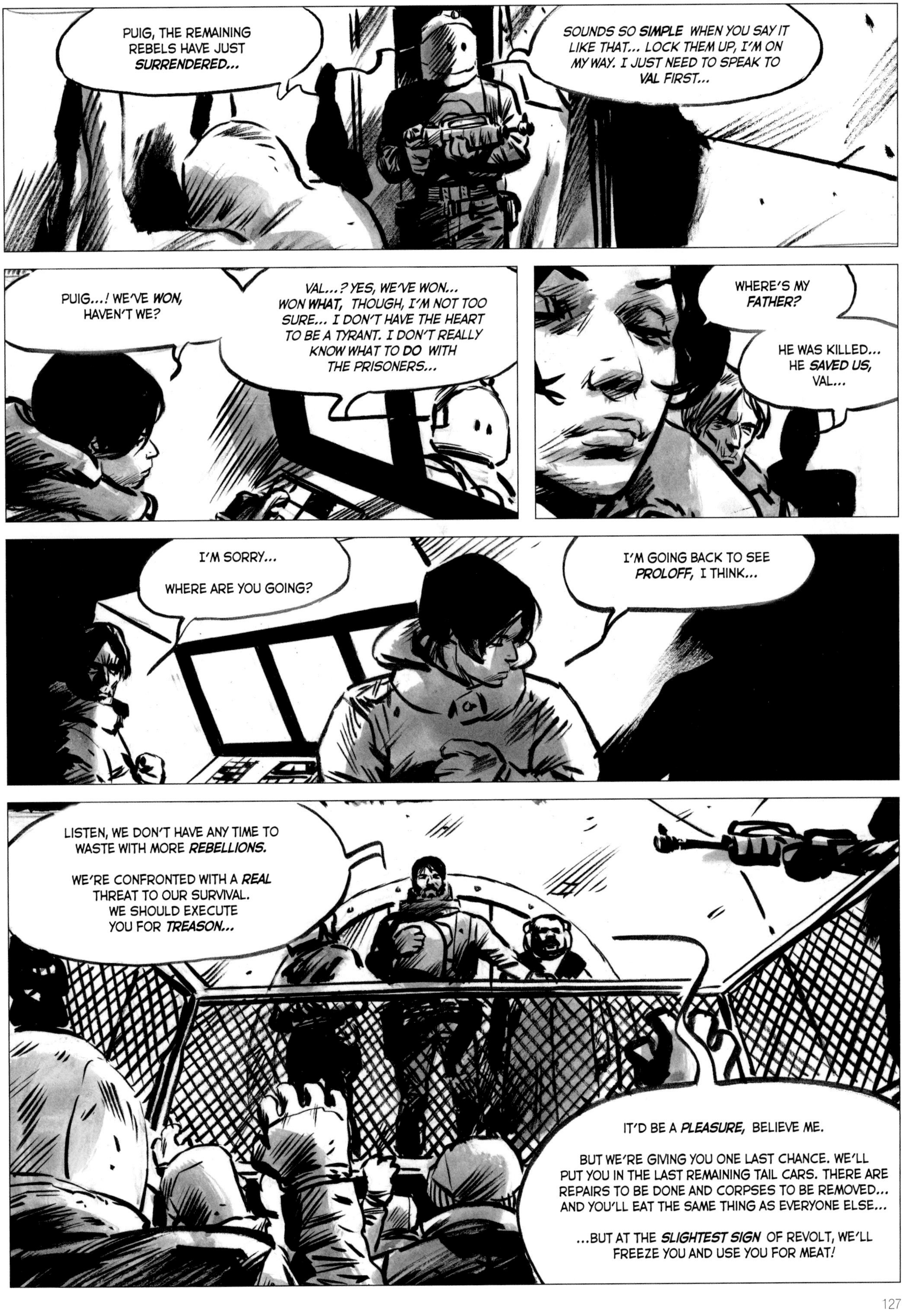
PUIG, THE REMAINING REBELS HAVE JUST SURRENDERED...
SOUNDS SO SIMPLE WHEN YOU SAY IT LIKE THAT... LOCK THEM UP, I'M ON MY WAY. I JUST NEED TO SPEAK TO VAL FIRST...
PUIG...! WE'VE WON, HAVEN'T WE?
VAL...? YES, WE'VE WON... WON WHAT, THOUGH, I'M NOT TOO SURE... I DON'T HAVE THE HEART TO BE A TYRANT. I DON'T REALLY KNOW WHAT TO DO WITH THE PRISONERS...
WHERE'S MY FATHER?
HE WAS KILLED... HE SAVED US, VAL...
I'M SORRY... WHERE ARE YOU GOING?
I'M GOING BACK TO SEE PROLOFF, I THINK...
LISTEN, WE DON'T HAVE ANY TIME TO WASTE WITH MORE REBELLIONS. WE'RE CONFRONTED WITH A REAL THREAT TO OUR SURVIVAL. WE SHOULD EXECUTE YOU FOR TREASON...
IT'D BE A PLEASURE, BELIEVE ME. BUT WE'RE GIVING YOU ONE LAST CHANCE. WE'LL PUT YOU IN THE LAST REMAINING TAIL CARS. THERE ARE REPAIRS TO BE DONE AND CORPSES TO BE REMOVED... AND YOU'LL EAT THE SAME THING AS EVERYONE ELSE... ...BUT AT THE SLIGHTEST SIGN OF REVOLT, WE'LL FREEZE YOU AND USE YOU FOR MEAT!

THE *SNOWPIERCER* TRAVELS SLOWLY... CRAWLING LIKE A CATERPILLAR ACROSS THE PALE, FROZEN OCEAN.

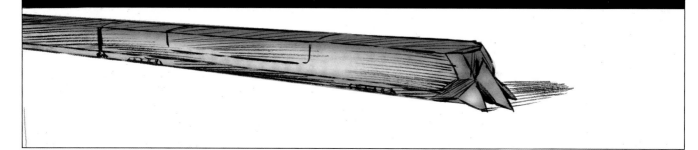

WHAT--?

...AFTER THE MUTINY, THERE'LL BE MORE PROBLEMS TO COME... THE *PROMISED LAND* STILL LIES A LONG WAY OFF...

PROLOFF... YOU'RE... *ALIVE?!* THAT'S INCREDIBLE... IT'S LIKE... YOU'RE *INSIDE* THE MACHINE!

DON'T CRY FOR ME, YOUNG LADY -- IT'S STILL A LONG TIME TILL WE REACH THE OTHER SIDE. FOR THE LONGEST TIME, I THOUGHT I WAS THE ONLY MAN FOR HER... BUT NOW THE ENGINE WANTS SOMEONE *ELSE.*

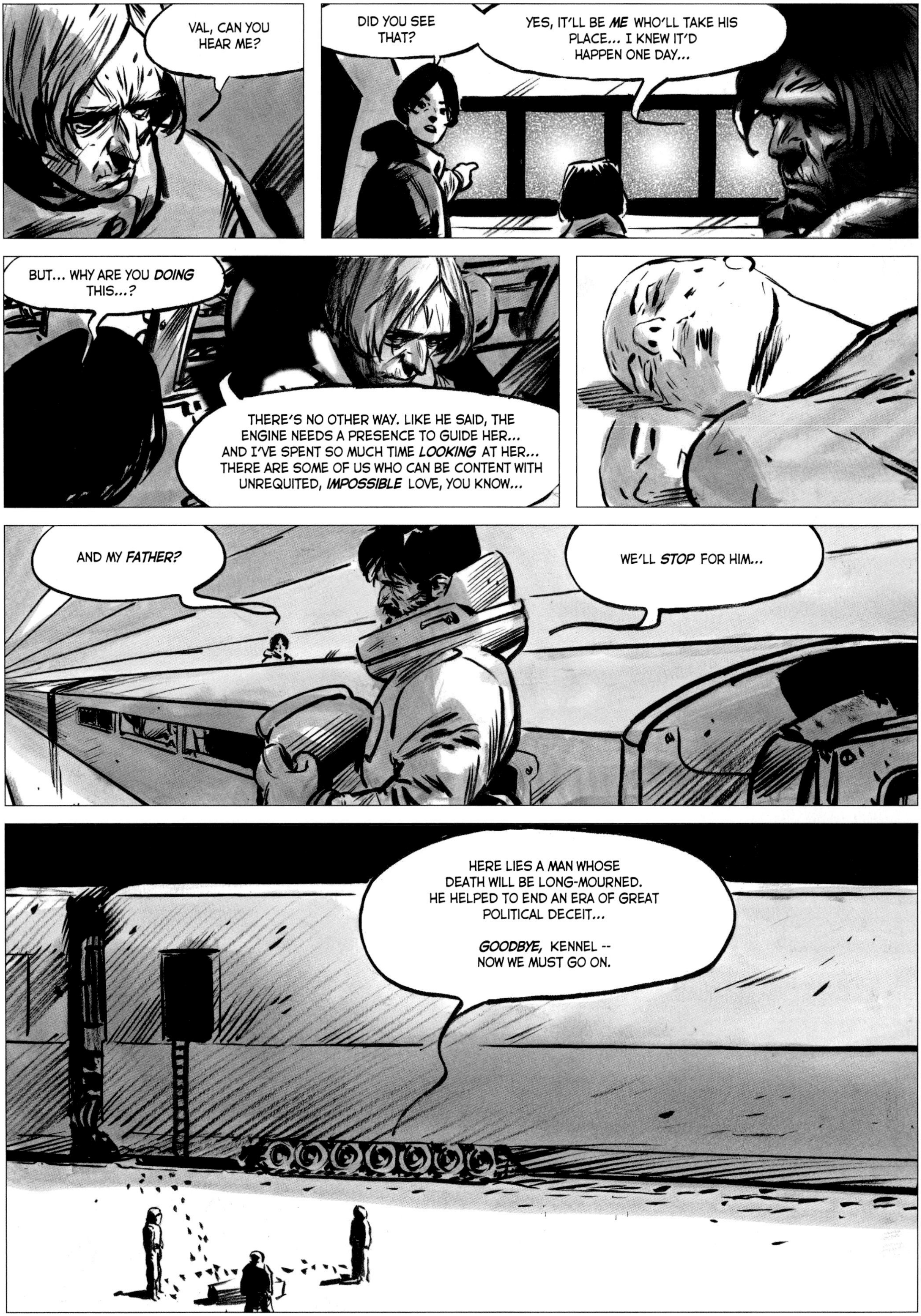
VAL, CAN YOU HEAR ME?
DID YOU SEE THAT?
YES, IT'LL BE *ME* WHO'LL TAKE HIS PLACE... I KNEW IT'D HAPPEN ONE DAY...
BUT... WHY ARE YOU *DOING* THIS...?
THERE'S NO OTHER WAY. LIKE HE SAID, THE ENGINE NEEDS A PRESENCE TO GUIDE HER... AND I'VE SPENT SO MUCH TIME *LOOKING* AT HER... THERE ARE SOME OF US WHO CAN BE CONTENT WITH UNREQUITED, *IMPOSSIBLE* LOVE, YOU KNOW...
AND MY *FATHER?*
WE'LL *STOP* FOR HIM...
HERE LIES A MAN WHOSE DEATH WILL BE LONG-MOURNED. HE HELPED TO END AN ERA OF GREAT POLITICAL DECEIT...
GOODBYE, KENNEL -- NOW WE MUST GO ON.

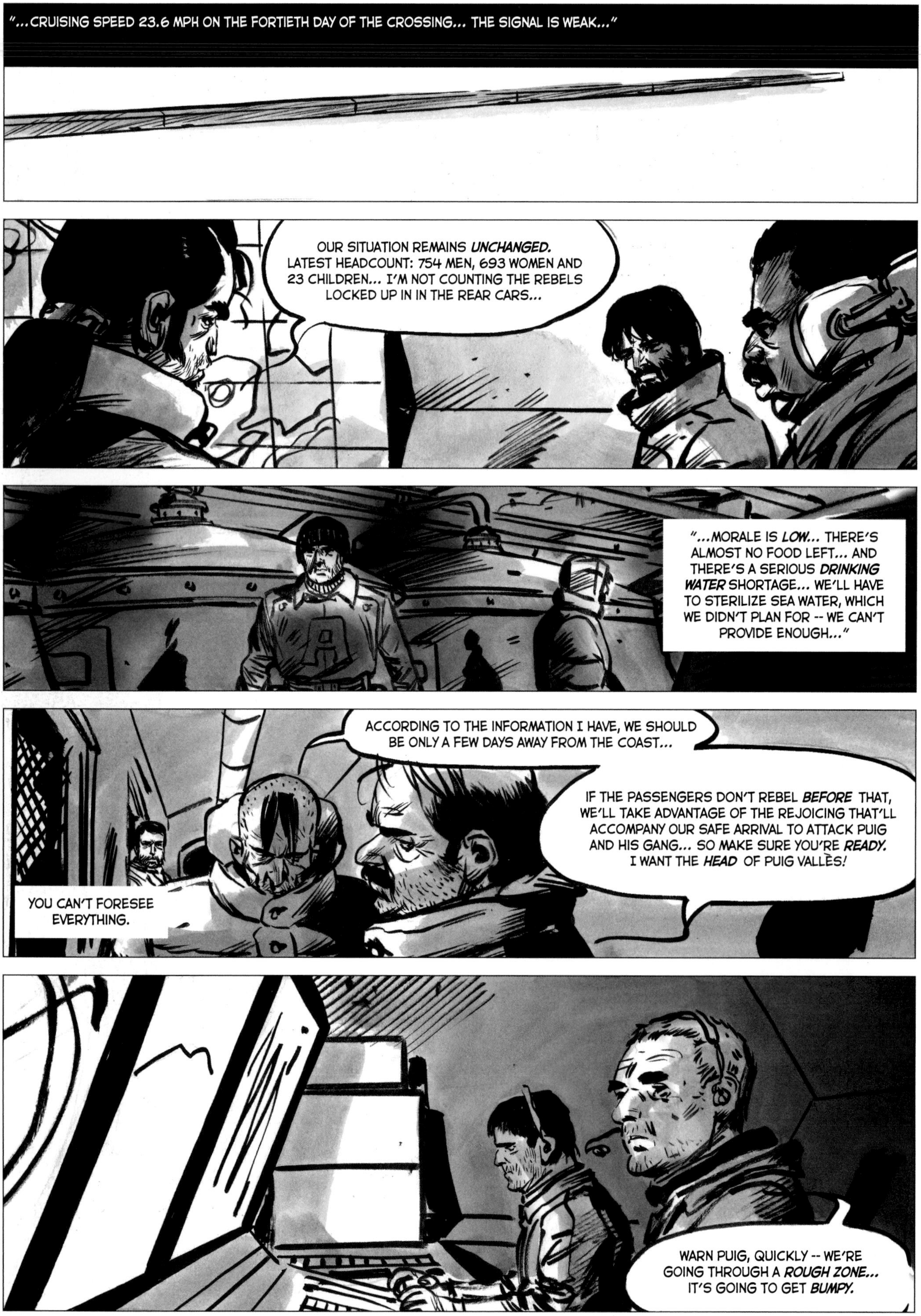
"...CRUISING SPEED 23.6 MPH ON THE FORTIETH DAY OF THE CROSSING... THE SIGNAL IS WEAK..."
OUR SITUATION REMAINS UNCHANGED. LATEST HEADCOUNT: 754 MEN, 693 WOMEN AND 23 CHILDREN... I'M NOT COUNTING THE REBELS LOCKED UP IN IN THE REAR CARS...
"...MORALE IS LOW... THERE'S ALMOST NO FOOD LEFT... AND THERE'S A SERIOUS DRINKING WATER SHORTAGE... WE'LL HAVE TO STERILIZE SEA WATER, WHICH WE DIDN'T PLAN FOR -- WE CAN'T PROVIDE ENOUGH..."
ACCORDING TO THE INFORMATION I HAVE, WE SHOULD BE ONLY A FEW DAYS AWAY FROM THE COAST...
IF THE PASSENGERS DON'T REBEL BEFORE THAT, WE'LL TAKE ADVANTAGE OF THE REJOICING THAT'LL ACCOMPANY OUR SAFE ARRIVAL TO ATTACK PUIG AND HIS GANG... SO MAKE SURE YOU'RE READY. I WANT THE HEAD OF PUIG VALLÈS!
YOU CAN'T FORESEE EVERYTHING.
WARN PUIG, QUICKLY -- WE'RE GOING THROUGH A ROUGH ZONE... IT'S GOING TO GET BUMPY.

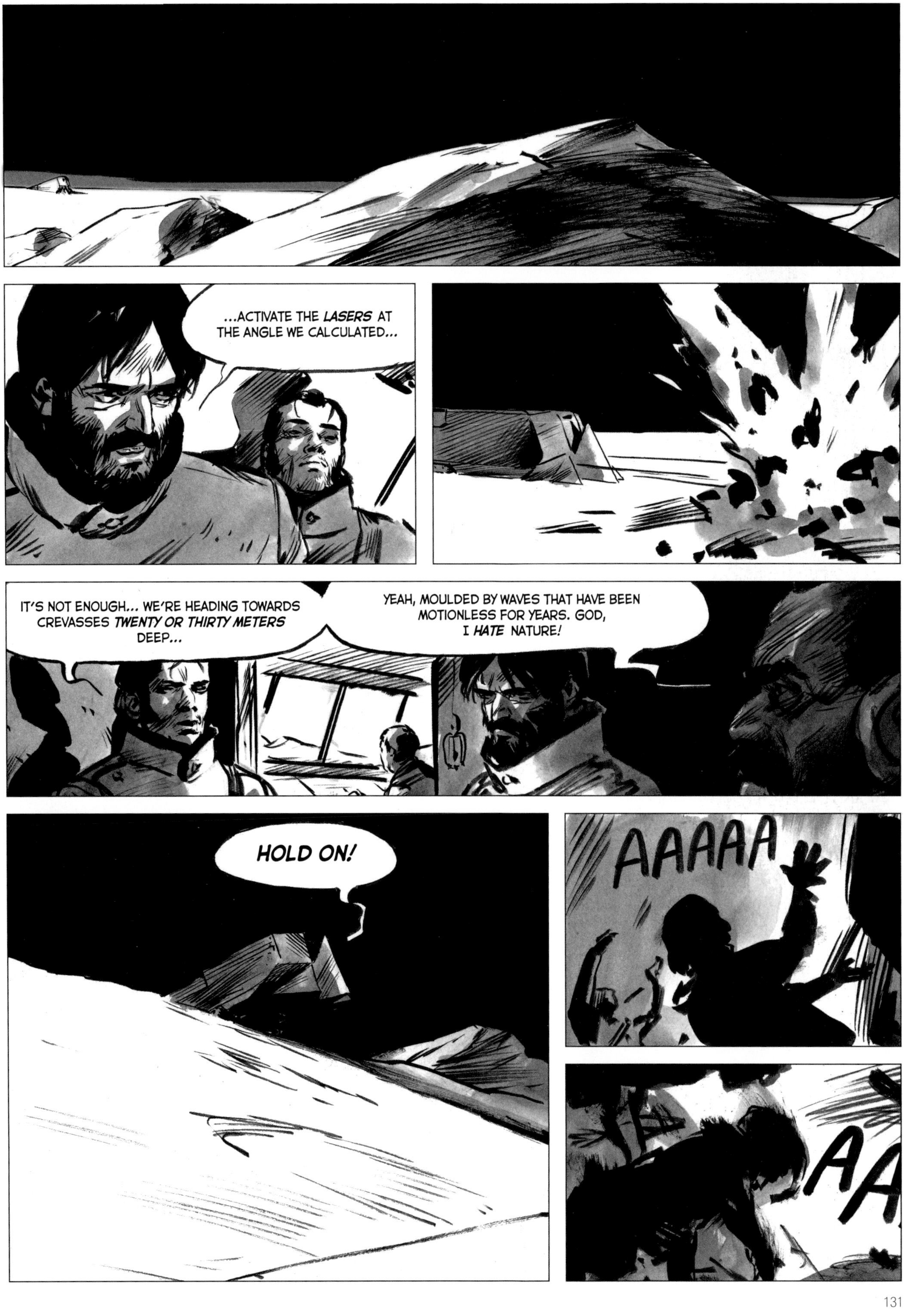
...ACTIVATE THE LASERS AT THE ANGLE WE CALCULATED...
IT'S NOT ENOUGH... WE'RE HEADING TOWARDS CREVASSES TWENTY OR THIRTY METERS DEEP...
YEAH, MOULDED BY WAVES THAT HAVE BEEN MOTIONLESS FOR YEARS. GOD, I HATE NATURE!
HOLD ON!
AAAAA
AA

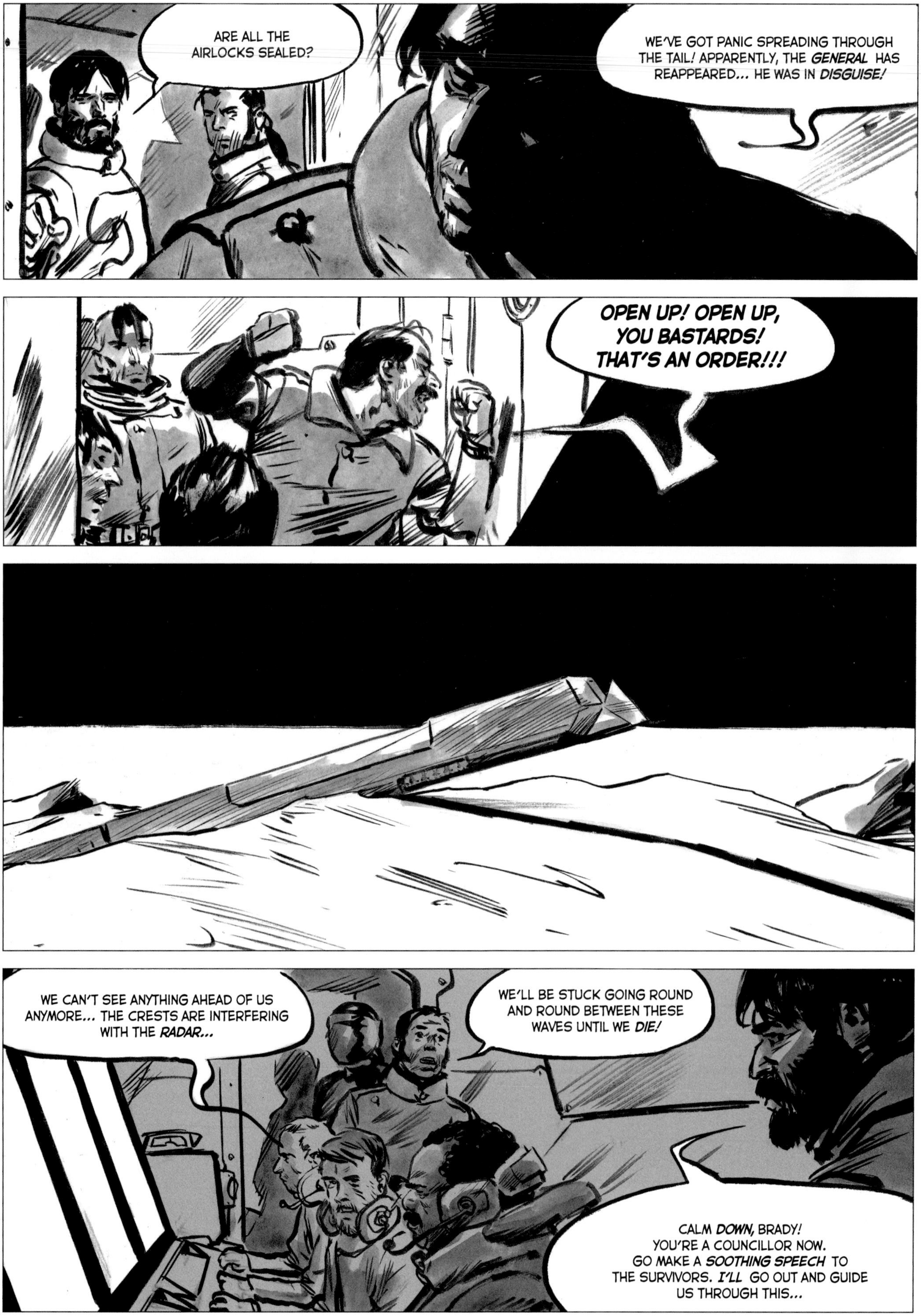
ARE ALL THE AIRLOCKS SEALED?
WE'VE GOT PANIC SPREADING THROUGH THE TAIL! APPARENTLY, THE *GENERAL* HAS REAPPEARED... HE WAS IN *DISGUISE!*
OPEN UP! OPEN UP, YOU BASTARDS! THAT'S AN ORDER!!!
WE CAN'T SEE ANYTHING AHEAD OF US ANYMORE... THE CRESTS ARE INTERFERING WITH THE *RADAR...*
WE'LL BE STUCK GOING ROUND AND ROUND BETWEEN THESE WAVES UNTIL WE *DIE!*
CALM *DOWN,* BRADY! YOU'RE A COUNCILLOR NOW. GO MAKE A *SOOTHING SPEECH* TO THE SURVIVORS. *I'LL* GO OUT AND GUIDE US THROUGH THIS...

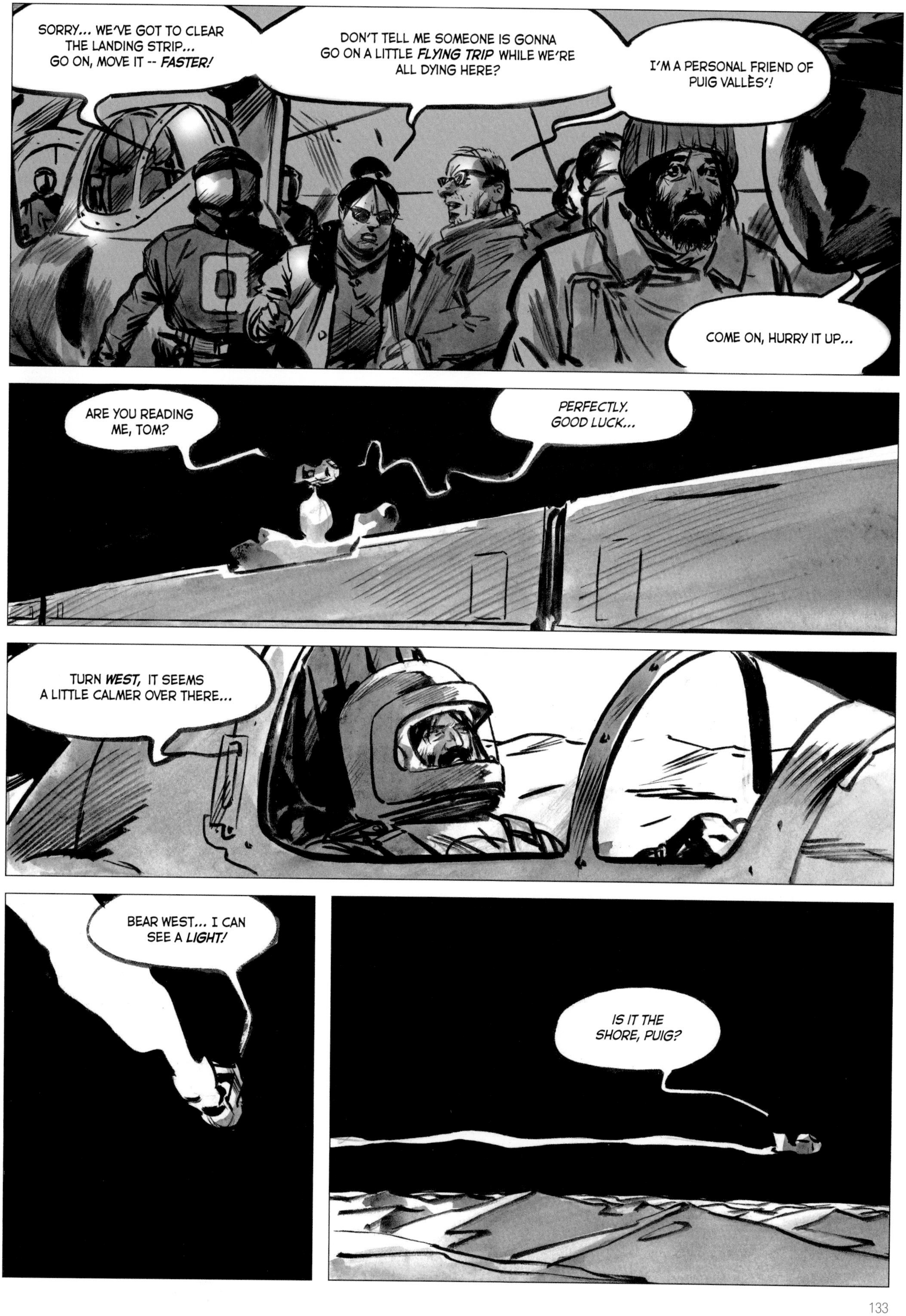
SORRY... WE'VE GOT TO CLEAR THE LANDING STRIP... GO ON, MOVE IT -- *FASTER!*
DON'T TELL ME SOMEONE IS GONNA GO ON A LITTLE *FLYING TRIP* WHILE WE'RE ALL DYING HERE?
I'M A PERSONAL FRIEND OF PUIG VALLÈS'!
COME ON, HURRY IT UP...
ARE YOU READING ME, TOM?
PERFECTLY. GOOD LUCK...
TURN *WEST,* IT SEEMS A LITTLE CALMER OVER THERE...
BEAR WEST... I CAN SEE A *LIGHT!*
IS IT THE SHORE, PUIG?

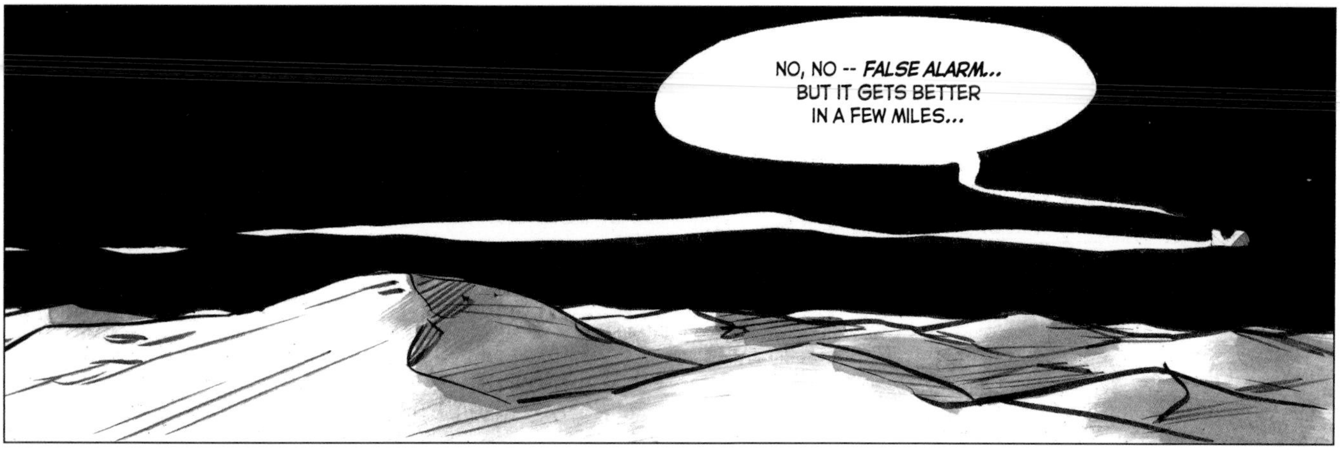
NO, NO -- FALSE ALARM... BUT IT GETS BETTER IN A FEW MILES...

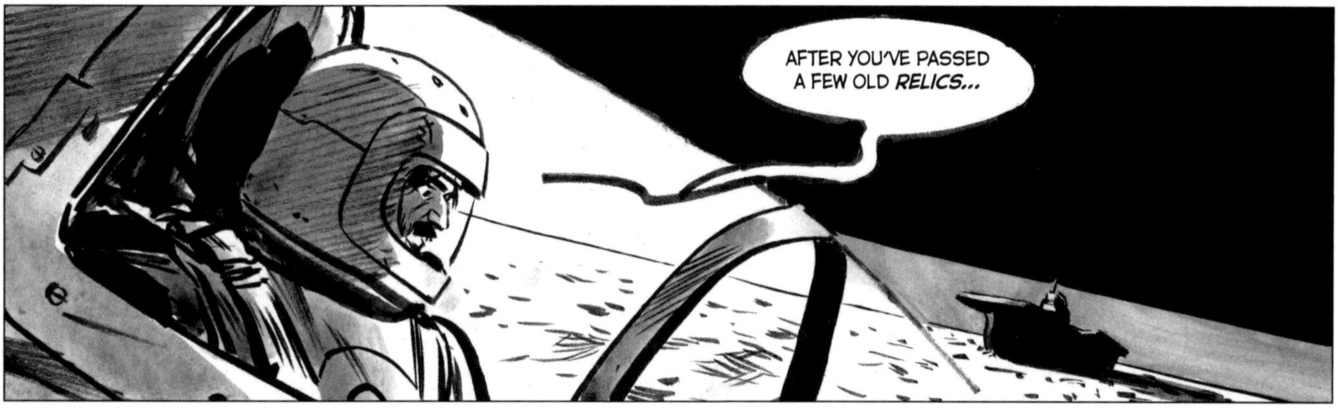
AFTER YOU'VE PASSED A FEW OLD RELICS...

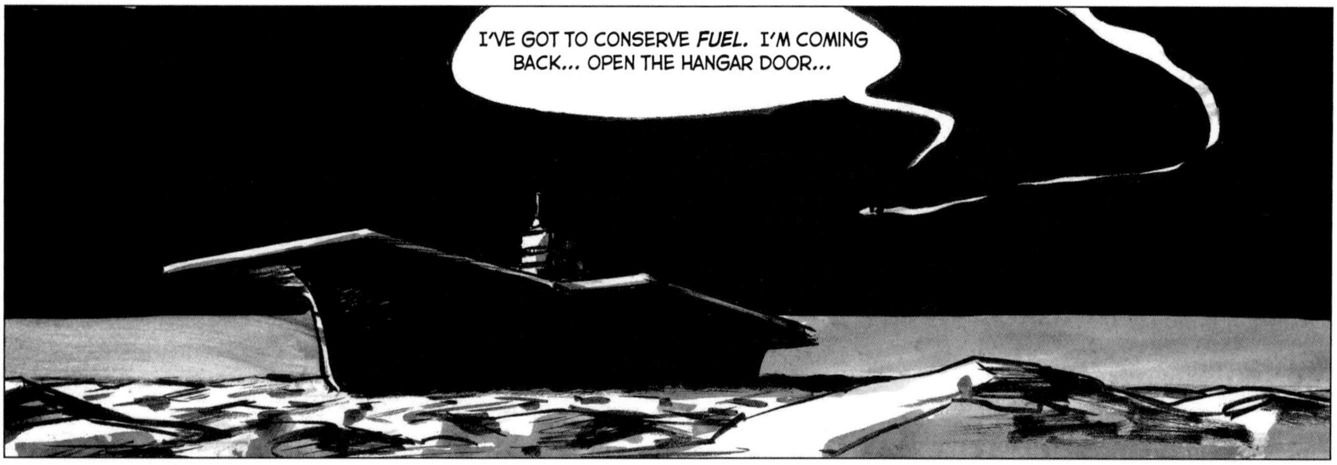
I'VE GOT TO CONSERVE FUEL. I'M COMING BACK... OPEN THE HANGAR DOOR...

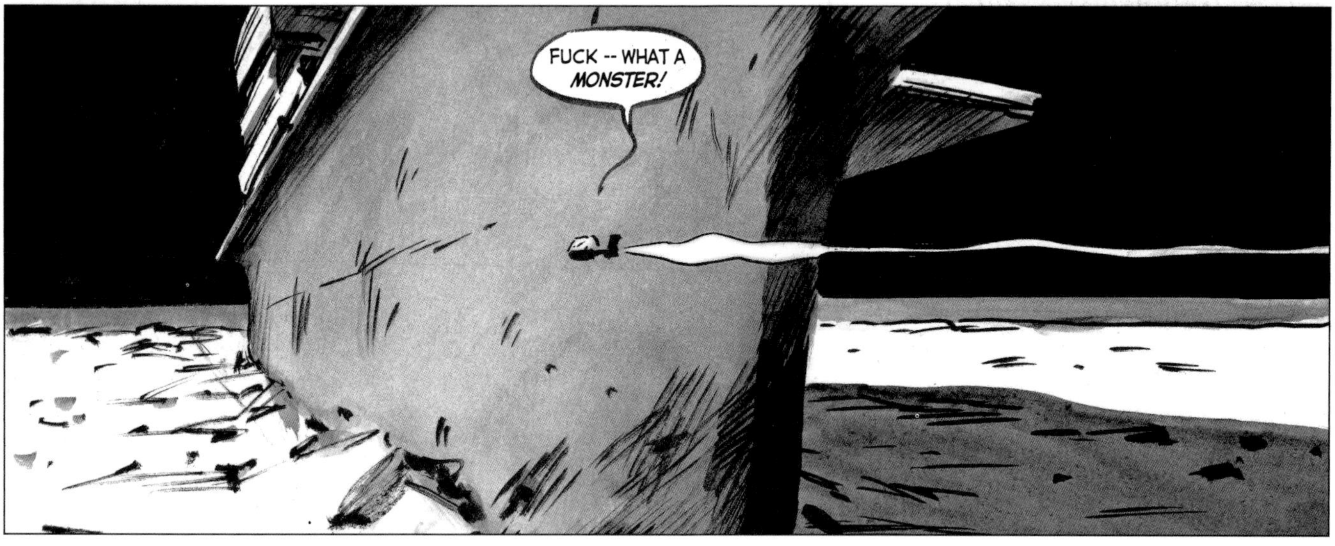
FUCK -- WHAT A MONSTER!

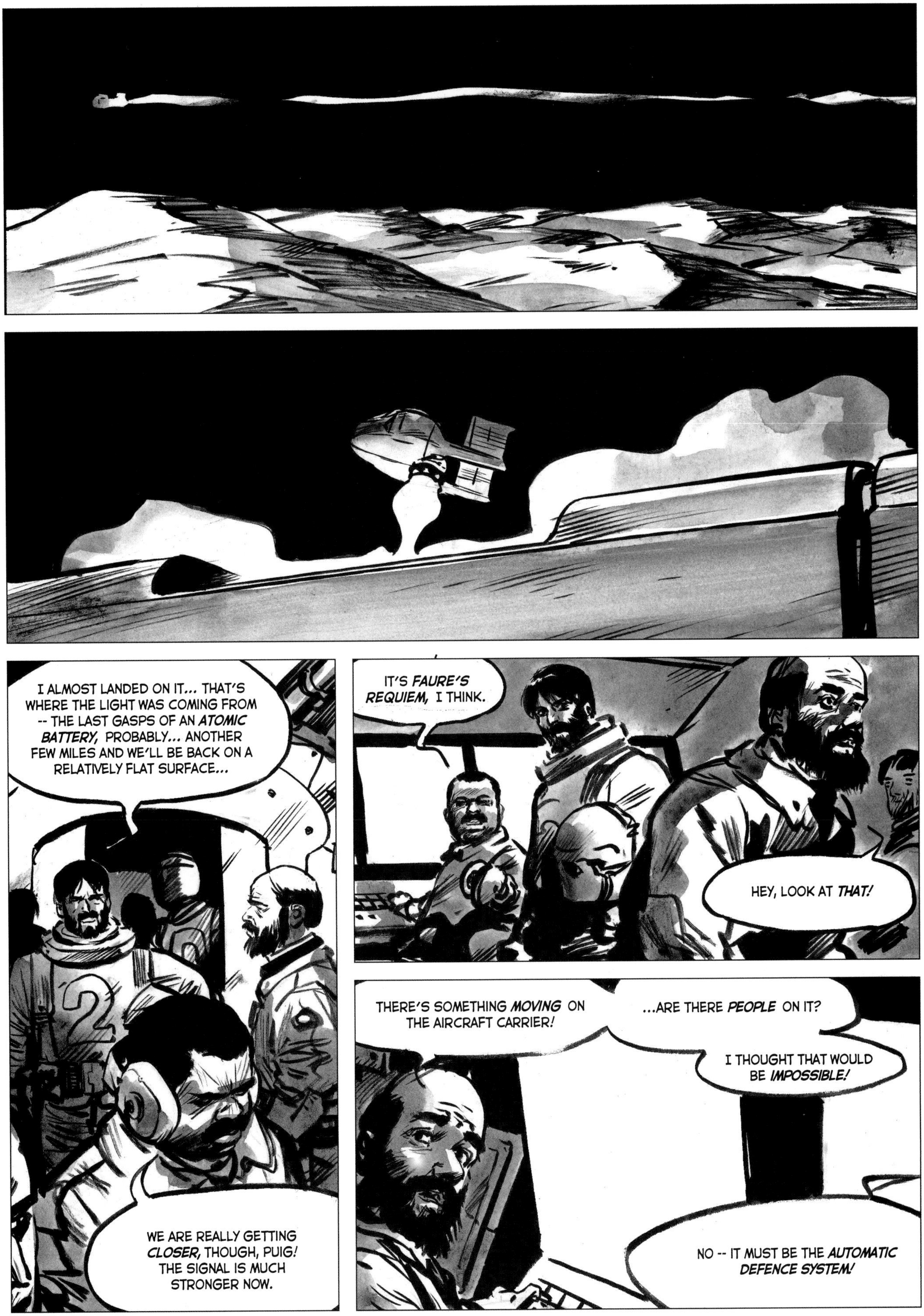
I ALMOST LANDED ON IT... THAT'S WHERE THE LIGHT WAS COMING FROM -- THE LAST GASPS OF AN ATOMIC BATTERY, PROBABLY... ANOTHER FEW MILES AND WE'LL BE BACK ON A RELATIVELY FLAT SURFACE...
WE ARE REALLY GETTING CLOSER, THOUGH, PUIG! THE SIGNAL IS MUCH STRONGER NOW.
IT'S FAURE'S REQUIEM, I THINK.
HEY, LOOK AT THAT!
THERE'S SOMETHING MOVING ON THE AIRCRAFT CARRIER!
...ARE THERE PEOPLE ON IT?
I THOUGHT THAT WOULD BE IMPOSSIBLE!
NO -- IT MUST BE THE AUTOMATIC DEFENCE SYSTEM!

SLOOF
THEY'RE FIRING AT US! MISSILES!
TWO OF THEM! I DON'T WANNA DIE!
WE'RE GONNA GET HIT... CLOSE ALL THE AIRLOCKS!
BEAR SOUTH-SOUTHWEST! THEN TURN TO THE RIGHT, FULL SPEED AHEAD!
AIRLOCKS SEALED! HOLD ON!
FOC FOC

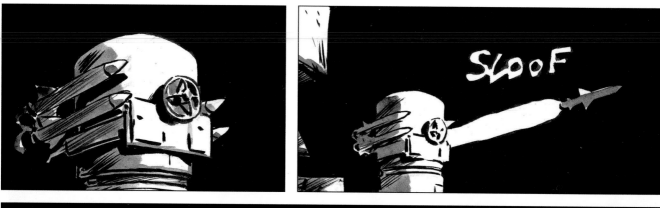

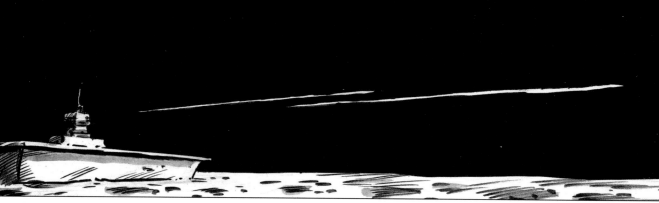

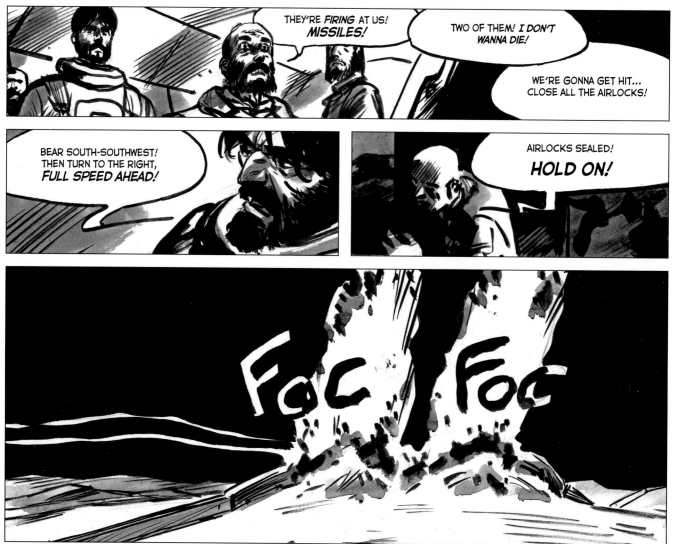

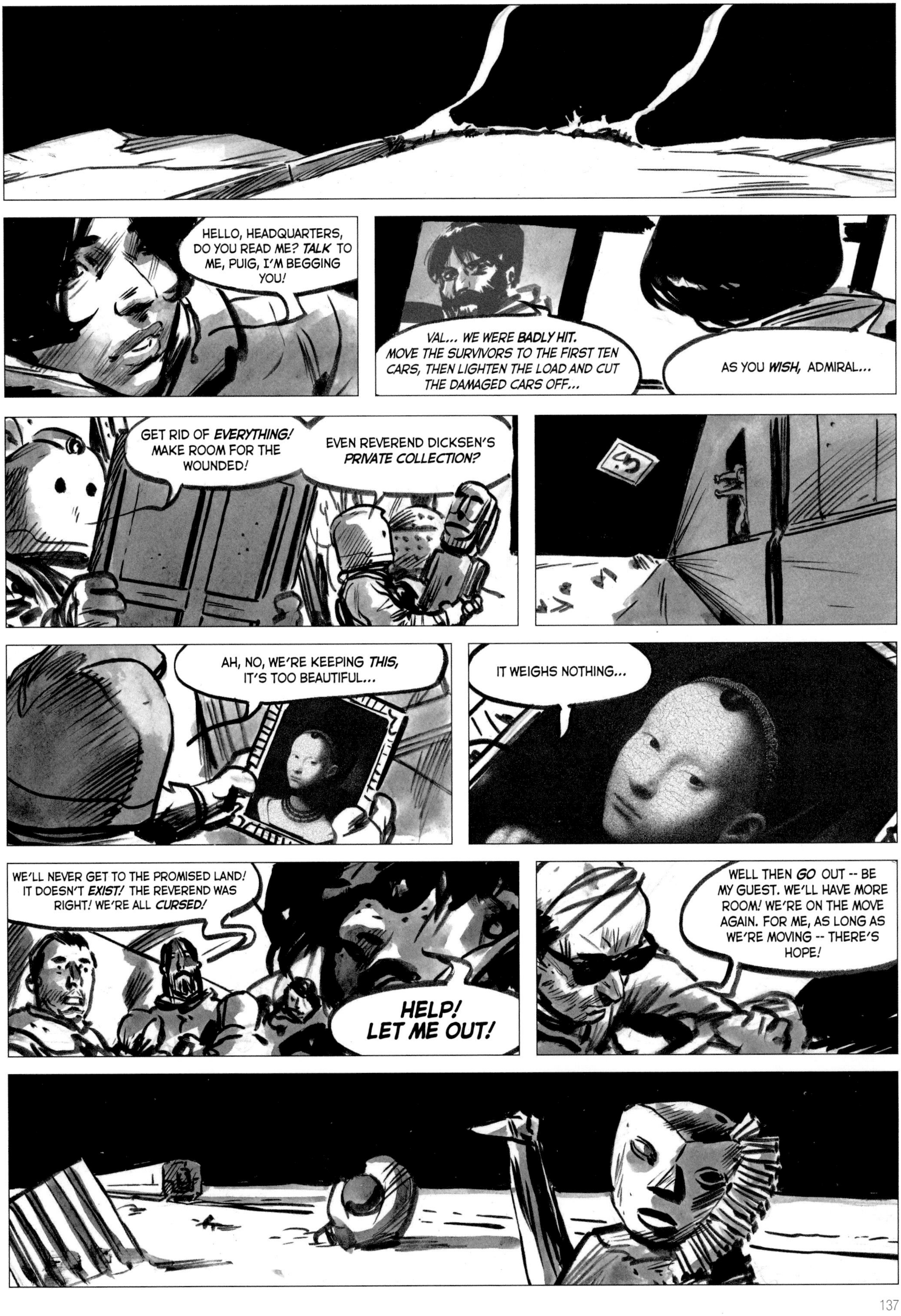
HELLO, HEADQUARTERS, DO YOU READ ME? TALK TO ME, PUIG, I'M BEGGING YOU!
VAL... WE WERE BADLY HIT. MOVE THE SURVIVORS TO THE FIRST TEN CARS, THEN LIGHTEN THE LOAD AND CUT THE DAMAGED CARS OFF...
AS YOU WISH, ADMIRAL...
GET RID OF EVERYTHING! MAKE ROOM FOR THE WOUNDED!
EVEN REVEREND DICKSEN'S PRIVATE COLLECTION?
AH, NO, WE'RE KEEPING THIS, IT'S TOO BEAUTIFUL...
IT WEIGHS NOTHING...
WE'LL NEVER GET TO THE PROMISED LAND! IT DOESN'T EXIST! THE REVEREND WAS RIGHT! WE'RE ALL CURSED!
HELP! LET ME OUT!
WELL THEN GO OUT -- BE MY GUEST. WE'LL HAVE MORE ROOM! WE'RE ON THE MOVE AGAIN. FOR ME, AS LONG AS WE'RE MOVING -- THERE'S HOPE!

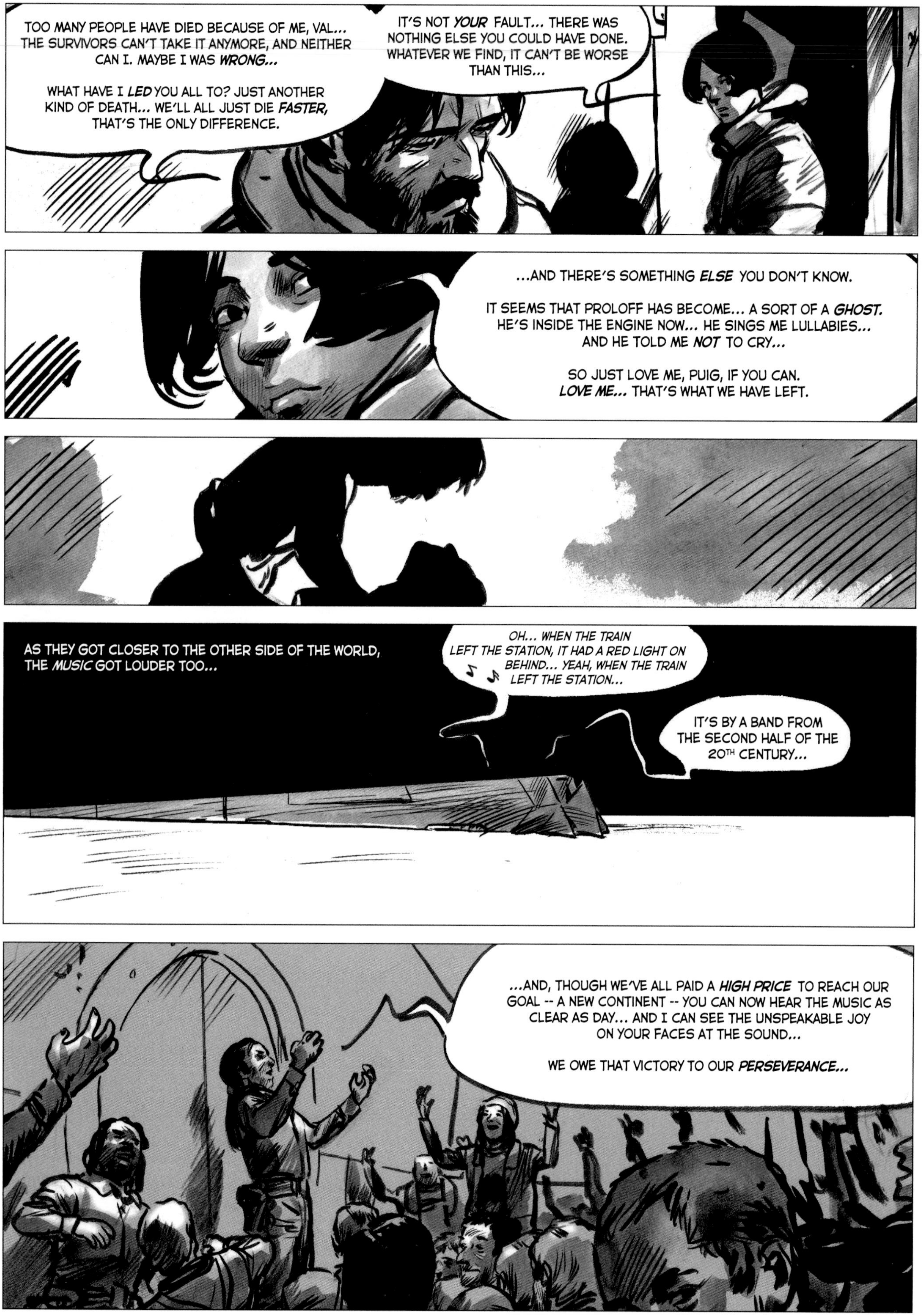
TOO MANY PEOPLE HAVE DIED BECAUSE OF ME, VAL... THE SURVIVORS CAN'T TAKE IT ANYMORE, AND NEITHER CAN I. MAYBE I WAS WRONG...
WHAT HAVE I LED YOU ALL TO? JUST ANOTHER KIND OF DEATH... WE'LL ALL JUST DIE FASTER, THAT'S THE ONLY DIFFERENCE.
IT'S NOT YOUR FAULT... THERE WAS NOTHING ELSE YOU COULD HAVE DONE. WHATEVER WE FIND, IT CAN'T BE WORSE THAN THIS...
...AND THERE'S SOMETHING ELSE YOU DON'T KNOW.
IT SEEMS THAT PROLOFF HAS BECOME... A SORT OF A GHOST. HE'S INSIDE THE ENGINE NOW... HE SINGS ME LULLABIES... AND HE TOLD ME NOT TO CRY...
SO JUST LOVE ME, PUIG, IF YOU CAN. LOVE ME... THAT'S WHAT WE HAVE LEFT.
AS THEY GOT CLOSER TO THE OTHER SIDE OF THE WORLD, THE MUSIC GOT LOUDER TOO...
OH... WHEN THE TRAIN LEFT THE STATION, IT HAD A RED LIGHT ON BEHIND... YEAH, WHEN THE TRAIN LEFT THE STATION...
IT'S BY A BAND FROM THE SECOND HALF OF THE 20TH CENTURY...
...AND, THOUGH WE'VE ALL PAID A HIGH PRICE TO REACH OUR GOAL -- A NEW CONTINENT -- YOU CAN NOW HEAR THE MUSIC AS CLEAR AS DAY... AND I CAN SEE THE UNSPEAKABLE JOY ON YOUR FACES AT THE SOUND...
WE OWE THAT VICTORY TO OUR PERSEVERANCE...

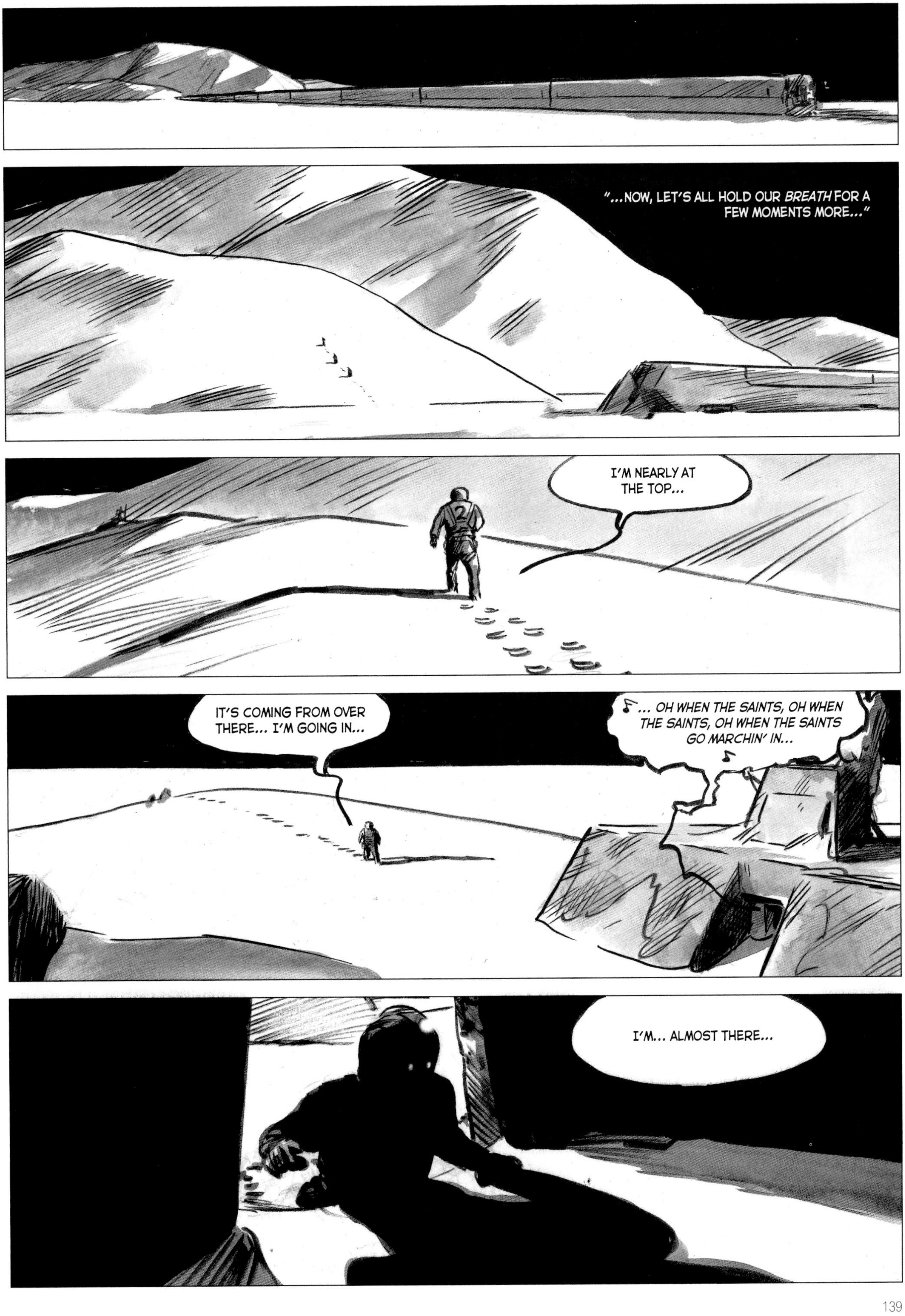
"...NOW, LET'S ALL HOLD OUR *BREATH* FOR A FEW MOMENTS MORE..."
I'M NEARLY AT THE TOP...
IT'S COMING FROM OVER THERE... I'M GOING IN...
... OH WHEN THE SAINTS, OH WHEN THE SAINTS, OH WHEN THE SAINTS GO MARCHIN' IN...
I'M... ALMOST THERE...

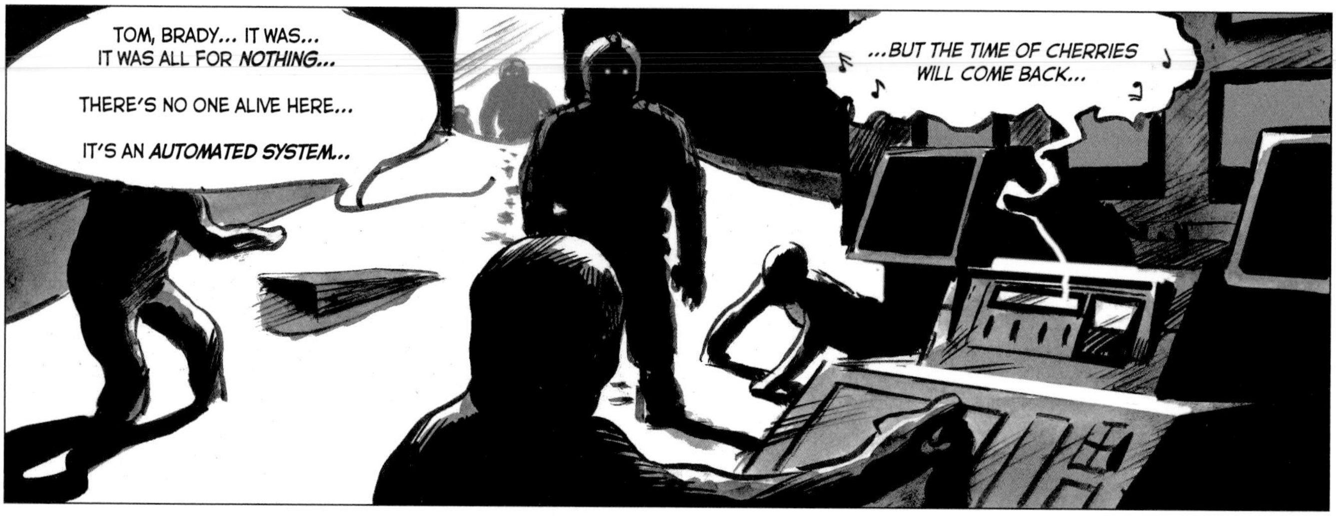
TOM, BRADY... IT WAS...
IT WAS ALL FOR ***NOTHING...***
THERE'S NO ONE ALIVE HERE...
IT'S AN ***AUTOMATED SYSTEM...***
...BUT THE TIME OF CHERRIES WILL COME BACK...

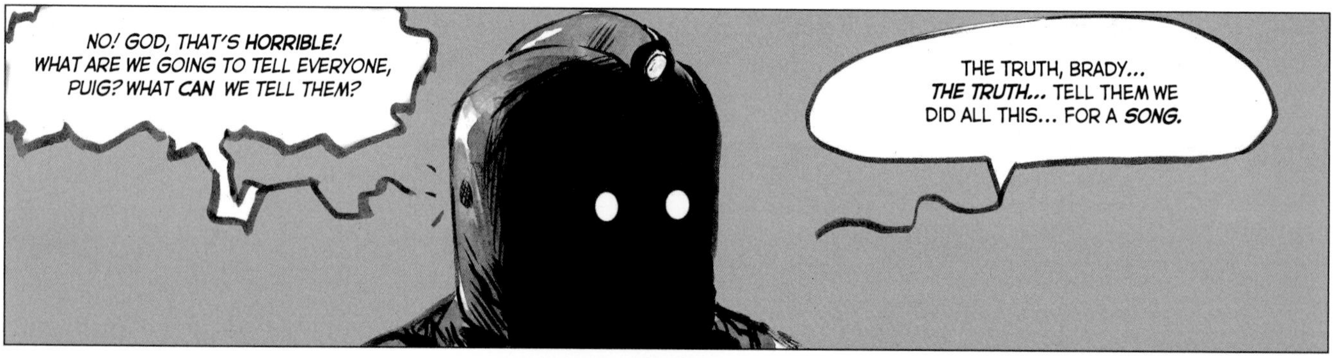
NO! GOD, THAT'S **HORRIBLE!** *WHAT ARE WE GOING TO TELL EVERYONE, PUIG? WHAT* **CAN** *WE TELL THEM?*
THE TRUTH, BRADY... ***THE TRUTH...*** TELL THEM WE DID ALL THIS... FOR A ***SONG.***

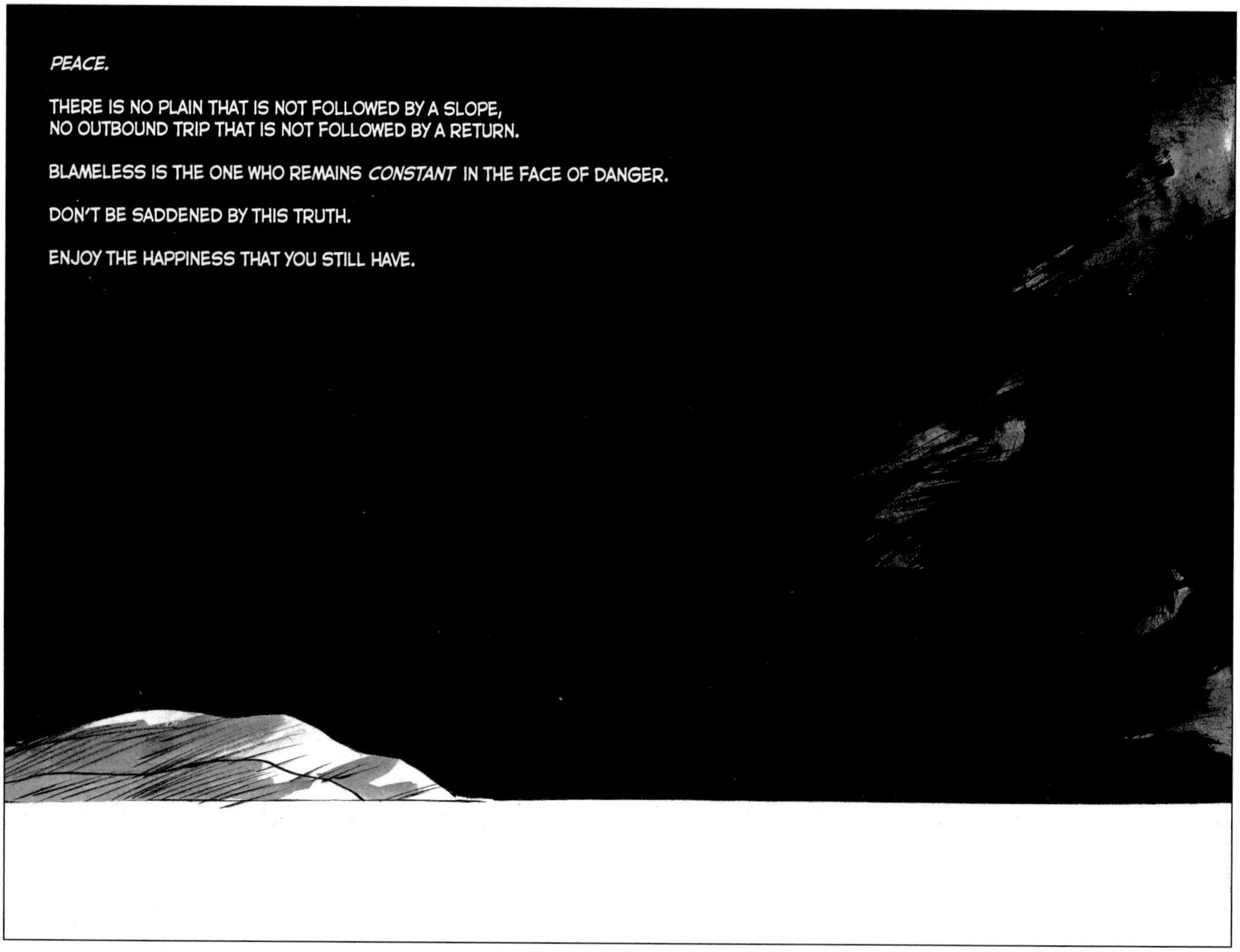
PEACE.
THERE IS NO PLAIN THAT IS NOT FOLLOWED BY A SLOPE,
NO OUTBOUND TRIP THAT IS NOT FOLLOWED BY A RETURN.
BLAMELESS IS THE ONE WHO REMAINS *CONSTANT* IN THE FACE OF DANGER.
DON'T BE SADDENED BY THIS TRUTH.
ENJOY THE HAPPINESS THAT YOU STILL HAVE.

AUTHOR BIOS

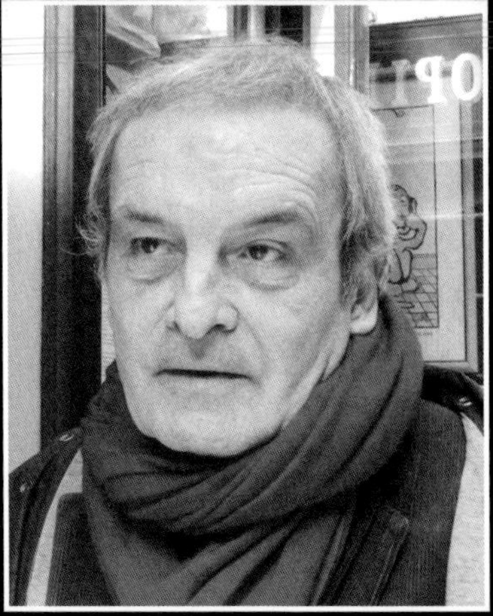

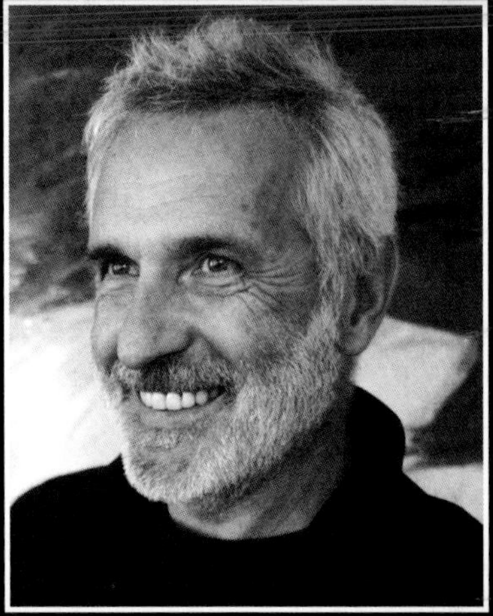

BENJAMIN LEGRAND is the author of numerous thriller novels, screenplays, and comic scripts. As well as his own original works, he is well-known as the French translator of the works of such authors as Tom Wolfe, Paul Cleave and Nelson DeMille. After Jacques Lob's death in 1990, Legrand continued the *Snowpiercer* series with a two-part sequel, collected by Titan in a single second volume.

JEAN-MARC ROCHETTE is a painter, illustrator and cartoonist. He has worked across a variety of projects and genres, from science fiction comics to children's cartoons – and including adaptations of Voltaire's *Candide* and Homer's *Odyssey* – but *Snowpiercer* remains the work by which he is most popularly known.

JACQUES LOB, winner of the Grand Prix de la ville d'Angoulême award, was a Franco-Belgian comic book author, best known for his *Superdupont* series. He began his career as an editorial cartoonist, before an editor suggested he focused on his writing, which bore rich fruit across a number of genres. He wrote the first volume of *Snowpiercer* between 1982 and 1983. He passed away in 1990.

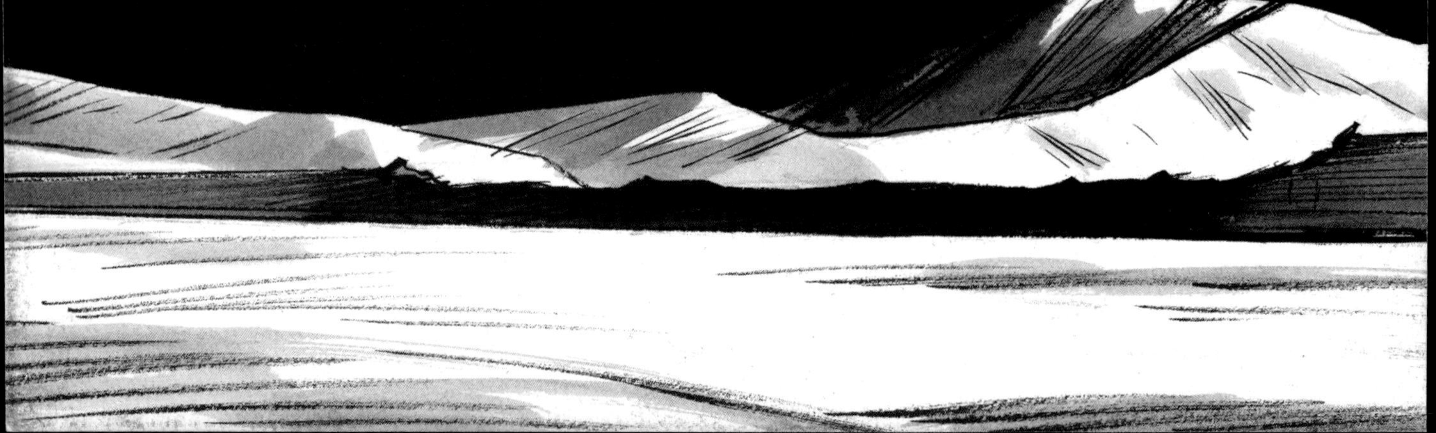

AN EPIC FANTASY
POST-APOCALYPTIC GRAPHIC NOVEL COLLECTION - 25 YEARS IN THE MAKING

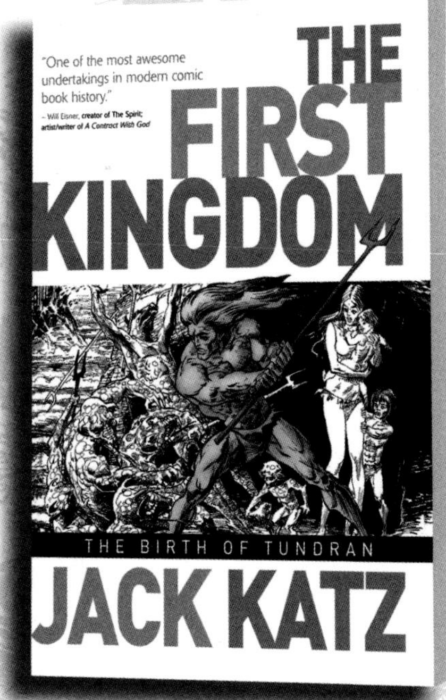
"One of the most awesome undertakings in modern comic book history."
– Will Eisner, creator of The Spirit; artist/writer of A Contract With God
THE FIRST KINGDOM
THE BIRTH OF TUNDRAN
JACK KATZ

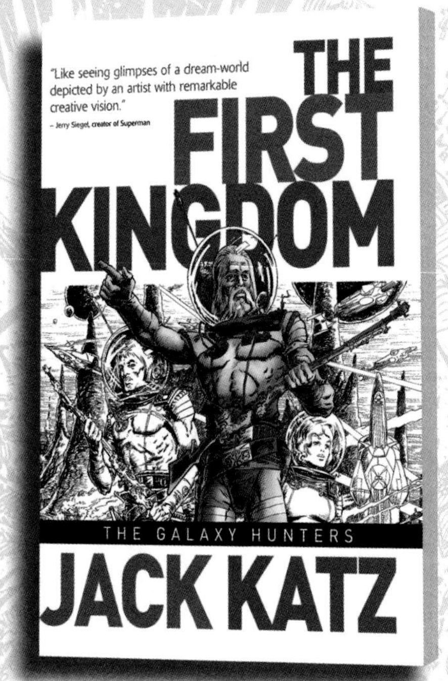
"Like seeing glimpses of a dream-world depicted by an artist with remarkable creative vision."
– Jerry Siegel, creator of Superman
THE FIRST KINGDOM
THE GALAXY HUNTERS
JACK KATZ

'One of the most awesome undertakings in modern comic book history!'
– Will Eisner, *The Spirit*

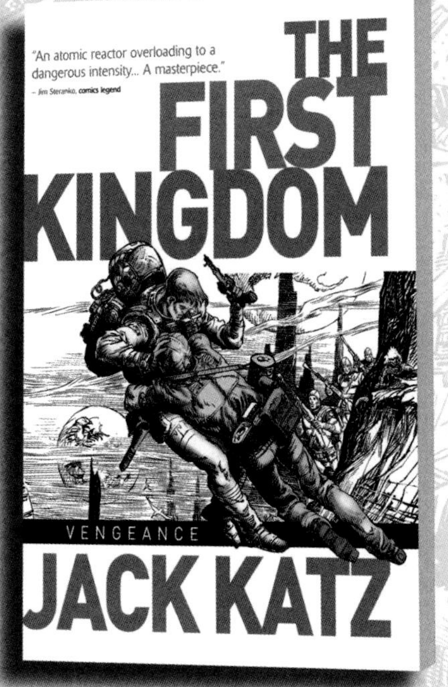
"An atomic reactor overloading to a dangerous intensity... A masterpiece."
– Jim Steranko, comics legend
THE FIRST KINGDOM
VENGEANCE
JACK KATZ

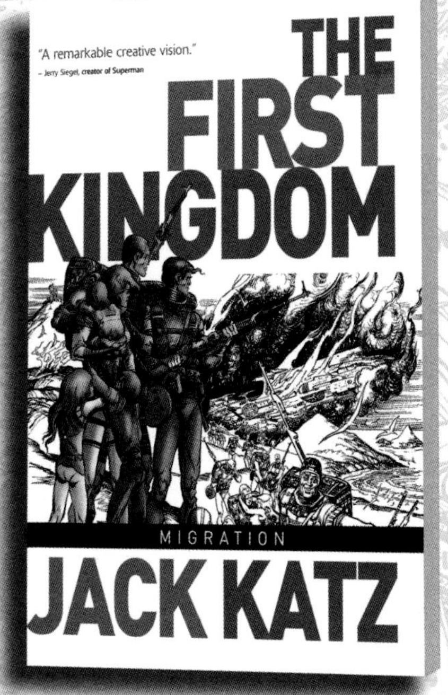
"A remarkable creative vision."
– Jerry Siegel, creator of Superman
THE FIRST KINGDOM
MIGRATION
JACK KATZ

AVAILABLE FROM ALL GOOD BOOKSTORES!

TITAN COMICS

TITAN-COMICS.COM

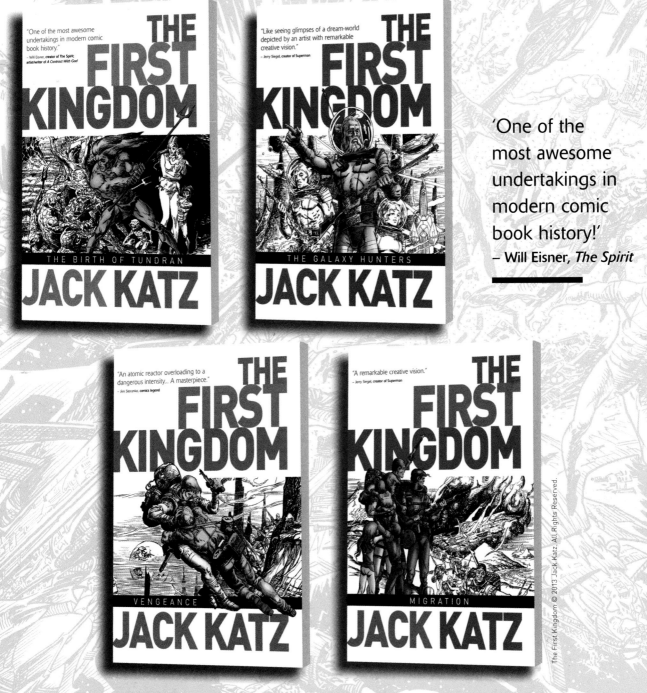

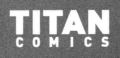